USER'S GUIDE

www.broderbund.com

383206-MAN

NOTE: DESIGN PLANS CREATED IN 3D HOME ARCHITECT® OR 3D HOME LANDSCAPE VERSIONS 4 OR EARLIER CANNOT BE IMPORTED INTO THIS PRODUCT.

IMPORTANT: READ CAREFULLY BEFORE USING THIS PRODUCT LICENSE AGREEMENT AND LIMITED WARRANTY

SINGLE-USER PRODUCTS

THIS IS A LEGAL AGREEMENT BETWEEN YOU (EITHER AN INDIVIDUAL OR AN ENTITY) AND RIVERDEEP, INC., AND ITS SUBSIDIARIES AND AFFILIATES ("RIVERDEEP"). THIS AGREEMENT IS GOVERNED BY THE INTERNAL SUBSTANTIVE LAWS OF THE STATE OF MASSACHUSETTS (AND NOT BY THE 1980 UNITED NATIONS CONVENTION ON CONTRACTS FOR THE INTERNATIONAL SALE OF GOODS, AS AMENDED). BY INSTALLING OR USING THE SOFTWARE, YOU AGREE TO BE BOUND BY THE TERMS OF THIS AGREEMENT. IF YOU DO NOT AGREE TO THE TERMS OF THIS AGREEMENT, REMOVE THE PRODUCT FROM YOUR HARD DRIVE AND PERMANENTLY ERASE ALL COPIES OF THE PRODUCT. IF YOU ARE THE ORIGINAL INSTALLER OF THE SOFTWARE YOU MAY PROMPTLY AFTER PURCHASE RETURN THE SOFTWARE (INCLUDING PRINTED MATERIALS) WITH PROOF OF PURCHASE TO THE PLACE WHERE IT WAS PURCHASED FOR A FULL REFUND OF THE AMOUNT PAID.

RIVERDEEP SOFTWARE LICENSE

GRANT OF LICENSE. This License Agreement permits you to use one copy of RIVERDEEP software (the "Software"), which may include electronic documentation, on a single computer/workstation. The Software is "in use" on a computer when it is loaded into the temporary memory (i.e., RAM or Cache) or installed into permanent memory (e.g., hard disk, CD-ROM drive, or other storage device) of that computer. This License does not constitute a sale and does not authorize a sale of the Software or anything created thereby. All intellectual property (including copyright, trademark and patent) in the Software, including all animations, audio, images, maps, music, photographs, video, and text incorporated into the Software, are owned by RIVERDEEP and its affiliates, suppliers and licensors, and are protected by United States laws and international treaty provisions. RIVERDEEP and its affiliates, suppliers and licensors retain all rights not expressly granted herein. You must treat the Software like any other copyrighted material, except that you may make one copy of the Software solely for backup or archival purposes. You may transfer your rights under this Agreement on a permanent basis provided you transfer the license granted by this Agreement, and the Software and all associated printed materials, and you retain no copies, and the recipient agrees to all of the terms of this Agreement.

- You may not use the software on or over a network or any other transfer device (including the Internet) except in a manner using the network and online functions included in the Software, if any. Use of the Software on more than one computer constitutes copyright infringement and may be punishable by civil fines, criminal penalties, or both.
- You may not rent or lease the Software, but schools and libraries may lend the Software to third parties provided the Software is in CD format and each end user is given a copy of this License Agreement which will govern the use of such Software.
- You may not modify, translate, reverse engineer, decompile, or disassemble the Software, except to the extent that this restriction is expressly prohibited by applicable law.
- You may not remove any proprietary notices or labels in the Software.
- You may not copy the printed materials accompanying the Software or distribute printed copies of any user documentation provided in electronic format.
- You may not publicly perform or publicly display the Software.

The restrictions contained herein apply equally to hybrid CD-ROMs which may contain multiple versions of the Software for use on different operating systems. Regardless of the type of media you receive, you may use only the portion appropriate for your single-user computer/workstation. In the event you fail to comply with any of the terms or conditions of this license, your rights to use the Software will end, you shall stop using the Software, remove the Software from your computer, and permanently erase all copies of the Software. You may not export or re-export the Software or any underlying information or technology except in full compliance with all United States and other applicable laws and regulations.

LIMITED WARRANTY

LIMITED WARRANTY. RIVERDEEP and its affiliates, suppliers and licensors warrant to the original installer of the Software, for a period of ninety (90) days from the date of purchase, that the media on which the Software is distributed is substantially free from defects in materials and workmanship under normal use. ANY AND ALL OTHER IMPLIED WARRANTIES, STATUTORY OR OTHERWISE, WITH RESPECT TO THE SOFTWARE AND THE ACCOMPANYING WRITTEN MATERIALS, INCLUDING BUT NOT LIMITED TO IMPLIED WARRANTIES OF MERCHANTABILITY, NON-INFRINGEMENT, AND FITNESS FOR A PARTICULAR PURPOSE, ARE HEREBY EXPRESSLY DISCLAIMED.

REMEDIES. Your exclusive remedy shall be, at RIVERDEEP's sole option, (a) the refund of the amount you paid for the Software or (b) repair or replacement of the Software, provided that the defective Software is returned to RIVERDEEP (at Riverdeep, Dock Door #9, 120 Hidden Lake Circle, Duncan, SC 29334. Telephone: (319) 378-7319) along with proof of the date of purchase within ninety (90) days from the date of purchase. This Limited Warranty is void if failure of the Software has resulted from accident, abuse, neglect or misapplication. Any replacement Software will be warranted for the remainder of the original warranty period or thirty (30) days, whichever is longer. Except as set forth above, the Software is sold "as-is", without any express or implied warranties of any kind.

LIMITATION OF LIABILITIES. IN NO EVENT WILL RIVERDEEP OR ITS AFFILIATES, SUPPLIERS AND LICENSORS BE LIABLE FOR ANY INDIRECT, SPECIAL, INCIDENTAL, ECONOMIC, COVER, CONSEQUENTIAL, EXEMPLARY OR PUNITIVE DAMAGES ARISING OUT OF THE USE OF OR INABILITY TO USE THE SOFTWARE, USER DOCUMENTATION, OR RELATED TECHNICAL SUPPORT, INCLUDING, WITHOUT LIMITATION, DAMAGES OR COSTS RELATING TO THE LOSS OF PROFITS, BUSINESS, GOODWILL, DATA, TIME OR COMPUTER PROGRAMS, EVEN IF ADVISED OF THE POSSIBILITY OF SUCH DAMAGES. IN NO EVENT WILL RIVERDEEP'S AND ITS AFFILIATES', SUPPLIERS' AND LICENSORS' LIABILITY EXCEED THE AMOUNT PAID BY YOU FOR THE SOFTWARE REGARDLESS OF THE FORM OF THE CLAIM (INCLUDING, WITHOUT LIMITATION, ANY CONTRACT, PRODUCT LIABILITY, OR TORT CLAIM). BECAUSE SOME JURISDICTIONS DO NOT ALLOW THE EXCLUSION OR LIMITATION OF LIABILITY FOR CONSEQUENTIAL OR INCIDENTAL DAMAGES, THE ABOVE LIMITATION MAY NOT APPLY TO YOU.

MISCELLANEOUS

RIVERDEEP may cancel, change, modify, discontinue, terminate or charge a fee at any time for any reason for the online services advertised as part of this product.

The links in the Software will allow third-party sites to be accessed. These linked sites are not under the control of RIVERDEEP, and RIVERDEEP is not responsible for the contents of any linked site, and any such inclusion of any link does not imply endorsement by RIVERDEEP of the site.

No change or modification of the License will be valid unless it is in writing and is signed by RIVERDEEP. The provisions of this Agreement are severable; if any provision is held to be invalid or unenforceable, it shall not affect the validity or enforceability of any other provision. If the Software was acquired outside the United States, then local law may apply.

U.S. GOVERNMENT RESTRICTED RIGHTS. The Software and user documentation is provided with RESTRICTED RIGHTS AND LIMITED RIGHTS. Use, duplication, or disclosure by the Government is subject to restrictions as set forth in subparagraph (c)(1)(ii) of the Rights in Technical Data and Computer Software clause at DFARS 252.227-7013 or subparagraphs (c)(1) and (2) of the Commercial Computer Software--Restricted Rights at 48 CFR 52.227-19, as applicable. Riverdeep, Inc., 125 Cambridge Park Drive, Cambridge, MA 02140 U.S.A.

Table of Contents

The Basics 1

Designing the Interior 109

Utilities 127

Chapter 28: Text & Dimensions 185

Chapter 29: Project Estimate 197

Chapter 30: 3DTrueView™ 201

Customization 219

Part 1

The Basics

Chapter 1

Welcome

Congratulations on purchasing *3D Home Architect® Home Design Deluxe 6*! We guarantee you are going to enjoy creating your dream design projects.

3D Home Architect® Home Design is for anyone who wants to design, renovate or decorate a home. This high-quality, multi-functional tool is easy to use and delivers the results you want — completely and accurately. It eliminates the monotonous labor involved in creating building plans, and frees you to devote your energy to the creative — and enjoyable — aspects of building design.

Whether you are just playing around with different design ideas, or preparing drawings for a building professional, *3D Home Architect® Home Design* makes it fun and easy.

Possible uses include:

- Home design
- Floor plans
- Interior design
- Remodeling
- 3D visualization
- Photorealistic rendering
- Budget and materials list
- Export to other file formats

Take a few minutes to familiarize yourself with the contents of this guide so you can quickly find the answers you need while working on your project.

Package Contents

Your *3D Home Architect® Home Design* package includes the following:

- 3D Home Architect Home Design installation CD
- 3D Home Architect Home Design User's Guide

System Requirements

In order to run *3D Home Architect® Home Design*, your system should include the following:

- Microsoft® Windows® 98SE/2000 SP4/XP SP1/ME
- 500Mhz or higher processor
- 128 MB RAM (256 MB recommended)
- 300MB free hard-disk space
- 4X CD-ROM drive or faster
- Video Card with OpenGL driver and at least 32MB RAM
- Color monitor with 1024x768 resolution or higher
- Mouse
- Microsoft® Internet Explorer 5.5 or higher to view tutorials and access online features (optional).

Important Notes for Previous 3D Home Users

If you are using *3D Home Architect Home Design Deluxe 6*, you can open drawings from *3D Home Design Suite Professional 5*, *3D Home Architect® 5* and *3D Home Landscape Designer 5*. Drawings from older versions of *3D Home Architect* or *3D Home Landscape Designer* (4.0 or earlier) are not accepted.

If you have projects from version 5 of a *3D Home Design* program and would like to be able to open them in version 6, it is recommended that you make the textures in the older version available in version 6 so that textures will appear properly in version 6. This is because textures in the older version are bitmap (BMP) files, and the textures in version 6 are JPG files. The JPG format was chosen for version 6 to reduce file size and improve program speed.

If you choose not to back up your old textures, you can still open a version 5 drawing in version 6. However, the model will have no textures applied to it when you open it in version 6, and you will have to apply new textures to your elements if you want textures in your drawing.

There are two ways to make textures from version 5 available in version 6:

- Back up your old Textures directory temporarily, then once version 6 is installed, copy the old textures into the new Textures directory of version 6. This method allows you to uninstall version 5 if you want. See *Backing Up Textures from Version 5* on page 2.
- Or, once version 6 is installed, set your Textures path in your program settings to the Textures folder in the older version. With this method you cannot uninstall the old version. Also, when working with new drawings in version 6, materials will not show up in your catalog or when using the Materials Paintbrush unless you switch the path back to the Textures directory of version 6. For more information, see *Specifying the Location of the Textures Directory* on page 264.

Backing Up Textures from Version 5

If you want to uninstall version 5 before installing version 6, and you want to be able to open version 5 drawings in version 6 with all your textures properly applied, you should back up your old textures. If you are not planning to uninstall version 5, backing up your Textures directory is not necessary because they will still be available on your system and can be copied to your new Textures directory.

To back up textures from version 5:

1. Open Windows® Explorer.
2. Locate the Textures directory. (e.g. *C:\Program Files\Broderbund\Broderbund Home Design 5.1\Textures.*)
3. Copy the folder to another location on your system, such as the root (e.g. C: drive).
4. You can now safely uninstall version 5 if you want.

Once you've installed version 6, you can copy the textures in the backed up Textures directory to your new Textures directory. The new directory will then contain textures from both version 5 and version 6. By default, textures are located in the following directory in version 6:

C:\\Program Files\3D Home Architect\Home Design Deluxe 6\Textures

Uninstalling a Previous Version

Note: If you have projects from version 5 that you would like to open in version 6, see *Important Notes for Previous 3D Home Users* on page 2 **before uninstalling.**

If you currently have any older *3D Home Design* products installed on your system, you may want to uninstall your current version before installing *3D Home Architect® Home Design Deluxe 6.*

To uninstall a previous version:

1. At your Windows® desktop, select **Start > Settings > Control Panel**.
2. In the *Control Panel* window, double-click the **Add/Remove Programs** icon.
3. In the *Add/Remove Programs* window, select the program to be deleted.
4. Click the **Change/Remove** button.
5. In the *InstallShield Wizard* window, enable the **Remove** radio button.
6. Click **Next**.
7. In the *Confirm Uninstall* window, click **Yes**. The uninstallation begins.
8. Follow any remaining instructions.

How the Uninstallation Works

When you uninstall an older version of the software, all program files, folders and icons are removed **unless** you modified your catalog and/or have projects residing in the program's **Projects** directory. In this case, the old program folder remains on your system with the old **Catalogs** and **Projects** directories in tact.

If you want you can replace the **Catalogs** and **Projects** directories in *3D Home Architect® Home Design* with the old directories after you've installed it.

Installing 3D Home Architect® Home Design Deluxe 6

To install *3D Home Architect® Home Design Deluxe 6*, you need to run Setup. Make sure you exit all other programs, applications and screensavers before installing.

To install the program:

1. Begin at the Windows® desktop.
2. Insert the installation CD into your CD-ROM drive. The *InstallShield Wizard* screen appears and loads the setup.
3. Follow the on-screen instructions to complete the installation.

Note: If the install screen does not appear automatically, you must install the program manually.

To install the program if installation does not begin automatically:

1. Make sure the installation CD is in your CD-ROM drive.
2. At the Windows® desktop, click the **Start** button, then select **Run**.
3. Type **D:\setup.exe** in the **Open** edit box. The letter **D** represents your CD-ROM drive. If you are installing from a different drive, substitute the correct letter for the letter **D**.
4. Click **OK**, then follow the on-screen instructions to complete the installation.

Starting the Program

You can start your program from your Windows® **Start** menu, or by double-clicking the *3D Home Architect® Home Design Deluxe 6* icon on your desktop.

Registering the Program

Take a moment to register online when you see the registration window. Once registered you are eligible for technical support, special offers, advance notice of upgrades, and more.

You can also register your software later in one of two ways:

- Select **Start > Programs > 3D Home Architect > Home Design Deluxe 6 > Register Online**.
- Click the **Register Online** button in the startup dialog that appears when you start the program.

Starting a New Project

Every time you start the program, a startup dialog appears. This dialog lets you start new drawings, or open saved drawings.

To start a new project, click the **Start a New Project** button in the startup dialog.

If the program is already running, you can start a new project by selecting **File > New** or clicking the New button on the Standard toolbar.

Using the House Builder Wizard

By default, the **House Builder** screen appears when you start a new project. The House Builder Wizard builds a basic structure for you based on factors that you specify, such as the building shape and size. For more information about the House Builder Wizard, see page 13.

Starting a Drawing from Scratch

If you prefer to start drawing from scratch, or you do not want to run the House Builder Wizard right away, just click **Cancel** or the Close button in the **House Builder** dialog. This leaves a new, blank drawing on the screen.

Note that you can stop the House Builder Wizard from appearing when starting new projects. This will let you start from scratch every time you open a new project. See *Preventing the House Builder Wizard from Launching* on page 16.

Disabling the Startup Dialog

You can disable the startup dialog that appears when you start the program. If you disable it, the House Builder Wizard will launch when you start the program. If you have disabled the House Builder Wizard, a blank project will open.

To disable the startup dialog:

1. Select **Settings > Program Settings** or click the Program Settings button on the Settings toolbar.
2. In the **Program Settings** dialog, select the General tab.
3. Uncheck the **Enable Startup Dialog** check box.
4. Click **OK**.

Adjusting Your Display Settings

You can control program performance by ensuring your Windows® display settings are set correctly.

To adjust your display settings:

1. From the Windows® **Start** menu, select **Settings > Control Panel**.

2. In the Control Panel window, double-click **Display**.
3. In the **Display Properties** dialog, select the **Settings** tab.
4. From the Color drop box, select **True Color (32 bit)**.

   Note: If 32-bit is unavailable, select 24-bit.
5. In the Screen area section, move the slider to display at least 1024 x 768 pixels.
6. Click **OK**.

Learning the Program

3D Home Architect® Home Design includes a **Learning Center** that contains a variety of videos and tutorials to help you get started and learn the program. It's a quick, fun and easy, and will get you up and running with your project in no time.

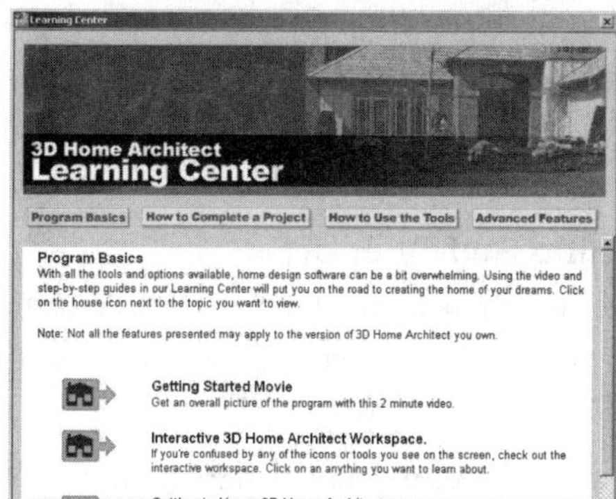

To access the Learning Center:

- When you start the program, click the **Learn to Use** button in the startup dialog, or
- If the program is running, make a selection from the **Learn** menu

Program Basics

The *Program Basics* page contains short videos, tools and guides to help get you up and running with the program.

How to Complete a Project

The *How to Complete a Project* page contains an excellent selection of project-specific tutorials that you can read and print out. Choose from the following:

- Completing a Home Design or Remodel
- Designing or Remodeling a Kitchen
- Designing or Remodeling a Bathroom
- Customizing Your Interiors

How to Use the Tools

The *How to Use the Tools* page lets you select a specific tool — anything from walls and floors to furniture and accessories, and view narrated videos on how to insert, edit and troubleshoot the element, and more.

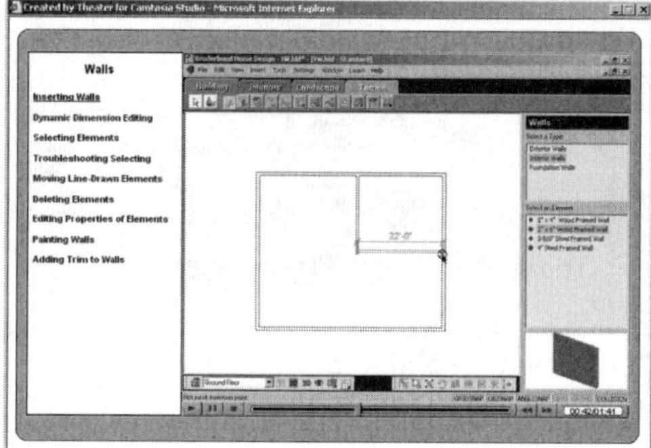

Advanced Features

The *Advanced Features* page offers insider's tips and instructions on performing more difficult tasks in the program. Choose from the following step-by-step guides:

- Visualizing Your Design in 3D
- Working with Catalogs and Elements
- Working on Multiple Floors & Split Levels
- Roofs, Ceilings, and Attics

Online Help

3D Home Architect® Home Design includes a comprehensive online help system that includes all of the information found in this User's Guide. You can browse through all help topics, or get help for a specific element, tool or dialog while you are designing.

To access the online help file:

- Select **Help > Program Help**, or
- Press **F1**, or
- Click the Program Help button on the Standard toolbar 

To get help for a specific part of your drawing:

1. Select the element you want help with.
2. Right-click and select the Tool Help option for that element (e.g. Walls Help). Help for the element is displayed. You can also access the Tool Help from the **Edit > Modify Elements** menu.

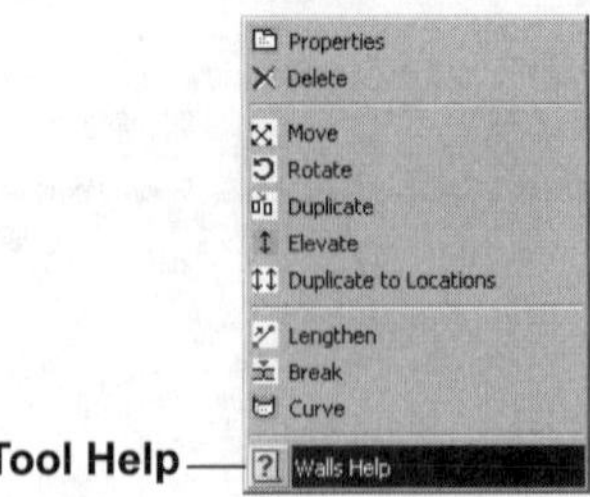

To get help in a dialog:

1. Click the Dialog Help button in the dialog. A window is displayed that describes the content of the dialog.

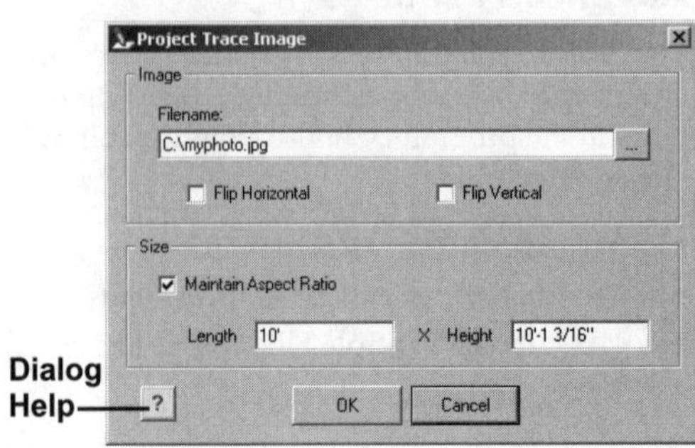

Troubleshooting Guide

3D Home Architect® Home Design's help tools include a Troubleshooting Guide that describes common problems in the program and how to solve them.

To access the Troubleshooting Guide:

1. Select **Help > Troubleshooting Guide**.

Glossary of Terms

You can instantly access a glossary of construction terms from the Help menu.

To view the Glossary of Terms:

1. Select **Help > Glossary of Terms**.

Technical Support

Our online technical support system offers 24-hour service and product information.

The online Support Center provides access to Online Self-Support, and lists contact information for E-mail Support and Telephone Support.

Online Self-Support

You can access troubleshooting guides, FAQs and downloads for *3D Home Architect® Home Design* 24 hours a day, 7 days a week.

To access free online software help:

1. Select **Help > Online Software Help**.
2. On the contact page, click the **Online Self-Support** link.

E-mail Support

You can contact technical support by e-mail provided you have registered your software and received a User Name and Password.

To contact technical support by e-mail:

1. Select **Help > Online Software Help**.
2. On the contact page, click the **E-mail Support** link.
3. On the Customer Support Login page, enter your User Name and Password. If you have

not yet registered your software, you can do so from the Customer Support Login page.

Telephone Support

If you contact technical support by telephone, be prepared to provide information about your computer name and model, and the brand name of the video card and sound card you are using, and a detailed description of your issue. We provide a form on our web site for your convenience. If possible, sit at your computer with the program running when you call.

To prepare for your call:

1. Select **Help > Online Software Help**.
2. On the contact page, click the **Telephone Support** link.
3. Fill out the *Technical Support Contact Form.*
4. Click **Print** to print the form.
5. Have the form with you when you call.

Note: If you want to submit your technical support contact form to technical support by e-mail, click the **Send E-mail** button at the bottom of the form.

To contact technical support by telephone:

1. Call **(319) 247-3333** during the following hours: Monday, Tuesday, Thursday, Friday 8:00 AM - 5:00 PM CST & Wednesday 9:00 AM - 5:00 PM CST

Note: Though technical support does not charge for support calls, this is a toll call that will be billed to your long distance carrier. Average hold times during peak periods can exceed 20 minutes.

3D Home Architect Online

The 3D Home Architect product page on our web site offers additional help, content and services related to the program.

To access the 3D Home Architect page:

1. Select **Help > 3D Home Architect Online**.

Broderbund.com

Visit the Broderbund® web site to view a complete listing of Broderbund products and services.

To instantly access the Broderbund web site:

1. Select **Help > Broderbund.com**, or go to http://www.broderbund.com in your Internet browser.

Satisfaction Guaranteed

If you are not completely satisfied with this product, Broderbund® will gladly exchange it for another title of equivalent value or refund your purchase price. Return the complete package to us at:

Broderbund
Dock Door # 9
120 Hidden Lake Circle
Duncan, SC 29334
U.S.A.

Make sure you include your store receipt showing the store name and location within 30 days of purchase. Please enclose an explanation for the return and specify the replacement title. Allow 4–6 weeks for refund or replacement title. Limit 1 per household. Dealers, wholesalers and their immediate families are not eligible.

Written inquires should be addressed to our corporate address at:

Broderbund
500 Redwood Boulevard
Novato, CA 94947
U.S.A.

Chapter 2

Screen Layout

The *3D Home Architect® Home Design* screen contains a variety of user-friendly features that make it easy to create precise home plans. This chapter describes everything you see on the screen so you can become familiar and comfortable with your work environment.

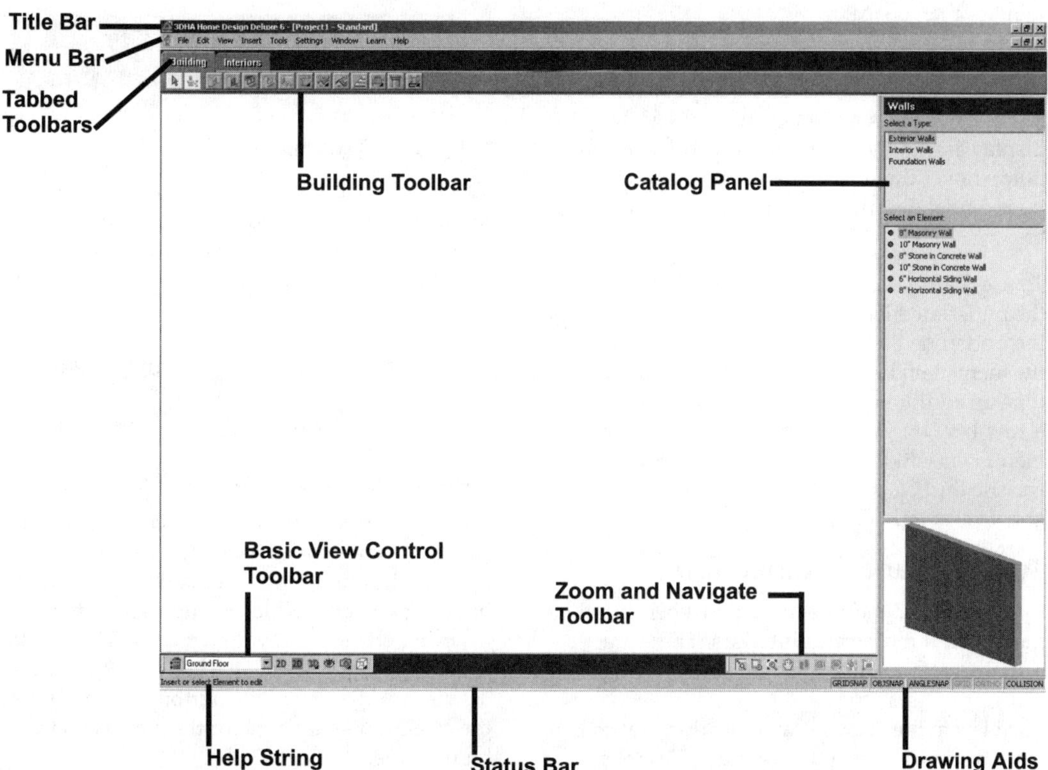

Title Bar

The title bar runs across the top of the screen. It displays the name of your program, the name of the current project, and the name of the current view.

You can minimize, maximize, restore or close the application window using the buttons at the right end of the title bar, or by clicking the Control menu button at the left end of the title bar. You can also maximize or restore the window by double-clicking the title bar. If the application window is not maximized, you can move the entire window around on your desktop by dragging the title bar.

Menu Bar

The menu bar is located directly below the title bar. You can select menu items using either the mouse or keyboard.

To use the mouse, simply click a menu name, then select an item from the menu that pops down. Menu items that have an arrow to the right display cascading menus when you place your pointer over them. When you highlight a menu item, a brief description is displayed on the status bar.

To use the keyboard, press the ALT key and type the underlined letter in the menu name, then type the underlined letter in the menu item name. If the menu item has a cascading menu, you need to type an additional letter. You can also use the arrow keys on your keyboard to move through menu items and press ENTER to select one. You can use the ESC key to back out of the menu items one level at a time.

Toolbars and Toolbar Tabs

By default, two tabs are located just beneath the menu bar: Building and Interiors. These are actually toolbars displayed in tabbed format.

The view in the drawing window does not change when you switch to a different tab. The tabs simply provide you with instant access to the specific toolbars you need, when you need them.

In addition to the two toolbar tabs, there are two free-standing toolbars displayed just below the drawing area: Basic View Control and Zoom and Navigate. Free-standing toolbars can be moved around on the screen. There are more toolbars available for display in your program settings. Each one can be displayed in tabbed or non-tabbed format — the choice is yours.

Note that you still have access to a complete set of Insert features on the **Insert** menu regardless of what tab you are on.

Building Toolbar

The Building toolbar contains the tools you need to build a home or any architectural structure. It includes tools such as Walls, Doors, Windows, and Roofs.

Interiors Toolbar

The Interiors toolbar contains the tools you need to furnish, decorate and equip the interior of your home. It contains tools such as Cabinets, Appliances, Furniture, Lighting and Plumbing Fixtures.

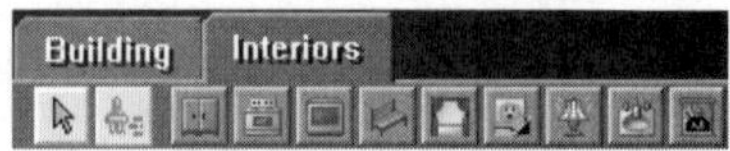

Basic View Control Toolbar

The Basic View Control toolbar contains several essential view-related tools. The toolbar's building location drop box displays the current building location, which is important when inserting elements in your drawing. The toolbar also lets you quickly switch between 2D view and 3D view. A display mode button lets you choose the current display type for the view (wireframe, hidden line, etc.).

Zoom and Navigate Toolbar

Zoom tools on the Zoom and Navigate toolbar include Zoom Realtime, Zoom Window, and Pan. Note that if you are in a 3D Perspective view, only the Zoom Realtime zoom tool is available. The navigation features on the toolbar (Walk Around, Fly Around, Look Around, Slide) are only active when you are in a 3D view. These tools let you change the view in real time using your mouse.

Catalog Panel

The catalog panel, located on the right side of the screen, displays the elements contained in the program's Master Catalog, or whatever catalog is currently open. This is where you select elements to insert into your drawing.

The content of the catalog panel changes depending on which Insert tool is currently selected, or was last selected. For example, if you select the Doors tool, you will see doors displayed in the catalog panel.

The top window of the catalog panel displays a list of groups specific to the current element type. For example, if Doors is the current tool, you will see groups such as Hinged, Entry and Bi-Fold.

The middle window of the catalog panel displays all the element types available in the currently selected group. For example, if the Hinged door group is currently selected, you will see a list of hinged door sizes in the element window.

The lower window of the catalog panel displays a 3D rendered preview of the currently selected element. You can rotate the image around by clicking and dragging with your mouse. Note, however, that the preview is for viewing purposes only within the catalog panel. The orientation of the element in the preview window has no effect on the orientation of the element when you insert it in your plan. You can change an element's orientation after you have inserted it in the plan.

You can also right-click in the preview window and select a different display mode for the image, or switch the preview to a 2D plan view.

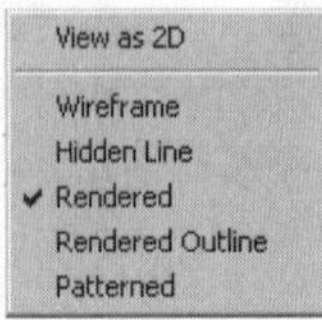

Status Bar

The Status bar is located at the bottom of the screen. It displays helpful prompts while you are working on your design project. For example, if you are inserting a wall, it may display *"Pick first insertion point"*. The Status bar also includes a selection of drawing aid buttons such as ORTHO and OBJSNAP.

Chapter 3

House Builder Wizard

The first question many people ask when they sit down with a new piece of software is, "Where do I start"? *3D Home Architect® Home Design*'s House Builder Wizard is the perfect way to start a project, because it builds a house for you instantly! All you need to do is specify how many stories you want to create, select a general house shape, define the building dimensions, then select the general style for the walls, roof, floors and foundation. In a few mouse clicks, you'll have a basic structure that you can edit and add to.

Once your basic model is built you can add things like interior walls, doors, windows, stairs and furnishings.

Using the House Builder Wizard

By default, the House Builder Wizard launches every time you start a new project.

The House Builder Wizard is a handy, easy-to-use tool that instantly builds a basic house for you based on factors that you specify while stepping through the Wizard. These factors include:

- number of floors
- wall height
- foundation type
- building shape
- building dimensions
- garage type and size
- materials used for walls, roof, floors, etc.

The resulting house includes exterior walls, footings and foundation walls (or concrete slab), a roof, and a floor.

Once the house has been created in your drawing area, you can edit all aspects of it and add to it to suit your needs.

To use the House Builder Wizard:

1. If you haven't already done so, click the **Start a New Project** button in the startup dialog, or select **File > New** if the program is already running.

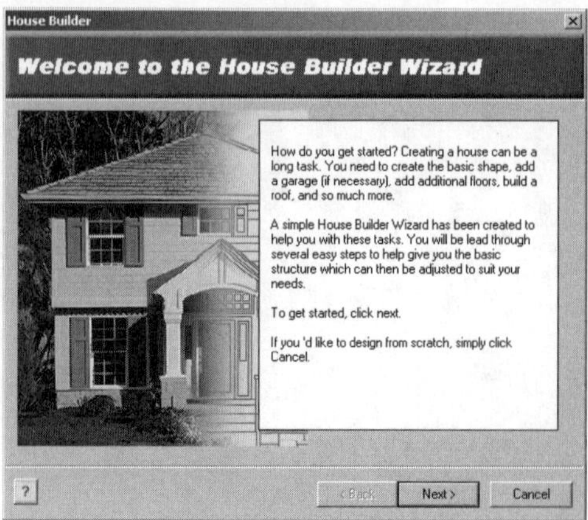

2. On the **House Builder** screen, click **Next**.

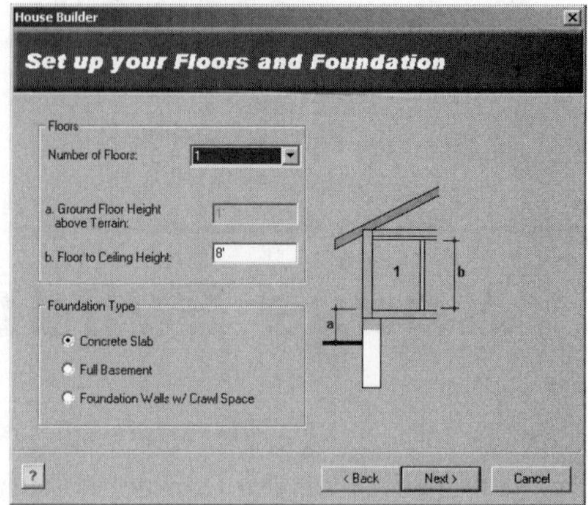

3. From the **Number of Floors** drop box, select the number of floors you would like the house to have (not including the basement level).
4. In the **Floor to Ceiling Height** edit box, type the desired wall height for each floor level.
5. In the *Foundation Type* area, select the type of foundation you want to create. Choose from Concrete Slab, Full Basement, or Foundation Walls w/ Crawl Space.
6. If you selected the Full Basement or Foundation Walls w/Crawl Space, specify the elevation of the ground floor relative to the ground in the **Ground Floor Height above Terrain** edit box.

7. Click **Next**.

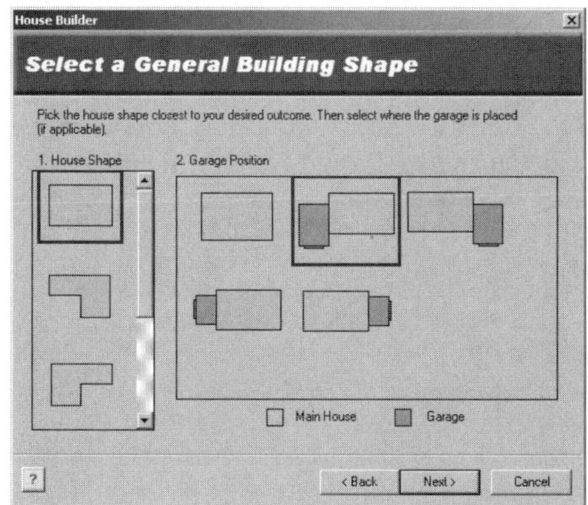

8. Select the general house shape by clicking one of the graphics in the *General House* pane.
9. Once you've selected a house shape, make a selection in the *Garage Position* pane to specify where you want to put the garage. If you don't want a garage, select the first option.
10. Click **Next**.

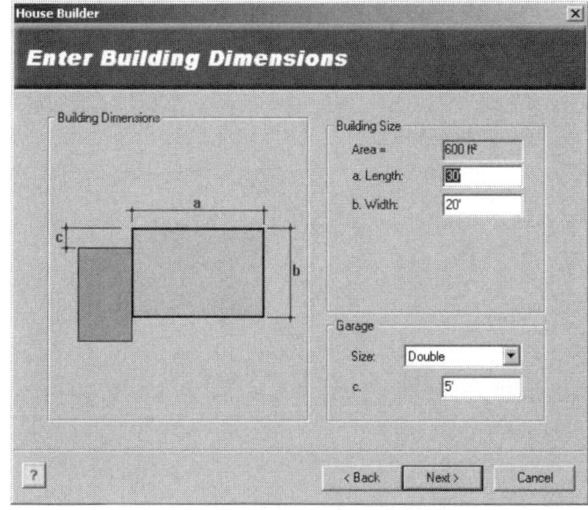

11. In the *Building Size* area, specify the desired dimensions for the house by entering values in the edit boxes. The edit box labels correspond to the labels on the image in the left pane.
12. In the *Garage* area, select either Single, Double or Triple from the **Type** drop box. Then, using the dimensioned graphic as an aid, specify the desired offset of the garage from the exterior wall corner.
13. Click **Next**.

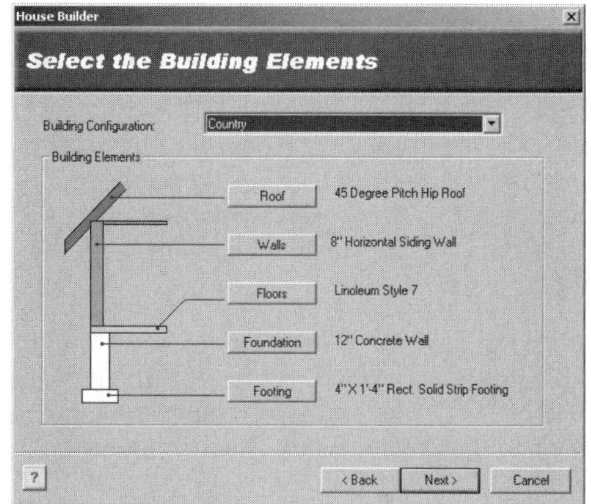

14. From the **Building Configuration** drop box, select the general style for your home (contemporary, country or traditional). The pre-set material selections for the elements in your house are displayed in the lower pane. You can select different materials if you want — just click the button of the element you want to change and make a selection from the catalog.
15. Click **Next**.

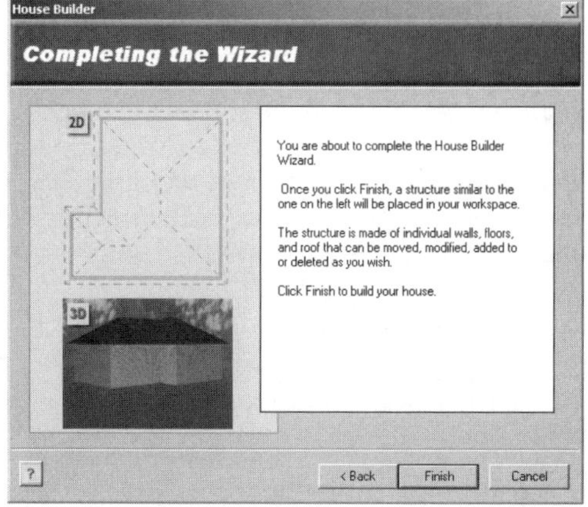

16. Click **Finish** to build the house.

Tip: You can create your own custom configuration of element styles that can be saved for use in any project. See *Creating a Custom House Builder Wizard Configuration* on page 288.

Running the House Builder Wizard When a Drawing is Open

If you have disabled the House Builder Wizard in your program settings, or have cancelled out of the House Builder Wizard when starting a new drawing, you can launch it manually from the Tools menu.

Note: Running the House Builder Wizard will delete all existing building elements in the current project. It will not, however, remove the terrain or any landscaping elements you have inserted.

To run the House Builder Wizard when a drawing is open:

1. Select **Tools > Design Wizards > House Builder.**

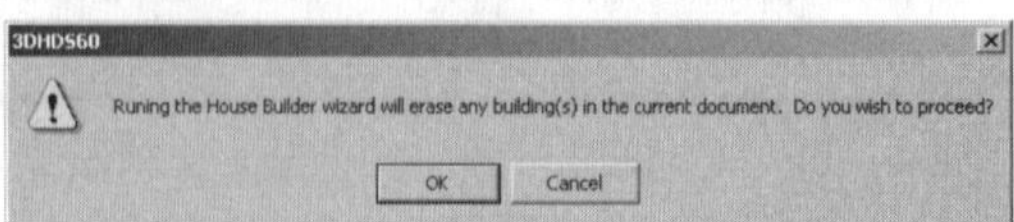

2. Click **OK** in the warning dialog. The House Builder Wizard launches.

Preventing the House Builder Wizard from Launching

By default, the House Builder Wizard launches every time you start a new project. You can stop the House Builder Wizard from appearing if you want. If you disable it, a new blank drawing will open when you start a new project.

To disable the House Builder Wizard:

1. Select **Settings > Program Settings** or click the Program Settings button on the Settings toolbar.
2. In the **Program Settings** dialog, select the General tab.
3. In the *Startup* area, uncheck the **Launch House Builder wizard when starting new drawing** check box.
4. Click **OK**.

Note: You can still run the House Builder Wizard from the Tools > Design Wizards menu when a drawing is open.

Chapter 4

Building Locations

When you insert an element in your drawing, it is inserted on the current building location. It is important to define your building locations before inserting elements, since building locations are the key to organizing elements and inserting them at the correct height in your model.

If you used the House Builder Wizard to start your project, your main building locations are set up for you. Their settings depend on the selections you made in the House Builder Wizard. If you are drawing from scratch, the program's default drawing templates have three pre-defined building locations: Foundation, Ground Floor, and Second Floor. You can change the settings for existing building locations as well as add and delete locations.

This chapter describes how to define your building locations, and identify the current building location when adding elements to your design.

Defining Building Locations

When you define building locations, you are basically doing two things:

- setting the wall height for each floor (level) in your model
- specifying where each floor is positioned relative to the ground (zero)

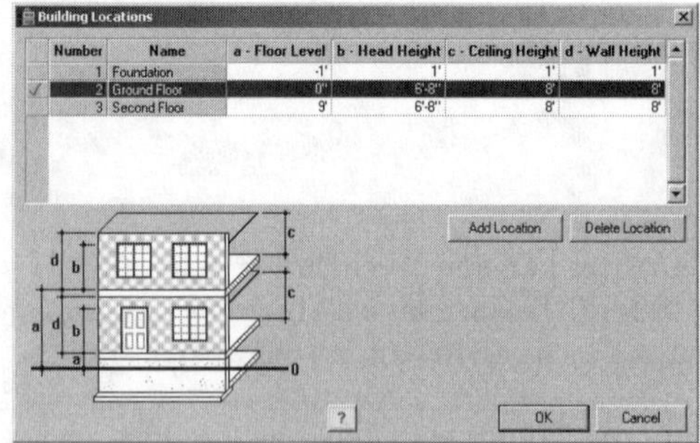

To view building location settings:

1. Select **Settings > Building Locations**, or click the Building Locations button on the Settings toolbar. 

Below is a brief description of each building location property.

Number. A reference number for the location.

Name. The location's name (e.g. Ground Floor).

Floor Level. Height of floor base above ground level (0).

Head Height. Height of tops of windows and wall openings relative to the floor level.

Ceiling Height. Height of underside of ceiling surface relative to the floor level.

Wall Height. Physical height of the walls on the location.

By default, if you are drawing from scratch, the Foundation location has a Floor Level of -1', meaning the base of the foundation starts one foot below the ground. (In other words, it is not a full basement.) The Wall Height of the Foundation location is 1', meaning the foundation wall runs 1' up from the foundation floor. The top of the foundation wall would be even with the ground. These are typical settings for someone who isn't interested in creating a basement. If you wanted to create a full basement, you could change the Floor Level to -8' and the Wall Height to 8'.

By default, the Ground Floor and Second Floor locations each have their Wall Height set to 8'. The Floor Level of the Ground Floor is set to 0. The Floor Level of the Second Floor location is set to 9'. This leaves a 12" space between the Ground Floor walls and Second Floor walls, which is needed to fit the floor structure of the ground floor.

To change the properties of a building location:

1. In the **Building Locations** dialog, click on the property you want to change. You can change location names or any of the numerical settings.
2. Type the value you want.
3. Press **Enter**.

To add a new building location:

1. In the **Building Locations** dialog, click the Add Location button. A new location is added to the bottom of the list.

   Note: By default the new location will adopt the numerical settings of the currently selected location.
2. Specify the location's properties. To specify a property, click on the current value, type the new value, then press **Enter**.

Note: When you add a location to your list, it does not become the current location unless you select it in the list or edit its properties.

To delete a building location:

1. In the **Building Locations** dialog, click on one of the location's fields to make it the current location.
2. Click **Delete Location**.

Note: You cannot delete a location if it contains any elements. Also, you cannot delete a location if it is the only one in the list.

Current Building Location

Before inserting an element in your drawing you should make sure that the building location you want to insert the element on is the *current* building location.

To identify the current building location:

- Take a look at the building locations drop box on the Basic View Control or Advanced View Control toolbar.

  or

- See which location is checked in the **Building Locations** dialog.

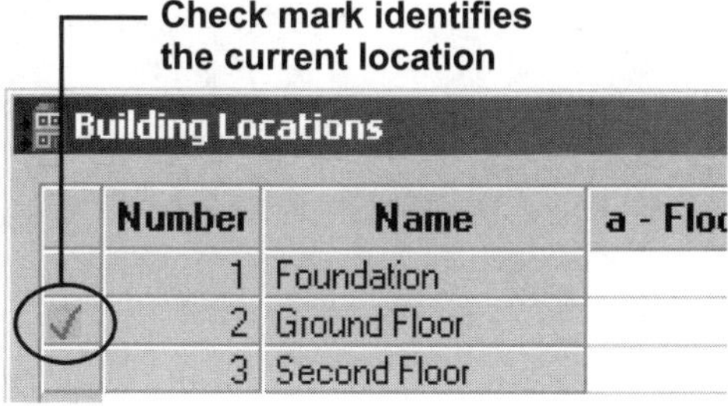

To make a different location current within the current view:

- Click on the building locations drop box on the Basic View Control or Advanced View Control toolbar and select the desired location.

  or

- In the **Building Locations** dialog, click in the far left field of the location you want to make current. A check mark indicates the location is now current.

Location Dimming

When a particular location is current, elements on all other visible locations are dimmed. This makes it easier to insert and edit elements on the current location because it is more obvious which elements are part of the current location.

By default, elements on other locations are dimmed by 90%. You can adjust the dimming so that it is lighter or darker according to your preference.

To change the dimming percentage:

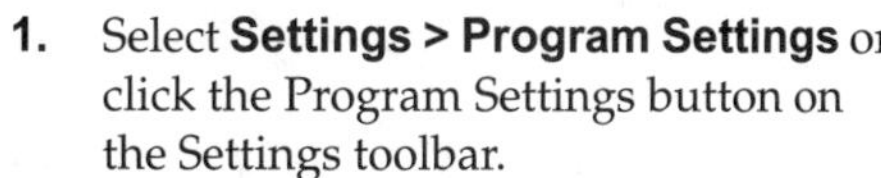

1. Select **Settings > Program Settings** or click the Program Settings button on the Settings toolbar. 
2. In the **Program Settings** dialog, select the Workspace tab.
3. Type the desired dimming percentage in the **Dimming Percentage** edit box, or use the arrows to scroll up or down through a list of values.
4. Click **OK**.

Chapter 5

Drawing & Editing Basics

Whether you have automatically built a house using the House Builder Wizard, or have started a drawing from scratch, you will insert a variety of elements to create your home design.

Everything is point-and-click in *3D Home Architect® Home Design*, making it extremely simple to use and leaving you free to be as creative as you like. All elements are intelligent and know what they are in relation to other elements. For example, a door can only be inserted in a wall. *3D Home Architect® Home Design* automatically displays dimensions as you draw, making it even easier to create accurate drawings right from the start.

While working on your project, you will probably want to edit it as you go. You can select elements by clicking on them, or by drawing a selection window around them.

This chapter describes the basics of inserting elements, and selecting them for editing.

Inserting Elements

When you select a tool from the **Insert** menu or one of the insertion toolbars, you are in Insertion mode. To insert an element, you select it in the catalog panel, then click in your drawing area.

Many elements can be inserted with a single mouse click. *Single-click* elements include doors, windows, stairs, columns, cabinets, furniture, appliances, light fixtures, electrical elements and plumbing fixtures. *Line-drawn* elements, like walls and railings, require that you select two points to define the element's start point and end point. The points you pick determine the element's length and angle. *Area-drawn* elements, such as floor and ceiling openings, are drawn by picking a series of points to define their outline.

In many cases, on-screen dimensions are displayed as you draw, making it easy to create line-drawn and area-drawn elements at the correct length or size, and insert elements like doors and windows precisely where you want them in a wall.

Once you insert an element in your drawing area, you can:

- Continue inserting the same element
- Select a different element in the catalog to insert
- Right-click and select **Finish** to end the command and return to Selection mode

Tip: When an Insert tool is active, double-clicking inserts the element and finishes the command at the same time. Note, however, that double-clicking after you've already inserted an element will, in most cases, insert another element.

Tip: If you are in Selection mode, you can insert any element currently accessible in the catalog by clicking the desired element in the catalog and dragging your pointer into the drawing area.

Note: If you don't see the exact element you want to insert in the catalog, you can create custom elements to suit your needs. See *Adding and Editing Elements in a Catalog* on page 247.

Selecting an Insertion Method for Line-Drawn Elements

Some elements, like walls and railings, are drawn by picking two or more points. By default, line-drawn elements use the **Pick and drag** insertion method. With this method, you keep the mouse button depressed after clicking the first point, drag the mouse to draw the element, then release your mouse button to select the next point.

If you prefer to pick points without dragging, you can select the **Pick Points** insertion method. With this method you do not have to keep your mouse button depressed to draw the element (i.e. you do not have to click and drag the mouse). Once you've selected the first point, you can simply move your mouse in the direction you want the element to run, then click to select the next point.

To select an insertion method for line-drawn elements:

1. Select **Settings > Program Settings** or click the Program Settings button on the Settings toolbar. 
2. In the **Program Settings** dialog, select the Drawing Aids tab.
3. In the *Insertion Method* area, select either **Pick Points** or **Pick and drag**.
4. Click **OK**.

Inserting Ceilings Automatically

If you want ceilings to be inserted automatically when you draw a wall layout, you need to enable the **Automatically Insert Ceilings** option. By default, a 1/2" drywall ceiling is inserted, or whatever ceiling type was last selected in the catalog. You can edit the ceiling type later if you want.

To enable or disable automatic ceiling insertion:

1. Select **Settings > Program Settings** or click the Program Settings button on the Settings toolbar. 
2. In the **Program Settings** dialog, select the Drawing Aids tab.

3. Check or uncheck the **Automatically Insert Ceilings** check box.
4. Click **OK**.

Note: You can also insert ceilings separately using one of the **Insert > Ceilings** tools.

Tip: The underside of a floor can also serve as a ceiling.

Going into Selection Mode for Editing

When you have finished using an insertion tool, either by double-clicking or selecting **Finish** from the right-click menu, you automatically go into Selection mode. When in Selection mode, you can select elements in your drawing area and edit them.

You can also go into Selection mode by clicking the Select/Edit button on any insertion toolbar, or by selecting **Select/Edit** from the **Edit** menu.

Disabling Pre-Selection

When pre-selection is turned on, elements highlight when you hover your cursor over them. Tooltips are also displayed that tell you what the elements are as they are highlighted. By default, pre-selection is enabled. On some systems, disabling pre-selection can help improve program speed.

To disable pre-selection:

1. Select **Settings > Program Settings** or click the Program Settings button on the Settings toolbar.
2. In the **Program Settings** dialog, select the Drawing Aids tab.
3. In the *Visual Aids* area, uncheck the **Enable Pre-Selection** check box.
4. Click **OK**.

Selecting Elements for Editing

When in Selection Mode, you can select elements for editing. You can select individual elements, a group of elements, or all elements.

When an element is selected, it is highlighted in a different color (usually light green). One or more handles are also displayed on the element.

When you are in 3D view, all elements on all locations are selectable. When you are in 2D plan view, only elements on the current building location are selectable. However, you can change this if you want. See *Making Elements on All Locations Selectable in 2D Plan View* on page 24.

If you are having trouble selecting the element you want, you may want to use the View Filter to make other elements non-selectable. This makes selection of the element much easier. See *Selection Filtering* on page 37.

Note: Automatic floors and ceilings cannot be selected in 2D. They can only be selected in 3D.

To select a single element:

1. Click on the element.

To select multiple elements by clicking:

1. Click the first element you want to select.
2. Hold down the **Shift** key and click on the rest of the elements you want to select. The most recent selection is green and prior selections are blue.

To select a group of elements by creating a selection window:

1. Going from either left to right, or right to left, drag a selection window around the elements you want to select. Any elements touching the selection window will be selected (they do not need to be totally enclosed).

To select all elements on the current location:

1. Select **Edit > Select All**.

To re-select the elements you last selected:

1. Select **Edit > Select Previous**.

Deselecting Elements

When you select elements, you can remove individual elements from your selection set. You can also deselect everything that is currently selected.

To deselect individual elements:

1. Hold down your **Shift** key.
2. Click the element you want to deselect.

To deselect everything in your selection set:

1. Select **Edit > Deselect All**, or right-click in the drawing area and select **Deselect All**, or simply click in a blank spot somewhere else in the drawing area.

Making Elements on All Locations Selectable in 2D Plan View

By default, only elements on the current building location can be selected in 2D plan view, even if elements on other locations are visible. If you want to make elements on all locations selectable, you need to change one of your program settings.

To make elements on all locations selectable in 2D plan view:

1. Select **Settings > Program Settings** or click the Program Settings button on the Settings toolbar. 
2. In the **Program Settings** dialog, select the Drawing Aids tab.
3. In the *Drawing Assistance* area, uncheck the **Select elements on current location only while in plan view** check box.
4. Click **OK**.

Accessing Edit Tools

Most elements can be moved once they are selected by simply clicking and dragging them. Some can also be stretched or rotated. You can access a full menu of edit tools by right-clicking in the drawing area, or by selecting **Edit > Modify Elements**.

Menus vary depending on the element selected. Typical tools are Properties, Move, Rotate, Duplicate, and Delete. If two types of elements are selected (such as a floor and a wall), only tools that are common to both element types are available.

Each chapter includes editing instructions specific to the contents of that chapter. For information about general editing, see *Editing Your Design* on page 165.

Part 2

Controlling the View

Chapter 6

2D and 3D Viewing

3D Home Architect® Home Design offers a variety of options for viewing your design in 2D and 3D.

When working in 2D plan view, you can magnify or reduce the view using the Zoom Realtime tool. You can also magnify a selected area using the Zoom Window tool. The Zoom to Fit tool magnifies your design so it fills the drawing area, creating the largest view possible. The Pan tool lets you pan the view in any direction by simply clicking and dragging.

You can instantly switch to 3D view with a couple of mouse clicks. You can choose from the realistic 3D Perspective view, which is like viewing your house from a distance, or 3D Overview, which eliminates distance from the view and lets you see the house from above.

While viewing in 3D you can choose from a variety of display types, including Wireframe, Patterned and Rendered.

Using the Framing Visibility options you can view your house frame, which consists of wall, roof, floor and ceiling framing.

This chapter describes all basic 2D and 3D viewing features. For information about advanced viewing features, see page 233.

Viewing the 2D Plan

When you start a drawing, the default view is a 2D plan view. It shows your model in a "flat" view, as if you were looking at it from above. 2D Plan view is ideal for creating a floor plan.

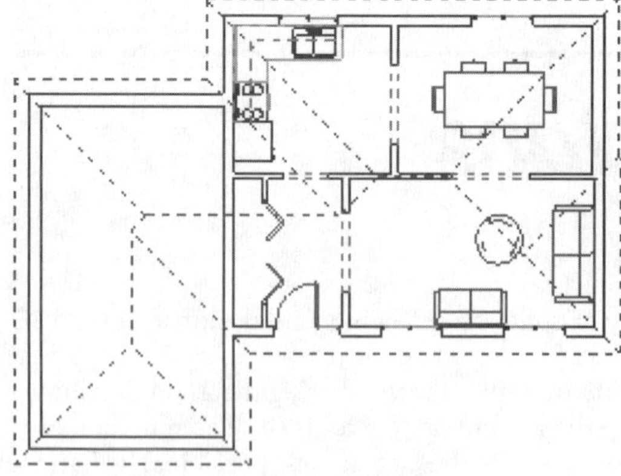

To display your model in 2D plan view:

- Select **View > 2D Plan View**, or
- Click the 2D Plan View button on the Basic View Control or Advanced View Control toolbar, or
- Right-click in the drawing area and select **2D Plan View**

By default, all locations are visible at the same time. However, any locations other than the current location are dimmed. You can control which elements and locations are displayed by using the View Filter. See *Filtering the Display* on page 34.

While in 2D plan view you can zoom in and out, and pan your drawing.

Viewing a 2D Designer's View

By default, your design is displayed in a wireframe 2D plan view. You can use the 2D Designer's View tool to quickly display a rendered version of the 2D plan view. In a rendered view, materials are applied to the elements and terrain, creating a more realistic view. For example, if you have a shingled roof on your model, you will actually see the shingles in 2D Designer's View.

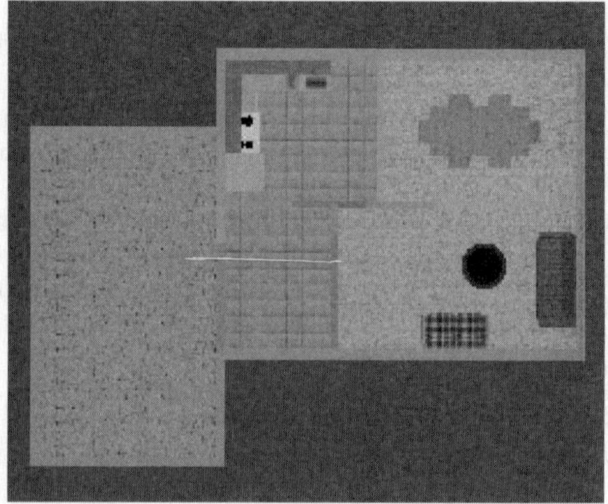

To view a 2D Designer's View:

1. Select **View > 2D Designer's View**, or click the 2D Designer's View button on the Basic View Control or Advanced View Control toolbar. 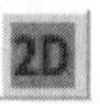

Note: If you want to be able to see inside the model, you can use the View Filter to hide elements like the roof or ceilings. See *Filtering the Display* on page 34.

Viewing in 3D

You can instantly switch to 3D view by selecting either the 3D Perspective or 3D Overview tool.

In a 3D Perspective view, the scale of an element decreases according to its distance from the viewer, creating a more real-world view.

To view a 3D perspective view:

1. Select **View > 3D Model View > 3D Perspective**, or click the 3D Model View button on the Basic View Control or Advanced View Control toolbar and select **3D Perspective**.

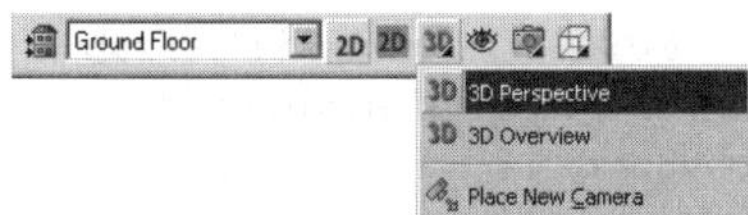

The 3D Overview is an orthographic view, where the view is set from a common angle, and distance is eliminated from the view. This creates an instant close-up of your design.

To view a 3D overview:

1. Select **View > 3D Model View > 3D Overview**, or click the 3D Model View button on the Basic View Control or Advanced View Control toolbar and select **3D Overview**.

Tip: If you have your cameras turned on in 2D, you can switch to a 3D view by selecting a camera, right-clicking it, then selecting **Look Through**.

Note: By default, 3D views are displayed in Rendered mode. For information about changing the display mode, see *Changing the Display Mode* on page 30. For information about moving around in a 3D view, or creating or customizing 3D views, see *Custom Viewing* on page 233.

Zooming In and Out

The Zoom Realtime tool continuously magnifies or shrinks the view as you click and drag with your mouse. You can zoom in and out in 2D plan view or any 3D view.

To zoom in and out:

1. Select **View > Zoom and Navigate > Zoom Realtime**, or click the Zoom Realtime button on the Zoom and Navigate toolbar. 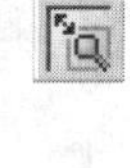
2. To zoom in, click and drag toward the top of the screen. To zoom out, click and drag toward the bottom of the screen.
3. When the view is the desired size, release your mouse button.

Tip: You can also zoom in and out using the scroll button on your mouse.

Zooming a Selected Area

Using the Zoom Window tool you can magnify a particular area of your design by drawing a selection window around it.

To zoom a selected area:

1. Select **View > Zoom and Navigate > Zoom Window**, or click the Zoom Window button on the Zoom and Navigate toolbar. Your cursor becomes a magnifying glass. 
2. Click and drag a selection window around the area you want to magnify.

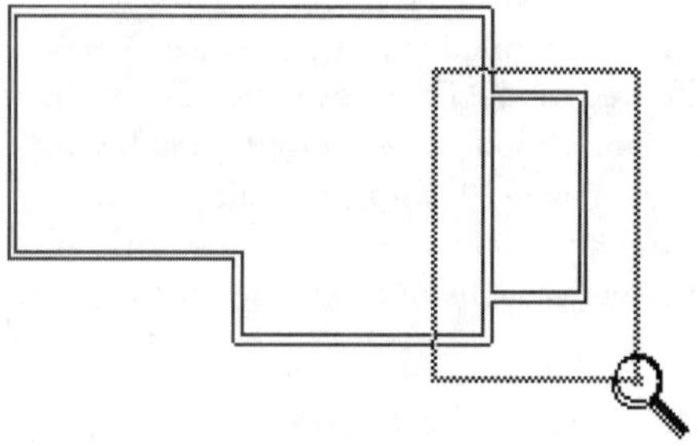

Note: The Zoom Window tool is not available in 3D perspective views.

Zooming to Fit the Drawing Area

The Zoom to Fit tool instantly extends your drawing to the edges of the drawing area. This ensures your entire drawing is visible at the most maximized view possible, and makes full use of the drawing area.

To zoom the drawing to fit the drawing area:

1. Select **View > Zoom and Navigate > Zoom to Fit**, or click the Zoom to Fit button on the Zoom and Navigate toolbar. 

Note that the terrain is considered part of your drawing. If you want to zoom your model to fit the drawing area, you need to turn the terrain off before using Zoom to Fit.

Note: The Zoom to Fit tool is not available in 3D perspective views.

Panning Across a Drawing

Using the Pan tool you can move the current view of your design to bring a particular part of your design into view. This is especially useful when the area you want to view is currently not visible because you have zoomed in on your drawing.

To pan the current view:

1. Select **View > Zoom and Navigate > Pan**, or click the Pan button on the Zoom and Navigate toolbar. 
2. Click in the drawing.
3. Hold your mouse button down.
4. Drag the view in the direction you want to pan.
5. Release the mouse button.

Note: The Pan tool is not available in 3D perspective views.

Changing the Display Mode

By default, your design is displayed in Wireframe mode when you are in 2D plan view. When you switch to a 3D view, the default display mode is Rendered mode. There are five display modes you can choose from.

Wireframe. Each line in your design is visible, creating a "see-through" view.

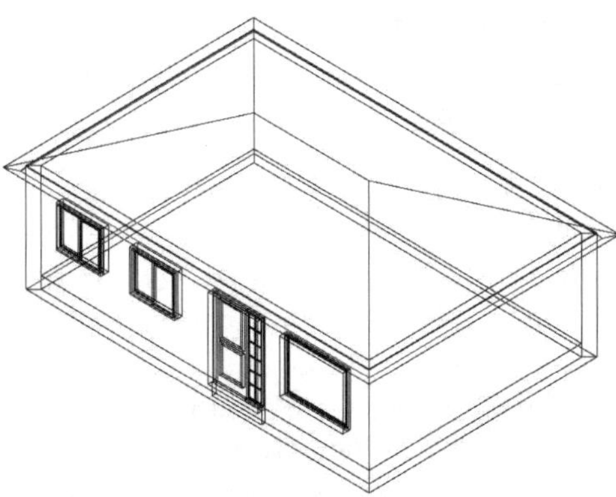

Hidden Line. Removes lines from the view that you would normally not see, creating an opaque view.

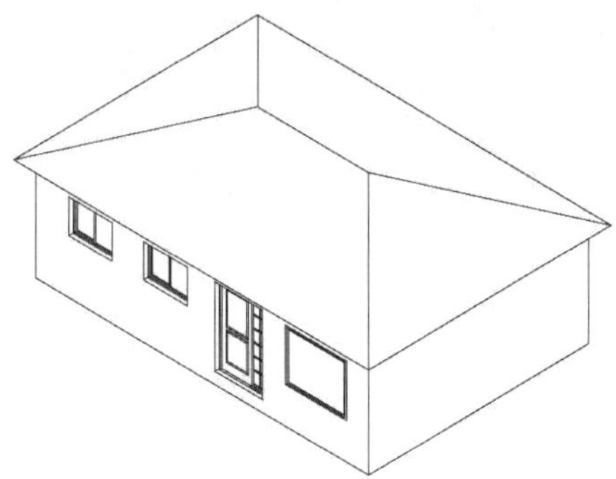

Rendered. Applies materials to the elements and terrain, creating a very realistic view.

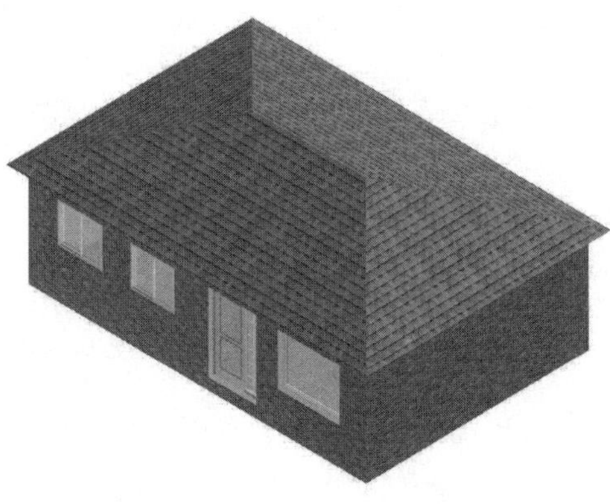

Rendered Outline. Applies materials to the elements and terrain, and outlines surface edges in a single, dark line for increased surface definition.

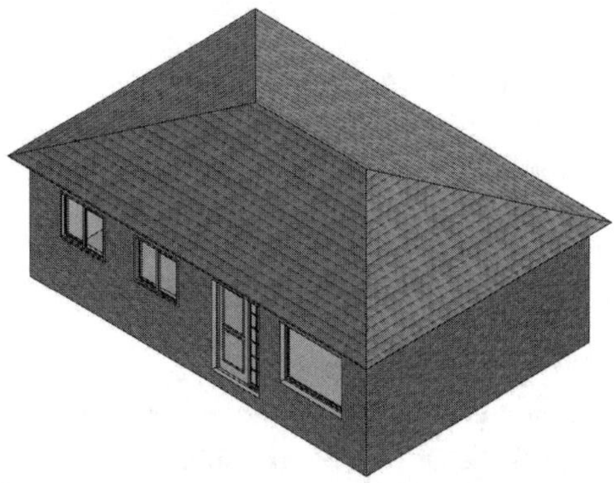

Patterned. Applies patterns of lines (hatching) to the surfaces of elements.

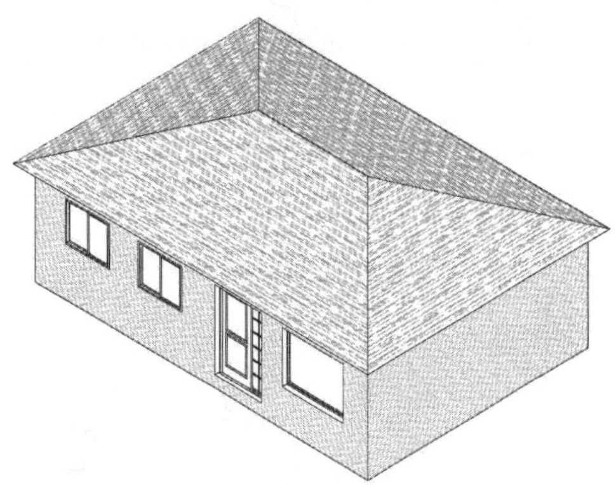

To view Wireframe mode:

- Select **View > Display Mode > Wireframe**, or
- Click the Display Mode button on the Basic View Control or Advanced View Control toolbar and select **Wireframe**

To view Hidden Line mode:

- Select **View > Display Mode > Hidden Line**, or
- Click the Display Mode button on the Basic View Control or Advanced View Control toolbar and select **Hidden Line**

To view Rendered mode:

- Select **View > Display Mode > Rendered**, or
- Click the Display Mode button on the Basic View Control or Advanced View Control toolbar and select **Rendered**

To view Rendered Outline mode:

- Select **View > Display Mode > Rendered Outline**, or
- Click the Display Mode button on the Basic View Control or Advanced View Control toolbar and select **Rendered Outline**

To view Patterned mode:

- Select **View > Display Mode > Patterned**, or
- Click the Display Mode button on the Basic View Control or Advanced View Control toolbar and select **Patterned**

Displaying Framing

Walls, floors, ceilings and roofs have a framing configuration assigned to them in their properties. You can instantly view just your house frame using the Display Framing tool, then return to a regular view of your model at any time.

To display framing:

1. Select **View > Framing Visibility > Display Framing**.

Note: You can also use the View Filter to display framing. However, the framing will not be displayed on its own unless you turn everything else off.

Note: Framing cannot be selected for editing. It is available for viewing purposes only.

To return to a non-framed view:

1. Select **View > Framing Visibility > Display All But Framing**.

To change framing members or member spacing:

1. In non-framed view, select the wall, floor, ceiling or roof whose framing you want to change.
2. Right-click and select **Properties**, or select **Edit > Modify Elements > Properties**.
3. On the Basic property page, click the **Specify Framing** button.

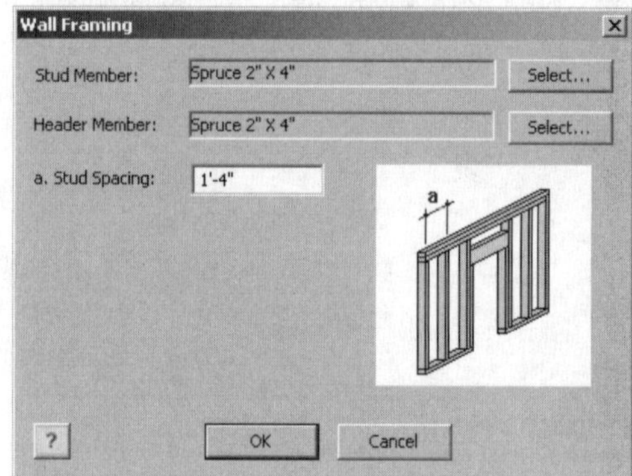

4. Select the desired framing members and specify the spacing you want.
5. Click **OK**.

Chapter 7

View Filter

The program's unique View Filter feature lets you decide which elements or locations you want displayed at any given time. For example, you may want to hide your roof and ceilings to be able to see inside the model. It also lets you make selected elements non-selectable, which is sometimes necessary when trying to select a particular element in your drawing, like a floor or ceiling.

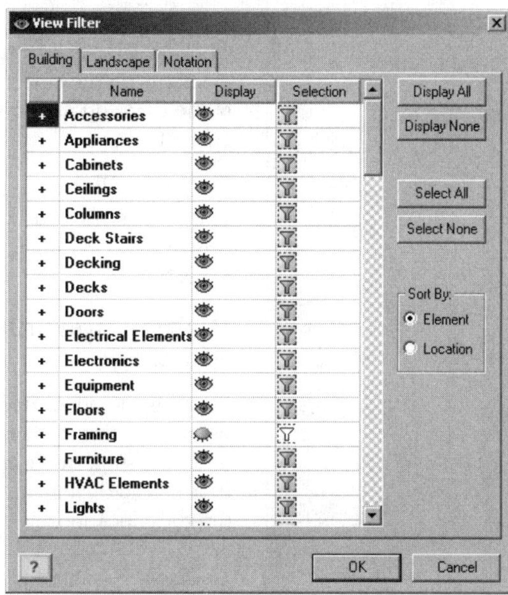

Filtering the Display

The View Filter provides precise control over what elements and locations are displayed in a view at any given time.

You can display/hide:

- an entire location, or multiple locations
- building elements on a specific location or multiple locations
- selected or all landscaping elements
- text and dimension elements

Note: Using the View Filter does not delete elements from your drawing. It just hides them from view.

To access the View Filter:

- Select **View > View Filter** or click the View Filter button on the Basic View Control or Advanced View Control toolbar. 

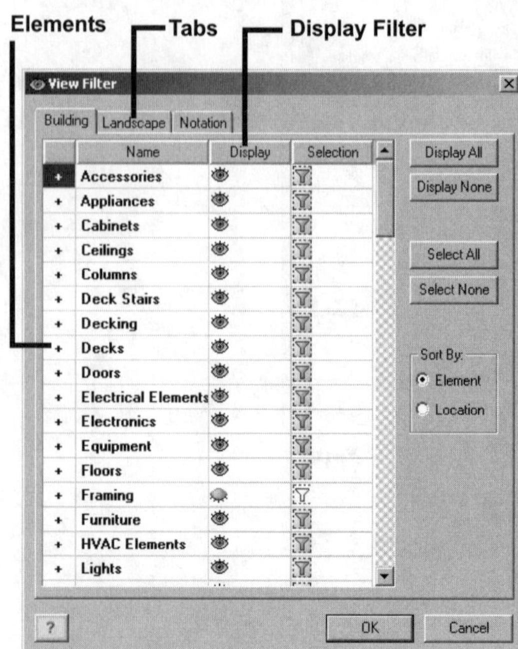

The **View Filter** dialog contains three tabs: Building, Landscape and Notation. The Building tab lists all elements types. If you expand an element, a list of building locations is displayed below the element name. If you choose to sort by location, a list of building locations is displayed with a list of elements under each one. The Landscape tab contains a list of exterior landscaping elements, and the Notation tab contains text, dimensions, project trace images, and electrical wiring.

The icons in the *Display* column indicate whether or not that location or element is currently displayed. Clicking an icon toggles the icon to the opposite state (on or off).

 Location or element is turned on

 Location or element is turned off

 If sorting by element, this means that the element is displayed on some locations and not on others. If sorting by location, it means that some elements on the location are displayed and some are not.

Clicking **Display All** turns on all locations and elements on the current tab. Clicking **Display None** turns off all locations and elements on the current tab.

The **View Filter** dialog also lets you control whether or not individual locations and elements can be selected. See *Selection Filtering* on page 37.

Displaying/Hiding Building Elements

Building elements are things like walls, doors and windows - things that make up an architectural model. Using the View Filter you can display or hide selected element types on all or selected building locations.

To display or hide building elements:

1. Select **View > View Filter** or click the View Filter button on the Basic View Control or Advanced View Control toolbar. 
2. In the **View Filter** dialog, select the Building tab.

3. In the *Sort By* area, make sure the **Element** radio button is selected.
4. If you want to change the visibility of an element on all locations, click the element's eye icon in the *Display* column. If you want to filter an element on a specific location, click the element's plus sign (+) to display a list of building locations. Then, click the location's eye icon in the *Display* column.

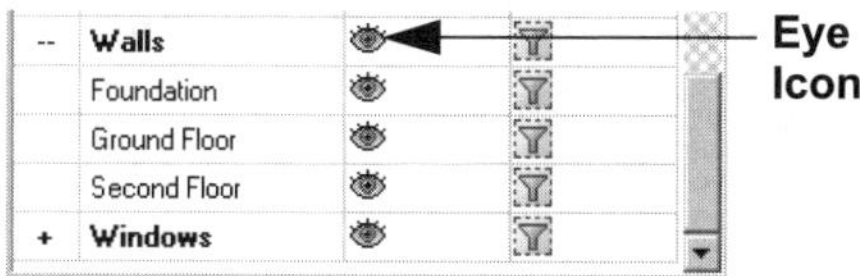

 Element is turned on

 Element is turned off

You can also filter elements by location. If you enable the **Location** radio button in the *Sort By* area, a list of building locations is displayed. You can then expand the location you want to filter elements on to display a list of elements. Toggling the eye icons of elements in this list filters elements on the selected location.

+	Foundation		
--	Ground Floor		
	Accessories		
	Appliances		
	Cabinets		

If you want to make all elements on all locations visible, click the **Display All** button. If you want to make all elements on all locations non-visible, click **Display None**.

5. Once you've selected what you want to filter, click **OK**.

Displaying/Hiding Building Locations

You can turn individual locations on or off. When you turn a location off, all elements on that location are hidden from view.

To display or hide entire locations:

1. Select **View > View Filter** or click the View Filter button on the Basic View Control or Advanced View Control toolbar. 
2. In the **View Filter** dialog, select the Building tab.
3. In the *Sort By* area, enable the **Location** radio button. A list of building locations is displayed in the window.

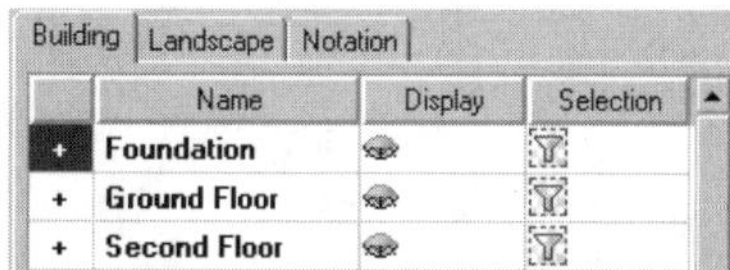

4. Click the eye icon next to the name of the location you want to display or hide.

 Location is turned on

 Location is turned off

5. Click **OK**.

Displaying/Hiding Landscape Elements

Landscape elements include things like the terrain, site boundary, paths and plants. Using the View Filter you can display or hide selected landscape element types. With the exception of the terrain, your project does not contain landscape elements unless you have opened a drawing from a program that is capable of producing landscaping, such as *3D Home Architect® Landscape Design*.

To filter landscape elements:

1. Select **View > View Filter** or click the View Filter button on the Basic View Control or Advanced View Control toolbar.

2. In the **View Filter** dialog, select the Landscape tab. A list of landscape elements is displayed.

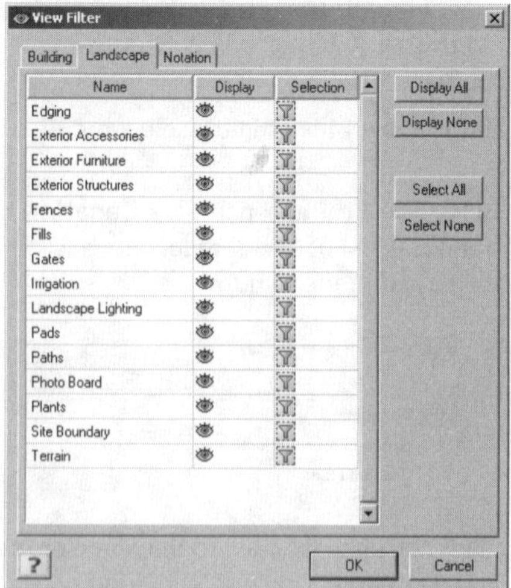

3. Click the eye icons in the *Display* column to turn elements on or off.

 Element is turned on

 Element is turned off

4. Click **OK**.

Displaying/Hiding Text

Using the View Filter you can display or hide text in your drawing.

To filter text from view:

1. Select **View > View Filter** or click the View Filter button on the Basic View Control or Advanced View Control toolbar.

2. In the **View Filter** dialog, select the Notation tab.

Building | Landscape | Notation

Name	Display	Selection
Dimension		
Electrical Wiring		
Project Trace Image		
Text		

3. In the **Text** row, click the eye icon in the *Display* column to turn text on or off.

 Text is turned on

 Text is turned off

4. Click **OK**.

Displaying/Hiding Dimensions

Using the View Filter you can display or hide dimensions in your drawing.

To filter dimensions from view:

1. Select **View > View Filter** or click the View Filter button on the Basic View Control or Advanced View Control toolbar.

2. In the **View Filter** dialog, select the Notation tab.

Building | Landscape | Notation

Name	Display	Selection
Dimension		
Electrical Wiring		
Project Trace Image		
Text		

3. In the **Dimension** row, click the eye icon in the *Display* column to turn dimensions on or off.

 Dimensions are turned on

 Dimensions are turned off

4. Click **OK**.

Displaying/Hiding Electrical Wiring

Using the View Filter you can display or hide electrical wiring in your drawing.

To filter electrical wiring from view:

1. Select **View > View Filter** or click the View Filter button on the Basic View Control or Advanced View Control toolbar. 
2. In the **View Filter** dialog, select the Notation tab.

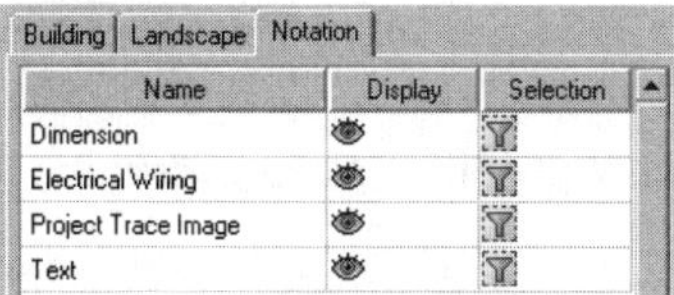

3. In the **Electrical Wiring** row, click the eye icon in the *Display* column to turn wiring on or off.

 Wiring is turned on

 Wiring is turned off

4. Click **OK**.

Displaying/Hiding Project Trace Images

If you have used the Project Trace Image tool to import a plan into your project, you can hide the image if you want using the View Filter. This is an alternative to deleting the image.

To filter project trace images from view:

1. Select **View > View Filter** or click the View Filter button on the Basic View Control or Advanced View Control toolbar. 
2. In the **View Filter** dialog, select the Notation tab.

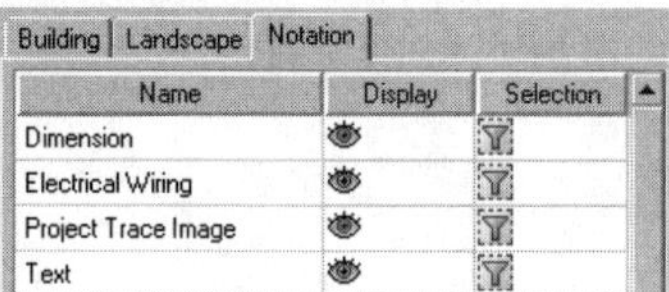

3. In the **Project Trace Image** row, click the eye icon in the *Display* column to turn wiring on or off.

 Project trace image is turned on

 Project trace image is turned off

4. Click **OK**.

Selection Filtering

When your model contains a number of elements, it can sometimes be difficult to select certain ones because of proximity or overlapping edges. Floors, for example, can be very difficult to select because floor edges are typically right up against your walls. Also, small elements can be hard to select in an extreme zoomed out view, even in 2D.

You can use the View Filter to stop certain elements from being selected. You can even prevent entire building locations from being selected.

To access the View Filter:

1. Select **View > View Filter** or click the View Filter button on the Basic View Control or Advanced View Control toolbar.

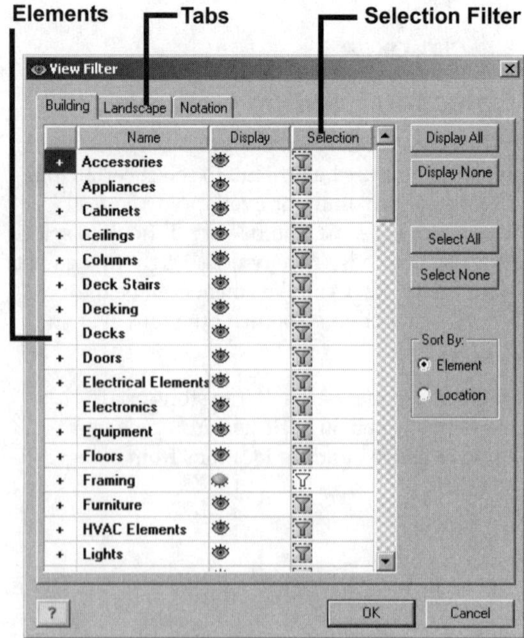

The **View Filter** dialog contains three tabs: Building, Landscape and Notation. The Building tab lists all element types. When you expand an element, all of your building locations are listed below the element. The Landscape tab contains a list of exterior landscaping elements, and the Notation tab contains text, dimensions, project trace images, and electrical wiring.

The icons in the *Selection* column indicate whether or not that location or element is currently selectable. Clicking an icon toggles the icon to the opposite state (selectable or non-selectable).

Element or location is selectable

Element or location is not selectable

Making Building Elements Selectable or Non-Selectable

Building elements are things like walls, doors and windows - things that make up an architectural model. Using the View Filter you can make individual element types selectable or non-selectable on all or selected building locations.

To change the selectability of building elements:

1. Select **View > View Filter** or click the View Filter button on the Basic View Control or Advanced View Control toolbar.

2. In the **View Filter** dialog, select the Building tab.
3. In the *Sort By* area, make sure the **Element** radio button is selected.
4. If you want to change the selectability of an element on all locations, click the element's filter icon in the *Selection* column. If you want to filter an element on a specific location, click the element's plus sign (+) to display a list of building locations. Then, click the location's filter icon in the *Selection* column.

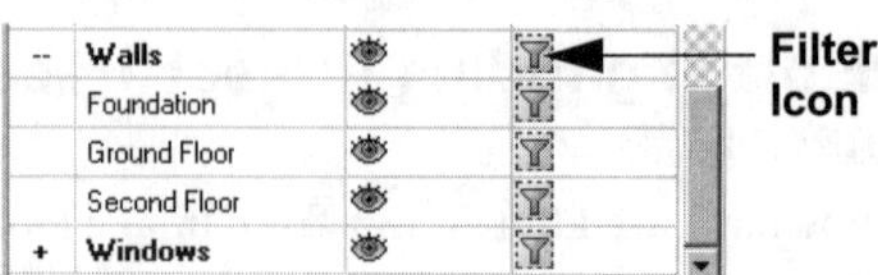

 Element is selectable

 Element is not selectable

You can also filter elements by location. If you enable the **Location** radio button in the *Sort By* area, a list of building locations is displayed. You can then expand the location you want to filter elements on to display a list of elements. Toggling the filter icons of elements in this list filters elements on the selected location.

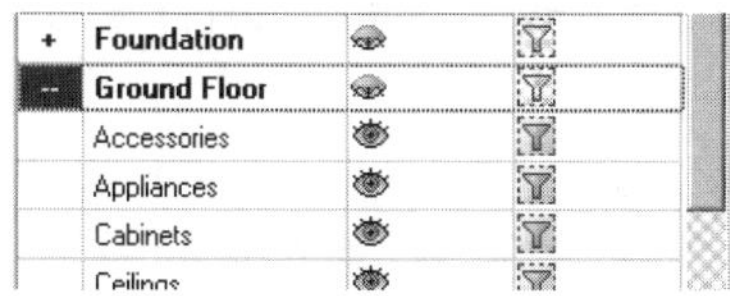

If you want to make all elements on all locations selectable, click the **Select All** button. If you want to make all elements on all locations non-selectable, click **Select None**.

5. Once you've selected what you want to filter, click **OK**.

Making Building Locations Selectable or Non-Selectable

When you make a location non-selectable, no elements on that location can be selected in any view.

To make a location selectable or non-selectable:

1. Select **View > View Filter** or click the View Filter button on the Basic View Control or Advanced View Control toolbar.
2. In the **View Filter** dialog, select the Building tab.
3. In the *Sort By* area, enable the **Location** radio button. A list of building locations is displayed in the window.

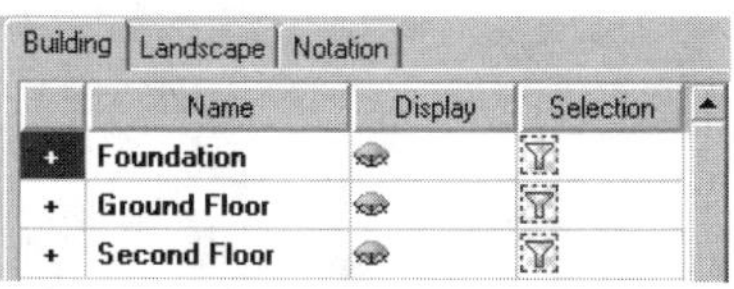

4. Click the filter icon next to the name of the location you want to make selectable or non-selectable.

 Location is selectable

 Location is not selectable

If you want to make all locations selectable, click the **Select All** button. If you want to make all locations non-selectable, click **Select None**.

5. Once you've made your selections, click **OK**.

Making Landscape Elements Selectable or Non-Selectable

Landscape elements include things like the terrain, site boundary, paths and plants. Using the View Filter you can make selected landscape element types selectable or non-selectable. With the exception of the terrain, your project does not contain landscape elements unless you have opened a drawing from a program that is capable of producing landscaping, such as *3D Home Architect® Landscape Design*.

To make landscape elements selectable or non-selectable:

1. Select **View > View Filter** or click the View Filter button on the Basic View Control or Advanced View Control toolbar. 
2. In the **View Filter** dialog, select the Landscape tab. A list of landscape elements is displayed.

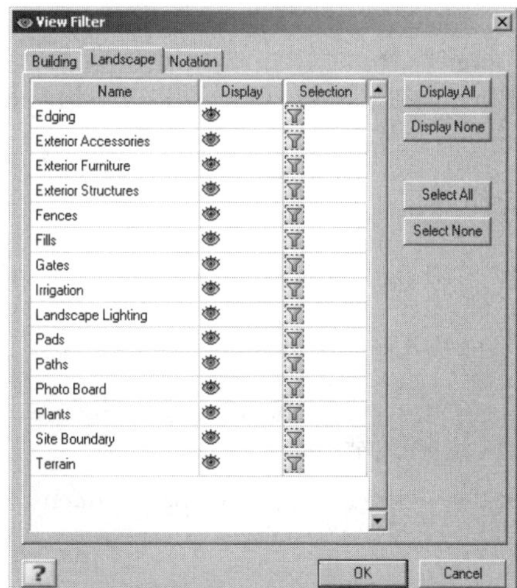

3. Click the filter icons in the Selection column to toggle selectability on or off.

 Element is selectable

Element is not selectable

4. If you want to make all landscape elements selectable, click the **Select All** button. If you want to make all landscape elements non-selectable, click **Select None**.
5. Click **OK**.

Making Text Selectable or Non-Selectable

Using the View Filter you can make text selectable or non-selectable.

To make text selectable or non-selectable:

1. Select **View > View Filter** or click the View Filter button on the Basic View Control or Advanced View Control toolbar. 
2. In the **View Filter** dialog, select the Notation tab.

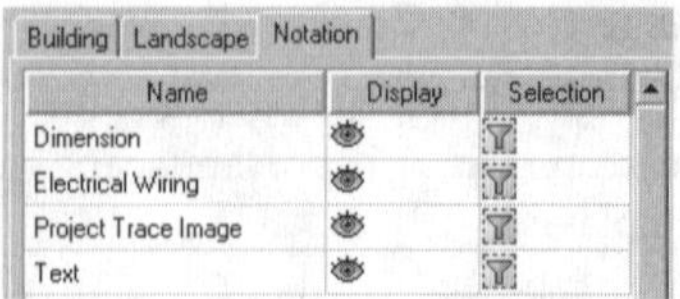

3. In the **Text** row, click the filter icon in the *Selection* column to toggle selectability on or off.

Text is selectable

Text is not selectable

4. Click **OK**.

Making Dimensions Selectable or Non-Selectable

Using the View Filter you can make dimensions selectable or non-selectable.

To make dimensions selectable or non-selectable:

1. Select **View > View Filter** or click the View Filter button on the Basic View Control or Advanced View Control toolbar. 
2. In the **View Filter** dialog, select the Notation tab.

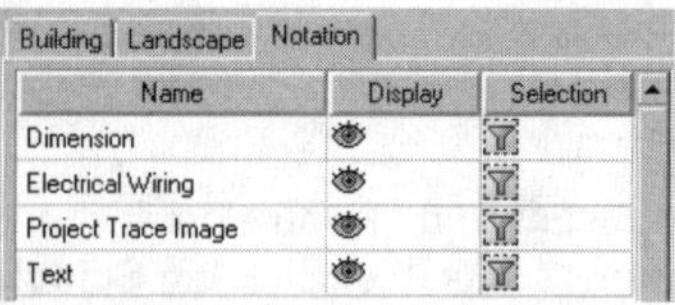

3. In the **Dimension** row, click the filter icon in the *Selection* column to toggle selectability on or off.

Dimensions are selectable

Dimensions are not selectable

4. Click **OK**.

Making Electrical Wiring Selectable or Non-Selectable

Using the View Filter you can make electrical wiring selectable or non-selectable.

To make electrical wiring selectable or non-selectable:

1. Select **View > View Filter** or click the View Filter button on the Basic View Control or Advanced View Control toolbar. 
2. In the **View Filter** dialog, select the Notation tab.

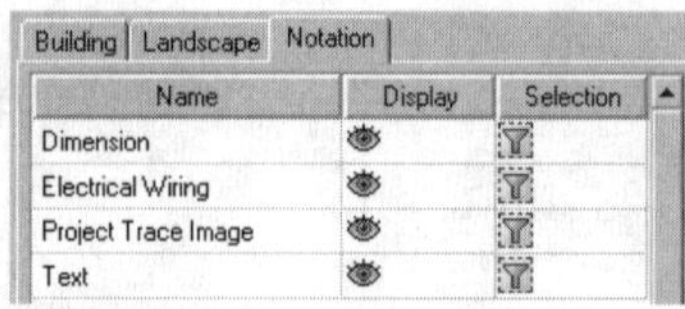

3. In the **Electrical Wiring** row, click the filter icon in the *Selection* column to toggle selectability on or off.

Wiring is selectable

Wiring is not selectable

4. Click **OK**.

Making Project Trace Images Selectable or Non-Selectable

If you have used the Project Trace Image tool to import a plan into your project, you can use the View Filter to make the image selectable or non-selectable.

To make project trace images selectable or non-selectable:

1. Select **View > View Filter** or click the View Filter button on the Basic View Control or Advanced View Control toolbar.

2. In the **View Filter** dialog, select the Notation tab.

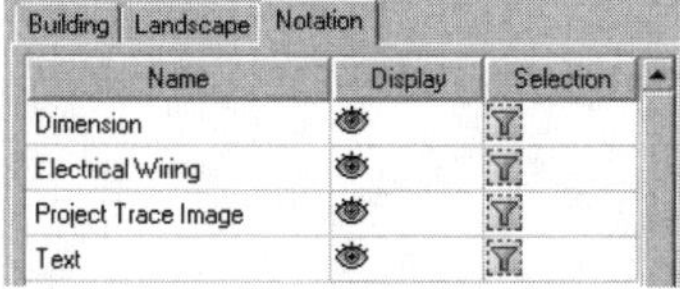

3. In the **Project Trace Image** row, click the filter icon in the *Selection* column to toggle selectability on or off.

   Project trace image is selectable

   Project trace image is not selectable

4. Click **OK**.

Part 3

Building Your Home

Chapter 8

Foundation

If you have decided to create your project from scratch, you can do what builders do in the real world — build from the ground up. *3D Home Architect® Home Design* offers the versatility of creating both full basements and crawlspace foundations.

First you need to define the foundation's building location, if you haven't already done so. The building location's Floor Level variable determines how far below the ground the foundation floor will be positioned, and the Wall Height variable determines how tall the walls will be. See *Defining Building Locations* on page 18.

To create a basement or crawlspace foundation, you start by drawing your foundation walls. A floor is created for you automatically. You can then add support columns where needed and quickly create footings beneath walls and columns.

To begin, set your current building location on the Basic View Control toolbar to the Foundation location, or whatever location you have set up for your foundation.

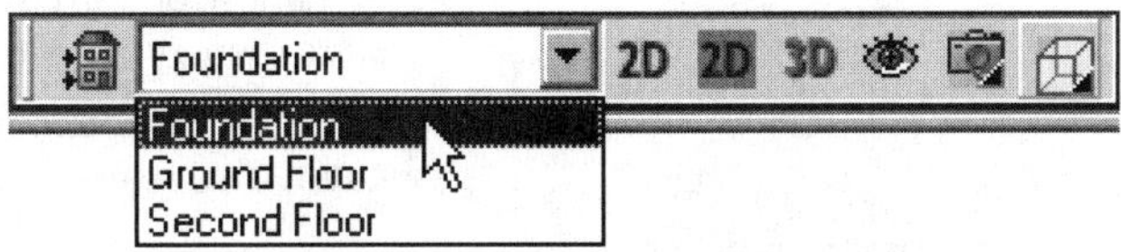

Creating a Basement or Crawlspace Foundation

The first step in creating a basement or crawlspace foundation is drawing the foundation walls, which are typically made of poured concrete or concrete blocks. You can draw the entire perimeter in seconds by just pointing and clicking with your mouse.

A floor is automatically inserted when you create a closed foundation wall layout. You can change the floor type after it has been inserted if you want. If you want you can also opt to insert ceilings automatically. See *Inserting Ceilings Automatically* on page 22.

To draw the foundation walls:

1. Make sure the current location in the Building Locations drop box is the Foundation location, or whatever location you have set up for your foundation elements. Make sure that you have defined the correct Floor Level and Wall Height for that location in the Building Locations dialog.
2. Select **Insert > Walls**, or click the Walls button on the Building toolbar.
3. In the catalog panel, select the Foundation Walls category, then select the type of wall you want to insert.

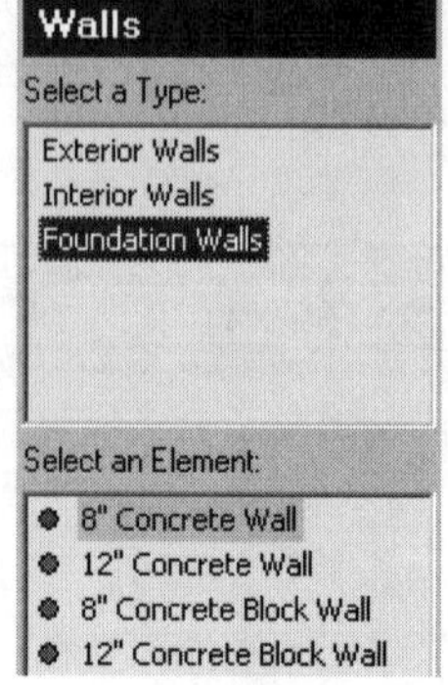

4. In the drawing area, select a start point for the first wall.
5. Move your pointer in the direction you want your wall to run. A dynamic dimension is displayed to indicate the length of the wall.

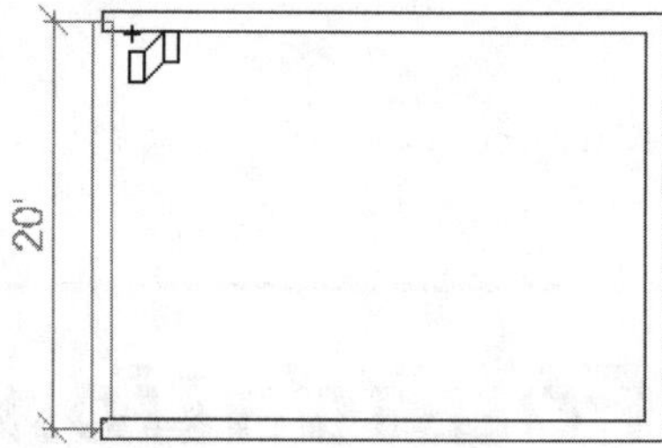

Note: By default, drawing is constrained to 5° angles. To release this constraint, turn off your Angle Snap.

6. When the wall is the length you want, click to set its endpoint.
7. Continue drawing walls until the perimeter is complete. You can add walls to the interior of the foundation layout if you want (if you are creating a cold cellar, for example).
8. Right-click and select **Finish** from the shortcut menu.

To move the foundation:

1. Click on one of the foundation walls to select it, then Shift+click to select the remaining walls.
2. Hover your pointer over the center grab handle on the currently selected wall to display the Move cursor.

3. Click and drag the foundation to where you want it, then release your mouse button.

To resize the foundation by stretching:

1. Select the foundation wall you want to move. All attached walls will stretch along with it when you move it.
2. Hover your pointer over the center grab handle to display the Move cursor.

3. Click and drag the wall to resize the wall layout, then release your mouse button.

Note: If you have footings attached to your walls, the footings will stretch along with the walls.

To resize the foundation by editing its dimensions:

1. Select one of the foundation walls. If you want to stretch the layout left or right, select a vertical wall. If you want to stretch the layout up or down, select a horizontal wall. Dimensions are displayed on the foundation. Positioning your cursor over one of the dimensions changes your cursor to a pointing finger.

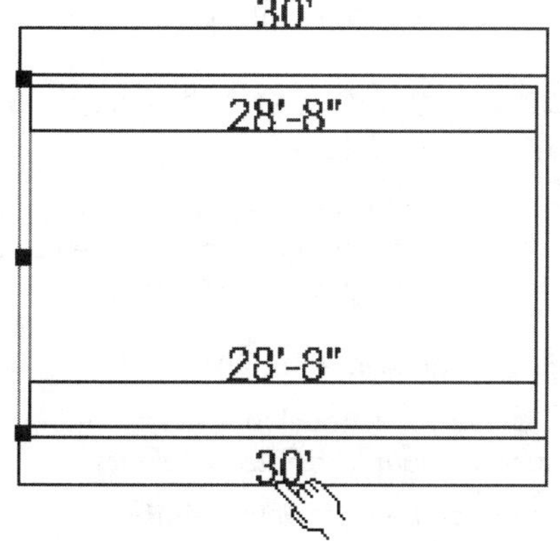

2. Click the dimension you want to edit. The **Edit Dimension** dialog appears.

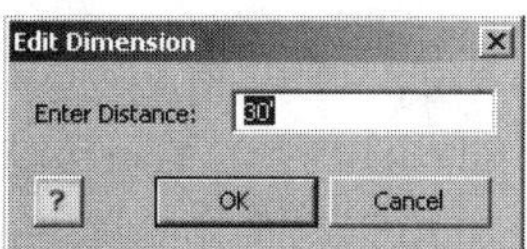

3. Enter the new value in the **Enter Distance** edit box, then press **Enter** or click **OK**. The walls update automatically.

To remove the foundation:

1. Select the foundation by dragging a *selection window* around it, or by clicking on one wall and using Shift+click to select the remaining walls.
2. Press the **Delete** key on your keyboard, or right-click and select **Delete**, or select **Edit > Modify Elements > Delete**.

Editing a Wall's Height, Width or Elevation

You can edit the size properties of a wall by making changes on the wall's Basic property page.

To edit a wall's size properties:

1. Select the wall whose properties you want to change. You can select multiple walls using Shift+click if you want.
2. Right-click and select **Properties**, or select **Edit > Modify Elements > Properties**.
3. In the **Walls** dialog, select the Basic tab.
4. Edit the properties as desired.

   Width. The thickness of the wall.

   Wall Height. The physical height of the wall.

   Extension Below Base. The height of the wall below floor level.
5. Once the properties are set, click **OK**.

Lengthening and Shortening Walls

You can lengthen or shorten an individual wall by clicking and dragging one of the wall's ends.

To lengthen or shorten a wall:

1. Select the wall. A grab handle is displayed at each wall end.
2. Hover your pointer over the wall end you want to stretch. The Stretch cursor is displayed. 
3. Click and drag the wall end until it has reached the desired length.
4. Release your mouse button.

Rotating a Wall

You can use the Rotate tool to rotate a wall about a selected point.

To rotate a wall:

1. Select the wall.
2. Right-click and select **Rotate**, or select **Edit > Modify Elements > Rotate**.

3. Position your pointer over the grab handle you want to rotate the wall around.
4. Click and drag to rotate the wall, then release your mouse button.

Curving a Wall

You can curve a wall using the Curve tool. Once the tool is active, you can click and drag the wall to curve it, or select a point to curve to.

To curve a wall by clicking and dragging:

1. Click the wall to select it.
2. Right-click and select **Curve**, or select **Edit > Modify Elements > Curve**.
3. Click and drag the wall to the desired curve.
4. Release your mouse button.

To curve a wall to a selected point:

1. Click the wall to select it.
2. Right-click in and select **Curve**, or select **Edit > Modify Elements > Curve**.
3. Select the point you want to curve to. The wall automatically curves to the point.
4. Click to finish.

Breaking a Wall

You can break a wall into two or more segments using the Break tool. The segments can then be edited individually.

To break a wall:

1. Click the wall to select it.
2. Right-click in the drawing area and select **Break**, or select **Edit > Modify Elements > Break**.
3. Double-click the point where you want to break the wall. This divides the wall into two segments that can be moved, stretched or manipulated individually.

Deleting a Wall

You can delete a wall in a couple of easy steps.

To delete a wall:

1. Select the wall to delete. You can select multiple walls using Shift+click.
2. Press the **Delete** key on your keyboard, or right-click and select **Delete**, or select **Edit > Modify Elements > Delete**.

Note: The floor will be deleted if the wall you are deleting opens up the wall layout.

Applying a Different Material to the Foundation Floor

You can use the Materials Paintbrush to quickly apply a different material such as poured concrete to the foundation floor.

To apply a material to the floor:

1. Display your model in 3D view and make sure the floor is visible in the view.
2. Select **Edit > Materials Paintbrush**, or click the Materials Paintbrush button on any tabbed toolbar.

3. In the catalog panel, select the material you want to apply.

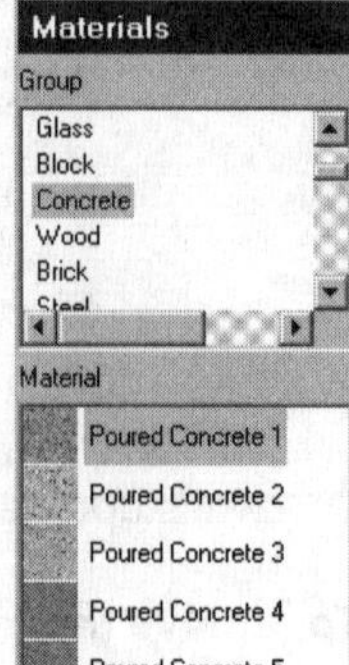

4. Click on the floor surface. The material is immediately applied.
5. Right-click and select **Finish**.

Inserting Strip Footings Beneath the Foundation Walls

Since foundation walls bear the weight of exterior walls above them, you need to insert footings beneath the foundation walls to transfer support for the vertical load.

Strip footings are easy to insert — just click on a wall and a footing is automatically inserted underneath the wall.

To insert strip footings under walls:

1. Select **Insert > Footings > Strip Footings Attached to Walls**, or click the Footings button on the Building toolbar and select **Strip Footings Attached to Walls**.

2. In the catalog panel, select the footing you want to insert. Typically you would choose one that is wider than the wall you are attaching it to.
3. Click on the wall you want to attach the footing to. The footing is inserted automatically. In plan view, strip footings are usually shown using a dashed line.
4. Continue inserting footings underneath each exterior foundation wall.
5. Right-click and select **Finish** from the shortcut menu.

Editing the Strip Footing Type

Strip footing types include rectangular, tapered and filleted. The footing type determines the footing's general appearance.

To edit the footing type:

1. Select the footing whose properties you want to change. You can select multiple footings using Shift+click if you want.
2. Right-click and select **Properties**, or select **Edit > Modify Elements > Properties**.
3. Select the Basic tab, then click on the appropriate graphic in the *Type* area.

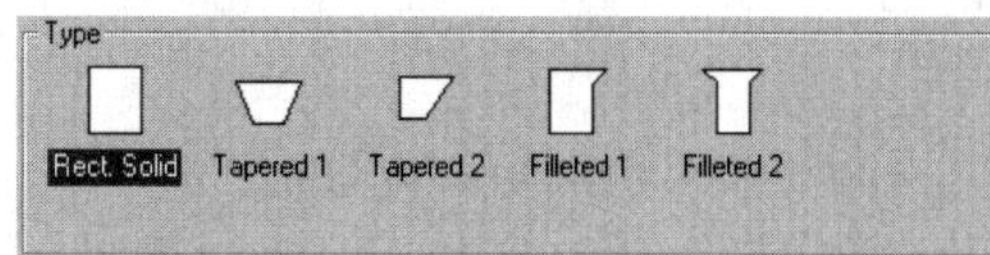

4. Click **OK**.

Editing the Size of Strip Footings

You can edit the dimensions of a footing on the footing's Basic property page.

To change the footing size:

1. Select the footing.
2. Right-click and select **Properties**, or select **Edit > Modify Elements > Properties**.
3. In the **Strip Footing** dialog, select the Basic tab.
4. Edit the dimensions of the footing.
5. Click **OK**.

Moving/Stretching Strip Footings

When you move a strip footing, all footings attached to it move with it for a stretching effect. You can move strip footings by just clicking and dragging.

To move/stretch strip footings:

1. Select the footing to move. You may need to make walls non-selectable to be able to select the footing.

2. Position your pointer over the center grab handle to display the Move cursor. 
3. Click and drag the footing to move it.
4. Release your mouse button.

Note: When you move a strip footing, it becomes detached from the wall. Therefore, if you move or stretch the wall, the footing will not go with it. If you want to re-attach a footing to a wall, you will need to delete the footing, then insert a new one.

Lengthening and Shortening Strip Footings

You can lengthen or shorten an individual footing by clicking and dragging one of the footing's ends.

To lengthen or shorten a footing:

1. Select the footing. A grab handle is displayed at each end.
2. Hover your pointer over the end you want to stretch. The Move cursor is displayed. 
3. Click and drag the footing end until it has reached the desired length.
4. Release your mouse button.

Breaking Strip Footings

You can break a footing into two or more segments using the Break tool. The segments can then be edited individually.

To break a footing:

1. Click the footing to select it.
2. Right-click in the drawing area and select **Break**, or select **Edit > Modify Elements > Break**.
3. Double-click the point where you want to break the footing.

Deleting Strip Footings

You can delete a strip footing in a couple of easy steps.

To delete strip footings:

1. Select the footing to delete. You can select multiple footings using Shift+click.
2. Press the **Delete** key on your keyboard, or right-click and select **Delete**, or select **Edit > Modify Elements > Delete**.

Inserting Columns

Typically, any bearing members in your basement require support. For example, if you have a W-type I-beam in your basement, it may be supported by steel posts at each end. Columns are an important consideration when designing your basement, especially if you intend to finish it.

When inserting columns, you can choose from a variety of wood, concrete, steel, brick and gypsum columns in various shapes and sizes.

To insert a column:

1. Select **Insert > Columns**, or click the Columns button on the Building toolbar. 
2. In the catalog panel, select the column you want to insert.
3. Position the column where you want it, then click to insert it.
4. Right-click and select **Finish** from the shortcut menu.

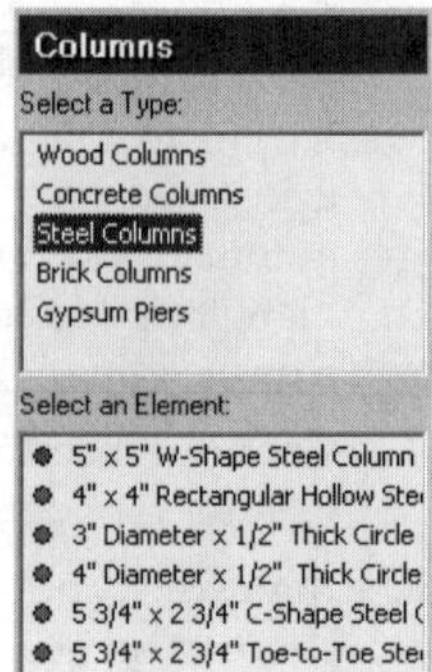

Editing the Column Type

Columns come in a variety of materials and shapes.

To edit the column type:

1. Select the column whose properties you want to change. You can select multiple columns using Shift+click if you want.
2. Right-click and select **Properties**, or select **Edit > Modify Elements > Properties**.
3. Select the Basic tab, then click on the appropriate graphic in the *Type* area.

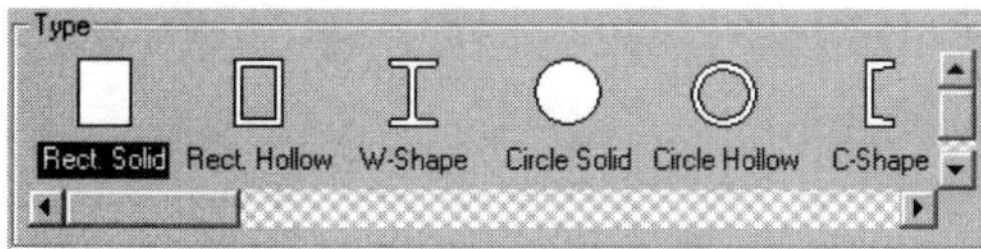

4. Click **OK**.

Editing the Size and Elevation of a Column

You can edit the dimensions of a column (e.g. height, width and depth) as well as its elevation height.

To edit the size properties of a column:

1. Click on the column to select it.
2. Right-click and select **Properties**, or select **Edit > Modify Elements > Properties**.
3. Edit the properties as desired. Different column shapes will have different dimension variables. If you want to offset the base of the column from the floor (so it sits higher or lower), enter a value in the **Base Offset** edit box.
4. Click **OK**.

Moving Columns

You can move a column by simply clicking and dragging it.

To move a column:

1. Click on the column to select it.
2. Hover your pointer over the center grab handle to display the Move cursor.
3. Click and drag the column to move it.
4. Release your mouse button.

Note: If you have a mono footing attached to the column, the footing will remain attached to the column and move with it.

Deleting a Column

You can remove a column in a couple of quick steps.

To remove a column:

1. Click on the column to select it.
2. Press the **Delete** key on your keyboard, or right-click and select **Delete**, or select **Edit > Modify Elements > Delete**.

Inserting Mono Footings Under Columns

Since support columns in your basement bear loads at a concentrated point, the load should be transferred to a proper footing.

Using the Mono Footings Attached to Columns tool you can insert a single pad footing beneath a selected column. All you have to do is select the column.

To insert a footing under a column:

1. Select **Insert > Footings > Mono Footings Attached to Columns**, or click the Footings button on the Building toolbar and select **Mono Footings Attached to Columns**.

2. In the catalog panel, select the footing you want to insert. Typically you would choose one that is wider than the column you are attaching it to.
3. Click on the column you want to attach the footing to. The footing is inserted automatically.
4. Right-click and select **Finish** from the shortcut menu.

Editing the Mono Footing Type

Mono footing types include rectangular, tapered, cylinder and cylinder tapered. The footing type determines the footing's general appearance.

To edit the footing type:

1. Select the footing whose properties you want to change. You can select multiple footings using Shift+click if you want.
2. Right-click and select **Properties**, or select **Edit > Modify Elements > Properties**.
3. Select the Basic tab, then click on the appropriate graphic in the *Type* area.

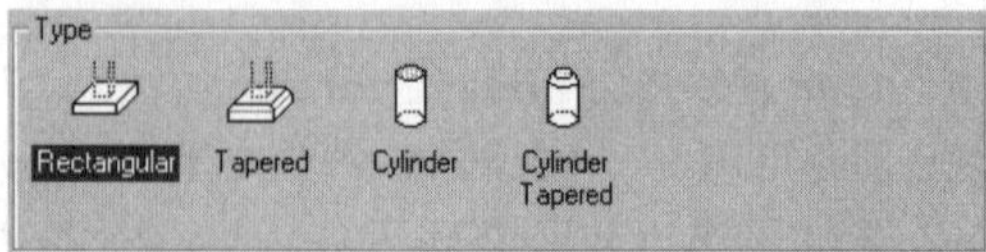

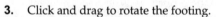

4. Click **OK**.

Editing the Size of Mono Footings

You can edit the dimensions of a footing on the footing's Basic property page.

To change the footing size:

1. Select the footing.
2. Right-click and select **Properties**, or select **Edit > Modify Elements > Properties**.
3. In the **Mono Footing** dialog, select the Basic tab.
4. Edit the dimensions of the footing.
5. Click **OK**.

Moving Mono Footings

You can move a mono footing by clicking and dragging it.

To move a mono footing by clicking and dragging:

1. Select the footing to move.
2. Position your pointer over the center grab handle to display the Move cursor.

3. Click and drag the footing to move it.
4. Release your mouse button.

Note: When you move a mono footing, it becomes detached from the column. Therefore, if you move the column, the footing will not go with it. If you want to re-attach a footing to a column, you will need to delete the footing, then insert a new one.

Rotating a Mono Footing

You can rotate a mono footing by simply clicking and dragging it.

To rotate a mono footing:

1. Select the footing.
2. Hover your pointer over the triangular grab handle to display the Rotate cursor.
3. Click and drag to rotate the footing.

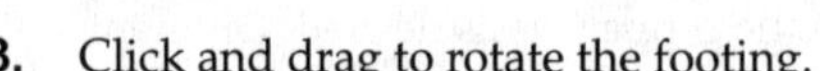

4. When the footing is at the desired rotation, release your mouse button.

Deleting Mono Footings

You can delete a mono footing in a couple of easy steps.

To delete mono footings:

1. Select the footing to remove. You can select multiple footings using Shift+click.
2. Press the **Delete** key on your keyboard, or right-click and select **Delete**, or select **Edit > Modify Elements > Delete**.

Chapter 9

Walls

Once you've created your foundation, the next step is to create the ground floor exterior walls as well as the exterior walls of any additional stories. You can then add interior walls on all stories.

Drawing walls is easy — just point and click. *3D Home Architect® Home Design* automatically displays dimensions as you draw, and connects corners for you. If the Object Snap is turned on, which by default it is, interior walls snap to other existing walls and create clean intersections with them.

Once inserted, any wall can be moved, rotated, lengthened, shortened, broken, curved or deleted. This lets you create the exact wall layout that you want.

The catalog contains a wide variety of wall types including brick, stone, sided, wood-framed and steel-framed. Once your walls are drawn, you can add paint, wallpaper, baseboards and other types of trim to them for a truly customized look.

Drawing the Ground Floor Exterior Walls

You can draw your ground floor exterior walls by simply pointing and clicking with your mouse. If you have created a foundation, you can just trace around the foundation.

A floor is automatically inserted when you create a closed foundation wall layout. You can change the properties of the floor after it has been inserted if you want. If you want you can also opt to insert ceilings automatically. See *Inserting Ceilings Automatically* on page 22.

To draw the ground floor exterior walls:

1. Make sure the current location is the Ground Floor location, or whatever location you have set up for your ground floor elements.

2. Select **Insert > Walls**, or click the Walls button on the Building toolbar. 
3. In the catalog, select the wall type you want to insert.

Walls
Select a Type:
Exterior Walls
Interior Walls
Foundation Walls
Select an Element:
8" Brick Wall
10" Brick Wall
8" Stone Wall
10" Stone Wall
6" Horizontal Siding Wall
8" Horizontal Siding Wall
6" Vertical Siding Wall
8" Vertical Siding Wall

4. Select a start point for the first wall.
5. Move your cursor in the direction you want your wall to run. Its length is shown as you draw the wall.

   Note: By default, drawing is constrained to 5° angles. To release this constraint, turn off your Angle Snap.
6. When the wall is the length you want, click to set its endpoint.
7. To add another wall to the one you have just drawn, move the mouse in the direction you want the new wall to run. When it is the right length, click to set its endpoint.

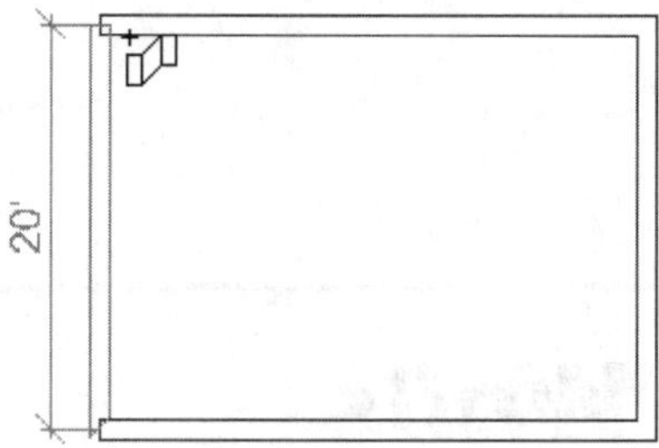

8. When the wall layout is complete, right-click and select **Finish**.

To move the entire wall layout:

1. Click on one of the exterior walls to select it, then Shift+click to select the remaining walls.
2. Hover your pointer over the center grab handle on the currently selected wall to display the Move cursor. 
3. Click and drag the layout to where you want it, then release your mouse button.

To resize the wall layout by stretching:

1. Select the exterior wall you want to move. All attached walls will stretch along with it when you move it.
2. Hover your pointer over the center grab handle to display the Move cursor. 
3. Click and drag the wall to resize the wall layout, then release your mouse button.

To resize the wall layout by editing its dimensions:

1. Select one of the exterior walls. If you want to stretch the layout left or right, select a vertical wall. If you want to stretch the layout up or down, select a horizontal wall. Dimensions are displayed on the wall layout.

2. Click the dimension you want to edit. The **Edit Dimension** dialog appears.

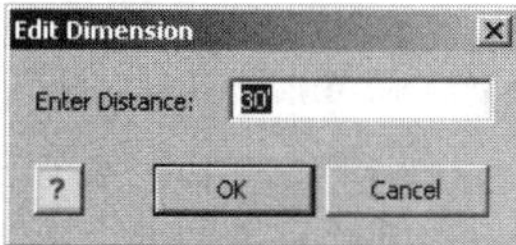

3. Enter the new value in the **Enter Distance** edit box, then press **Enter** or click **OK**. The walls update automatically.

To remove the wall layout:

1. Click on one of the walls, then Shift+click to select the remaining walls.
2. Press the **Delete** key on your keyboard, or right-click and select **Delete**, or select **Edit > Modify Elements > Delete**.

Adding a Story

Once you have created your ground floor exterior walls, adding more levels to your design is easy. You can draw the layout just like you did to create the ground floor, or you can use the Duplicate to Locations tool to copy the ground floor exterior walls to the second floor location.

To create a new story by drawing the walls:

1. Make sure the current location is the Second Floor location, or whatever location you have set up for the story you are creating.

2. Select **Insert > Walls**, or click the Walls button on the Building toolbar. 
3. In the catalog, select the wall type you want to insert.
4. Select a start point for the first wall.
5. Move your cursor in the direction you want your wall to run. Its length is shown as you draw the wall.

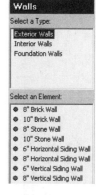

   Note: By default, drawing is constrained to 5° angles. To release this constraint, turn off your Angle Snap.
6. When the wall is the length you want, click to set its endpoint. Your cursor will snap to the dimmed image of the walls below for ease.
7. To add another wall to the one you have just drawn, move the mouse in the direction you want the new wall to run. When it is the right length, click to set its endpoint.

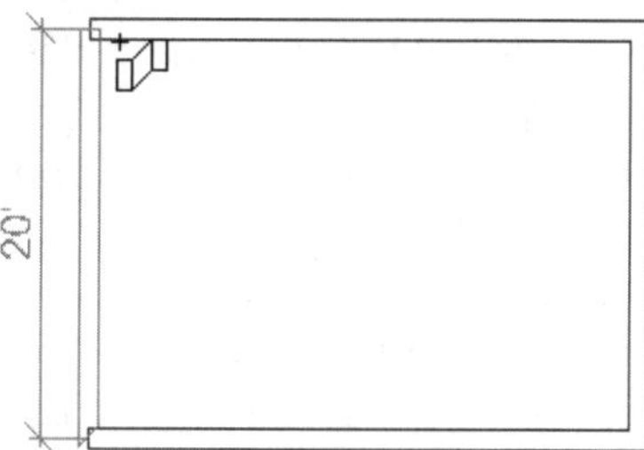

8. When the wall layout is complete, right-click and select **Finish**.

To create a new story by duplicating walls on the ground floor:

1. Make sure the current location is the Ground Floor, or whatever location that contains the walls to copy.
2. Click one of the walls to copy, then Shift+click to select the remaining walls.
3. Right-click and select **Duplicate to Locations**, or select **Edit > Modify Elements > Duplicate to Locations**.

4. In the **Duplicate to Locations** dialog, select the Second Floor (or whatever location you are copying to).

5. Click **OK**. The walls are copied, and you now have a new story.

Note: When you copy a wall layout, a floor with the default material is automatically created on the location you are copying to.

To resize the wall layout by stretching:

1. Select the exterior wall you want to move. All attached walls will stretch along with it when you move it.
2. Hover your pointer over the center grab handle to display the Move cursor.
3. Click and drag the wall to resize the wall layout, then release your mouse button.

To resize the wall layout by editing its dimensions:

1. Select one of the exterior walls. If you want to stretch the layout left or right, select a vertical wall. If you want to stretch the layout up or down, select a horizontal wall. Dimensions are displayed on the wall layout.
2. Click the dimension you want to edit. The **Edit Dimension** dialog appears.

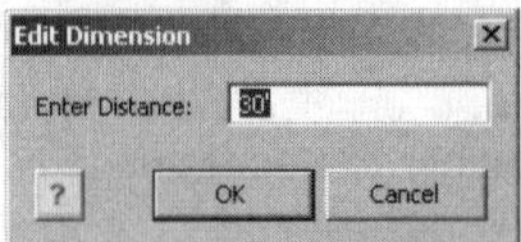

3. Enter the new value in the **Enter Distance** edit box, then press **Enter** or click **OK**. The walls update automatically.

To remove the wall layout:

1. Click on one of the walls, then Shift+click to select the remaining walls.
2. Press the **Delete** key on your keyboard, or right-click and select **Delete**, or select **Edit > Modify Elements > Delete**.

Applying Different Finishes to Exterior Walls

You can apply different finishes to your exterior walls using the handy Materials Paintbrush. The materials catalog contains an excellent selection of brick, concrete, stone and siding.

To apply a finish to an exterior wall:

1. Display your model in 3D, and make sure the wall face you want to apply the material to is visible in the view.
2. Select **Edit > Materials Paintbrush**, or click the Materials Paintbrush button on any tabbed toolbar.

3. In the catalog panel, select the material you want to apply.

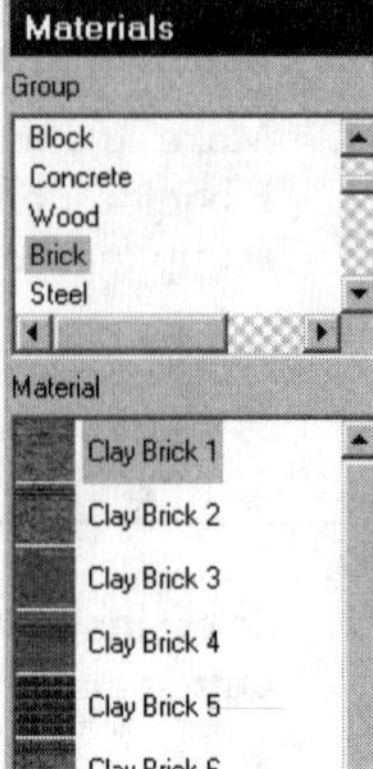

4. Click on the wall face that you want to apply the material to. The material is immediately applied. You can continue applying the material to other walls if you want.
5. Right-click and select **Finish**.

Drawing Interior Walls

Once you've created your exterior walls, you can start drawing interior walls. Walls snap to other walls automatically, creating clean corners and intersections.

As you create rooms in your model, the floor is split up into separate floors that you can edit individually.

To draw interior walls:

1. From the location drop box, select the location where you want to draw interior walls.

2. Select **Insert > Walls**, or click the Walls button on the Building toolbar.
3. In the catalog panel, select the wall type you want to insert.

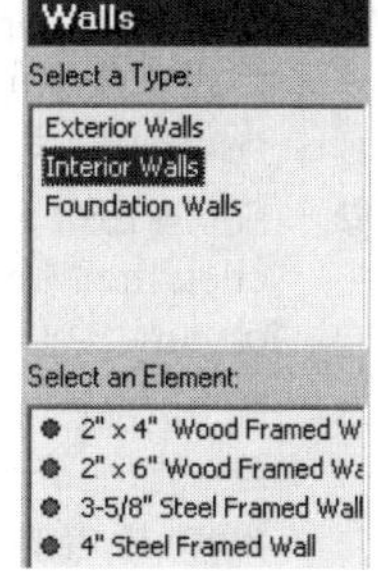

4. Select a start point for the first wall.
5. Move your cursor in the direction you want your wall to run. Its length is shown as you draw the wall.

   Note: By default, drawing is constrained to 5° angles. To release this constraint, turn off your Angle Snap.
6. When the wall is the length you want, click to set its endpoint.
7. When you are done, right-click and select **Finish**.

Editing a Wall's Height, Width or Elevation

You can edit the size properties of a wall by making changes on the wall's Basic property page.

To edit a wall's size properties:

1. Select the wall whose properties you want to change. You can select multiple walls using Shift+click if you want.
2. Right-click and select **Properties**, or select **Edit > Modify Elements > Properties**.
3. In the **Walls** dialog, select the Basic tab.
4. Edit the properties as desired:

   Width. The thickness of the wall.

   Wall Height. The physical height of the wall.

   Extension Below Base. The height of the wall below floor level.
5. Once the properties are set, click **OK**.

Lengthening and Shortening Walls

You can lengthen or shorten an individual wall by clicking and dragging one of the wall's ends.

To lengthen or shorten a wall:

1. Select the wall. A grab handle is displayed at each wall end.
2. Hover your pointer over the wall end you want to stretch. The Stretch cursor is displayed.

3. Click and drag the wall end until it has reached the desired length.
4. Release your mouse button.

Rotating a Wall

You can use the Rotate tool to rotate a wall about a selected point.

To rotate a wall:

1. Select the wall. A grab handle is displayed at each wall end.
2. Right-click and select **Rotate**, or select **Edit > Modify Elements > Rotate**.

3. Position your pointer over the grab handle you want to rotate the wall around.
4. Click and drag to rotate the wall, then release your mouse button.

Curving a Wall

You can curve a wall using the Curve tool. Once the tool is active, you can click and drag the wall to curve it, or select a point to curve to.

To curve a wall by clicking and dragging:

1. Click the wall to select it.
2. Right-click and select **Curve**, or select **Edit > Modify Elements > Curve**.
3. Click and drag the wall to the desired curve.
4. Release your mouse button.

To curve a wall to a selected point:

1. Click the wall to select it.
2. Right-click in and select **Curve**, or select **Edit > Modify Elements > Curve**.
3. Select the point you want to curve to. The wall automatically curves to the point.
4. Click to finish.

Breaking a Wall

You can break a wall into two or more segments using the Break tool. The segments can then be edited individually. You may, for example, want to apply different materials to each new individual wall.

To break a wall:

1. Click the wall to select it.
2. Right-click in the drawing area and click **Break**, or select **Edit > Modify Elements > Break**.
3. Double-click the point where you want to break the wall. This divides the wall into two segments that can be moved, stretched or edited individually.

Deleting a Wall

You can delete a wall in a couple of easy steps.

To delete a wall:

1. Select the wall to delete. You can select multiple walls using Shift+click.
2. Press the **Delete** key on your keyboard, or right-click and select **Delete**, or select **Edit > Modify Elements > Delete**.

Note: If a floor was inserted automatically when you created your wall layout, the floor will be deleted if the wall you are deleting opens up the wall layout.

Adding Paint and Wallpaper

You can use the Materials Paintbrush to quickly apply custom paint, wallpaper or wood paneling to a wall.

To apply paint or wallpaper to walls:

1. Display your model in 3D, and make sure the wall face you want to apply the paint or wallpaper to is visible in the view.
2. Select **Edit > Materials Paintbrush**, or click the Materials Paintbrush button on any tabbed toolbar.

3. In the catalog panel, select the material you want to apply. Paint colors are located in the Paint category, and wallpaper can be found in the Finishes category. You can apply any material in the catalog that you want.
4. Click on the wall face that you want to apply the paint or wallpaper to. The material is immediately applied. You can continue applying the material to other walls if you want.
5. Right-click and select **Finish**.

Adding Trim to Walls

Trim types include baseboards, crown molding, chair rails, door/window trim, cove molding, wainscoting and decorative wallpaper borders. You can add as many types of trim to a wall as you want, and even add different materials to either side of the wall.

Trim selections are made on a wall's Trim property page.

To add trim to walls:

1. Select the wall you want to add trim to.
2. Right-click and select **Properties**, or select **Edit > Modify Elements > Properties**.
3. In the **Walls** dialog, select the Trim tab.

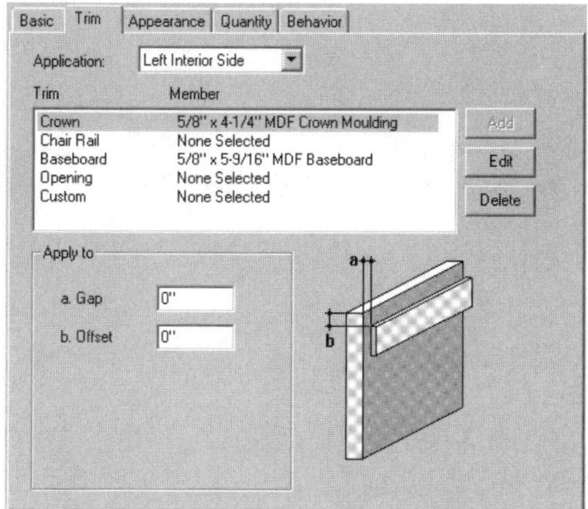

4. From the *Application* drop box, select the wall side you want to add trim to.

   Exterior Side. The exterior side of an exterior wall.

   Left Interior Side. If a wall was drawn left to right, this is the north side of the wall, or the side closest to the top of the screen. If a wall was drawn right to left, this is the south side of the wall, or the side closer to the bottom of the screen. If a wall was drawn vertically from the top downward, the left side is the eastern side of the wall, or the side closest to the right side of the screen. If a wall was drawn vertically from the bottom up, the left side is the western side of the wall, or the side closest to the left side of the screen.

   Right Interior Side. If a wall was drawn left to right, this is the south side of the wall, or the side closest to the bottom of the screen. If a wall was drawn right to left, this is the north side of the wall, or the side closest to the top of the screen. If a wall was drawn vertically from the top downward, the right side is the western side of the wall, or the side closest to the left side of the screen. If a wall was drawn vertically from the bottom up, the right side is the eastern side of the wall, or the side closest to the right side of the screen.

5. In the list of trim types, select the trim you would like to select a member for, then click **Add**.
6. In the catalog, select the trim you want to use, then click **OK**. The trim list displays the member you selected.

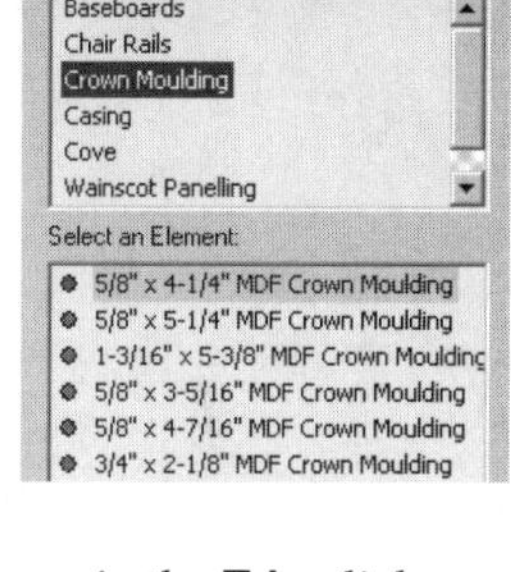

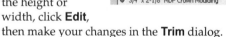

7. If you want to edit the properties of the selected member, such as the height or width, click **Edit**, then make your changes in the **Trim** dialog.
8. To delete the member from the trim list, select it, then click **Delete**.
9. In the *Apply to* area, specify how you would like the trim applied to the wall. Different variables are available depending on the trim type.

   Gap. For trim around door and window openings, this is the offset of the trim from the opening. For crown moldings, baseboards and chair rails, this is the offset of the trim from the wall face.

   Offset. For crown moldings, this is the offset of the molding from the top of the wall. For baseboards and chair rails, this is the offset of the member from the bottom of the wall.

Offset from wall. If creating custom trim, this determines where the member is offset from when an offset is specified. Choose from Wall Bottom, Wall Top, Ceiling or Floor.

Trim basepoint. If creating custom trim, this determines which edge of the trim is used to measure the offset. Choose either Top of Trim or Bottom of Trim.

10. Once you've selected your trim, click **OK**. The walls are updated automatically.

Chapter 10

Doors, Windows & Openings

Once you've drawn walls, you can insert a variety of doors, windows and openings in them to create the exact design you want.

Like all elements in *3D Home Architect® Home Design*, doors, windows and openings are intelligent. They know that they can only be inserted in walls. As soon as your pointer gets close to a wall, they snap into place. All you have to do is position it where you want it along the wall, then click to insert it. Dimensions are displayed as you are positioning the element so you can get the precise placement you want.

Even though doors, windows and openings automatically become associated with the walls they are inserted in, you can edit them independently if you want.

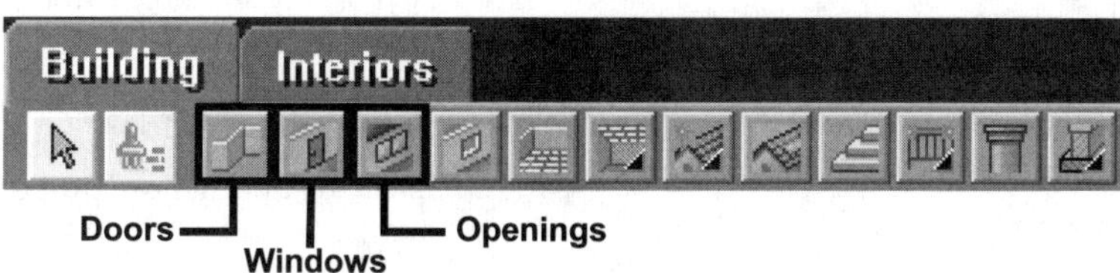

Inserting Doors

The catalog contains a wide variety of doors for you to insert, including hinged, bi-fold, pocket, sliding glass and garage doors. You can point and click to insert a door, or offset the door a specific distance from the end of a wall.

Doors are inserted at floor level. You can raise or lower a door after you have inserted it if you need to.

To insert a door:

1. Make sure the location you want to insert doors on is the current location in the building locations drop box.
2. Select **Insert > Doors**, or click the Doors button on the Building toolbar.
3. In the catalog, select the door you want to insert.

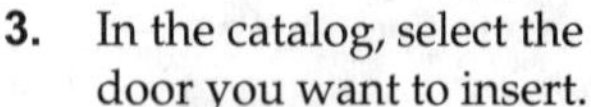

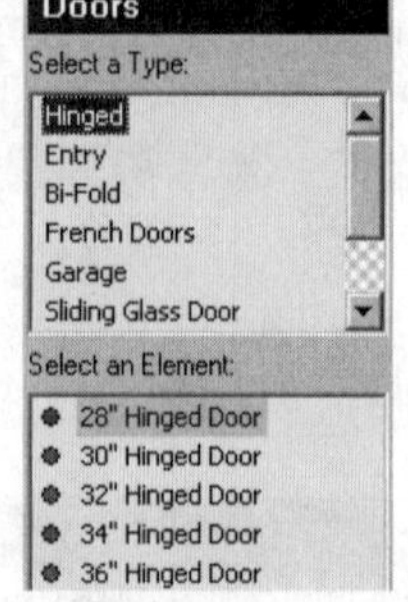

4. If you want to offset the door a specific distance from the end of the wall, right-click and select **Enter insertion offset**.

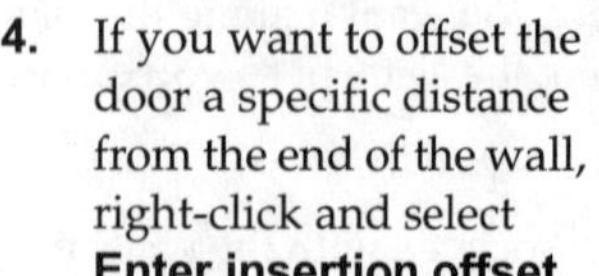

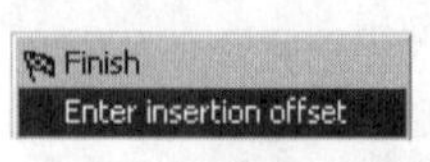

Enter the offset distance in the **Enter insertion offset** dialog, then click **OK**.

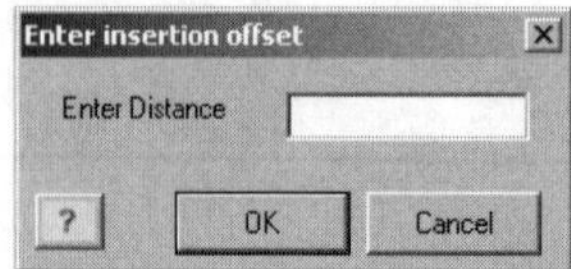

5. Position the door in the receiving wall. If you are using an insertion offset, position the door close to the end you want to offset it from. The door will snap inside the wall. Dimensions are displayed that show you the distance on either side of the door.
6. With your door positioned where you want it, click to insert it.
7. Right-click and select **Finish**.

Editing Door Types

Door types include hinged, bi-fold, pocket, face slider, track slider, fold-up, tilt, and roller. You can edit a door's type on the door's Basic property page.

To edit a door type:

1. Select the door whose properties you want to change.
2. Right-click and select **Properties**, or select **Edit > Modify Elements > Properties**.
3. In the **Doors** dialog, select the Basic tab.
4. In the *Type* area, click on the desired door type to select it.

5. Click **OK**.

Editing the Size and Shape of a Door

You can edit the shape of a door, its height and width, and swing type.

To edit the size of a door:

1. Select the door whose properties you want to change.
2. Right-click and select **Properties**, or select **Edit > Modify Elements > Properties**.

3. In the **Doors** dialog, select the Basic tab.

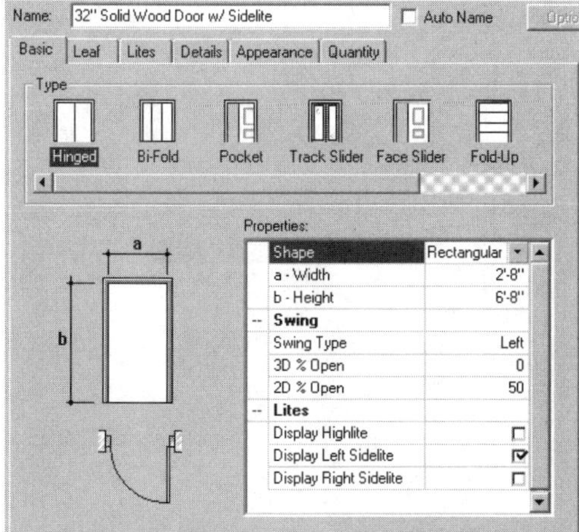

4. Edit the shape and dimensions as desired. Clicking a dimension marked with an alphabetical character (a, b, c, etc.) highlights the corresponding dimension in the door graphic, and vice versa.

   Shape. Choose from Rectangular, Arched or Apexed.

   Width. The width of the door leaf.

   Height. The height of the door leaf.

   Swing Type. Choose from *Left*, *Right* or *Double*. A door with a left door swing will have its hinges on the right.

   3D % Open. How much the door is shown swung open in 3D view. By default, doors are shown closed in 3D view.

   2D % Open. How much the door is swung open in 2D plan view.

Editing a Door's Sidelites and Highlites

A sidelite is a fixed glass panel set on one or both sides of a door (usually an entry door). A highlite is a fixed glass panel above a door. You can create a custom configuration of sidelites and/or highlights for a door.

To display lites on a door:

1. Select the door.
2. Right-click and select **Properties**, or select **Edit > Modify Elements > Properties**.
3. In the **Doors** dialog, select the Basic tab.
4. To display a highlite over the door, enable the **Display Highlite** check box.
5. To display a sidelite on the left side of the door, enable the **Display Left Sidelite** check box.
6. To display a sidelite on the right side of the door, enable the **Display Right Sidelite** check box.

To edit sidelites and highlites:

1. Select the door whose properties you want to change.
2. Right-click and select **Properties**, or select **Edit > Modify Elements > Properties**.
3. In the **Doors** dialog, select the Lites tab.

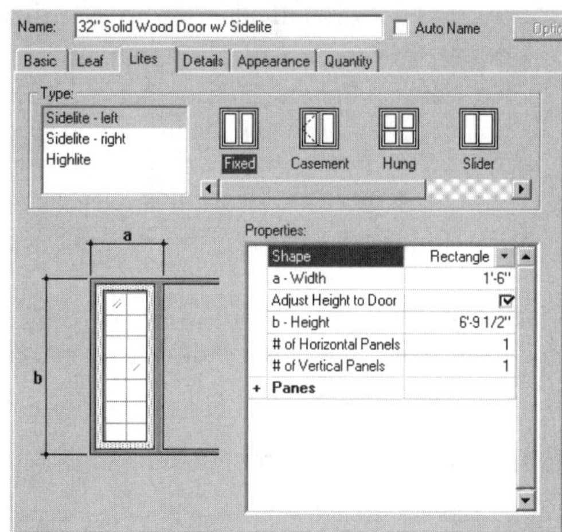

4. In the *Type* window, select the lite you want to specify settings for. Note that the lite must be enabled on the Basic property page before it can be edited.
5. To select a specific window type for the currently selected lite, click on the appropriate graphic in the *Type* area.
6. Edit the dimensions of the lite in the *Properties* area if desired. Clicking a dimension marked with an alphabetical character (a, b, c, etc.) highlights the

corresponding dimension in the sidelite/ highlite graphic, and vice versa.

Shape. Choose from *Rectangle*, *Arched* or *Trapezoid*.

(highlite) **Adjust Width**. Selecting *Opening* adjusts the width of the highlite to match the width of the opening (including any sidelites). Selecting *Door* adjusts the width of the highlite to match the width of the door (excluding any sidelites). Selecting *User Defined* lets you specify a precise width for the highlite in the **Width** edit box.

Width. The total width of the lite.

(sidelites) **Adjust Height to Door**. Automatically adjusts the height of a sidelite to match the height of the door.

Height. The overall height of the lite.

# of Horizontal Panels. The number of panels across the lite. If you specify more than one panel, vertical dividers are added inside the lite's frame.

# of Vertical Panels. The number of panels running vertically along the lite. If you specify more than one panel, horizontal dividers are added inside the lite's frame.

# of Horizontal Panes. The number of panes of glass across the lite.

# of Vertical Panes. The number of panes of glass running vertically along the lite.

7. Click **OK**.

Editing a Door Leaf

You can choose from a variety of door leaf types and change the thickness of the leaf.

To edit a door's leaf:

1. Select the door whose properties you want to change.
2. Right-click and select **Properties**, or select **Edit > Modify Elements > Properties**.
3. In the **Doors** dialog, select the Leaf tab.

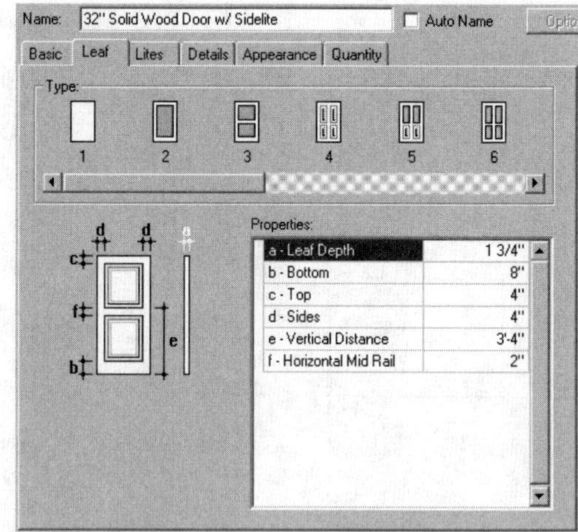

4. In the *Type* area, click on the leaf type you want.
5. If you want to change the thickness of the leaf, enter the thickness in the **Leaf Depth** edit box.
6. Each door leaf type has its own set of dimensions that you can define. These dimensions vary according to how many panels the leaf has. Clicking a dimension marked with an alphabetical character (a, b, c, etc.) highlights the corresponding dimension in the door leaf graphic, and vice versa.
7. Click **OK**.

Editing Door Details

You can specify precise dimensions and offsets for the door frame, sash, mullions and transoms.

To edit door details:

1. Select the door whose properties you want to change.
2. Right-click and select **Properties**, or select **Edit > Modify Elements > Properties**.

3. In the **Doors** dialog, select the Details tab.

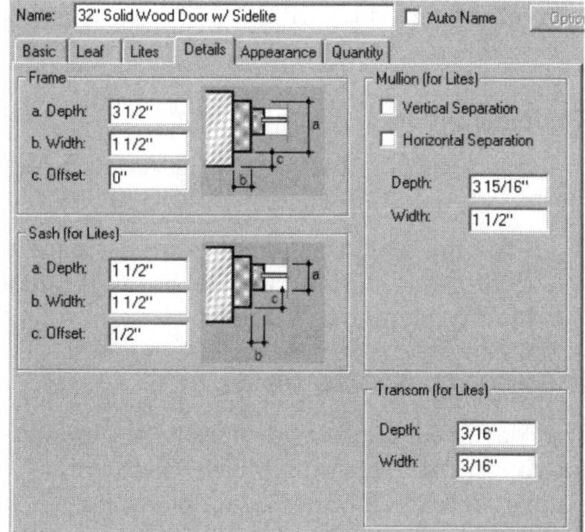

4. Edit the dimensions as desired. They are described below.

   <u>Frame</u>

   Depth. The depth of the frame members as seen from an overhead view.

   Width. The width of the frame members as seen from an overhead view.

   Offset. The offset of the door frame from the wall face.

   <u>Sash</u>

   Depth. The depth of sash members (sidelite/highlite frame) as seen from an overhead view.

   Width. The width of sash members as seen from an overhead view.

   Offset. The offset of the sash from the front of the door frame, i.e. how far back it sits in the door frame.

   <u>Mullion</u>

   Vertical Separation. If a lite has two or more panels running across it, this adds vertical dividers between the panels.

   Horizontal Separation. If a lite has two or more stacked panels, this adds horizontal dividers between them.

   Depth. The front-to-back thickness of the mullion as seen from an overhead view.

   Width. The width (left-to-right distance) of the mullion as seen from an overhead view.

   <u>Transom</u>

   Depth. The front-to-back thickness of the transom member as seen from an overhead view. The transom is the member between the door and the sidelite or highlite frame.

   Width. The width of the transom as seen from an overhead view.

5. Click **OK**.

Flipping a Door

You can use the Flip Opening tool to flip an entire door around. If the door originally opened out, it now opens in; if it was hinged on the left, it is now hinged on the right (and vice versa).

To flip a door:

1. Click the door to select it.
2. Right-click in the drawing area and select **Flip Opening**, or select **Edit > Modify Elements > Flip Opening**.

Flipping a Door Swing

Use the Flip Swing tool to flip only the swing of a door. The door will be hinged on the opposite side, but it will still open in the same direction, either in or out.

To flip a door swing:

1. Click the door to select it.
2. Right-click in the drawing area and select **Flip Swing**, or select **Edit > Modify Elements > Flip Swing**.

Moving a Door

You can move a door by clicking and dragging it inside the wall, or by editing the dynamic dimensions on either side of the door.

To move a door by clicking and dragging:

1. Click on the door to select it.
2. Click and drag the door to move it, then release your mouse button.

To move a door by editing dimensions:

1. Click on the door. Dimensions appear on either side of the door.
2. Click on the dimension you want to edit.

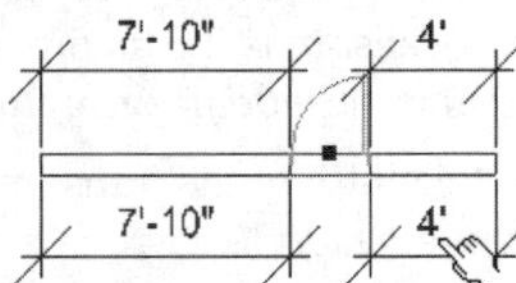

3. In the **Edit Dimension** dialog, enter the new value, then press **Enter** or click **OK**. The door position updates automatically.

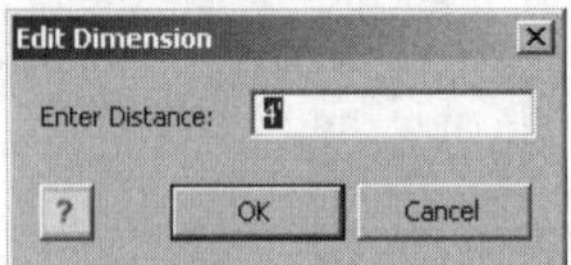

Raising or Lowering a Door

You can raise or lower a door in a wall using the Elevate tool on the door's right-click menu. You may, for example, want to lower your garage door if your ground floor sits above the ground.

To raise or lower a door:

1. Select the door whose elevation you want to edit.
2. Right-click and select **Elevate**, or select **Edit > Modify Elements > Elevate**.

   The value currently shown in the **Elevate** dialog is the current elevation of the door above or below the floor level.
3. In the **Elevate** dialog, specify the desired elevation of the door base above the floor. You can enter a negative value to move the door down.
4. Click **OK**.

Deleting a Door

You can delete a door with a couple of mouse clicks.

To delete a door:

1. Select the door to delete. To select multiple doors, use Shift+click.
2. Click the **Delete** button on your keyboard, or right-click and select **Delete**, or select **Edit > Modify Elements > Delete**.

Inserting Windows

The catalog contains a wide variety of windows for you to insert, including fixed, casement, double casement, hopper, awning, sliding, double-hung, single-hung, bay, bow and louvered windows.

You can point and click to insert a window, or offset the window a specific distance from the end of a wall.

Windows are inserted at the Head Height defined for the building location you insert the window on. You can raise or lower a window after you have inserted it if you need to.

Note: If you want to insert a skylight, see *Inserting Skylights* **on page 106**.

To insert a window:

1. Make sure the location you want to insert windows on is the current location in the building locations drop box.
2. Select **Insert > Windows**, or click the Windows button on the Building toolbar. 
3. In the catalog, select the window you want to insert.

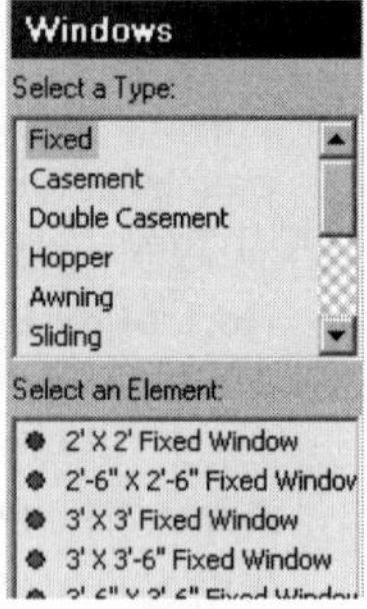

4. If you want to offset the window a specific distance from the end of

the wall, right-click and select **Enter insertion offset**.

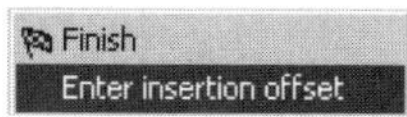

Enter the offset distance in the **Enter insertion offset** dialog, then click **OK**.

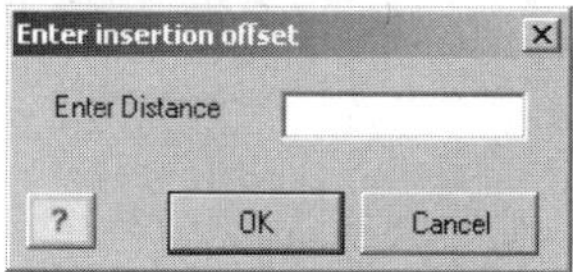

5. Position the window in the receiving wall. If you are using an insertion offset, position the window close to the end you want to offset it from. The window will snap inside the wall. Dimensions are displayed that show you the distance on either side of the window.
6. With your window positioned where you want it, click to insert it.
7. Right-click and select **Finish**.

Editing Window Types

Window types include fixed, casement, hung, sliding, awning, hopper, vent, bay, bow and louvre. You can edit a window's type on the window's Basic property page.

To edit a window type:

1. Select the window whose properties you want to change.
2. Right-click and select **Properties**, or select **Edit > Modify Elements > Properties**.
3. In the **Windows** dialog, select the Basic tab.
4. In the *Type* area, click on the desired window type to select it.

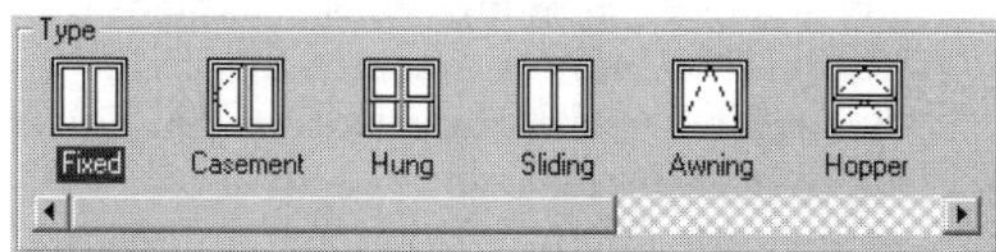

5. Click **OK**.

Editing a Window's Size Properties

You can edit the height and width of a window. You can also control the number of horizontal and vertical panes in the window. Some window types have additional properties that define their geometry.

To edit the size of a window:

1. Select the window whose properties you want to change.
2. Right-click and select **Properties**, or select **Edit > Modify Elements > Properties**.
3. In the **Windows** dialog, select the Basic tab.

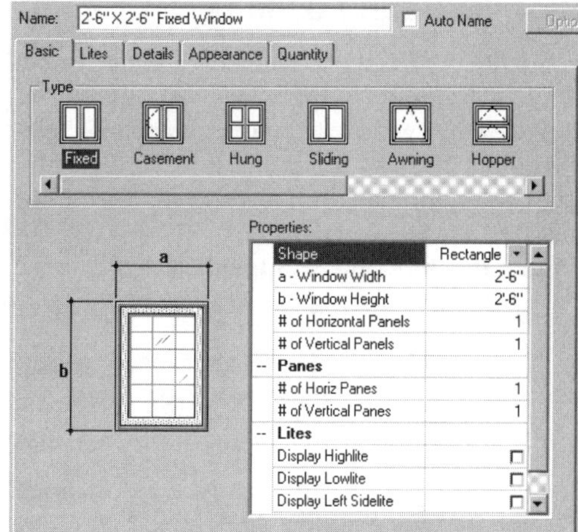

4. Edit the dimensions as desired. Most windows have the common dimensions listed below. Some have additional settings to define their geometry. Clicking a dimension marked with an alphabetical character (a, b, c, etc.) highlights the corresponding dimension in the window graphic, and vice versa.

   Window Width. The width of the window, not including the frame.

   Window Height. The height of the window.

   # of Horizontal Panels. The number of window panels running horizontally across the window frame. If you specify more than one panel, vertical dividers are added inside the window frame.

# of Vertical Panels. The number of window panels running vertically along the window frame. If you specify more than one panel, horizontal dividers are added inside the window frame.

# of Horizontal Panes. The number of panes of glass across each window panel.

# of Vertical Panes. The number of panes of glass running vertically along each window panel.

5. Click **OK**.

Editing a Window's Sidelites, Highlites and Lowlites

A sidelite is a fixed glass panel set on one or both sides of a window. A highlite is a glass panel above a window. A lowlite is a glass panel below a window. You can create a custom configuration of sidelites, highlites and lowlites for a window.

To display lites on a window:

1. Select the window.
2. Right-click and select **Properties**, or select **Edit > Modify Elements > Properties**.
3. In the **Windows** dialog, select the Basic tab.
4. To display a highlite over the window, enable the **Display Highlite** check box.
5. To display a lowlite under the window, enable the **Display Lowlite** check box.
6. To display a sidelite on the left side of the window, enable the **Display Left Sidelite** check box.
7. To display a sidelite on the right side of the window, enable the **Display Right Sidelite** check box.
8. Click **OK**.

To edit a window's lites:

1. Select the window whose properties you want to change.
2. Right-click and select **Properties**, or select **Edit > Modify Elements > Properties**.
3. In the **Windows** dialog, select the Lites tab.

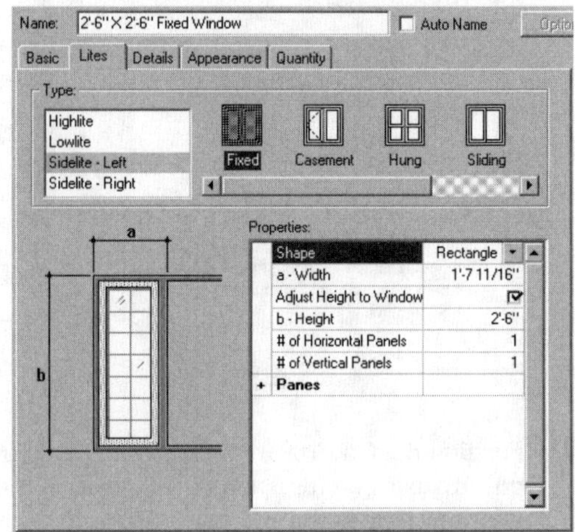

4. To display a highlite, sidelite or lowlite, check the appropriate box in the *Type* area (Highlite, Lowlite, Sidelite - left, Sidelite - right). You can select as many as you want.
5. In the *Type* window, select the lite you want to specify settings for.
6. To select a specific window type for the currently selected lite, click on the appropriate graphic in the *Type* area.
7. Edit the dimensions of the lite in the *Properties* area if desired. Clicking a dimension marked with an alphabetical character (a, b, c, etc.) highlights the corresponding dimension in the sidelite/highlite graphic, and vice versa.

   Shape. Choose from *Rectangle, Arched* or *Trapezoid*.

   (highlite/lowlite) **Adjust Width**. Selecting *Opening* adjusts the width of the highlite to match the width of the opening (including any sidelites). Selecting *Window* adjusts the width of the highlite to match the width of the window (excluding any sidelites). Selecting *User Defined* lets you specify a precise width for the highlite/lowlite in the **Width** edit box.

   Width. The total width of the lite.

(sidelites) **Adjust Height to Window**. Automatically adjusts the height of a sidelite to match the height of the window.

Height. The overall height of the lite.

# of Horizontal Panels. The number of panels across the lite. If you specify more than one panel, vertical dividers are added inside the lite's frame.

# of Vertical Panels. The number of panels running vertically along the lite. If you specify more than one panel, horizontal dividers are added inside the lite's frame.

# of Horizontal Panes. The number of panes of glass across the lite.

# of Vertical Panes. The number of panes of glass running vertically along the lite.

8. Click **OK**.

Editing Window Details

You can specify precise dimensions and offsets for the window frame, sash, mullions and transoms.

To edit window details:

1. Select the window whose properties you want to change.
2. Right-click and select **Properties**, or select **Edit > Modify Elements > Properties**.
3. In the **Windows** dialog, select the Details tab.

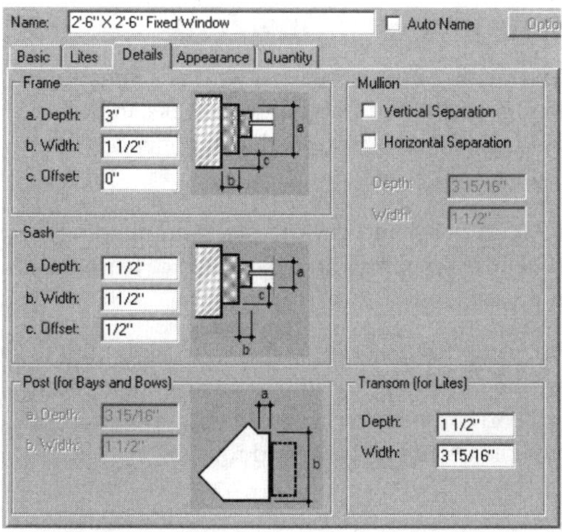

4. Edit the dimensions as desired. They are described below.

<u>Frame</u>

Depth. The depth of the frame members as seen from an overhead view.

Width. The width of the frame members as seen from an overhead view.

Offset. The offset of the window frame from the wall face.

<u>Sash</u>

Depth. The depth of sash members (sidelite/highlite/lowlite frame) as seen from an overhead view.

Width. The width of sash members as seen from an overhead view.

Offset. The offset of the sash from the front of the window frame, i.e. how far back it sits in the window frame.

<u>Post (for Bays and Bows)</u>

Depth: The thickness of posts in bay and bow windows.

Width: The width of posts in bay and bow windows.

<u>Mullion</u>

Vertical Separation. If a lite has two or more panels running across it, this adds vertical dividers between the panels.

Horizontal Separation. If a lite has two or more stacked panels, this adds horizontal dividers between them.

Depth. The front-to-back thickness of the mullion as seen from an overhead view.

Width. The width (left-to-right distance) of the mullion as seen from an overhead view.

<u>Transom (for Lites)</u>

Depth. The front-to-back thickness of the transom member as seen from an overhead view. The transom is the member between the window and the sidelite, highlite or lowlite frame.

Width. The width of the transom as seen from an overhead view.

5. Click **OK**.

Flipping a Window

You can use the Flip Opening tool to instantly flip a window around in the wall. If the window has a swing, the swing is also flipped.

To flip a window:

1. Select the window.
2. Right-click in the drawing area and select **Flip Opening**, or select **Edit > Modify Elements > Flip Opening**.

Moving a Window

You can move a window by clicking and dragging it inside the wall, or by editing the dynamic dimensions on either side of the window.

To move a window by clicking and dragging:

1. Click on the window to select it.
2. Click and drag the window to move it.

To move a window by editing dimensions:

1. Click on the window. Dimensions appear on either side of the window.
2. Click on the dimension you want to edit.

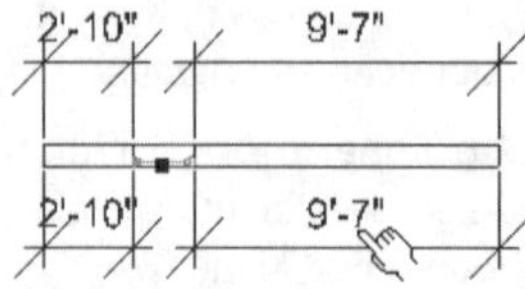

3. In the **Edit Dimension** dialog, enter the new value, then press **Enter** or click **OK**. The window position updates automatically.

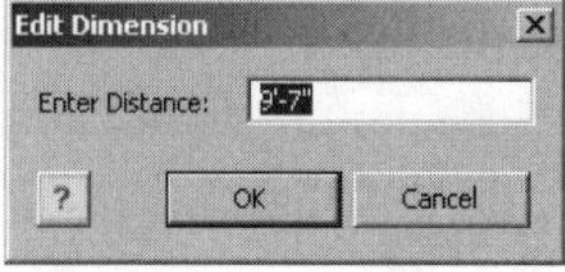

Raising or Lowering a Window

You can raise or lower a window in a wall using the Elevate tool on the window's right-click menu.

To raise or lower a window:

1. Select the window whose elevation you want to edit.
2. Right-click and select **Elevate**, or select **Edit > Modify Elements > Elevate**.
   The value currently shown in the **Elevate** dialog is the current elevation of the window top above the floor level.
3. In the **Elevate** dialog, specify the desired elevation of the top of the window above the floor.
4. Click **OK**.

Deleting a Window

You can delete a window with a couple of mouse clicks.

To delete a window:

1. Select the window to delete. To select multiple windows, use Shift+click.
2. Click the **Delete** button on your keyboard, or right-click and select **Delete**, or select **Edit > Modify Elements > Delete**.

Inserting Wall Openings

An opening is a cutout in a wall of a specific shape, width and height. Openings can be rectangular, round, arched, octagonal or trapezoidal.

You can point and click to insert an opening, or offset the opening a specific distance from the end of a wall.

Openings are inserted at the Head Height defined for the building location you insert the opening on. You can raise or lower an opening after you have inserted it if you need to.

To insert an opening:

1. Make sure the location you want to insert openings on is the current location in the building locations drop box.
2. Select **Insert > Openings**, or click the Openings button on the Building toolbar. 
3. In the catalog, select the opening you want to insert.

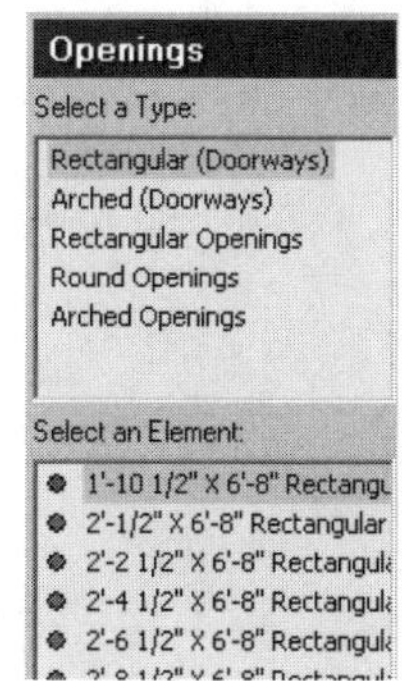

4. If you want to offset the opening a specific distance from the end of the wall, right-click and select **Enter insertion offset**.

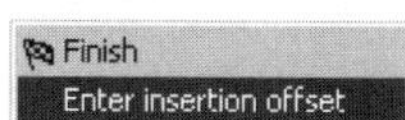

Enter the offset distance in the **Enter insertion offset** dialog, then click **OK**.

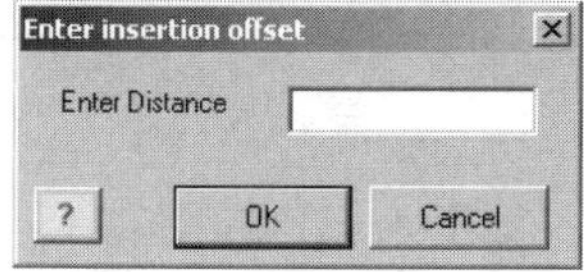

5. Position the opening in the receiving wall. If you are using an insertion offset, position the opening close to the end you want to offset it from. The opening will snap inside the wall. Dimensions are displayed that show you the distance on either side of the opening.
6. With your opening positioned where you want it, click to insert it.
7. Right-click and select **Finish**.

Editing the Shape of a Wall Opening

Openings can be rectangular, round, arched, octagonal or trapezoidal.

To change the shape a wall opening:

1. Select the opening whose properties you want to change.
2. Right-click and select **Properties**, or select **Edit > Modify Elements > Properties**.
3. In the *Type* area, click on the shape you want.

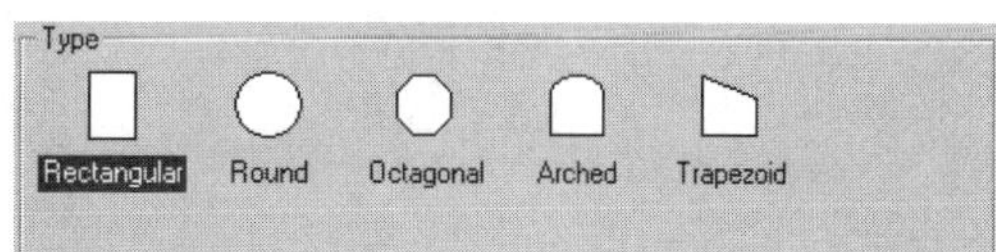

4. Click **OK**.

Editing the Size of a Wall Opening

You can edit the dimensions of a wall opening by changing the properties on the opening's Basic property page.

To edit the size of a wall opening:

1. Select the opening whose properties you want to change.
2. Right-click and select **Properties**, or select **Edit > Modify Elements > Properties**.
3. In the *Properties* area, edit the dimensions of the opening. Dimensions vary according to the shape of the opening.
4. Click **OK**.

Tip: If you want the bottom of your opening to be level with the floor, change the height of opening to match the Head Height of the building location it is inserted on. Alternatively you can lower the opening using the Elevate tool.

Moving a Wall Opening

You can move a wall opening by clicking and dragging it inside the wall, or by editing the dynamic dimensions on either side of the opening.

To move an opening by clicking and dragging:

1. Click on the opening to select it.
2. Click and drag the opening to move it.

To move an opening by editing dimensions:

1. Click on the opening. Dimensions appear on either side of the opening.

2. Click on the dimension you want to edit.

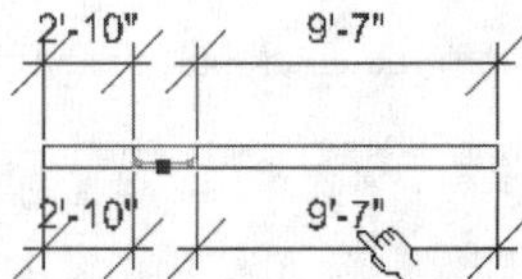

3. In the **Edit Dimension** dialog, enter the new value, then press **Enter** or click **OK**. The opening position updates automatically.

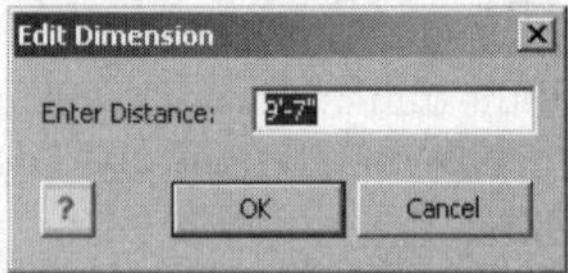

Raising or Lowering a Wall Opening

You can raise or lower an opening in a wall using the Elevate tool on the opening's right-click menu.

To raise or lower a wall opening:

1. Select the opening whose elevation you want to edit.
2. Right-click and select **Elevate**, or select **Edit > Modify Elements > Elevate**.

   The value currently shown in the **Elevate** dialog is the current elevation of the opening top above the floor level.
3. In the **Elevate** dialog, specify the desired elevation of the top of the opening above the floor.
4. Click **OK**.

Deleting a Wall Opening

You can delete a wall opening with a couple of mouse clicks.

To delete an opening:

1. Select the opening to delete. To select multiple openings, use Shift+click.
2. Click the **Delete** button on your keyboard, or right-click and select **Delete**, or select **Edit > Modify Elements > Delete**.

Chapter 11

Floors & Ceilings

A floor is inserted automatically when you connect three or more walls to create a closed wall layout. When you insert interior walls, the floor is split as new rooms are created. If you want different flooring types in different rooms, you can use the Materials Paintbrush to quickly apply different types of carpet, tiles, wood flooring, vinyl flooring, linoleum, or concrete to individual floors.

Ceilings are not created automatically unless you turn on the Insert Ceilings Automatically option in your program settings before drawing walls. Alternatively you can point and click to insert ceilings using one of the handy Ceiling tools.

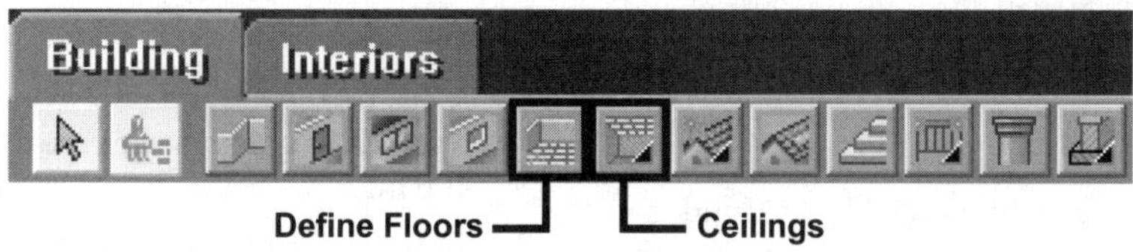

How Floors are Created

A floor is automatically inserted throughout your model when you connect three or more walls to create a closed exterior wall layout.

The material applied to the floor depends on the house style you selected when using the House Builder Wizard. If you created your model from scratch, a nylon carpet was applied.

When you draw interior walls, the floor is split into individual floors as new rooms are created provided the room's walls are all connected. You can also manually split any floor surface using the Define Floors tool.

Floors cannot be selected in 2D plan view. They can only be selected in 3D view. The only exception are floor edges that have been defined using the Define Floors tool. Such edges are marked with a dashed line in 2D view, and can be moved if necessary.

Floors are directly associated with the walls that contain them. If you stretch your wall layout, the floor stretches with it. If you open up your wall layout by deleting a wall, the floor will be deleted. You cannot re-insert a floor manually.

Tip: For projects in which you plan to use the House Builder Wizard, you can change the default floor type by editing the House Builder Wizard element configuration before running the Wizard. See *Creating a Custom House Builder Wizard Configuration* on page 288. If you plan to create a model from scratch, you can change the default floor type by selecting the desired floor type in the Catalog Manager before creating your wall layout. See *Using the Catalog Manager* on page 246.

Defining Individual Floor Areas

As you draw interior walls, the floor is split into individual floors as new rooms are created provided the rooms are completely enclosed by walls. You can manually split a floor if you want. You may, for example, want to create two different floor areas in one room. You can also use the Define Floors tool to define an opening in your floor. Floor edges defined with the Define Floors tool can be moved to increase or decrease the size of the individual floor area. They can also be deleted if necessary.

To define individual floor areas:

1. Select **Insert > Define Floors**, or click the Define Floors button on the Building toolbar. 
2. Select points to define the split line.

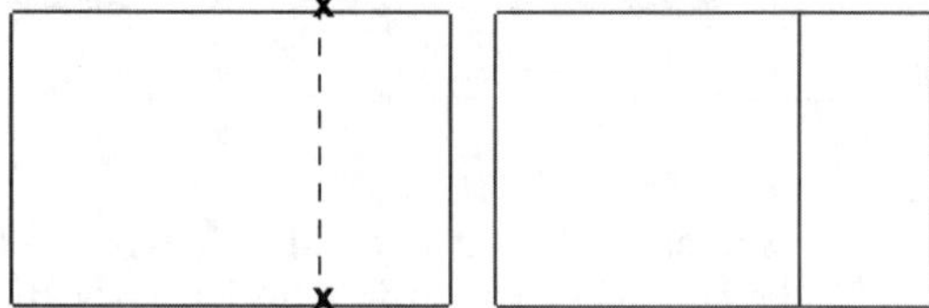

   Note that the start point and end point of the line must be on an existing floor edge, although intermediate points are permitted anywhere on the floor surface (if you are creating a custom floor shape, for example).

3. Right-click and select **Finish**.

To move a defined floor edge:

1. Click on the dashed floor edge in 2D plan view. Blue grab handles are displayed along the line.
2. Hover your pointer over the center grab handle, then click and drag to move the line.
3. Release your mouse button.

Raising or Lowering a Floor

You can raise or lower a floor using the Elevate tool.

To raise or lower a floor:

1. Select the floor in 3D.
2. Right-click and select **Elevate**, or select **Edit > Modify Elements > Elevate**.
3. In the **Elevate** dialog, specify the desired elevation of the floor above the floor level defined for the current building location.
4. Click **OK**.

Editing the Thickness of a Floor

You can edit the thickness of a floor on its Basic property page.

To edit the thickness of a floor:

1. Select the floor in 3D.
2. Right-click and select **Properties**, or select **Edit > Modify Elements > Properties**.
3. Edit the value in the **Thickness** edit box on the Basic page.
4. Click **OK**.

Applying Different Materials to Floors

You can use the Materials Paintbrush to quickly apply different types of materials to floors, such as different colors or patterns of carpet, tile or linoleum.

To apply a material to a floor:

1. Display your model in 3D view and make sure the floor is visible in the view. You may need to use the View Filter to hide the roof and ceilings.
2. Select **Edit > Materials Paintbrush**, or click the Materials Paintbrush button on any tabbed toolbar. 
3. In the catalog panel, select the material you want to apply. Categories that contain flooring include Wood, Concrete, Carpet, Tile and Linoleum.
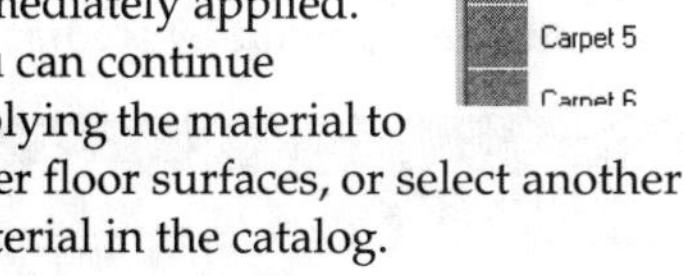

4. Click on the floor surface you want to apply the material to. The material is immediately applied. You can continue applying the material to other floor surfaces, or select another material in the catalog.
5. Right-click and select **Finish**.

Inserting Openings in Floors

You can insert an opening of any shape and size in a floor. You may need to do this to accommodate a staircase.

To insert an opening in a floor:

1. Select **Insert > Define Floors**, or click the Define Floors button on the Building toolbar. 
2. Select points to define the outline of the opening, ensuring the outline is a closed shape.
3. Right-click and select **Finish**. An outline is created on the floor surface. You can stretch, move and curve the opening if necessary to get the exact size and shape you want. Note that you cannot edit the size, shape or position of the opening later, so make sure it's correct before proceeding.
4. Go into 3D view and make sure the floor is visible and accessible.
5. Click in the center of the outline you drew to select the outline.
6. Press the **Delete** key on your keyboard, or right-click and select **Delete**, or select **Edit > Modify Elements > Delete**.

Deleting a Floor

You can delete a floor while in 3D view.

Warning: There is no method of inserting floors manually. They can only be created while drawing walls.

To delete a floor:

1. Select the floor in 3D.
2. Press the **Delete** key on your keyboard, or right-click and select **Delete**, or select **Edit > Modify Elements > Delete**.

How Ceilings Are Created

If you turn on the Insert Ceilings Automatically feature in your Program Settings before drawing walls, a ceiling is automatically created when you connect three or more walls to form a closed wall layout.

The type of ceiling that is inserted depends on the house style you select when using the House Builder Wizard. If you create your model from scratch, a 1/2" drywall material is applied to the ceiling, or whatever ceiling material was last selected in the catalog. When you draw interior walls, the ceiling is split into individual ceilings as new rooms are created provided the room's walls are all connected.

Automatic ceilings can only be selected and edited in 3D view.

If you did not turn on the Insert Ceilings Automatically feature before drawing walls, or you have deleted a ceiling, you can insert ceilings using any of the handy Ceiling tools — Ceiling by Room, Ceiling by Perimeter, or Ceiling by Picking Points.

You can edit the thickness and appearance of any ceiling as well as lower it to create a suspended ceiling, regardless of how you created it. You can also use the Materials Paintbrush to apply different colors or materials to individual ceilings.

Tip: The underside of an upper-story floor can also serve as a ceiling. By the same token, the top side of a lower-story ceiling can serve as a floor.

Inserting Ceilings by Perimeter

You can use the Ceiling by Perimeter tool to instantly insert a ceiling of your choice inside the perimeter of your model. This means that every room on a selected location will have the same ceiling. Also, the ceiling will be considered one element, even though it is present in individual rooms.

To instantly add a ceiling to the entire perimeter of a location:

1. Make sure the location you want to insert the ceiling on is the current location in the building locations drop box.
2. Select **Insert > Ceilings > Ceiling by Perimeter**, or click the Ceilings button on the Building toolbar and select **Ceiling by Perimeter**.

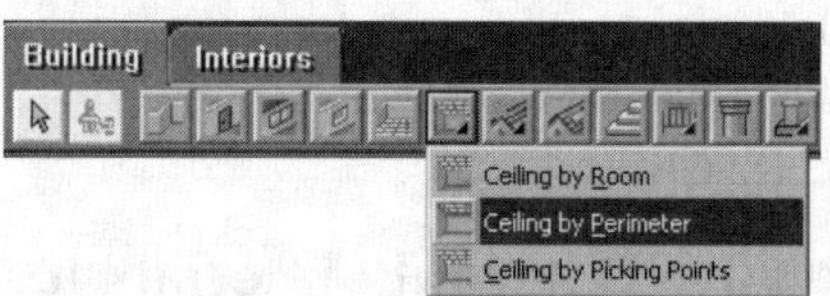

3. In the catalog, select the ceiling type you want to insert.
4. Click anywhere inside the perimeter of the model. The ceiling is added automatically.
5. Right-click and select **Finish** from the shortcut menu.

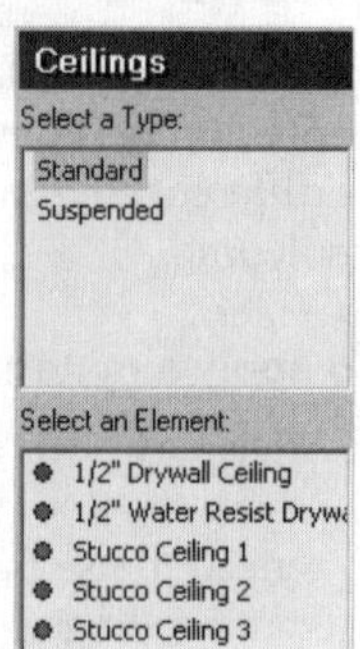

Inserting Ceilings by Room

The **Ceiling by Room** option inserts a ceiling inside the perimeter of a room provided all the walls are connected. Adding ceilings by room allows you to have different ceiling types in different rooms.

To insert a ceiling inside a room:

1. Make sure the location you want to insert the ceiling on is the current location in the building locations drop box.
2. Select **Insert > Ceilings > Ceiling by Room**, or click the Ceilings button on the Building toolbar and select **Ceiling by Room**.

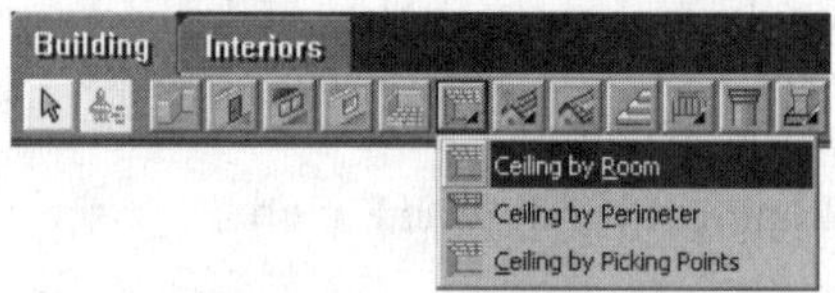

3. In the catalog, select the ceiling type you want to insert.
4. Click inside the room that you want to add the ceiling to. The ceiling is added automatically. (If you want, you can continue adding ceilings to other rooms.)
5. Right-click and select **Finish** from the shortcut menu.

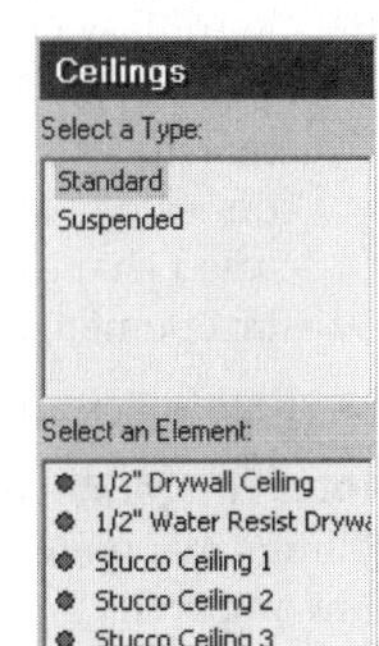

Inserting a Ceiling by Picking Points

Using the Ceiling by Picking Points tool you can insert a ceiling by picking points to define the ceiling's outline. This lets you create a ceiling of any shape and size, anywhere in the drawing area.

To create a ceiling by picking points:

1. Make sure the location you want to insert the ceiling on is the current location in the building locations drop box.
2. Select **Insert > Ceilings > Ceiling by Picking Points**, or click the Ceilings button on the Building toolbar and select **Ceiling by Picking Points**.

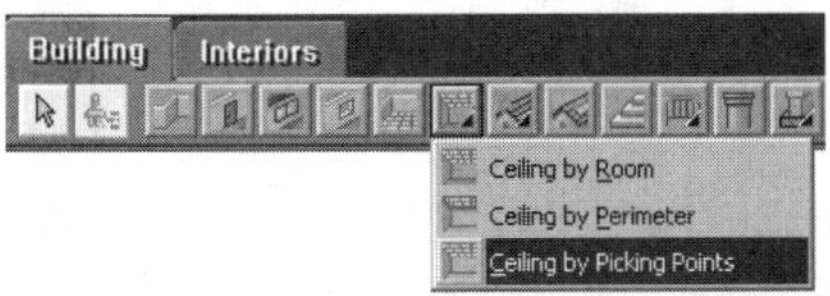

3. In the catalog, select the ceiling type you want to insert.
4. Select a start point for the ceiling outline.
5. Continue selecting points until the outline is defined. (You do not have to select the start point again because the last point you pick is always closed back to the start point.)
6. Right-click and select **Finish**.

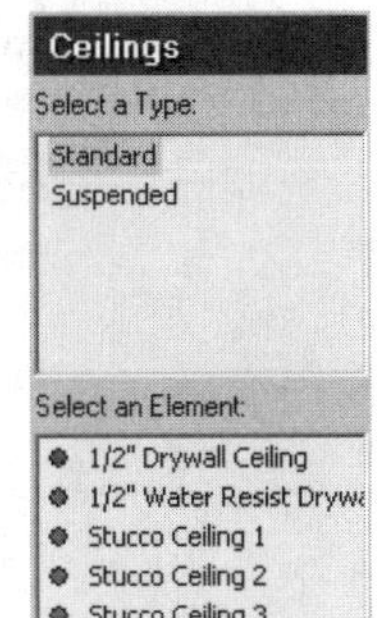

Raising or Lowering a Ceiling

You can change the height of a ceiling using the Elevate tool.

To raise or lower a ceiling:

1. Select the ceiling you want to raise or lower by clicking on the edge of it. If the ceiling was created automatically when drawing walls, you need to select it in 3D view.
2. Right-click and select **Elevate**, or select **Edit > Modify Elements > Elevate**.

   The current value in the **Elevate** dialog is the current elevation of the ceiling above the floor level.
3. In the **Elevate** dialog, specify the height you want the ceiling to sit at above the floor.
4. Click **OK**.

Curving a Ceiling Edge

You can curve a ceiling edge using the Curve tool. Once the tool is active, you can click and drag the edge to curve it, or select a point to curve to.

To curve a ceiling edge by clicking and dragging:

1. Click on the edge you want to curve.
2. Right-click and select **Curve**, or select **Edit > Modify Elements > Curve**.
3. Click and drag the ceiling edge to the desired curve.
4. Release your mouse button.

To curve a ceiling edge to a selected point:

1. Click on the ceiling edge you want to curve.
2. Right-click in and select **Curve**, or select **Edit > Modify Elements > Curve**.
3. Select the point you want to curve to. The ceiling edge automatically curves to the point.
4. Click to finish.

Inserting Openings in Automatic Ceilings

If you opted to insert a ceiling automatically before drawing walls, you can create a custom opening in the automatic ceiling using the Define Floors and Delete tools.

To insert an opening in an automatic ceiling:

1. In 2D plan view, select **Insert > Define Floors**, or click the Define Floors button on the Building toolbar.
2. Select points to define the outline of the opening, ensuring the outline is a closed shape.
3. Right-click and select **Finish**. An outline is created on both the floor and ceiling of the current location. If necessary you can move, stretch or curve edges to get the exact size and shape you want. Note that you cannot edit the size, shape or position of the opening later, so make sure it's correct before proceeding.
4. Go into 3D view and make sure the ceiling is visible.
5. Click in the center of the outline you drew to select the outline.
6. Press the **Delete** key on your keyboard, or right-click and select **Delete**, or select **Edit > Modify Elements > Delete**.

Inserting Openings in Manually Inserted Ceilings

If you used a Ceiling tool to insert a ceiling, you can insert a custom opening in it of virtually any shape and size using the Cut Opening tool.

You create the opening by picking points to define its outline.

To insert an opening in a ceiling:

1. Select the ceiling by clicking on one of its edges.
2. Right-click and select **Cut Opening**, or select **Edit > Modify Elements > Cut Opening**.
3. Select a start point for the opening.
4. Continue selecting points to define the opening. As you select points, the opening is created. The last point picked is always connected back to the start point to form a closed shape, so you don't have to select the start point again.
5. Right-click and select **Finish**.

Note: You cannot insert openings this way in ceilings that were created automatically when drawing walls.

Resizing a Ceiling Opening

If you created a ceiling opening in a manually inserted ceiling, you can resize the opening by clicking and dragging one of its edges.

Note: You cannot edit an opening created in an automatic ceiling.

To stretch a ceiling opening:

1. In 2D plan view, click on the opening edge you want to move. The entire opening is highlighted, and a blue grab handle appears at the center of the opening edge you selected.

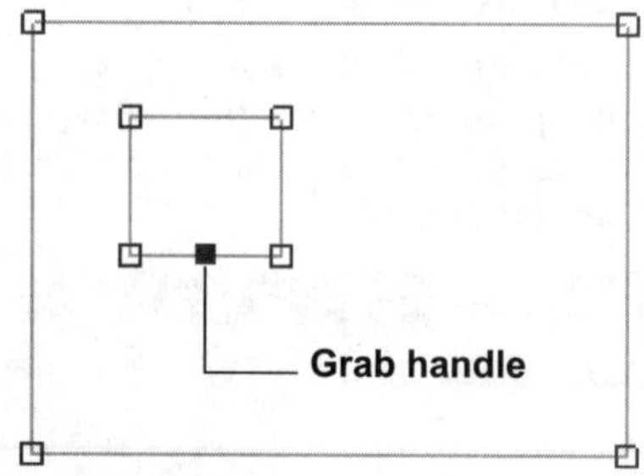

2. Hover your pointer over the center grab handle to display the Move cursor. 

3. Click and drag in the direction you want to stretch.

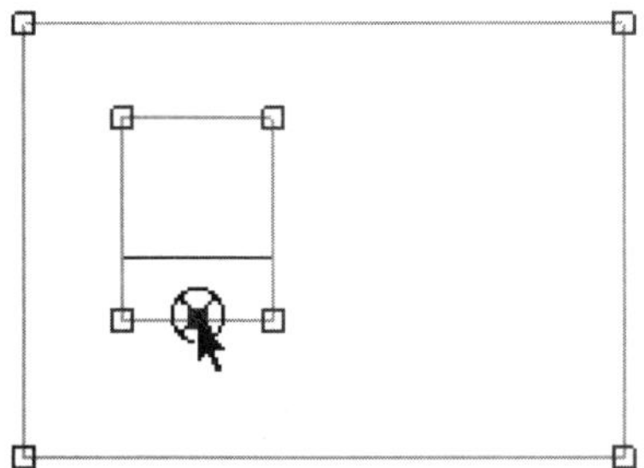

4. When the opening is the correct size, release your mouse button.

Tip: You can also reshape a ceiling opening by clicking and dragging its corner grab handles.

Curving a Ceiling Opening Edge

You can curve an opening edge in a manually inserted ceiling using the Curve tool. Once the tool is active, you can click and drag the opening edge to curve it, or select a point to curve to.

Note: You cannot edit an opening created in an automatic ceiling.

To curve an opening edge by clicking and dragging:

1. Click on the opening edge you want to curve.
2. Right-click and select **Curve**, or select **Edit > Modify Elements > Curve**.
3. Click and drag the opening edge to the desired curve.
4. Release your mouse button.

To curve an opening edge to a selected point:

1. Click on the opening edge you want to curve.
2. Right-click in and select **Curve**, or select **Edit > Modify Elements > Curve**.
3. Select the point you want to curve to. The opening edge automatically curves to the point.
4. Click to finish.

Removing Ceiling Openings

You can remove an opening from a manually inserted ceiling by selecting all sides of the opening, then clicking and dragging it away from the ceiling.

Note: You cannot remove an opening using Delete. Also, you cannot remove an opening created in an automatic ceiling.

To remove a ceiling opening:

1. Click on one of the opening's edges.
2. Shift+click to select the remaining sides.
3. Hover your pointer over one of the grab handles to display the Move cursor. 
4. Click and drag the opening off the ceiling surface until it disappears.

Applying Different Colors and Materials to Ceilings

You can use the Materials Paintbrush to quickly apply different colors or materials to ceilings. The paintbrush intelligently applies the material to the underside of the ceiling, even if you select the top side of the ceiling.

To apply a material to a ceiling:

1. Display your model in 3D view and make sure the ceiling is visible in the view. You may need to use the View Filter to hide the roof.
2. Select **Edit > Materials Paintbrush**, or click the Materials Paintbrush button on any tabbed toolbar. 

3. In the catalog panel, select the material you want to apply. Paint colors are located in the Paint category, and Stucco and Drywall can be found in the Finishes category.
4. Click on the ceiling you want to apply the material to. The material is immediately applied to the underside of the ceiling. You can continue applying the material to other ceiling surfaces, or select another material in the catalog.
5. Right-click and select **Finish**.

Deleting a Ceiling

You can delete a ceiling in a couple of easy steps.

To delete a ceiling:

1. Select the ceiling. If the ceiling was created automatically when drawing walls, you need to select it in 3D view.
2. Press the **Delete** key on your keyboard, right-click and select **Delete**, or select **Edit > Modify Elements > Delete**.

Chapter 12

Stairs, Ramps & Railings

If your design has more than one floor, you'll want to insert a staircase. The catalog contains a variety of stair and ramp styles, including straight, spiral, fold-back, L-shaped, L-winder. You can edit the composition and dimensions of each component in your staircase to create the exact look you want.

Stairs and ramps are inserted as solid objects with point-and-click simplicity. Just select the staircase or ramp you want to insert in the catalog, then click to insert it in your model.

The catalog also contains an excellent selection of railing types. A railing can be just a handrail, or a balustrade with posts, top/bottom rails and newels. You can insert railings on a staircase automatically. You can choose to put it on both sides, the left side, the right side, or the center. You can also draw a horizontal railing by picking points.

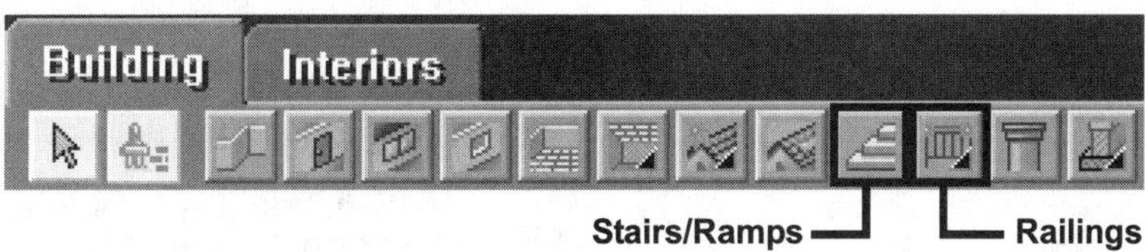

Inserting Stairs and Ramps

You can insert a staircase or ramp with a single mouse click. If you place the staircase near a wall, the staircase will automatically snap to the wall. Once you have inserted a staircase, you can edit its size, style and geometry.

To insert a staircase or ramp:

1. In the building locations drop box, select the location where you want to insert the base of the staircase.
2. Select **Insert > Stairs/Ramps**, or click the Stairs/Ramps button on the Building toolbar.

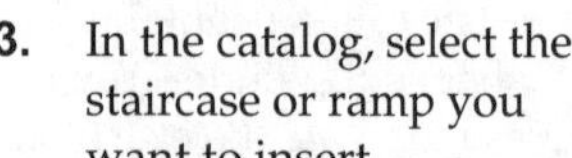

3. In the catalog, select the staircase or ramp you want to insert.
4. Position the staircase and click to insert it.
5. Right-click and select **Finish**.

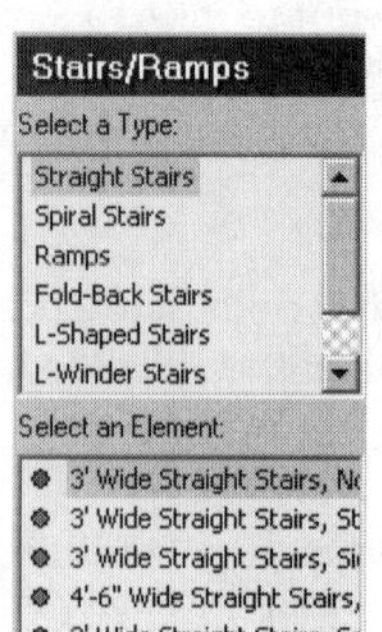

Parts of a Staircase

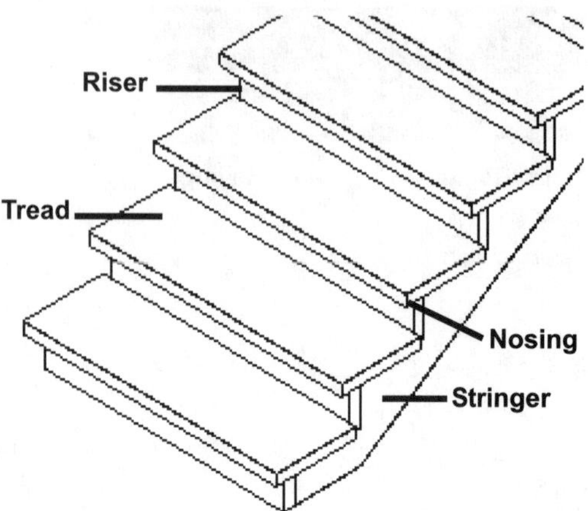

Editing Stair Size Properties

By default, most stairs (except porch stairs) have an overall height of 9′ and have 18 steps. You can edit the general dimensions of a staircase, such as height, width, and number of steps.

To edit stair size properties:

1. Select the staircase whose stair properties you want to edit.
2. Right-click and select **Properties**, or select **Edit > Modify Elements > Properties**.

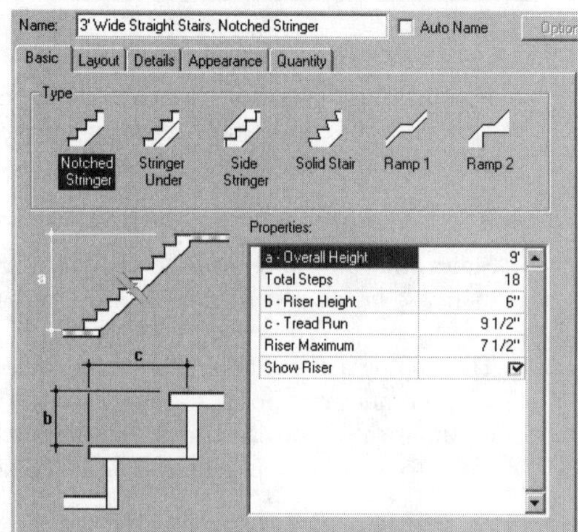

3. In the **Stairs/Ramps** dialog, edit the dimensions in the *Properties* window.

   Overall Height. The vertical distance from the base of the staircase to the top of the staircase. Generally this is the distance from one floor to the next.

   Total Steps. The total number of steps in the staircase including all treads and landings. This value is controlled by the Overall Height and Riser Maximum, so you can only go so high or so low when specifying the total number of steps.

   Riser Height. The distance from the top of one tread to the top of the next tread. The riser height adjusts if you edit the Overall Height or Total Steps, making this a read-only value.

Tread Run. The width of a step from the nose of the step to the riser of the next step.

Riser Maximum. The maximum height allowed for risers. The riser height adjusts when you change the Overall Height or Total Steps variables.

Show Riser. Inserts vertical boards under the treads. If turned off, the stairs are open under the treads.

Editing a Staircase Layout

You can choose from a multitude of preset staircase layouts and edit the dimensions of individual segments to suit your needs.

To edit a staircase layout:

1. Select the staircase whose stair properties you want to edit.
2. Right-click and select **Properties**, or select **Edit > Modify Elements > Properties**.
3. In the **Stairs/Ramps** dialog, select the Layout tab.
4. To change the layout of the staircase, make a selection from the **Preset Layouts** drop box, or click the graphic to display the available layouts and select the one you want.

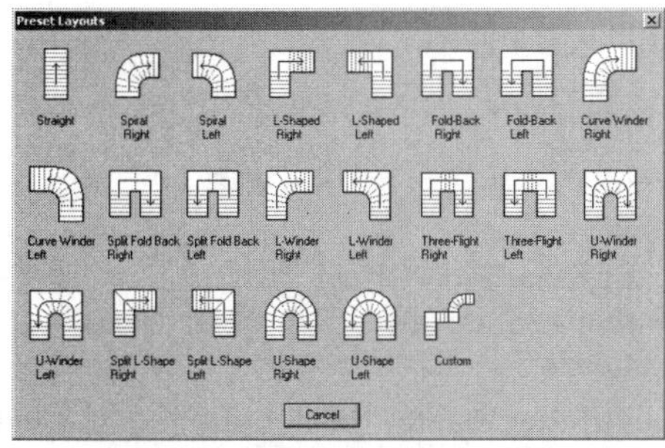

5. To edit the dimensions of a particular segment, select the segment in the *Layout Segments* window. For example, an L-shaped staircase will have three segments: *Stair 1*, *Landing 2* and *Stair 3*. The Stair 1 segment is the lower flight of stairs, Landing 2 is the central landing between the two flights, and Stair 3 is the upper flight of stairs.
6. Different layouts will have different parameters. Common ones are described below. Clicking a dimension marked with an alphabetical character (a, b, c, etc.) highlights the corresponding dimension in the stair graphic, and vice versa.

Stair Segments

Number of Steps. The number of steps in the flight.

Position Offset. Shifts the base of the staircase left or right from the center line. A positive value shifts it right, a negative value shifts it left. If the Upper Offset is set to 0, the entire staircase is moved.

Lower Width. The width of the bottom step.

Upper Width. The width of the top step.

Upper Offset. Shifts the top of the stair segment left or right to create an angled flight. A positive value shifts it right, a negative value shifts it left.

Landing Connection. Choose from *Front*, *Bottom* or *Under* to determine how the stairs attach to the landing.

Adjust Width. Adjusts the width of attached landings and stair flights to match the width settings of the current segment.

Adjust Segment. When editing the number of risers or height of the segment, this determines which other segments (or all others) are to be adjusted to make up the overall height of all segments.

Landing Segments (vary per style)

Position Offset. Shifts the landing left or right. A positive value moves the landing right. A negative value moves it left.

Width. The width of the landing along the lower flight of stairs. By default this matches the Upper Width setting of the lower stair flight.

Depth 1. The width of the landing along the upper flight of stairs. By default this matches the Lower Width setting of the upper stair flight.

Depth 2. The width of the exposed side of the landing.

Adjust Width. Adjusts the width of attached stair flights to match the width of the landing.

7. To add a flight or landing to your staircase, click **Add** in the *Layout Segments* area. Select the segment you want to add in the **Add/Edit Segment** dialog.

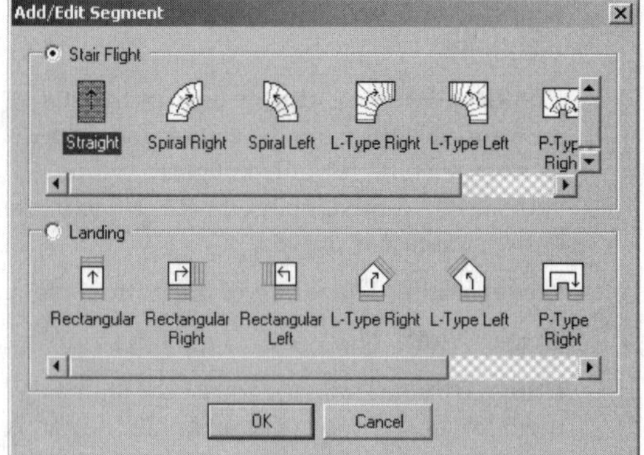

The segment is added to your list of segments in the *Layout Segments* window. Proceed with defining the parameters for the new segment in the *Parameters* window.

8. To change an existing segment to another type, select the segment in the *Layout Segments* window, then click **Edit**. Select the new segment type in the **Add/Edit Segment** dialog.
9. To delete a segment from the staircase, select the segment in the *Layout Segments* window, then click **Delete**.
10. Once you are satisfied with your layout settings, click **OK**.

Editing Stair Details

Editing stair details lets you precisely control the size and position of treads, risers, stringers and landing platforms.

To edit stair details:

1. Select the staircase whose stair properties you want to edit.
2. Right-click and select **Properties**, or select **Edit > Modify Elements > Properties**.
3. To change the stringer style or create a solid stair, click the appropriate graphic in the *Type* area.

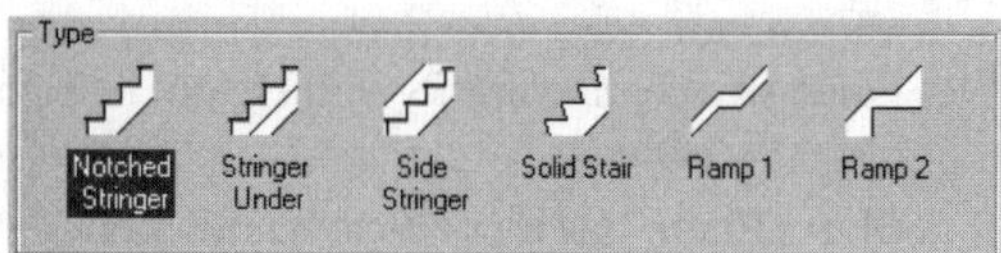

4. To edit tread, riser, stringer and landing details, select the Details tab. Clicking a dimension marked with an alphabetical character (a, b, c, etc.) highlights the corresponding dimension in the stair graphic, and vice versa.
5. Edit the properties in the *Properties* area.

Tread Thickness. The thickness of each step.

Nosing Depth. The distance the step extends past the riser.

Riser Angle. The tilt of the riser board. A value of 0 means the board is perpendicular to the step (straight up and down). A value above 0 tilts the riser down toward the back of the staircase. The maximum angle allowed is 20°.

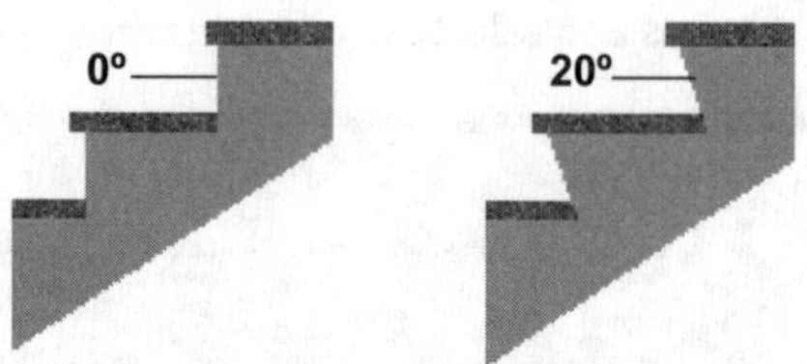

Stringer Side Offset. The distance the side stringers are offset from the ends of the treads.

Stringer Waste. The distance from the bottom of the stringer to the underside of the tread/riser intersection. Setting the stringer waste to match the height of your staircase creates a stringer that runs from the staircase right to the floor.

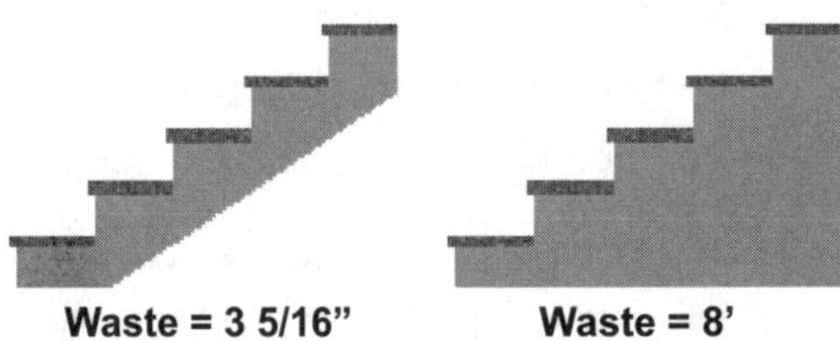

Stringer Thickness. The thickness of the stringer member.

Max Stringer Spacing. The maximum distance allowed between stringers. If you increase the width of the staircase, additional stringers will be inserted if this spacing is exceeded.

Landing Thickness. The thickness of the landing platform.

6. Click **OK**.

Editing the Appearance of the Cut Line

When viewing a staircase in 2D plan view you can see a cut line through the staircase. The cut line is a standard drafting symbol for stairs.

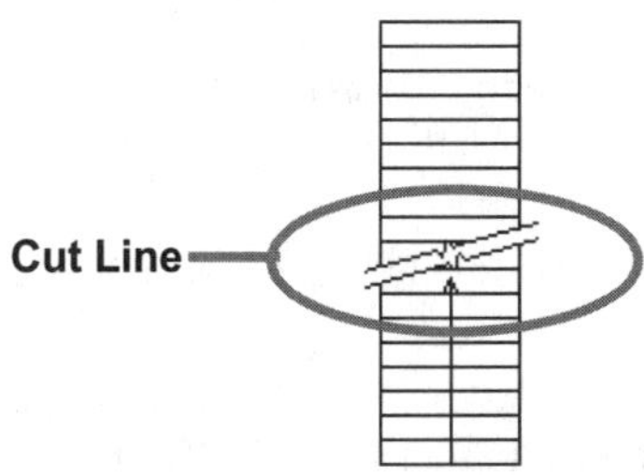

You can change the cut line's position, size, angle and style. You can also hide it from view if you want.

To edit the appearance of the cut line:

1. Select the staircase.
2. Right-click and select **Properties**, or select **Edit > Modify Elements > Properties**.
3. In the **Stairs/Ramps** dialog, select the Details tab.
4. Make your changes in the *Cut Line* area.

   Show Cut Lines. Shows or hides the cut lines in 2D plan view.

   Extension. The distance the cut line extends past the edge of the staircase in 2D plan view.

   Angle. The angle of the cut line in 2D plan view.

   Spacing. If using the Double or Double Arch style, this is the distance between the lines.

   Elevation. How high up the staircase the cut line sits.

   Style. Choose from Single, Single Architectural, Double and Double Architectural. The default is Double Architectural.
5. Once you've defined your cut line, click **OK**.

Editing General Ramp Properties

If editing a ramp, you can select a uniform or full style, and edit the ramp thickness and landing thickness. If you want to change the layout (shape) of the ramp or edit properties such as the height or slope, see *Editing the Layout of a Ramp* on page 88.

To edit ramp properties:

1. Select the ramp.
2. Right-click and select **Properties**, or select **Edit > Modify Elements > Properties**.
3. In the **Stairs/Ramps** dialog, select the Basic tab.
4. If you want to change the ramp type, click on the type you want in the Type area. The first type is a ramp with uniform thickness, while the second is a full, wedge-style ramp.

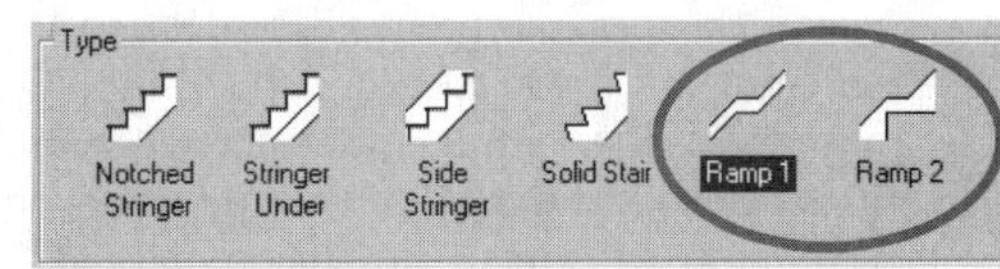

5. If you selected the uniform ramp style, you can change its thickness by entering the desired thickness in the **Ramp Thickness** edit box.

6. To change the thickness of the landing, enter a value in the **Landing Thickness** edit box.
7. Click **OK**.

Editing the Layout of a Ramp

You can choose from a multitude of preset ramp layouts as well as edit various layout properties such as length and slope.

To edit the layout of a ramp:

1. Select the ramp.
2. Right-click and select **Properties**, or select **Edit > Modify Elements > Properties**.
3. In the **Stairs/Ramps** dialog, select the Layout tab.
4. To change the layout of the ramp, make a selection from the **Preset Layouts** drop box, or click the graphic to display the available layouts and select the one you want.

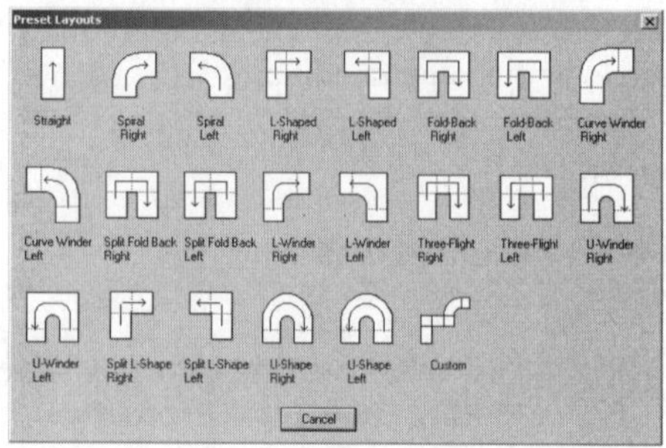

5. To edit the dimensions of a particular segment, select the segment in the *Layout Segments* window. A straight ramp will have one segment, named *Ramp 1*. Other ramp styles will have more segments. For example, an L-shaped ramp will have three segments: *Ramp 1*, *Landing 2* and *Ramp 3*. The Ramp 1 segment is the lower section of the ramp, Landing 2 is the central landing between the two sections, and Ramp 3 is the upper section of the ramp. Clicking a dimension marked with an alphabetical character (a, b, c, etc.) highlights the corresponding dimension in the ramp graphic, and vice versa.
6. Edit the variables in the *Parameters* window.

   Ramp segments

   Slope. The angle of the ramp's incline.

   Length. The length of the ramp's surface.

   Position Offset. Shifts the base of the ramp left or right from the center line. A positive value shifts it right, a negative value shifts it left. If the Upper Offset is set to 0, the entire ramp is moved.

   Lower Width. The width of the bottom of the ramp.

   Upper Width. The width of the top of the ramp.

   Upper Offset. Shifts the top of the ramp segment left or right to create an angled ramp. A positive value shifts it right, a negative value shifts it left.

   Landing Segments (vary per style)

   Position Offset. Shifts the landing left or right from the center line. A positive value moves it right, a negative value moves it left.

   Width. The width of the landing along the lower ramp section. By default this matches the Upper Width setting of the lower ramp section.

   Depth 1. The width of the landing along the upper ramp section. By default this matches the Lower Width setting of the upper ramp section.

   Depth 2. The width of the exposed side of the landing.

   Adjust Width. Adjusts the width of attached ramp segments to match the width of the landing.
7. To add a segment or landing to your ramp, click **Add** in the *Layout Segments* area. Select

the segment you want to add in the **Add/Edit Segment** dialog.

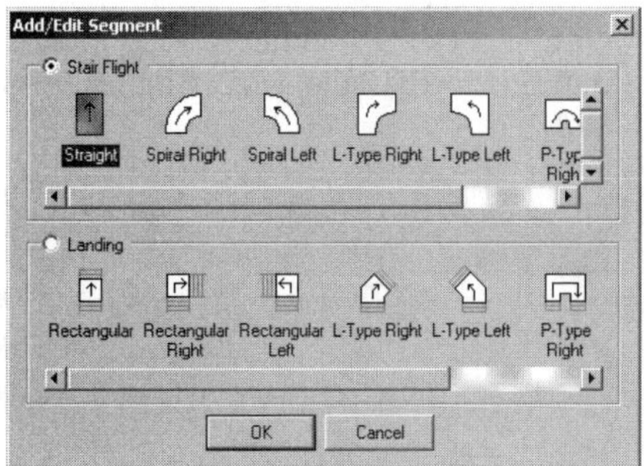

The segment is added to your list of segments in the *Layout Segments* window. Proceed with defining the parameters for the new segment in the *Parameters* window.

8. To change an existing segment to another type, select the segment in the *Layout Segments* window, then click **Edit**. Select the new segment type in the **Add/Edit Segment** dialog.
9. To delete a segment from the ramp, select the segment in the *Layout Segments* window, then click **Delete**.
10. Once you are satisfied with your layout settings, click **OK**.

Moving a Staircase or Ramp

You can move a staircase or ramp by clicking and dragging it.

To move a staircase or ramp:

1. Click on the staircase or ramp to select it.
2. Hover your pointer over the center grab handle to display the Move cursor.
3. Click and drag the staircase/ramp to move it.
4. Release your mouse button.

Rotating a Staircase or Ramp

You can rotate a staircase or ramp by simply clicking and dragging it.

To rotate a staircase or ramp:

1. Select the staircase or ramp.
2. Hover your pointer over the triangular grab handle to display the Rotate cursor.
3. Click and drag to rotate the staircase or ramp.
4. When the staircase or ramp is at the desired rotation, release your mouse button.

Deleting a Staircase or Ramp

You can delete a staircase or ramp in a couple of easy steps.

To delete a staircase or ramp:

1. Select the staircase or ramp.
2. Press the **Delete** key on your keyboard, right-click and select **Delete**, or select **Edit > Modify Elements > Delete**.

Inserting Railings on Staircases and Ramps

A railing can be just a handrail, or a balustrade with posts, top/bottom rails and newels. You can insert railings on both sides of a staircase or ramp automatically. Or you can very easily draw one on the left side, the right side, or the center.

To insert railings on both sides of a staircase or ramp automatically:

1. Select **Insert > Railings > Railings on Stairs Automatically**, or click the Railings button on the Building toolbar and select **Railings on Stairs Automatically**.

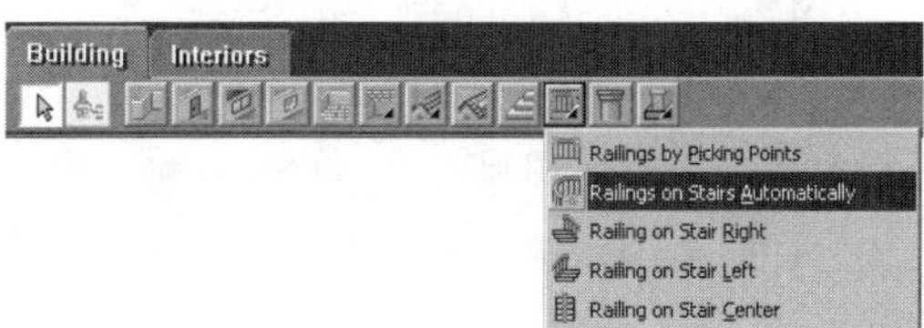

2. In the catalog, select the railing type you want to insert.
3. Click on the staircase. The railings are inserted automatically on both sides.
4. Right-click and select **Finish**.

To insert a railing on the right side of a staircase or ramp:

1. Select **Insert > Railings > Railing on Stair Right**, or click the Railings button on the Building toolbar and select **Railing on Stair Right**.

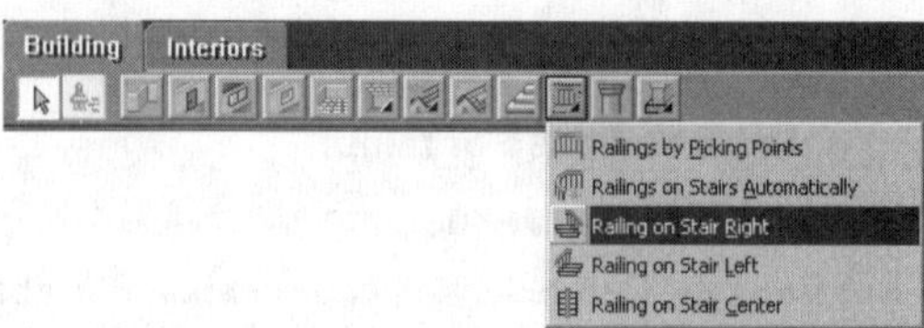

2. In the catalog, select the railing type you want to insert.
3. Select a point anywhere along the bottom of the staircase (or along the tread where you want the bottom of the railing to sit) to define the level of the railing's bottom post. Your cursor will snap to the right side of the staircase as you start to draw the railing.
4. Select a point anywhere along the top of the staircase (or along the tread where you want the top of the railing to sit) to define the level of the railing's top post.
5. Right-click and select **Finish**.

To insert a railing on the left side of a staircase or ramp:

1. Select **Insert > Railings > Railing on Stair Left**, or click the Railings button on the Building toolbar and select **Railing on Stair Left**.

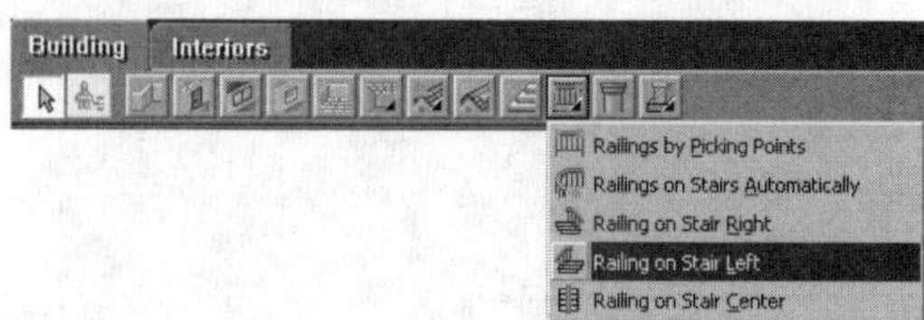

2. In the catalog, select the railing type you want to insert.

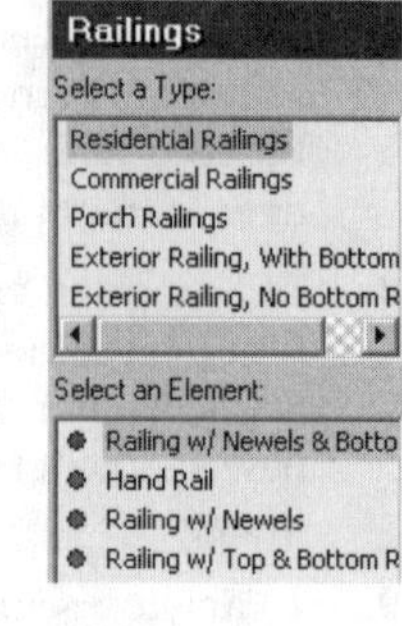

3. Select a point anywhere along the bottom of the staircase (or along the tread where you want the bottom of the railing to sit) to define the level of the railing's bottom post. Your cursor will snap to the left side of the staircase as you start to draw the railing.
4. Select a point anywhere along the top of the staircase (or along the tread where you want the top of the railing to sit) to define the level of the railing's top post.
5. Right-click and select **Finish**.

To insert a railing along the center of a staircase or ramp:

1. Select **Insert > Railings > Railing on Stair Center**, or click the Railings button on the Building toolbar and select **Railing on Stair Center**.

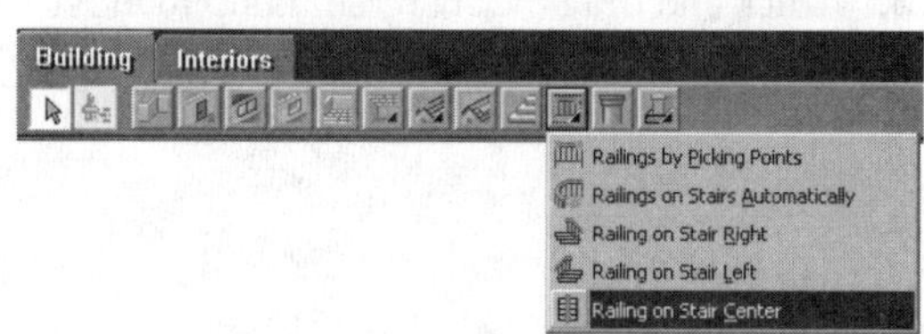

2. In the catalog, select the railing type you want to insert.
3. Select a point anywhere along the bottom of the staircase (or along the tread where you want the bottom of the railing to sit) to define the level of the railing's bottom post. Your cursor will snap to the center of the staircase as you start to draw the railing.
4. Select a point anywhere along the top of the staircase (or along the tread where you want the top of the railing to sit) to define the level of the railing's top post.
5. Right-click and select **Finish**.

Inserting a Horizontal Railing

You can use the Railing by Picking Points tool to create a horizontal railing anywhere in your model. You may, for example, want to create a railing around a stairwell, or insert a railing to separate two rooms in your house. You create the railing by picking the start point and end point of the railing. Each point you pick serves as a main post point.

To insert a railing along a floor:

1. Make sure the building location that you want to insert the railing on is current.
2. Select **Insert > Railings > Railings by Picking Points**, or click the Railings button on the Building toolbar and select **Railings by Picking Points**.

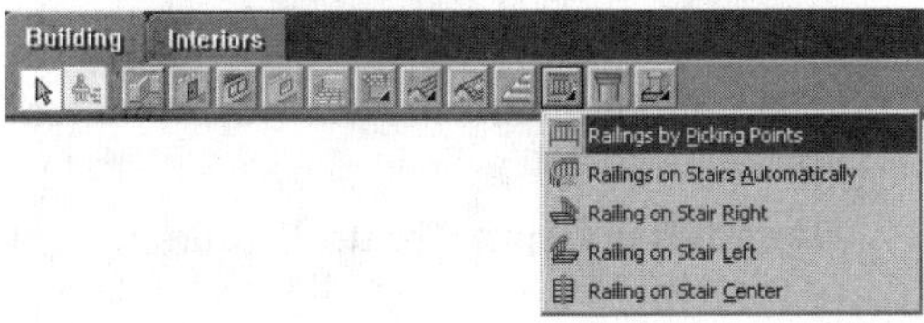

3. In the catalog, select the railing type you want to insert.
4. Select the start point for the railing.
5. Select an end point for the railing. You can continue adding sections to the railing if you want.
6. Right-click and select **Finish**.

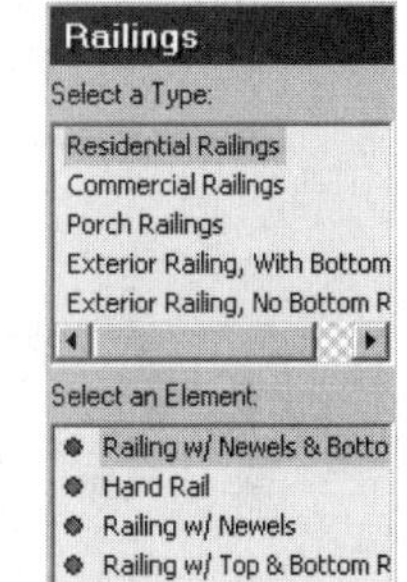

Parts of a Railing

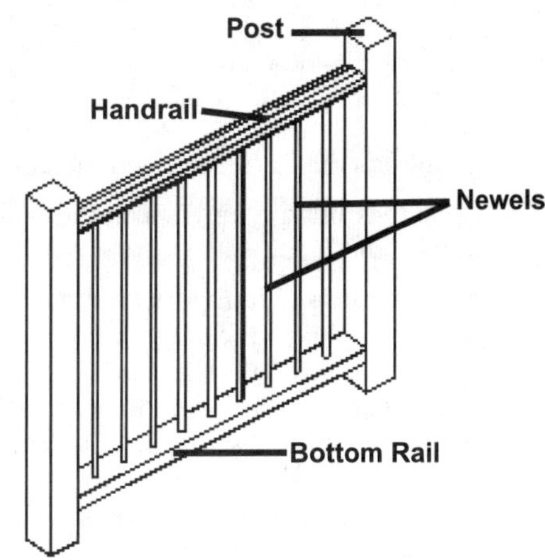

Editing Railing Properties

When editing a railing, you can choose a different railing type as well as control the dimensions and settings of posts, rails and newels.

To edit railing properties:

1. Select the railing. If the railing has multiple segments, use Shift+click to select the remaining segments.

2. Right-click and select Properties, or select **Edit > Modify Elements > Properties**.

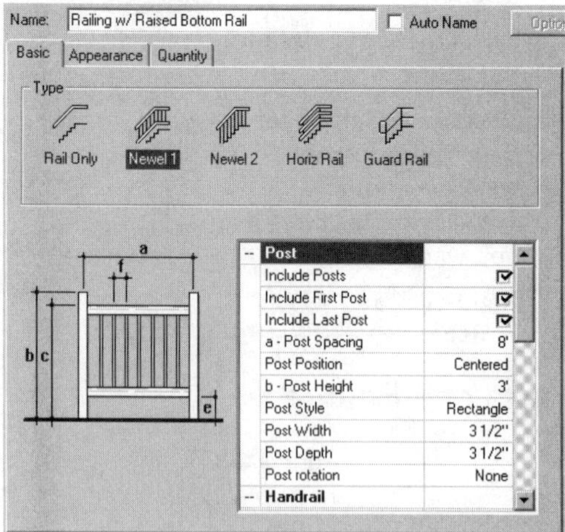

3. In the **Railings** dialog, select the Basic tab.
4. To change the railing type, click on the type you want in the *Type* area.
5. To edit the settings of individual railing components, make your changes in parameters window. The available parameters vary depending on the railing type. Below is a brief description of typical parameters you might see. Clicking a dimension marked with an alphabetical character (a, b, c, etc.) highlights the corresponding dimension in the railing graphic, and vice versa.

Posts

Include Posts. Inserts a post at the railing's start point and endpoint, and at points in between defined by the Post Spacing.

Include First Post. If disabled, eliminates the post at the start point of the railing.

Include Last Post. If disabled, eliminates the post at the end point of the railing.

Post Spacing. The distance between intermediate posts in your railing.

Post Position. Choosing *From Start* measures the intermediate posts from the start point of the railing. Choosing *Centered* inserts an intermediate post at the center of the railing and measures other intermediate posts from there.

Post Height. This value is determined by the handrail and bottom rail heights, and cannot be edited.

Post Style. Choose either *Rectangle* or *Round* for the post shape.

Post Width. The width of the post.

Post Depth. The depth of the post.

Post Rotation. Determines the rotation of the connecting post where two railings connect. Choosing *Half Way* rotates the connecting post half way between the angle. Choosing *None* leaves the connecting post aligned to the first railing.

Handrail

Handrail Height. The height of the handrail above the insertion surface.

Make Continuous. Makes the handrail cut through all posts, creating a continuous, solid member.

Handrail Style. Choose either a *Rectangle* or *Round* shape.

Handrail Width. The width of the handrail (as seen in 2D plan view).

Handrail Depth. The depth (thickness) of the handrail.

Bottom Rail

Bottom Rail Height. The height of the bottom rail from the insertion surface.

Bottom Rail Style. Choose either a *Rectangle* or *Round* shape for the rail.

Bottom Rail Width. The width of the bottom (as seen in 2D plan view).

Bottom Rail Depth. The depth (thickness) of the bottom rail.

Newels

Newel Spacing. The horizontal distance between newels.

Newel Style. Choose either *Rectangle* or *Round* for the newel shape.

Newel Width. The width of the newel.

Newel Depth. The depth (thickness) of the newel.

Stair Insertion

Post Offset. The horizontal offset of the first post from the bottom of the staircase. Only a positive value can be specified, which moves the post further back along the stairs.

Side Offset. Offset of railing from the sides of the treads.

Connection. Determines how railings are connected to the staircase. Connection 2 maintains the distance from the nosing to the railing at all times. Connection 1 breaks this rule to create a nicer-looking railing.

Stretching a Railing

You can stretch a railing by clicking and dragging one of its end points. Note that if your railing has multiple segments, you can stretch the individual segments.

To stretch a railing:

1. Select the railing. A grab handle is displayed at each railing end.
2. Hover your pointer over the end you want to stretch to display the Stretch cursor.
3. Click and drag to stretch the railing. Note that you can adjust the rotation of the railing as well as its length.
4. When the railing is the desired length, release your mouse button.

Rotating a Railing

You can rotate a railing using the Rotate tool.

To rotate a railing:

1. Select the railing.
2. Right-click and select **Rotate**, or select **Edit > Modify Elements > Rotate**.
3. Click on the point you want to rotate around, then move your mouse to rotate the railing around the selected point.
4. When the railing is at the desired rotation, click to finish.

Deleting Railings

You can delete a railing in a couple of easy steps.

To delete a railing:

1. Select the railing. If a railing has multiple segments you can Shift+click to select all the segments you want to remove.
2. Press the **Delete** key on your keyboard, or right-click and select **Delete**, or select **Edit > Modify Elements > Delete**.

Chapter 13

Roofs

To complete your structural model, you want to insert a roof over it. The design of your roof can be a major factor in the overall look and feel of your home. Inserting a roof in *3D Home Architect® Home Design* is incredibly simple. Just click inside your model and the roof is inserted.

Roofs are inserted by location. Therefore, if you have a two-story house, each story may require its own roof. The great thing about roofs in *3D Home Architect® Home Design* is that you can edit each roof edge individually to achieve the precise geometry, dimensions and appearance you want. This means that virtually any roof configuration is possible, including multiple pitch, multiple plate height roofs. And with a wide selection of roof styles to choose from, including hip, gable, mansard and arched, you can be as creative as you want.

To give your roof design that extra edge, you can add things like dormers, skylights and openings, all of which are completely customizable to suit your needs.

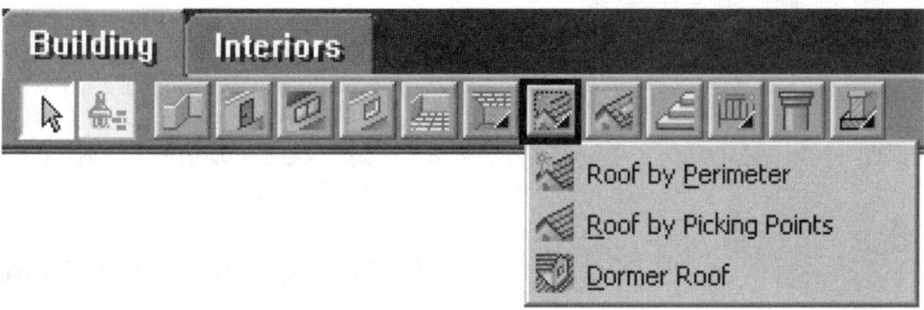

Inserting an Automatic Roof Over Perimeter Walls

You can use the Roof by Perimeter tool to automatically insert a roof over the perimeter wall layout of a selected building location. If you have a two-story home where the ground floor wall layout is different than the upper story wall layout, and you want each story to have its own roof, you will need to insert a roof on each location.

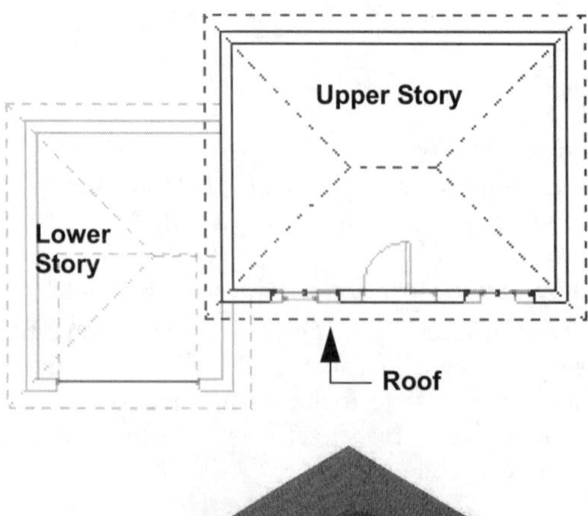

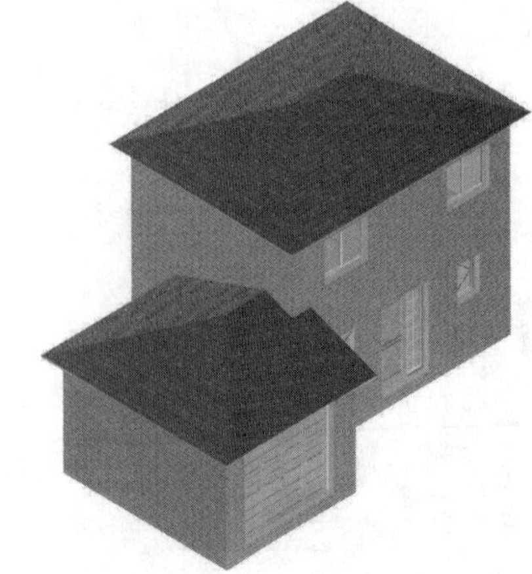

By default, the roof is inserted directly on top of the walls of the current building location. You can edit the support height as well as change the roof's style and dimensions after it has been inserted.

To insert a roof over an entire wall layout:

1. Make sure the current location is the location containing the walls you want to insert the roof over.
2. Select **Insert > Roofs > Roof by Perimeter**, or click the Roofs button on the Building toolbar and select **Roof by Perimeter**.

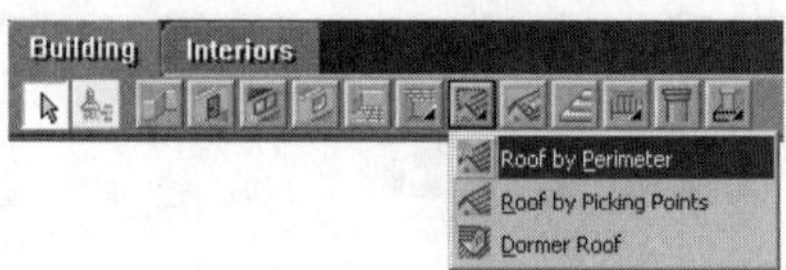

3. In the catalog, select the roof type you want to insert. Note that the catalog does not contain gable roofs. If you want to create a gable roof, insert a hip roof first, then convert it to a gable. (See *Converting a Hip Roof to a Gable Roof* on page 98.)

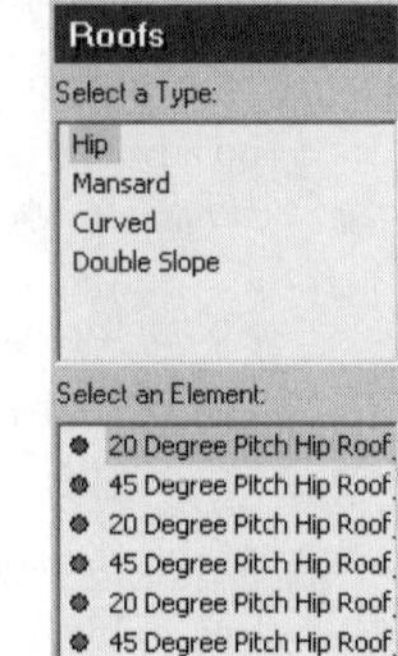

4. Click inside the wall perimeter. The roof is inserted automatically.

Note: If the roof you are inserting will run up against any upper-story walls, the roof cuts around the walls and may adjust to avoid saddle situations. If you do not want the roof to adjust, or you want the roof to ignore the walls, you need to change the roof's Solution Type before inserting the roof. See *Changing the Way a Lower-story Roof is Created* on page 97.

Inserting a Roof by Picking Points

You can use the Roof by Picking Points tool to create a roof of a custom size and shape by drawing the basic outline of the roof. This option is ideal when you want the roof to cover only a specific area, such as a porch.

To create a roof by picking points:

1. Make sure the current location is the location containing the walls you want to insert the roof over.

2. Select **Insert > Roofs > Roof by Picking Points**, or click the Roofs button on the Building toolbar and select **Roof by Picking Points**.

3. In the catalog, select the roof type you want to insert. Note that the catalog does not contain gable roofs. If you want to create a gable roof, insert a hip roof first, then convert it to a gable. (See *Converting a Hip Roof to a Gable Roof* on page 98.)

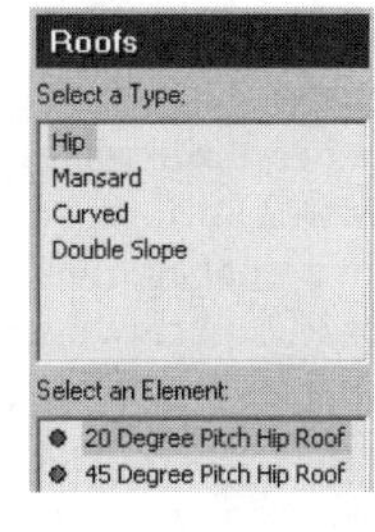

4. Select a start point for the roof boundary. Typically you would select an exterior wall corner. Continue selecting points until the boundary is defined. (You do not have to select the start point again because the last point you pick is always closed back to the start point.)
5. Right-click and select **Finish**.

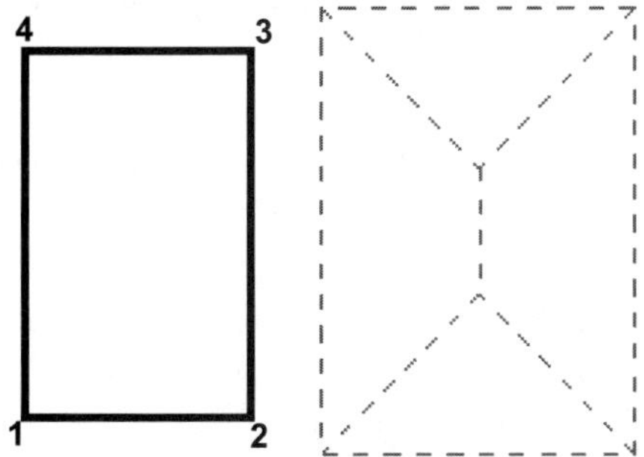

Note: If the roof you are inserting will run up against any upper-story walls, the roof cuts around the walls and may adjust to avoid saddle situations. If you do not want the roof to adjust, or you want the roof to ignore the walls, you need to change the roof's Solution Type before inserting the roof. See *Changing the Way a Lower-story Roof is Created* on page 97.

Changing the Way a Lower-story Roof is Created

By default, a lower-story roof cuts around upper-story walls and is adjusted to avoid saddle situations where it runs up against upper-story walls. A saddle situation is one where rain or snow runs down the roof slope and collects in areas where the roof meets a wall. If you prefer, you can have the roof cut around walls but not adjust to avoid saddle situations, or you can have the roof ignore the upper-story walls completely. You must change the solution type before inserting the roof — you can't change it after it's been inserted.

To change the way a lower-story roof is created:

1. In the catalog, select the roof type you want to insert.
2. Right-click and select **Catalog Manager**.
3. In the **Catalog Manager** dialog, select **Catalog > Element Properties**.
4. In the **Roofs** dialog, click the **Solution Type** button.
5. In the **Solution Type** dialog, click on the solution you want.

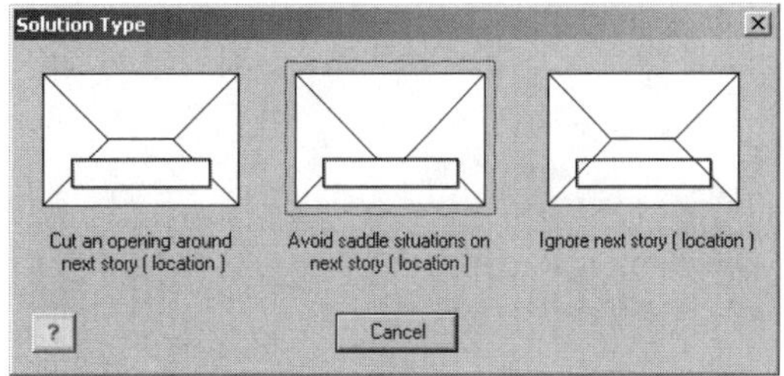

6. Click **OK** in the **Roofs** dialog.
7. Click **OK** in the **Catalog Manager** dialog. You can now insert the roof.

Converting a Hip Roof to a Gable Roof

To convert a hip roof to a gable roof, you need to select two hip ends, then select the gable roof type in the roof properties.

To convert a hip roof to a gable roof:

1. Click on the roof edge of one of the ends you want to convert. A blue grab handle appears on the plate line of that hip end. Holding down your Shift button, click on the plate line on the opposite side of the roof.

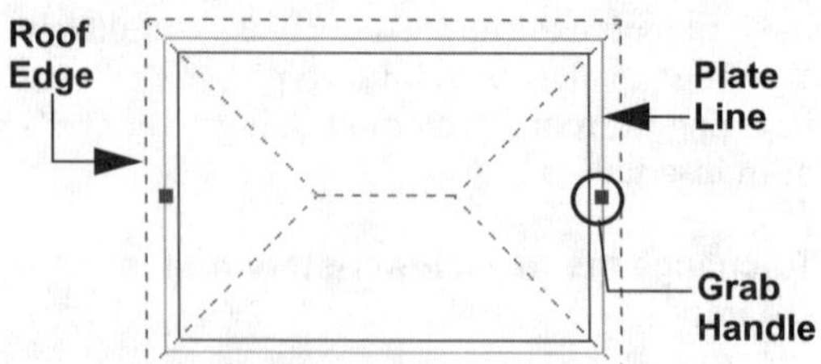

2. Right-click and select **Properties**, or select **Edit > Modify Elements > Properties**.
3. In the **Roofs** dialog, click the Hip button in the *Roof Shape* area of the Basic page.

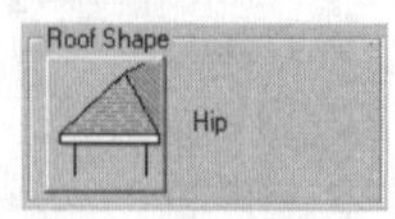

4. In the **Roof Shape** dialog, click the Gable graphic.

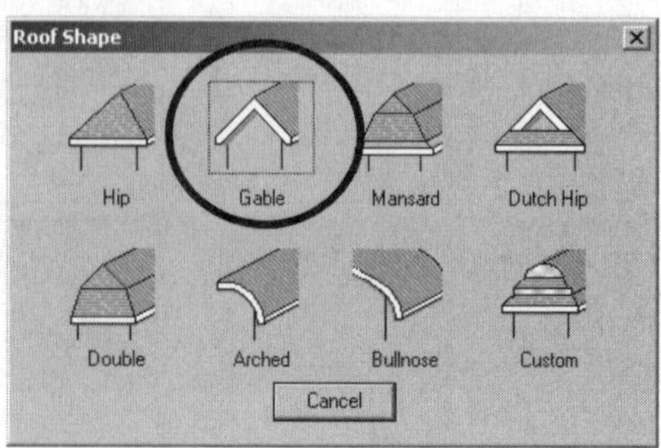

5. Click **OK** in the **Roofs** dialog. The roof is converted.

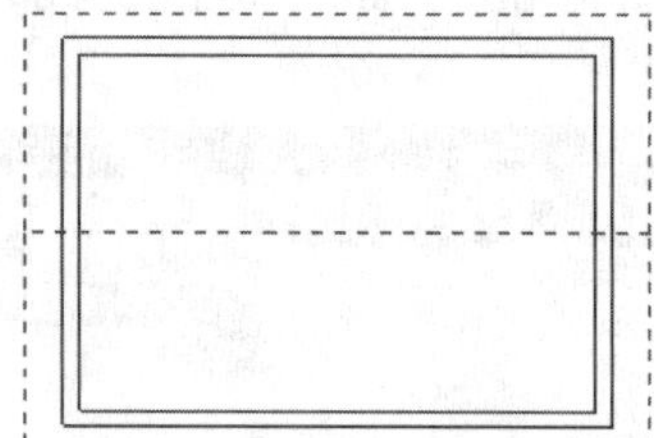

Note: When you create a gable roof, the areas beneath the pitched ends of the roof are filled in with a surface, such as siding. This surface is not an actual element — it is there for appearance only. You can change the appearance of the surface (see *Changing the Appearance of Raked Surfaces Under Gable Ends* on page 98), or extend your exterior walls to meet the pitched ends of the gable roof (see *Extending Walls Beneath Gable Ends* on page 99).

Changing the Appearance of Raked Surfaces Under Gable Ends

If you have created a gable roof, you can change the appearance of the raked surfaces beneath the pitched ends of the roof by editing the material selection for the roof's Gable End component.

To change the appearance of raked surfaces under gable ends:

1. Click on a roof edge to select the roof.
2. Right-click and select **Properties**, or select **Edit > Modify Elements > Properties**.

3. In the **Roofs** dialog, select the Appearance tab.

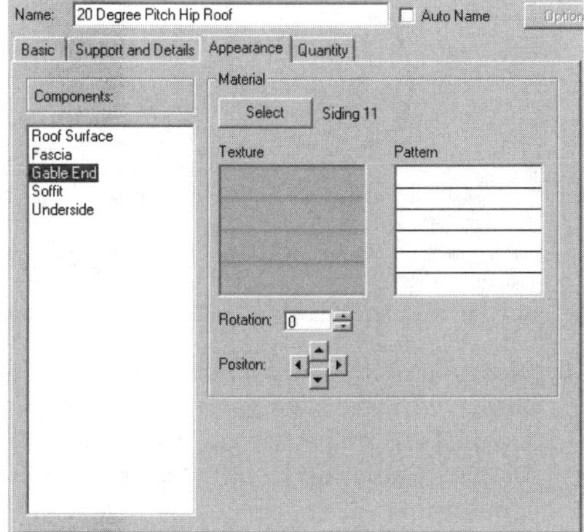

4. In the *Components* list, select **Gable End**.
5. In the *Material* area, click the **Select** button.
6. In the **Materials** dialog, select the material you would like to use, then click **OK**.
7. Click **OK** in the **Roofs** dialog.

Extending Walls Beneath Gable Ends

When you create a gable roof, a false surface such as siding is created beneath the pitched ends of the gable roof. You can get rid of this false surface by raking your exterior walls so that they extend to the roof's pitch.

To extend gable end walls to the roof:

1. Select the wall beneath the gable end. You can select additional gable end walls using Shift+click.
2. Right-click and select **Properties**, or select **Edit > Modify Elements > Properties**.
3. In the **Walls** dialog, select the Behavior tab.

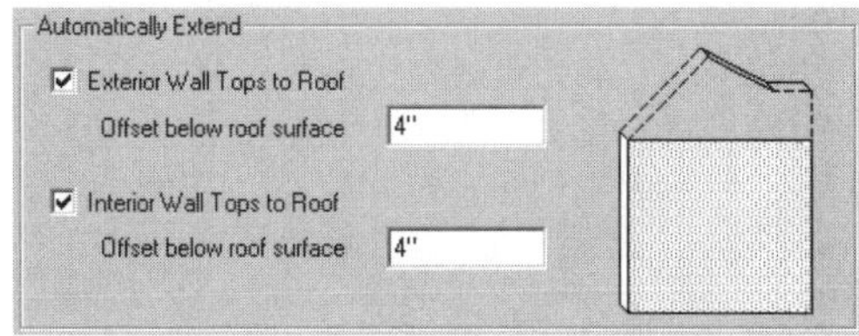

4. To rake the external side of the wall, check the **Exterior Wall Tops to Roof** check box. If you want to offset the wall a specific distance from the roof surface, enter a value in the **Offset below roof surface** edit box.
5. To rake the internal side of the wall, check the **Interior Wall Tops to Roof** check box. If you want to offset the wall a specific distance from the roof surface, enter a value in the **Offset below roof surface** edit box.
6. Click **OK**. The walls are adjusted.

Creating a Porch Roof

A typical porch roof is a simple roof having only one slope. Also known as a shed roof or lean-to roof, this type of roof can be attached to a wall face and be completely independent from the main roof. You create a porch roof by inserting a hip roof, then converting three sides to gables.

To create a porch roof:

1. Select **Insert > Roofs > Roof by Picking Points**, or click the Roofs button on the Building toolbar and select **Roof by Picking Points**.

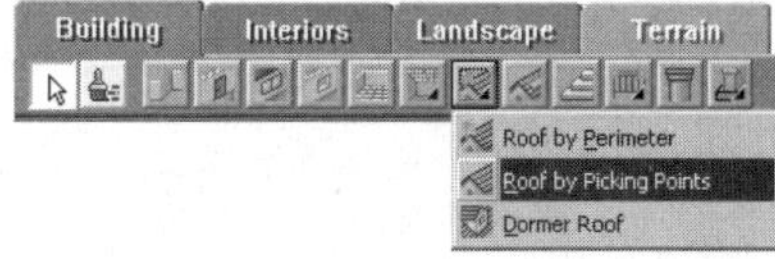

2. In the catalog, select a hip roof to insert.
3. Select four points to define the outline of the roof. It may be easier to draw the roof out in

space (away from the model), then move it into place later.

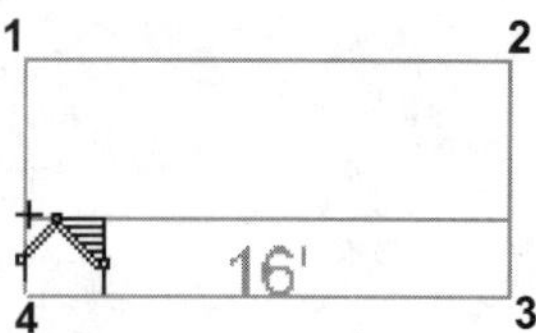

4. Right-click and select **Finish**.

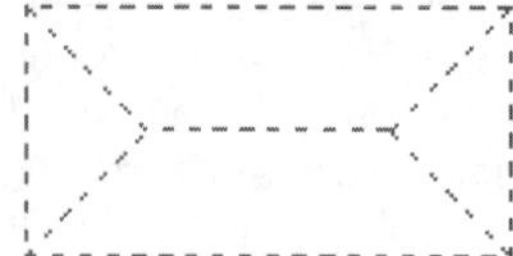

5. Click on the roof edge that will be attached to the wall, or that will be the high side of the roof. The roof is selected.
6. Hold down the Shift key, then click on the plate line at each end of the roof. Blue grab handles appear on each of the three selected sides.

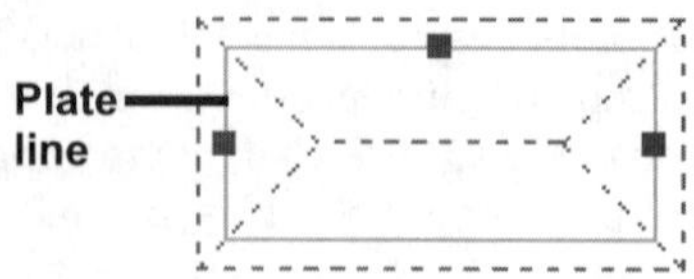

7. Right-click and select **Properties**, or select **Edit > Modify Elements > Properties**.
8. In the **Roofs** dialog, click the Hip button in the *Roof Shape* area of the Basic page.

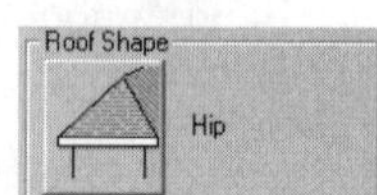

9. In the **Roof Shape** dialog, click the Gable graphic.

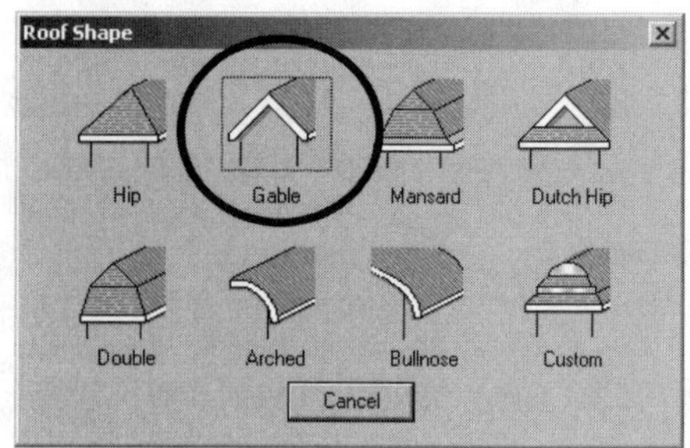

10. Next you need to turn off the surfaces displayed beneath the gable ends of the roof. On the Basic property page, disable the **Display Gable** check box in the *Parameters* window.

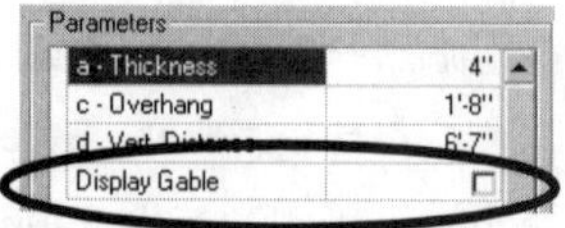

11. Click **OK**.

12. Deselect the roof by clicking in the drawing area.
13. Click on the front edge (low side) of the roof.
14. Right-click and select **Properties**, or select **Edit > Modify Elements > Properties**.
15. If you want to change the elevation of the roof at this point, select the Support and Details tab, then edit the value in the **Support Height** edit box.
16. On the Support and Details page, enable the **Raked** radio button in the *Soffit* area.
17. Click **OK**.
18. Now all that's left is to move the roof into place. With the roof selected, right-click and select **Move Whole Element**, or select **Edit >**

Modify Elements > Move Whole Element. Click and drag the roof into position. If you need to you can adjust the length and width of the roof by stretching it. Just remember to select the appropriate edge first.

If you want to insert support columns under the porch roof, see *Inserting Columns* on page 50.

Selecting a Roof for Editing

A roof can be edited as one unit, or by one or more of its segments. When you click on a roof edge, the entire roof becomes selected. This is indicated by the plate line being highlighted in green. You'll also notice a small blue grab handle on the green line. This handle indicates the currently selected roof segment. In the figure below, the blue handle on the right side indicates that the user clicked on the right hip end to select the roof.

Green line indicates roof is selected

Blue handle indicates currently selected segment

At this point, general editing tools like **Move Whole Element** and **Rotate** will affect the roof as a whole, as will editing the roof's Support Height, Support Type (rafters or trusses), and framing configuration. However, changes to other roof properties, such as the roof type, slope, and overhang distance, affect only the currently selected roof segment (which is marked by the blue handle).

You can select additional roof segments by holding down your Shift key and clicking on a segment's plate line. When you select a segment, it is marked with a blue handle. If you do select multiple segments, changes to roof properties (except for Support Height, Support Type and framing) affect all selected segments.

Stretching a Roof

You can stretch a roof by clicking and dragging one of its edges. Note that if you stretch your exterior wall layout, the roof stretches with it, eliminating the need to stretch the roof separately.

To stretch a roof:

1. Click on the roof edge you want to stretch.
2. Hover your pointer over the blue grab handle to display the Move cursor. 
3. Click and drag to stretch the roof segment, then release your mouse button.

Moving a Roof

To move an entire roof you need to select all roof segments, then click and drag it to where you want it. You can do this quickly using the Move Whole Element tool. Note that if you move your exterior wall layout, the roof will go with it, eliminating the need to move it separately.

To move an entire roof:

1. Click on one of the roof's edges to select the roof.
2. Right-click and select **Move Whole Element**, or select **Edit > Modify Elements > Move Whole Element**.
3. Click and drag to move the roof, then release your mouse button.

Rotating a Roof

You can rotate an entire roof about a selected point using the Rotate tool.

To rotate a roof:

1. Click on one of the roof's edges to select the roof.
2. Right-click and select **Rotate**, or select **Edit > Modify Elements > Rotate**.
3. Hover your pointer over the point you want to rotate around.
4. Click and drag to rotate the roof, then release your mouse button.

Editing a Roof's Shape and Size

You can change a roof's shape, slope, overhang distance, fascia distance, etc. You can specify different settings for different segments if you want.

To edit a roof's shape or size:

1. Click on the roof edge whose properties you want to edit. You can select additional segments using Shift+click.
2. Right-click and select **Properties**, or select **Edit > Modify Elements > Properties**.

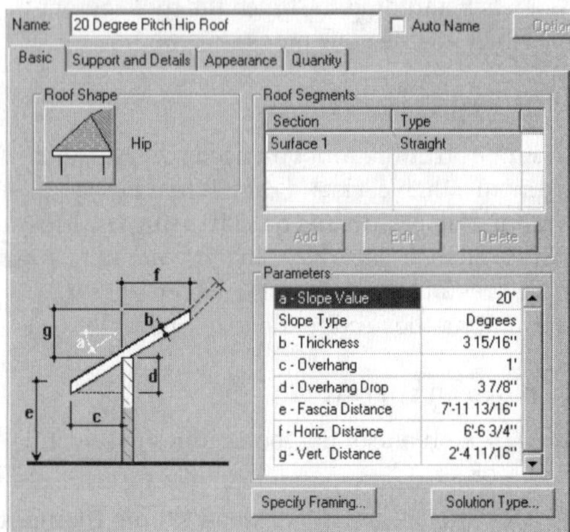

3. To convert the currently selected segments to a different roof type, click the graphical button in the *Roof Shape* area, then select a roof type in the **Roof Shape** dialog.

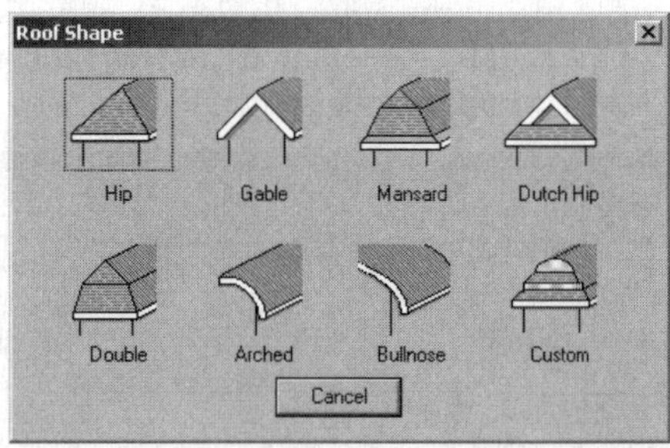

4. To edit the general dimensions and geometry of the roof, edit the values on the Basic page. These are described below. Note that a gable roof will have fewer properties.

   Thickness. The combined thickness of all roofing materials, such as shingles and sheathing.

   Slope Type. The method used to measure the pitch of the roof. Choose from *Degrees, ? in 12, 1 in ?*, or *Percent*.

   Slope Value. The pitch of the roof measured using the Slope Type method selected above.

   Overhang. The distance from the side wall to the fascia.

   Overhang Drop. The distance measured vertically from the support point to the underside of the fascia.

   Horiz. Distance. The maximum horizontal distance allowed from the support point the uppermost point of the underside of the rafter. This is a calculated result from the Slope Value and Vert. Distance variables.

   Vert. Distance. The maximum vertical distance allowed from the support point to the uppermost point of the underside of the rafter.

   Fascia Distance. The distance from the ground to the top edge of the fascia board.
5. Click **OK**.

Editing the Height of a Roof

You can raise or lower a roof by editing its Support Height variable.

To edit the height of a roof:

1. Click on a roof edge to select the roof.
2. Right-click and select **Properties**, or select **Edit > Modify Elements > Properties**.
3. In the **Roofs** dialog, select the Support and Details tab.
4. Edit the value in the **Support Height** edit box.
5. Click **OK**.

Editing a Roof's Frame Details

You can choose to frame with rafters or trusses. You can also select the members you want to use and edit the precise dimensions of your roof's framing configuration.

To edit a roof's framing details:

1. Click on a roof edge to select the roof.
2. Right-click and select **Properties**, or select **Edit > Modify Elements > Properties**.
3. To select a member type for your rafters or trusses, click the **Specify Framing** button on the Basic page. In the **Roof Framing** dialog, click **Select** to select a member from the catalog, then specify the spacing between the members in the **Member Spacing** edit box. Click **OK**.

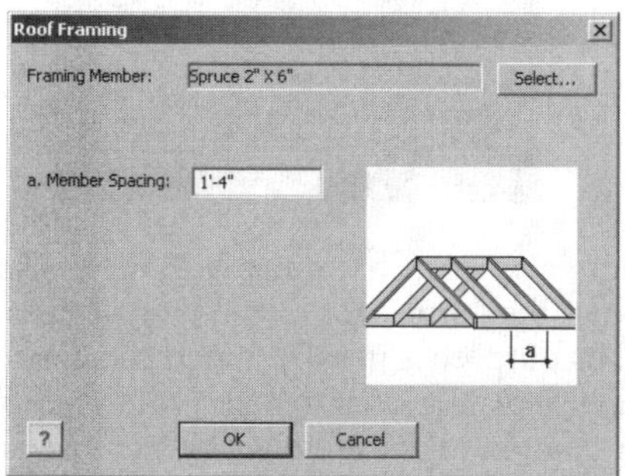

4. In the **Roofs** dialog, select the Support and Details tab.
5. Edit the parameters as desired. They are described below.

   Support Type. Choose Truss or Rafter.

   Raised Heel. The portion of the rafter that rests on the wall plate.

   Birds Mouth. The notch cut in the lower end of a rafter to fit it to the top plate of a wall.

   Seat. The horizontal cut that is made when cutting a bird's mouth in a rafter.

   <u>Fascia</u>

   Depth. The thickness of the fascia board.

   Plumb. The ends of the rafters are cut vertically resulting in a 90°
   fascia board.

   Raked. the ends of the rafters have an angled cut.

   <u>Soffit</u>

   Plumb. Creates a flat soffit that is parallel with the ground.

   Raked. Creates a soffit that is angled to match the roof slope.

   <u>Gable</u>

   Type. Choose either Plain, Squared, Full Hip or Half Hip for the gable return.

   Horizontal. The horizontal distance of the return when looking at the gable end face on.

   Depth. The depth of the return.
6. Once you have set your properties, click **OK**.

Applying a Different Roofing Material

You can use the Materials Paintbrush to quickly apply different shingles or tiles to a roof.

To apply a different material to a roof:

1. Display your model in 3D view and make sure the roof is visible in the view.
2. Select **Edit > Materials Paintbrush**, or click the Materials Paintbrush button on any tabbed toolbar. 

3. In the catalog panel, select the material you want to apply. You can find a wide selection of shingles and tiles in the Roofing category.
4. Click anywhere on the roof surface. The material is immediately applied to the entire roof.
5. Right-click and select **Finish**.

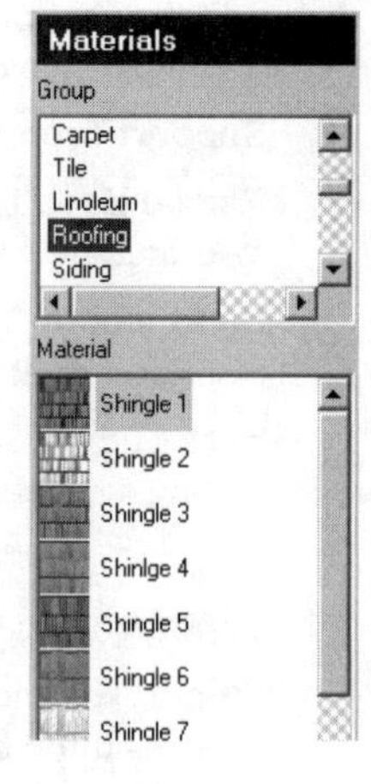

Cutting an Opening in a Roof

Once you have created a roof, you can create a custom opening in it of virtually any shape and size using the Cut Opening tool.

You create the opening by picking points to define its outline.

To insert an opening in a roof:

1. Select the roof by clicking on one of its edges.
2. Right-click and select **Cut Opening**, or select **Edit > Modify Elements > Cut Opening**.
3. Select a start point for the opening.
4. Continue selecting points to define the opening. As you select points, the opening is created. The last point picked is always connected back to the start point to form a closed shape, so you don't have to select the start point again.
5. When you have selected your final point, right-click and select **Finish**.

Removing Roof Openings

You can remove an opening from a roof by dragging it off the roof surface.

Note: You cannot use Delete to remove a roof opening.

To remove a roof opening:

1. Select the roof by clicking on one of its edges.
2. Press the Shift key and click on each of the roof opening edges.
3. Hover your pointer over one of the opening's grab handles to display the Move cursor. 
4. Click and drag the opening off the roof surface, then release your mouse button.

Deleting a Roof

You can delete a roof in a couple of easy steps.

To delete a roof:

1. Click on one of the roof's edges to select the roof.
2. Press the **Delete** key on your keyboard, right-click and select **Delete**, or select **Edit > Modify Elements > Delete**.

Inserting Dormers

A dormer is a small structure that projects from a roof slope. Dormers are often used to extend the usable floor area of a second story that is under a moderate to steeply pitched roof. They can be quite effective in opening up cramped rooms under the roof. A typical dormer consists of a roof and three walls. One of the most common dormer types is the gable dormer, characterized by the front gable in the roof.

You can also create a dormer without walls. In this case the dormer roof sits on top of the main roof. Its purpose is usually to add character to an otherwise plain roof or to make your roof design more complex. For example, you can insert a dormer roof on your main roof and stretch it to create a porch roof or gable extension.

Dormers are easy to insert - just point and click. You can control the dormer's width, roof type, wall type, and wall height.

To create a dormer:

1. In the building locations drop box, select the location containing the roof you want to add the dormer to.
2. Select **Insert > Roofs > Dormer Roof**, or click the Roofs button on the Building toolbar and select **Dormer Roof**.

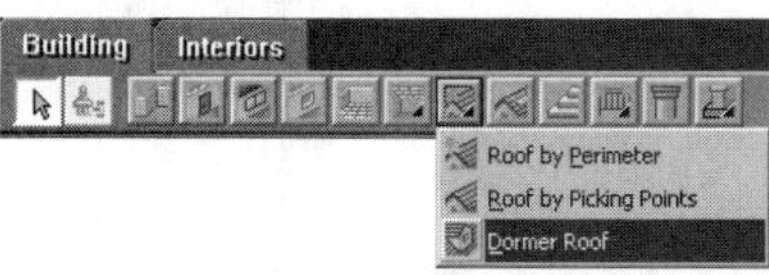

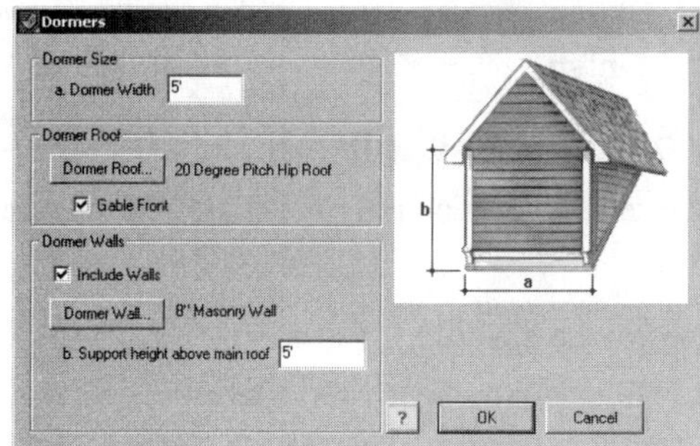

3. In the **Dormers** dialog, specify the desired width for the dormer in the **Dormer Width** edit box.
4. Click the **Dormer Roof** button, then select the desired roof type for the dormer. By default, the roof will have a gable front, regardless of the roof type. If you do not want it to have a gable front, uncheck the **Gable Front** check box.
5. If you want your dormer to have walls, check the **Include Walls** check box. Then, click the **Dormer Wall** button and select the desired wall type from the catalog. If you do not want your dormer to have walls, disable the **Include Walls** check box.
6. In the **Support height above main roof** edit box, type the height of the dormer's front wall, not including the raked portion between the two roof slopes. You can use this option even if you are not inserting walls to control the position of the bottom of the dormer roof. Note that dormer walls extend only to the roof surface.
7. Click **OK**. The dormer's wall footprint is attached to your cursor.
8. Position the dormer where you want it, then click to insert it. In most cases you would place the front dormer wall directly on top of the exterior wall.

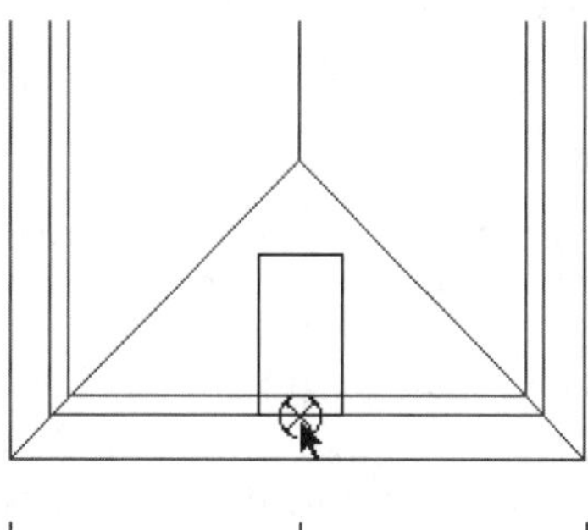

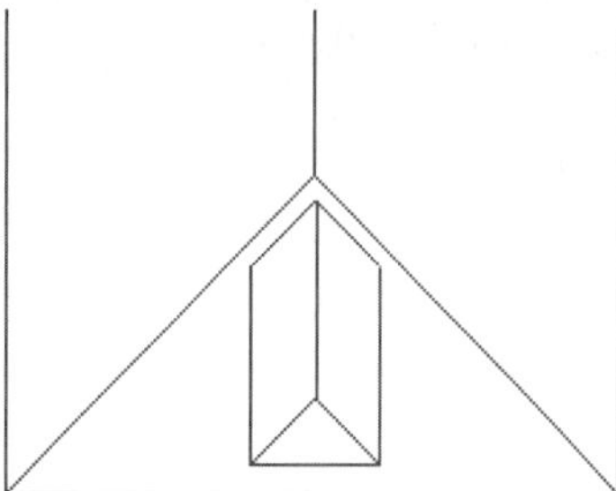

9. Right-click and select **Finish**.

Note: If you can't seem to insert the dormer, it means that the dormer is too large for the surface you are inserting it on. You may want to try decreasing the wall height before inserting it.

Moving a Dormer Roof

You can use the Move Whole Element tool to move a dormer roof to another spot on your roof.

To move a dormer roof:

1. Click on the edge of the dormer roof to select it.

2. Right-click and select **Move Whole Element**, or select **Edit > Modify Element > Move Whole Element**.
3. Click anywhere on the screen, then drag to move the dormer roof.
4. When the dormer roof is where you want it, release your mouse button.

Note: If the dormer has walls, you need to move the walls separately. To move the dormer walls, click on one wall, Shift+click to select the remaining walls, right-click and select Move, then click and drag the walls into place.

Stretching a Dormer Roof

You can stretch the front or sides a dormer roof by clicking and dragging the appropriate roof edge.

To stretch a dormer roof:

1. Click on the roof edge you want to stretch. A blue grab handle appears on the footprint line of the selected roof edge.
2. Position your pointer over the grab handle to display the Move cursor.

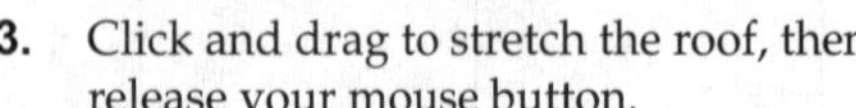

3. Click and drag to stretch the roof, then release your mouse button.

Note: If your dormer has walls, the dormer roof will not adjust if you stretch the dormer walls.

Deleting a Dormer

You can delete a dormer roof in a couple of easy steps. If the dormer has walls, they need to be deleted separately.

To delete a dormer:

1. Click on the edge of the dormer roof to select it.
2. Press the **Delete** key on your keyboard, or right-click and select **Delete**, or select **Edit > Modify Element > Delete**.
3. If the dormer has walls, select one of the walls, then Shift+click to select the remaining walls. Use the Delete tool to delete the selected walls.

Inserting Skylights

You can insert a skylight in your roof with point-and-click simplicity. The catalog contains a long list of skylights in a variety of sizes.

To insert a skylight:

1. Select **Insert > Skylights**, or click the Skylights button on the Building toolbar.

2. In the catalog, select the skylight you want to insert.

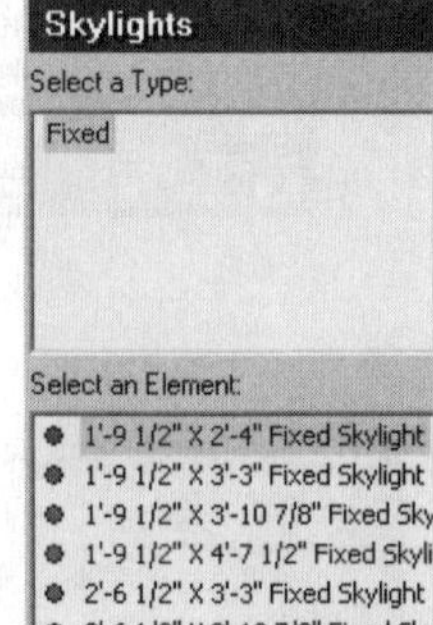

3. Position the skylight on the roof.
4. Click to insert the skylight.
5. Right-click and select **Finish**.

Moving a Skylight

You can move a skylight by clicking and dragging it.

To move a skylight:

1. Click on the skylight to select it.
2. Hover your pointer over the center grab handle to display the Move cursor.

3. Click and drag the skylight to move it.
4. Release your mouse button.

Rotating a Skylight

You can rotate a skylight using the Rotate tool.

To rotate a skylight:

1. Click on the skylight to select it.
2. Right-click and select **Rotate**, or select **Edit > Modify Elements > Rotate**.
3. Hover your pointer over the point you want to rotate around.
4. Click and drag to rotate the skylight, then release your mouse button.

Editing the Properties of a Skylight

Skylight properties include height and width, as well as dimensions for the frame and sash.

To edit the properties of a skylight:

1. Click on the skylight to select it.
2. Right-click and select **Properties**, or select **Edit > Modify Elements > Properties**.

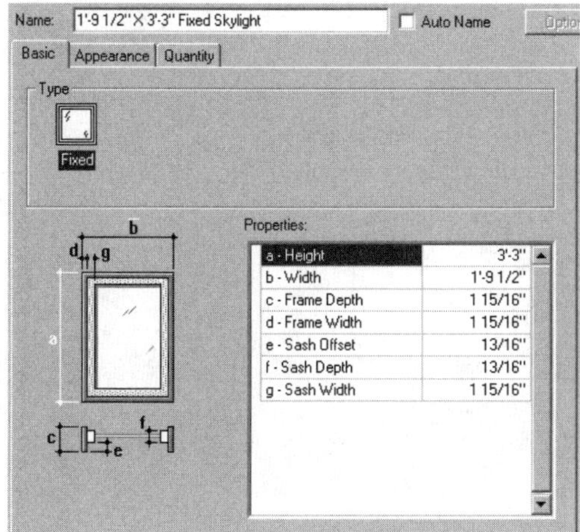

3. Edit the properties in the *Properties* window.

   Height. The overall height of the skylight window opening.

   Width. The overall width of the skylight window opening.

   Frame Depth. The depth of the window frame.

   Frame Width. The thickness of the window frame.

   Sash Offset. The distance the sash sits back in the window frame. The sash is the frame that holds the glass.

   Sash Depth. The thickness of the sash in plan view.

   Sash Width. The width of the sash in elevation.

4. Once you've set your properties, click **OK**.

Deleting a Skylight

You can delete a skylight in a couple of easy steps.

To delete a skylight:

1. Select the skylight.
2. Press the **Delete** key on your keyboard, or right-click and select **Delete**, or select **Edit > Modify Elements > Delete**.

Part 4

Designing the Interior

Chapter 14

Kitchen Builder Wizard

The structural elements of your home are built — now it's time to start designing the interior. One of the best places to start is the kitchen, since it is generally the room that's used the most in a house.

3D Home Architect® Home Design's Kitchen Builder Wizard creates a kitchen for you in a few easy steps. All you have to do is select the general shape and layout you want. Then, just point and click to insert all of your cupboards and appliances in one shot. It couldn't be easier!

Once you've inserted the kitchen you can move things around and edit individual elements to create a look that's customized to your taste and needs.

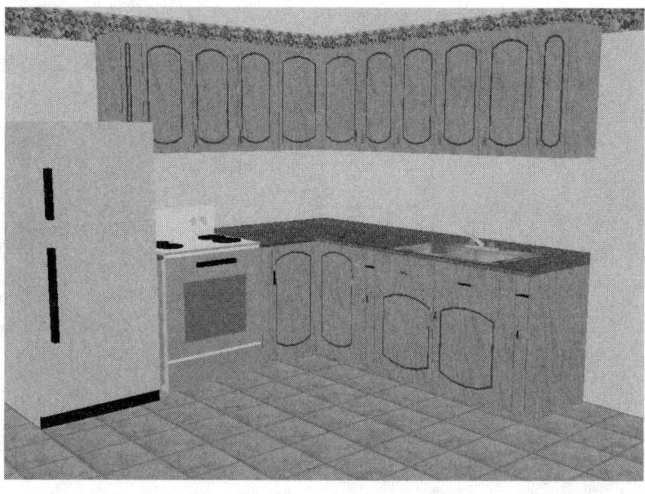

Creating a Kitchen with the Kitchen Builder Wizard

Using the Kitchen Builder Wizard you can quickly create a kitchen layout that includes upper and lower cabinets, a sink, refrigerator and stove. There are a number of layouts and styles to choose from.

To create a kitchen with the Kitchen Builder Wizard:

1. Select **Tools > Design Wizards > Kitchen Builder**.

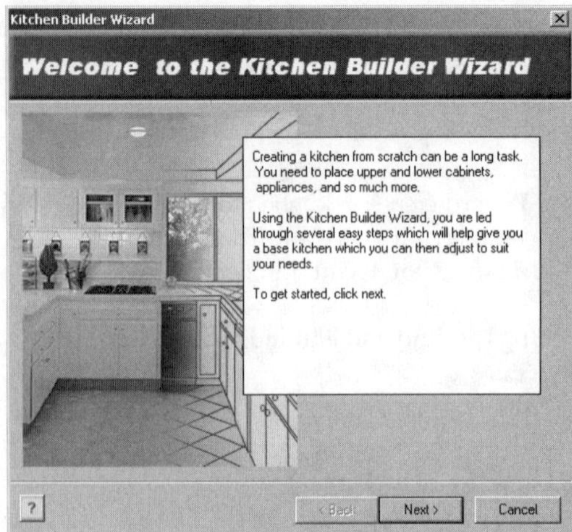

2. Click **Next**.

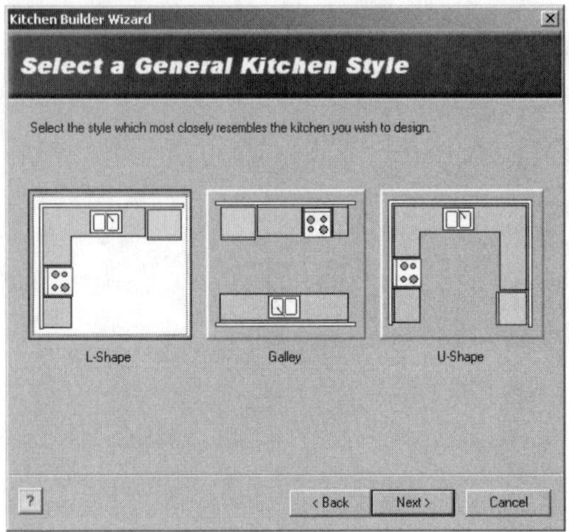

3. Click on the general style of kitchen you want — L-Shape, Galley or U-Shape.
4. Click **Next**.

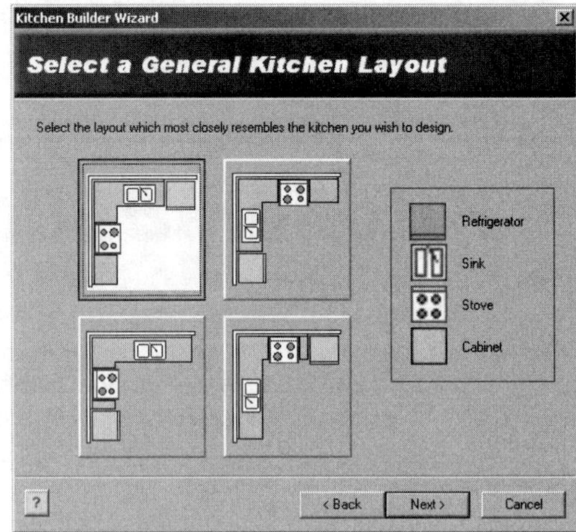

5. Select the layout that most closely resembles the layout you want. Remember that you can move and edit things later.
6. Click **Next**.

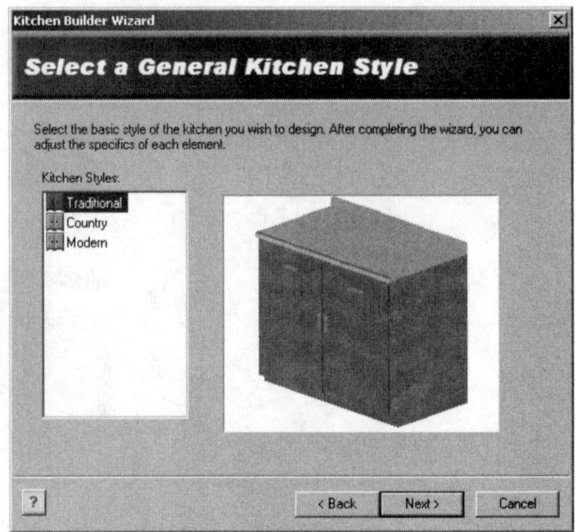

7. Select a general style for your kitchen. The selection you make mainly determines the materials and colors used for the cupboards and countertops.

8. Click **Next**.

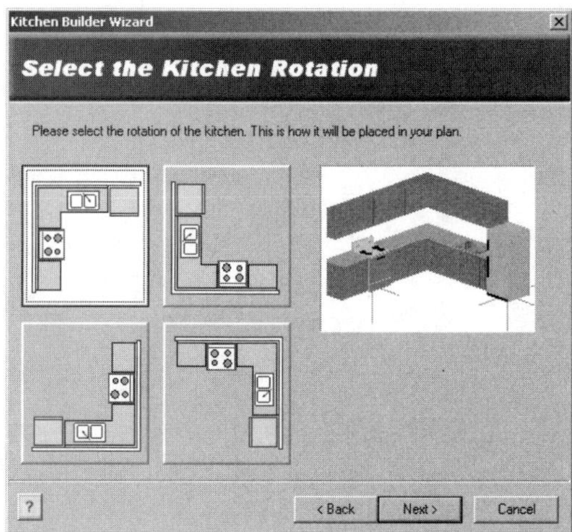

9. Select the desired rotation for the kitchen layout by clicking the appropriate graphic. This is how it will be attached to your cursor prior to insertion.
10. Click **Next**.

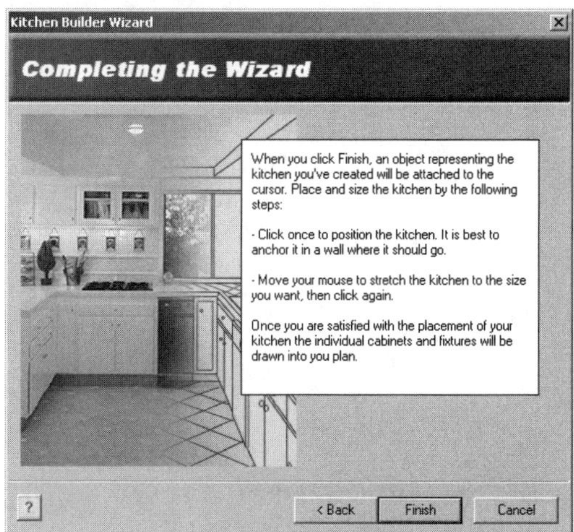

11. Click **Finish**. The kitchen configuration is attached to your cursor.
12. Position the kitchen layout in your kitchen area. It will automatically snap to the walls when you get close to them. Click to anchor the kitchen elements. Dynamic dimensions are displayed to show you the size of the layout.
13. If you want you can stretch the layout by simply moving your pointer in the direction you want to stretch.
14. Once the dimensions are correct, click to finish the insertion.

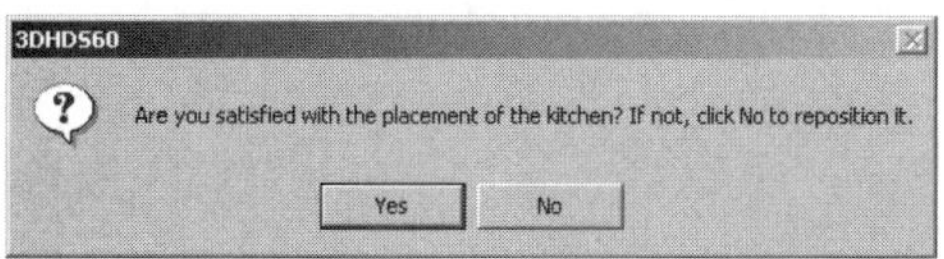

15. Click **Yes** to finish the task. If you click **No** you can reposition and reinsert the kitchen.

Tip: You can create your own custom configuration that can saved for use in any project. See *Creating a Custom Kitchen Builder Wizard Configuration* on page 288.

Chapter 15

Cabinets

Cabinets are essential for storage and can also contribute to the overall look and feel of a room. The catalog contains a huge selection of cabinet types, styles and sizes, all customizable to suit your taste and needs.

Cabinet types include base cabinets, corner cabinets, upper cabinets, islands, pantry cabinets and bathroom vanities.

You can insert cabinets in any room in your house with just a click of your mouse. Cabinets are designed to snap to walls and other cabinets, making insertion even easier.

Inserting Cabinets

You can insert a wide variety of cabinets in your design by simply pointing and clicking with your mouse. Cabinets automatically snap to walls and other elements when you get close to them provided Collision Control is turned on.

To insert a cabinet:

1. Select **Insert > Interiors > Cabinets**, or click the Cabinets button on the Interiors toolbar.

2. In the catalog, select the cabinet you want to insert.

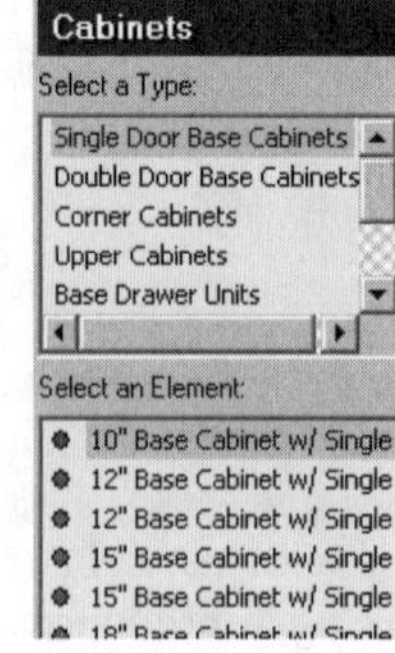

3. Position the cabinet where you want it, then click to insert it.
4. Right-click and select **Finish**.

Moving Cabinets

You can move individual or multiple cabinets by clicking and dragging them.

To move cabinets:

1. Select the cabinet you want to move. If you want to move multiple cabinets, use Shift+click to select the additional cabinets.
2. Hover your pointer over the cabinet's center grab handle to display the Move cursor.

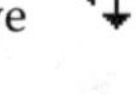

3. Click and drag to move the cabinet.
4. When the cabinet is where you want it, release your mouse button.

Rotating Cabinets

You can rotate cabinets by clicking and dragging them.

To rotate a cabinet:

1. Select the cabinet you want to rotate.
2. Hover your pointer over the triangular grab handle to display the Rotate cursor.
3. Click and drag to rotate the cabinet.
4. When the cabinet is at the desired rotation, release your mouse button.

Raising or Lowering a Cabinet

You can raise or lower a cabinet using the Elevate tool on the cabinet's right-click menu.

To edit a cabinet's elevation:

1. Select the cabinet whose elevation you want to edit.
2. Right-click and select **Elevate**, or select **Edit > Modify Elements > Elevate**. The value shown in the **Elevate** dialog is the current elevation of the cabinet.
3. In the **Elevate** dialog, specify the desired elevation of the bottom of the cabinet above the floor.
4. Click **OK**.

Tip: You can also change a cabinet's elevation by changing the **Distance above current location or terrain** variable on the cabinet's Behavior property page.

Editing Cabinet Properties

Cabinet properties include cabinet type, size, and leaf style, as well as settings for the counter, shelves, toe space and hardware.

To edit cabinet properties:

1. Select the cabinet whose properties you want to edit.
2. Right-click and select **Properties**, or select **Edit > Modify Elements > Properties**.
3. To change the cabinet type or dimensions, select the Basic tab. Cabinet types include Base, Upper and Pantry. Cabinet styles and size properties will vary depending on the cabinet type selected. Use the graphics as guides when determining the cabinet's properties. Clicking a dimension marked with an alphabetical character (a, b, c, etc.)

highlights the corresponding dimension in the cabinet graphic, and vice versa.

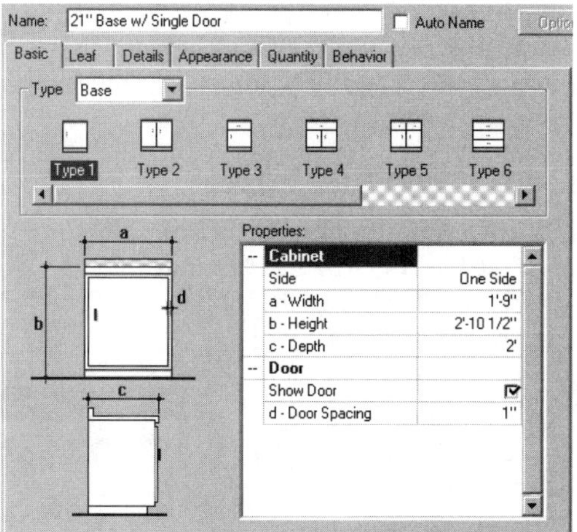

4. To change the cabinet's leaf style, select the Leaf tab.

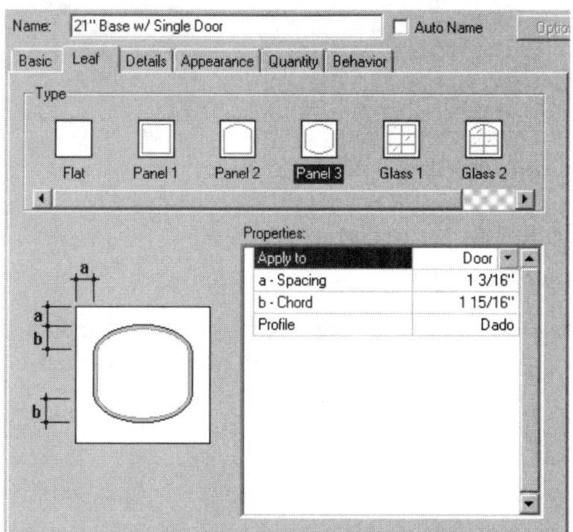

To select a leaf style for the door, select **Door** from the **Apply to** drop box, then make your selections. To select a leaf style for the drawers, if applicable, select **Drawer** from the **Apply to** drop box.

Leaf properties vary depending on the leaf style selected. Use the graphics as guides when setting these properties.

5. To edit the counter, shelving, toe space or hardware details, select the Details tab.

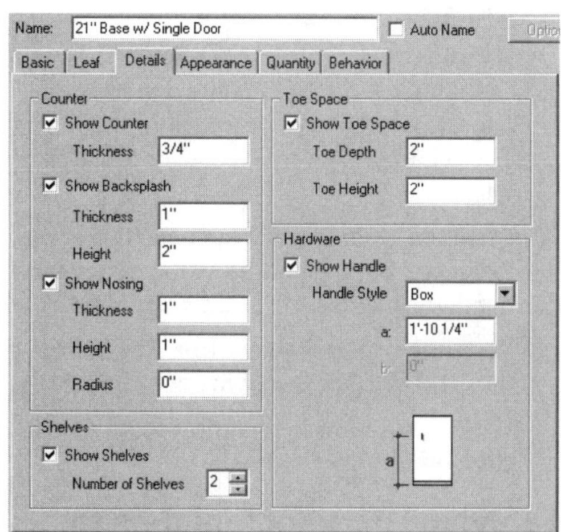

Show Counter. Displays a counter on the cabinet.

Thickness. The thickness of the counter material.

Show Backsplash. Displays a backsplash on the cabinet. The backsplash is a vertical surface designed to protect the wall behind a countertop.

Thickness. The thickness of the backsplash material.

Height. The distance from the countertop to the top of the backsplash.

Show Nosing. Displays nosing (moulded projection) on the front edge of the counter.

Thickness. The depth of the nosing.

Height. The height of the nosing.

Radius. The radius of the curve.

Show Shelves. Displays shelves inside the cabinet. The shelves would be visible if the cabinet door is glass.

Number of Shelves. The number of shelves you would like to display inside the cabinet.

Show Toe Space. Causes the bottom of the cabinet to recess so you can stand close to the cabinet without contacting it with their toes.

Toe Depth. The depth of the recess.

Toe Height. The height of the recess.

Show Handle. Displays handles on the cabinet door and drawers, if present.

Handle Style. Choose from Box, Circle or Cylinder. A box style creates a rectangular handle. A circle style creates a round knob. The cylinder style creates a cylindrical handle.

Distance a. For pantry cabinets, this is the distance from the bottom of the upper cabinet portion to the top of the door handle.

Distance b. The distance from the bottom of the cabinet to the top of the door handle.

6. When you're finished editing properties, click **OK**.

Applying Different Finishes to Cabinets

You can use the Materials Paintbrush to quickly apply a different finish to a cabinet, such as a different type of wood, or another type of material altogether.

To apply a different finish to a cabinet:

1. Display your model in 3D, and make sure the cabinet is visible in the view.
2. Select **Edit > Materials Paintbrush**, or click the Materials Paintbrush button on any tabbed toolbar.
3. In the catalog panel, select the material you want to apply.

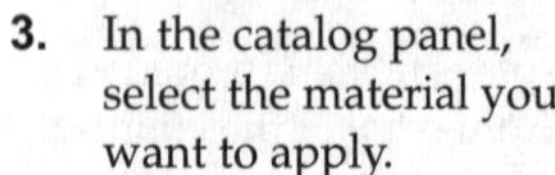

4. Click on the cabinet component you want to apply the material to. Materials are applied separately to the individual parts of the cabinet (frame, door, counter, handles, etc.).

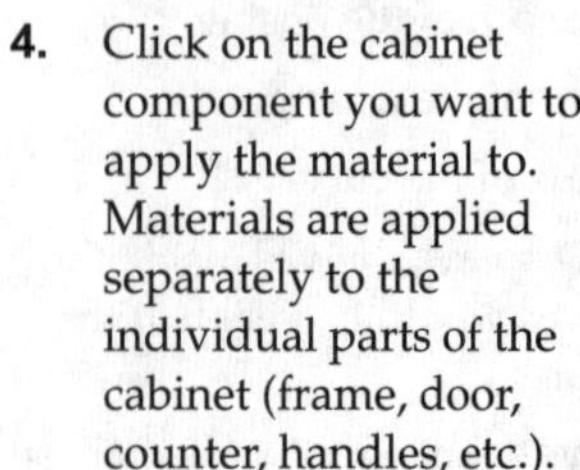

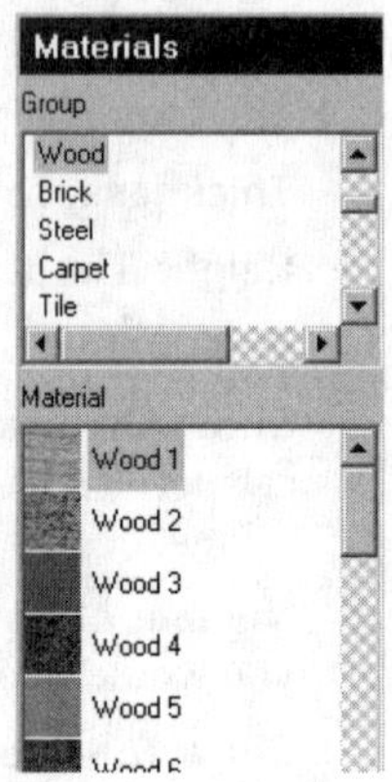

5. When you are finished applying materials, right-click and select **Finish**.

Inserting a Sink into a Cabinet

You can insert a kitchen or bathroom sink into a cabinet that you have inserted in your drawing by simply pointing and clicking. The sink automatically snaps itself into place at the center of the cabinet top.

To insert a sink into a cabinet:

1. Select **Insert > Interiors > Plumbing Fixtures**, or click the Plumbing Fixtures button on the Interiors toolbar.

2. In the catalog, select the Sinks category, then select the sink you want to insert.

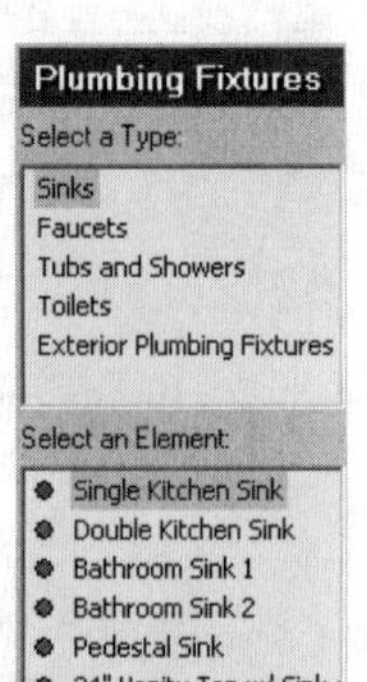

3. Position the fixture inside the cabinet, then click to insert it.
4. Right-click and select **Finish**.

Deleting a Cabinet

You can delete a cabinet in a couple of easy steps.

To delete a cabinet:

1. Select the cabinet.
2. Press the **Delete** key on your keyboard, or right-click and select **Delete**, or select **Edit > Modify Elements > Delete**.

Chapter 16

Appliances

Most home plans usually show the location of appliances in the kitchen and laundry room. Inserting appliances in your project can obviously enhance the design of a room, and can also help identify where electrical outlets are needed.

The *3D Home Architect® Home Design* catalog offers an excellent selection of kitchen and laundry appliances, including refrigerators, dishwashers, ovens, ranges, washers, dryers — even toasters. And of course, just like everything else, you can customize appliances to create the exact look you want.

Inserting appliances is easy — just point and click. Most major appliances are set to snap to walls and other elements when you get close to them.

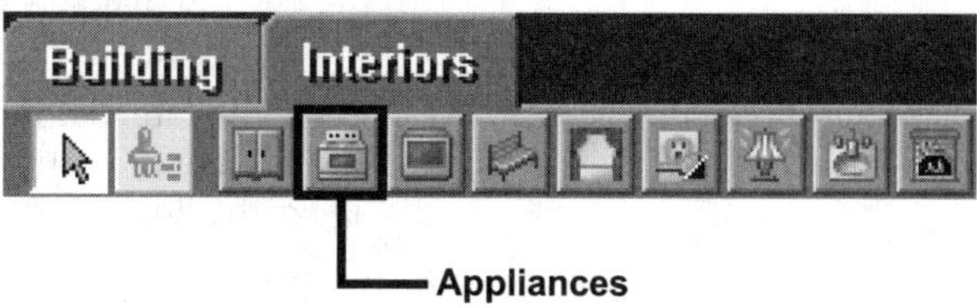

Inserting Appliances

You can insert a wide variety of kitchen and laundry appliances in your design by simply pointing and clicking with your mouse. Appliances automatically snap to walls and other elements when you get close to them provided Collision Control is turned on.

To insert an appliance:

1. Select **Insert > Interiors > Appliances**, or click the Appliances button on the Interiors toolbar.
2. In the catalog, select the appliance you want to insert.

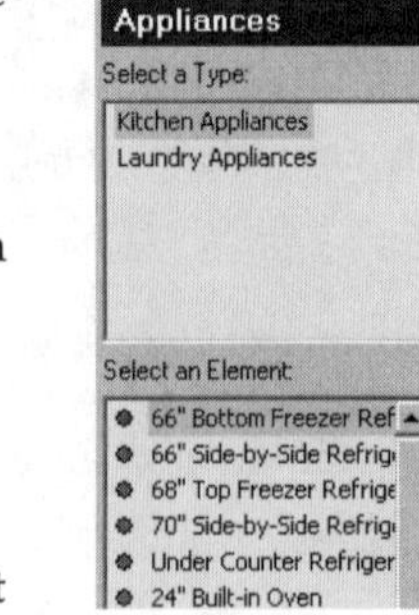

3. Position the appliance where you want it, then click to insert it.
4. Right-click and select **Finish**.

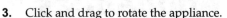

Note: If you are inserting a built-in oven, just position it where you want it in the wall and it will snap into place correctly with only the oven door and controls protruding from the wall.

Moving Appliances

You can move individual appliances by clicking and dragging them.

To move an appliance:

1. Select the appliance you want to move.
2. Hover your pointer over the appliance's center grab handle to display the Move cursor.

3. Click and drag to move the appliance.
4. When the appliance is where you want it, release your mouse button.

Rotating Appliances

You can rotate appliances by clicking and dragging them.

To rotate an appliance:

1. Select the appliance you want to rotate.
2. Hover your pointer over the triangular grab handle to display the Rotate cursor.

3. Click and drag to rotate the appliance.
4. When the appliance is at the desired rotation, release your mouse button.

Raising or Lowering an Appliance

You can raise or lower an appliance using the Elevate tool on the element's right-click menu. For example, you might want to place a microwave on the kitchen counter.

To raise or lower an appliance:

1. Select the appliance whose elevation you want to edit.
2. Right-click and select **Elevate**, or select **Edit > Modify Elements > Elevate**. The value in the **Elevate** dialog is the current elevation of the appliance.
3. In the **Elevate** dialog, specify the desired elevation of the bottom of the appliance above the floor.
4. Click **OK**.

Tip: You can also change an appliance's elevation by changing the **Distance above current location or terrain** variable on the appliance's Behavior property page.

Editing Appliance Size Properties

You can edit the height, width and depth of most appliances. Some appliances have additional properties that define their size and style.

To edit appliance properties:

1. Select the appliance whose properties you want to edit.

2. Right-click and select **Properties**, or select **Edit > Modify Elements > Properties**.
3. To change the size or style of the appliance, select the Basic tab. Appliance styles and size properties will vary depending on the appliance. Use the graphics as guides when determining the appliance's properties. Clicking a dimension marked with an alphabetical character (a, b, c, etc.) highlights the corresponding dimension in the appliance graphic, and vice versa.

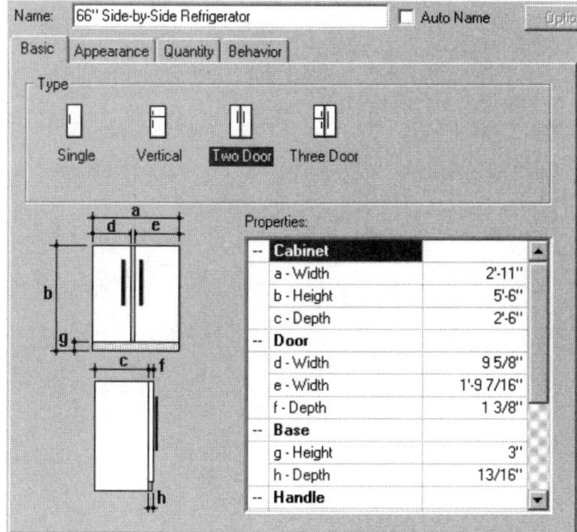

4. Once you've specified the properties, click **OK**.

Applying a Different Color or Finish to Appliances

You can use the Materials Paintbrush to quickly change the color or finish of an appliance.

To apply a color or finish to an appliance:

1. Display your model in 3D, and make sure the appliance is visible in the view.
2. Select **Edit > Materials Paintbrush**, or click the Materials Paintbrush button  on any tabbed toolbar.
3. In the catalog panel, select the color or finish you want to apply. You can find an assortment of colors in the Paint category. For the stainless steel look you may want to try the Silver material in the Finishes category.

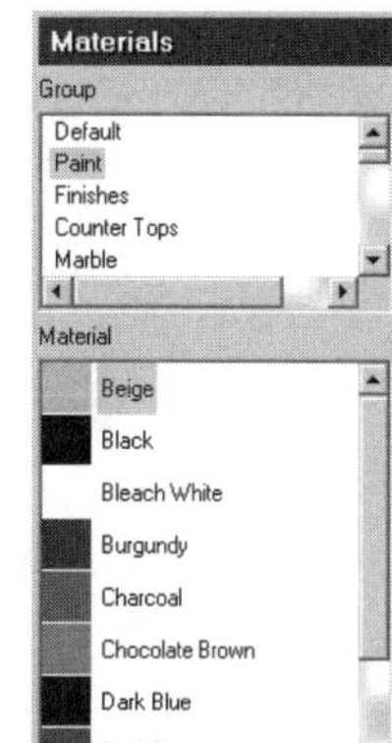

4. Click on the appliance component you want to apply the material to. Materials are applied separately to the individual parts of the appliance. For example, you can select a different color just for a knob or handle.
5. When you are finished applying materials, right-click and select **Finish**.

Deleting an Appliance

You can delete an appliance in a couple of easy steps.

To delete an appliance:

1. Select the appliance.
2. Press the **Delete** key on your keyboard, right-click and select **Delete**, or select **Edit > Modify Elements > Delete**.

Chapter 17

Furniture, Electronics & Accessories

Once you've got your cabinets and appliances in place, you can jump right into the fun stuff — furnishing and decorating your home. The catalog contains so many different types of furniture, electronics and decorative accessories, the possibilities are endless. And with easy, point-and-click insertion, you can play around with different design ideas and quickly decorate every room of your home, just the way you want it.

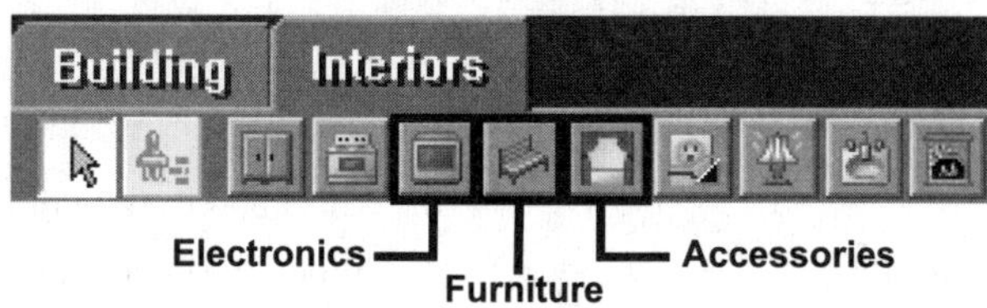

Inserting Furniture

The catalog contains a variety of furnishings for every room in your home — everything from beds to CD stands. Furnishings automatically snap to walls and other elements when you get close to them provided Collision Control is turned on.

To insert furniture:

1. Select **Insert > Interiors > Furniture**, or click the Furniture button on the Interiors toolbar.
2. In the catalog, select the element you want to insert.
3. Position the element where you want it, then click to insert it.
4. Right-click and select **Finish**.

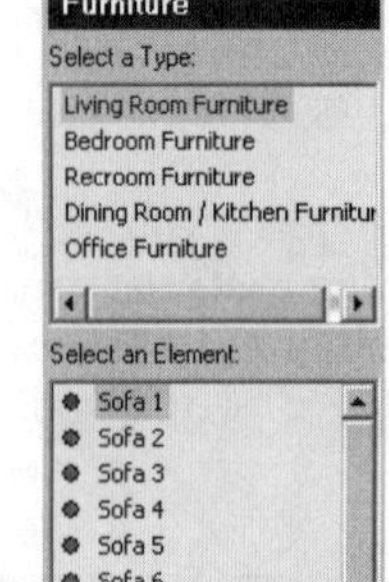

Inserting Electronics

Electronics include televisions, computers, clocks and telephones.

To insert electronics:

1. Select **Insert > Interiors > Electronics**, or click the Electronics button on the Interiors toolbar.
2. In the catalog, select the element you want to insert.
3. Position the element where you want it, then click to insert it.
4. Right-click and select **Finish**.

Inserting Accessories

Accessories are those small, personal touches that really pull a room together. They are things like curtains, blinds, towel racks, shower curtains, medicine cabinets, plates, bowls, cups, mirrors and pictures.

To insert accessories:

1. Select **Insert > Interiors > Accessories**, or click the Accessories button on the Interiors toolbar.

2. In the catalog, select the element you want to insert.
3. Position the element where you want it, then click to insert it.
4. Right-click and select **Finish**.

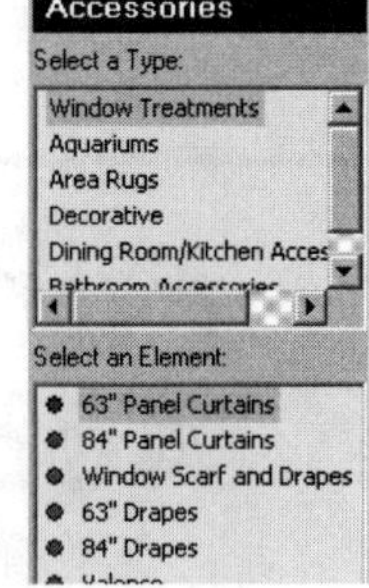

Moving Furnishing Elements

You can move furniture, electronics and accessories by clicking and dragging them.

To move an element:

1. Select the element you want to move.
2. Hover your pointer over the cabinet's center grab handle to display the Move cursor.

3. Click and drag to move the element.
4. When the element is where you want it, release your mouse button.

Rotating Furnishing Elements

You can rotate furniture, electronics and accessories by clicking and dragging them.

To rotate an element:

1. Select the element you want to rotate.
2. Hover your pointer over the triangular grab handle to display the Rotate cursor.

3. Click and drag to rotate the element.
4. When the element is at the desired rotation, release your mouse button.

Raising or Lowering a Furnishing Element

You can raise or lower furniture, electronics and accessories using the Elevate tool on the element's right-click menu. For example, you might want to adjust the height of a picture on the wall.

To edit the elevation of a furnishing element:

1. Select the element whose elevation you want to edit.
2. Right-click and select **Elevate**, or select **Edit > Modify Elements > Elevate**. The value shown in the **Elevate** dialog is the current elevation of the element.
3. In the **Elevate** dialog, specify the desired elevation of the bottom of the element above the floor.
4. Click **OK**.

Tip: You can also change a furnishing element's elevation by changing the **Distance above current location or terrain** variable on the element's Behavior property page.

Editing the Size of Furnishing Elements

You can edit the height, width and depth of most furnishing elements. Some elements have additional properties that define their size and style.

To edit the size of furnishing elements:

1. Select the element whose properties you want to edit.
2. Right-click and select **Properties**, or select **Edit > Modify Elements > Properties**.
3. To change the dimensions of the element, select the Basic tab. Size properties will vary depending on the element.

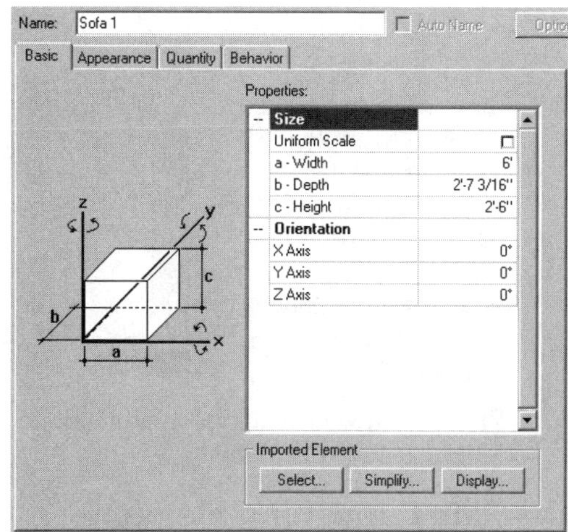

4. Once you've specified the properties, click **OK**.

Applying Different Colors, Fabrics and Finishes to Furnishing Elements

You can use the Materials Paintbrush to quickly apply a color, fabric or finish to any furnishing element.

To apply a material to a furnishing element:

1. Display your model in 3D, and make sure the furnishing element is visible in the view.
2. Select **Edit > Materials Paintbrush**, or click the Materials Paintbrush button  on any tabbed toolbar.

3. In the catalog panel, select the color or material you want to apply. You can find an assortment of colors in the Paint category.

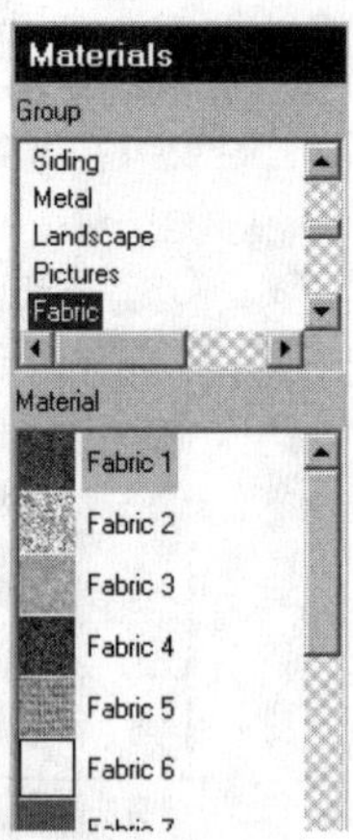

4. Click on the component you want to apply the material to. Materials are applied separately to the individual parts of the element. For example, you can apply a specific fabric to the bedspread on a bed.
5. When you are finished applying materials, right-click and select **Finish**.

Deleting Furnishing Elements

You can delete furniture, electronics or accessories in a couple of easy steps.

To delete a furnishing element:

1. Select the element.
2. Press the **Delete** key on your keyboard, right-click and select **Delete**, or select **Edit > Modify Elements > Delete**.

Part 5

Utilities

Chapter 18

Interior Lighting

Interior lighting can drastically change the look and atmosphere of a room. They also play an important part when you create interior 3DTrueView™ renderings. *3D Home Architect® Home Design* provides an excellent selection of ceiling lights, wall lights, track lights, recessed lights and lamps for you to insert. You can even turn them on and off!

Lights are inserted at a logical height in your plan depending on their type, making accurate placement easy. Also, ceiling lights snap to ceilings, and wall lights snap to walls. Just point and click!

Inserting Interior Light Fixtures

3D Home Architect® Home Design offers a good selection of lighting fixtures for the interior of your home. Interior light fixtures include ceiling lights, wall lights, track lighting, recessed lights, and lamps.

Each lighting fixture has a light source in its property definition, such as an incandescent light bulb. Lights are particularly important if you plan to create a 3DTrueView™ of your model, since the program uses light to calculate and create the rendered view.

With the exception of lamps, light fixtures are set to snap to either ceilings or walls depending on what kind of fixture they are.

To insert a light fixture:

1. Select **Insert > Interiors > Lighting**, or click the Lighting button on the Interiors toolbar.
2. In the catalog, select the light fixture you want to insert.

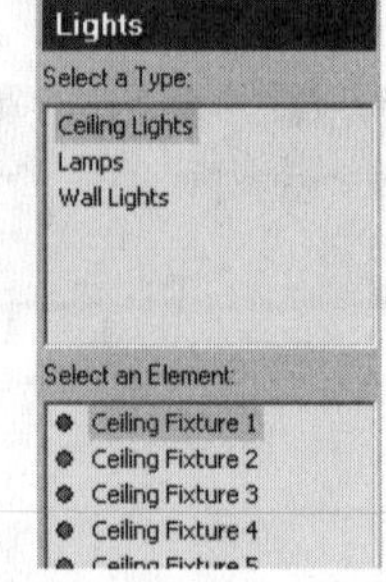

3. Position the light where you want it, then click to insert it. If you want the light to snap to a ceiling or wall and it isn't, or you want to stop the light from snapping, see *Changing the Way a Light Snaps on Insertion* below.
4. Right-click and select **Finish**.

Changing the Way a Light Snaps on Insertion

By default, ceiling lights are set to snap to ceilings, and wall lights are set to snap to walls. Lamps have no snap setting so that you can place them anywhere in a room. You can change a light fixture's snap setting on the fixture's Behavior property page.

To change the way a light snaps on insertion:

1. In the catalog, select the light fixture whose snap setting you want to change.
2. Right-click and select **Catalog Manager**. You can also access the Catalog Manager by selecting **File > Catalogs > Catalog Manager**.
3. In the **Catalog Manager** dialog, make sure the correct fixture is selected, then select **Catalog > Element Properties**.
4. In the **Lights** dialog, select the Behavior tab.
5. From the **Snap Light to** drop box, select either *Ceiling*, *Wall* or *None*.
6. Click **OK** in the **Lights** dialog.
7. Click **OK**.

Raising or Lowering a Light Fixture

You can raise or lower a light fixture using the Elevate tool on the fixture's right-click menu.

To raise or lower a light fixture:

1. Select the fixture whose elevation you want to edit.
2. Right-click and select **Elevate**, or select **Edit > Modify Elements > Elevate**. The value shown in the **Elevate** dialog is the current elevation of the light fixture.
3. In the **Elevate** dialog, specify the desired elevation of the fixture above the floor.
4. Click **OK**.

Tip: You can also change a light fixture's elevation by changing the **Distance above current location or terrain** variable on the fixture's Behavior property page.

Moving Light Fixtures

You can move light fixtures by clicking and dragging them.

To move a light fixture:

1. Select the light fixture you want to move.

2. Hover your pointer over the fixture's center grab handle to display the Move cursor.
3. Click and drag to move the light fixture.
4. When the light fixture is where you want it, release your mouse button.

Rotating Light Fixtures

You can rotate light fixtures by clicking and dragging them.

To rotate a light fixture:

1. Select the light fixture you want to rotate.
2. Hover your pointer over the triangular grab handle to display the Rotate cursor.
3. Click and drag to rotate the light fixture.
4. When the light fixture is at the desired rotation, release your mouse button.

Editing the Size of Light Fixtures

You can edit the dimensions of a light fixture on its Basic property page.

To edit the size of a light fixture:

1. Select the light fixture whose properties you want to edit.
2. Right-click and select **Properties**, or select **Edit > Modify Elements > Properties**.

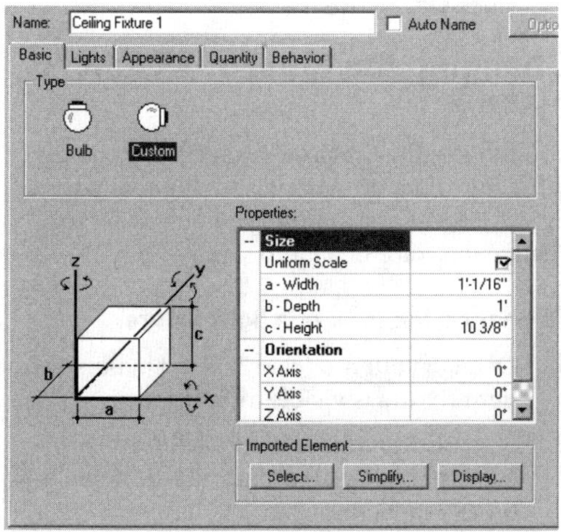

3. Select the Basic tab. Size properties will vary depending on the type of fixture. Use the diagram as a guide when determining the fixture's properties. Clicking a dimension marked with an alphabetical character (a, b, c, etc.) highlights the corresponding dimension in the light fixture diagram, and vice versa.
4. Click **OK**.

Editing a Light Fixture's Light Source

A light source is usually a type of light bulb. You can edit a light fixture's light source to achieve a different lighting effect.

To edit a light fixture's light source:

1. Select the light fixture whose properties you want to edit.
2. Right-click and select **Properties**, or select **Edit > Modify Elements > Properties**.
3. Select the Lights tab.

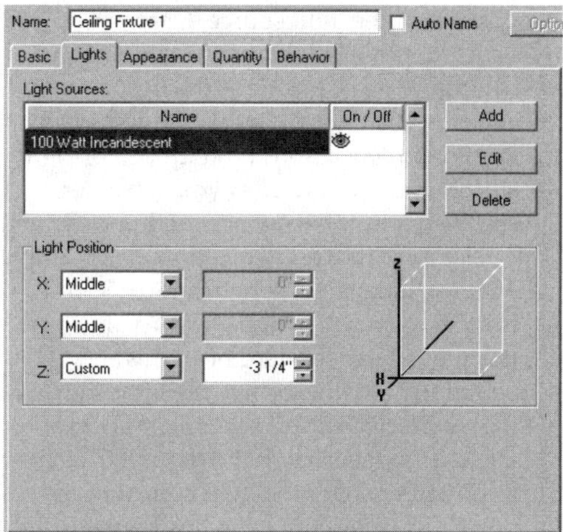

4. To replace the currently selected light source with another type, click **Edit**, then select a light source from the **Light Sources** dialog. To add a light source to the fixture, click **Add**,

then select a light source from the **Light Sources** dialog.

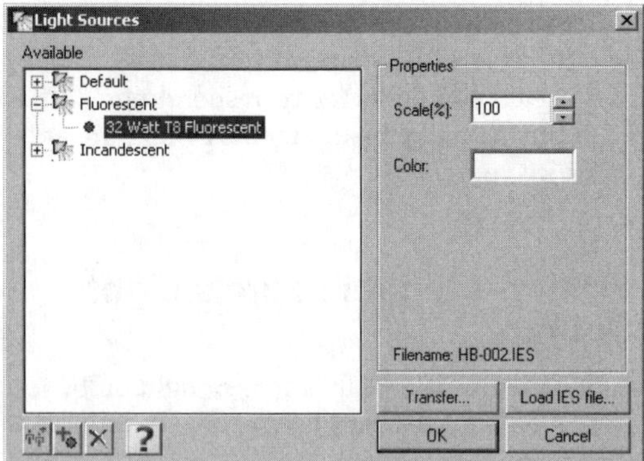

5. To delete a light source from the light fixture, click **Delete**.
6. To edit the position of the light source in relation to the light fixture, specify the X, Y and Z coordinates in the *Light Position* area. Coordinates are measured from the bottom center of the fixture. The small red box in the preview window indicates the current position of the light source. Changing the **X** value moves the light source left or right. Selecting *Middle* positions the light in the center of the fixture, and selecting *Minimum* or *Maximum* positions it on the left or right side. If you select *Custom* you can enter a specific value in the adjacent edit box which is relative to the center position. For example, entering **-3** moves the light source 3" left from the center. Changing the **Y** value moves the light source forward or backward. Selecting *Minimum* brings the light source all the way forward, and selecting *Maximum* moves it to the back of the fixture. Changing the **Z** value moves the light source up or down. Selecting *Minimum* positions the light source at the bottom of the fixture, while selecting *Maximum* positions it at the top of the fixture.
7. Once you've specified the properties, click **OK**.

Turning a Light On or Off

By default, lights are on when you insert them. You can virtually turn a light off by disabling its light source.

To turn a light on or off:

1. Select the light fixture you want to turn on or off.
2. Right-click and select **Properties**, or select **Edit > Modify Elements > Properties**.
3. Select the Lights tab.

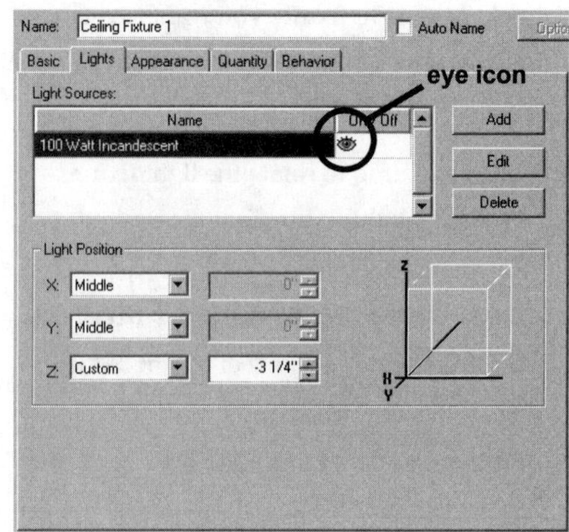

4. To turn the light on or off, click the eye icon next to the light source name.
5. Click **OK**.

Changing the Look of a Light Fixture

You can use the Materials Paintbrush to apply different colors or materials to different parts of a light fixture. For example, you may want to change the color of a lamp shade.

To change the look of a light fixture:

1. Display your model in 3D, and make sure the light fixture is visible in the view.
2. Select **Edit > Materials Paintbrush**, or click the Materials Paintbrush button on any tabbed toolbar. 

3. In the catalog panel, select the material you want to apply.
4. Click on the component you want to apply the material to. Materials are applied separately to the individual parts of the light fixture.
5. When you are finished applying materials, right-click and select **Finish**.

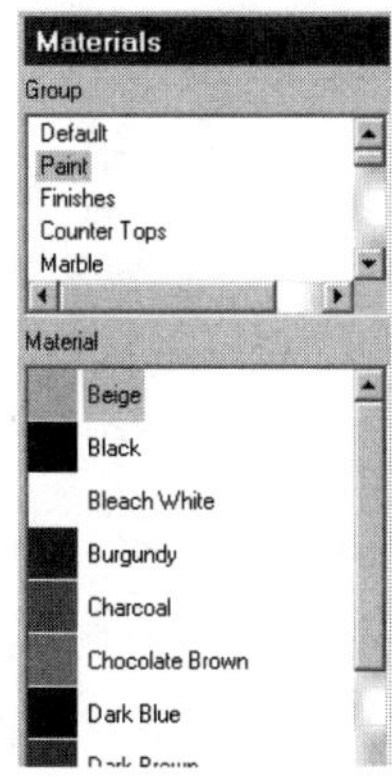

Deleting Light Fixtures

You can delete a light fixture in a couple of easy steps.

To delete a light fixture:

1. Select the fixture.
2. Press the **Delete** key on your keyboard, right-click and select **Delete**, or select **Edit > Modify Elements > Delete**.

Chapter 19

Electrical

3D Home Architect® Home Design makes it easy to insert electrical outlets, switches, thermostats and smoke detectors in your plan — just point and click. Electrical elements automatically snap to walls and are inserted at a logical height depending on their type, making it easy to place them accurately.

Once you've inserted electrical elements you may want to draw wiring in your 2D plan. All it takes is a few clicks of the mouse.

Inserting Outlets and Switches

You can insert electrical outlets and light switches in your plan with a single mouse click. The backs of these elements automatically snap to walls and are inserted at a logical height on the wall, making accurate placement effortless. You can move, raise and lower these elements after you have inserted them.

To insert outlets and switches:

1. Select **Insert > Interiors > Electrical > Electrical Elements**, or click the Electrical button on the Interiors toolbar and select **Electrical Elements.**

2. In the catalog, select the element you want to insert.
3. Position the element where you want it, then click to insert it.
4. Right-click and select **Finish**.

Inserting Thermostats and Smoke Detectors

To insert a thermostat or smoke detector, all you need to do is point and click. Thermostats are set to automatically snap to walls and are inserted at a default height of 5'. Smoke detectors insert a default height of 8'. You can move, raise or lower thermostats and smoke detectors after you have inserted them.

To insert thermostats and smoke detectors:

1. Select **Insert > Interiors > Electrical > Electrical Elements**, or click the Electrical button on the Interiors toolbar and select **Electrical Elements.**

2. In the catalog, select the Sensors category, then select the element you want to insert.
3. Position the element where you want it, then click to insert it.
4. Right-click and select **Finish**.

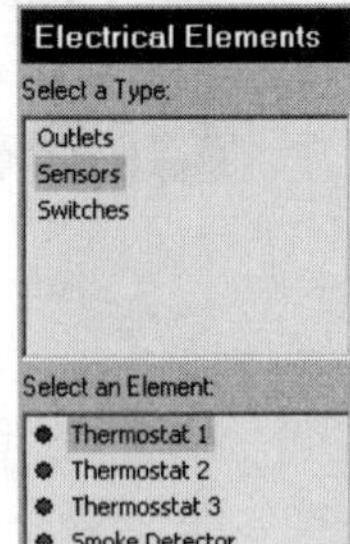

Raising or Lowering an Electrical Element

You can raise or lower an outlet, switch, thermostat or smoke detector using the Elevate tool.

To raise or lower an electrical element:

1. Select the element whose elevation you want to edit.
2. Right-click and select **Elevate**, or select **Edit > Modify Elements > Elevate**. The value shown in the **Elevate** dialog is the current elevation of the element.
3. In the **Elevate** dialog, specify the desired elevation of the bottom of the element above the floor.
4. Click **OK**.

Tip: You can also change an element's elevation by changing the **Distance above current location or terrain** variable on the element's Behavior property page.

Moving an Electrical Element

You can move outlets, switches, thermostats and smoke detectors in plan view by simply clicking and dragging them.

To move an element:

1. Select the element you want to move.
2. Hover your pointer over the element's center grab handle to display the Move cursor. 
3. Click and drag to move the element.
4. When the element is where you want it, release your mouse button.

Editing the Size of an Electrical Element

You can edit the height, width and depth of most electrical elements. Some elements have additional dimensions for individual components in the element.

To edit the size of an electrical element:

1. Select the element whose size you want to edit.
2. Right-click and select **Properties**, or select **Edit > Modify Elements > Properties**.

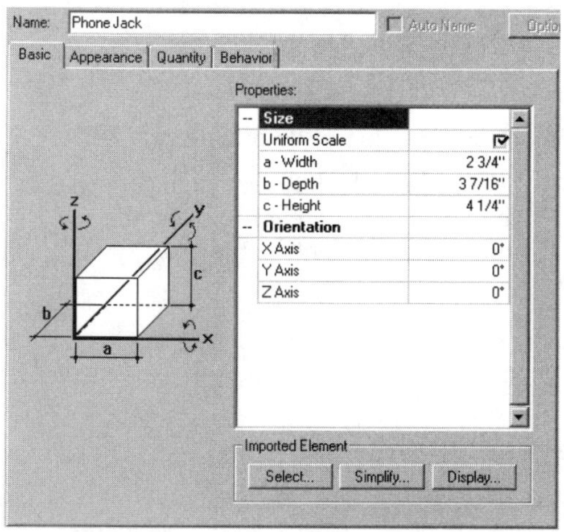

3. Edit the properties as desired.
4. Click **OK**.

Applying a Different Color or Material to an Electrical Element

You can use the Materials Paintbrush to apply a different color or material to an electrical element.

To apply a color or material to an electrical element:

1. Display your model in 3D, and make sure the electrical element is visible in the view.
2. Select **Edit > Materials Paintbrush**, or click the Materials Paintbrush button on any tabbed toolbar. 
3. In the catalog panel, select the color or material you want to apply. You can find an assortment of colors in the Paint category.

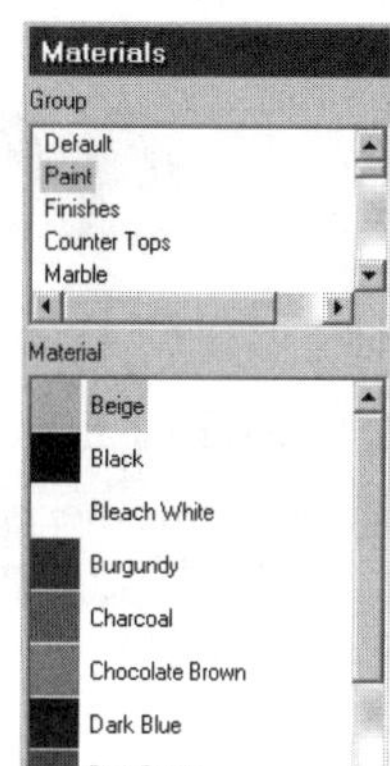

4. Click on the electrical element. The color or material is applied immediately.
5. Right-click and select **Finish**.

Deleting Electrical Elements

You can delete an outlet, switch, thermostat or smoke detector in a couple of easy steps.

To delete an electrical element:

1. Select the element.
2. Press the **Delete** key on your keyboard, right-click and select **Delete**, or select **Edit > Modify Elements > Delete**.

Inserting Wiring

Once you've inserted electrical elements, you can use the Wiring tool to indicate the location of electrical wiring in your 2D plan. By default, wiring lines have arched segments and use a dashed linestyle. You can stretch and reshape individual segments after you've inserted the line. You can also edit the linestyle. Wiring is only visible in 2D plan view.

To add electrical wiring:

1. Select **Insert > Interiors > Electrical > Wiring**, or click the Electrical button on the Interiors toolbar and select **Wiring**.

2. Select a start point for the wiring line.
3. Select the next point for the wiring line. An arched line segment is created between the two points.

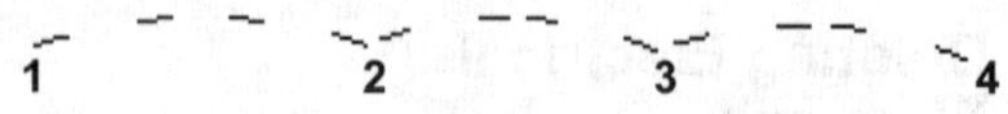

4. Continue selecting points to add more segments.
5. Right-click and select **Finish**.

Note: You can change the line style of individual wires if you want. See *Changing the Line Style of Wiring* on page 138. You can also mark your wiring lines with text. See *Adding Text to Your Drawing* on page 186.

Stretching and Reshaping Wiring Segments

You can stretch individual segments in a wiring line by clicking and dragging their grab handles. Stretching wiring segments can change their length or shape.

To stretch a wiring segment:

1. Select the segment you want to stretch. Grab handles are displayed along the segment.
2. Hover your pointer over the grab handle you want to grab and stretch.

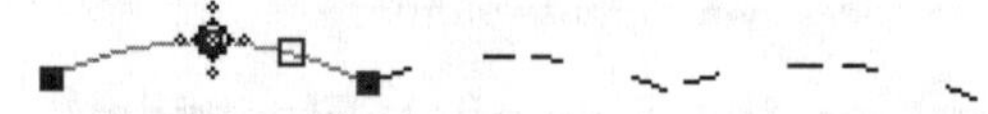

3. Click and drag to stretch the line, then release your mouse button.

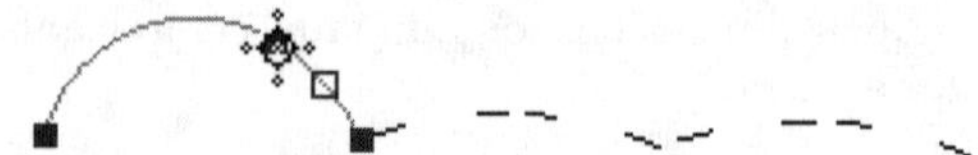

Changing the Line Style of Wiring

By default, electrical wiring is displayed using the Electrical Power Distribution line style, which is a brown, dashed line. You can select a different line style for selected wiring segments if you want. For example, you may want to select the Telephone line style for your telephone lines.

To change the line style of wiring:

1. Select one of the line segments you want to change. Use Shift+click to select the remaining segments in the line.

2. Right-click and select **Properties**, or select **Edit > Modify Elements > Properties**.

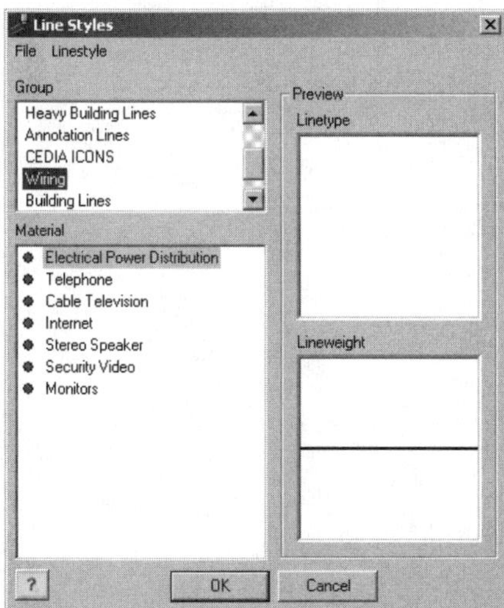

3. In the **Line Styles** dialog, select the line style you want to use.

   If you want to edit a line style, click one of the swatches to access the **Edit Line Styles** dialog. To add a new line style to the list, select **Linestyle > Add Linestyle**. For more information, see the Line Styles chapter page 267.

4. Click **OK**. The line style is updated in your drawing.

Deleting Wiring

You can delete individual wiring segments or an entire wire in a couple of easy steps.

To delete wiring:

1. Select the wiring segment you want to delete. To select an entire wire, drag a selection window around it.
2. Press the **Delete** key on your keyboard, right-click and select **Delete**, or select **Edit > Modify Elements > Delete**.

Chapter 20

Plumbing

3D Home Architect® Home Design offers a complete selection of sinks, faucets, tubs, showers, toilets and bidets to help you properly equip your home. Plumbing fixtures are inserted with a single mouse click and will automatically snap to walls if Collision Control is turned on. You can control which edge of a fixture snaps to the wall, as well as edit the fixture's size, style and elevation.

Inserting Plumbing Fixtures

Placing plumbing fixtures in your plan is easy — just select what you want to insert, then point and click. With Collision Control turned on, fixtures will automatically snap to walls when you get close to them. Also, fixtures will insert at a logical height. For example, a toilet will insert on the floor, while a sink may insert 3' off the floor. You can edit a fixture's size and elevation, as well as move and rotate it.

Note: The first four sinks in the Sinks category (kitchen and bathroom sinks) can only be inserted into a cabinet. Also, the cabinet must be large enough to house the sink.

To insert plumbing fixtures:

1. Select **Insert > Interiors > Plumbing Fixtures**, or click the Plumbing Fixtures button on the Interiors toolbar.

2. In the catalog, select the fixture you want to insert.
3. Position the fixture where you want it, then click to insert it.
4. Right-click and select **Finish**.

Plumbing Fixtures
Select a Type:
Sinks
Faucets
Tubs and Showers
Toilets
Exterior Plumbing Fixtures
Select an Element:
Single Kitchen Sink
Double Kitchen Sink
Bathroom Sink 1
Bathroom Sink 2
Pedestal Sink

Raising or Lowering a Plumbing Fixture

You can raise or lower a plumbing fixture using the Elevate tool on the fixture's right-click menu.

To edit a plumbing fixture's elevation:

1. Select the fixture whose elevation you want to edit.
2. Right-click and select **Elevate**, or select **Edit > Modify Elements > Elevate**. The value shown in the **Elevate** dialog is the current elevation of the element.
3. In the **Elevate** dialog, specify the desired elevation of the bottom of the fixture above the floor.
4. Click **OK**.

Tip: You can also change a plumbing fixture's elevation by changing the **Distance above current location or terrain** variable on the fixture's Behavior property page.

Moving Plumbing Fixtures

You can move plumbing fixtures by clicking and dragging them.

To move a plumbing fixture:

1. Select the plumbing fixture you want to move.
2. Hover your pointer over the fixture's center grab handle to display the Move cursor.

3. Click and drag to move the fixture.
4. When the fixture is where you want it, release your mouse button.

Rotating Plumbing Fixtures

You can rotate plumbing fixtures by clicking and dragging them.

To rotate a plumbing fixture:

1. Select the fixture you want to rotate.
2. Hover your pointer over the triangular grab handle to display the Rotate cursor.

3. Click and drag to rotate the fixture.
4. When the fixture is at the desired rotation, release your mouse button.

Editing the Size of a Plumbing Fixture

You can edit the height, width and depth of a plumbing fixture.

To edit the properties of a plumbing fixture:

1. Select the plumbing fixture whose properties you want to edit.

2. Right-click and select **Properties**, or select **Edit > Modify Elements > Properties**.

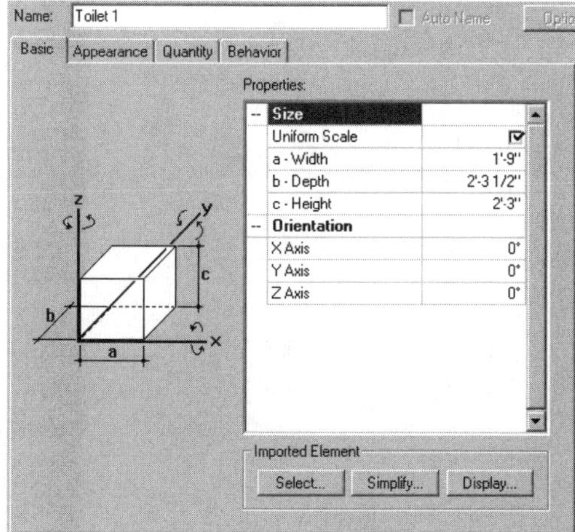

3. Edit the properties as desired.
4. Click **OK**.

Applying a Different Color or Finish to Plumbing Fixtures

You can use the Materials Paintbrush to apply different colors or finishes to different parts of a plumbing fixture.

To apply a color or finish to a plumbing fixture:

1. Display your model in 3D, and make sure the fixture is visible in the view.
2. Select **Edit > Materials Paintbrush**, or click the Materials Paintbrush button on any tabbed toolbar. 
3. In the catalog panel, select the color or finish you want to apply. You can find an assortment of colors in the Paint category.

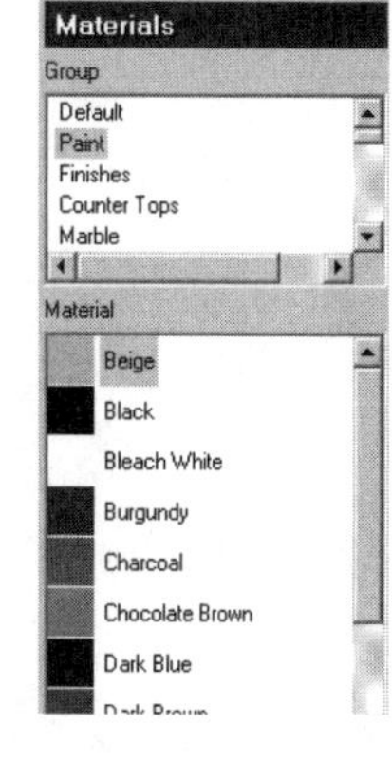

4. Click on the component you want to apply the material to. Materials are applied separately to the individual parts of the plumbing fixture. For example, you can select a different color just for a tap or handle.
5. When you are finished applying materials, right-click and select **Finish**.

Deleting Plumbing Fixtures

You can delete a plumbing fixture in a couple of easy steps.

To delete a plumbing fixture:

1. Select the fixture.
2. Press the **Delete** key on your keyboard, right-click and select **Delete**, or select **Edit > Modify Elements > Delete**.

Chapter 21

Heating & Ventilation

The correct placement of heating and ventilation elements is an important part of the home design process. Laying out HVAC elements in *3D Home Architect® Home Design* is quick and easy - just point and click.

The catalog contains just about anything you'd need — furnaces, fireplaces, wood stoves, chimneys, water heaters, floor registers and cold air returns. Of course, just like anything else, you can move, rotate and edit these elements if you change your mind.

Inserting Heating Elements

You can insert heating elements with a click of your mouse. Heating elements include fireplaces, wood stoves, furnaces and water heaters. By default, heating elements are inserted on the floor and will snap to walls if Collision Control is turned on.

To insert a heating element:

1. Select **Insert > Interiors > HVAC Elements**, or click the HVAC Elements button on the Interiors toolbar.

2. In the catalog, select the Heating category, then select the element you want to insert.
3. Position the element where you want it, then click to insert it.
4. Right-click and select **Finish**.

Inserting Floor Registers and Cold Air Returns

Registers and air returns come in a variety of sizes, but you can create a different size if you need to. Wall air returns will insert directly onto walls. You can change the height of them later if you want.

To insert a ventilation element:

1. Select **Insert > Interiors > HVAC Elements**, or click the HVAC Elements button on the Interiors toolbar.

2. In the catalog, select the Ventilation category, then select the element you want to insert.
3. Position the element where you want it, then click to insert it.
4. Right-click and select **Finish**.

Inserting a Chimney

Chimneys by default are 12' tall, but you can change this before or after you insert the chimney to create the correct height needed for your house. By default, the chimney in the catalog has a brick base and concrete cap. You can edit the appearance of the chimney to match the exterior of your home if you are inserting the chimney on the outside.

To insert a chimney:

1. Select **Insert > Interiors > HVAC Elements**, or click the HVAC Elements button on the Interiors toolbar.

2. In the catalog, select the Ventilation category, then select the Chimney element.

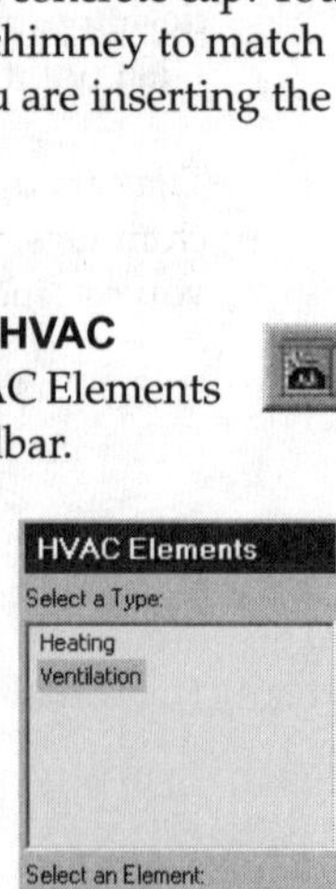

3. Position the chimney where you want it, then click to insert it.
4. Right-click and select **Finish**.

To edit the height of the chimney:

1. Select the chimney.
2. Right-click and select **Properties**, or select **Edit > Modify Elements > Properties**.
3. On the Basic property page, change the value in the **Base Height** edit box.
4. Click **OK**.

To apply different materials to the chimney:

1. Display your model in 3D, and make sure the chimney is visible in the view.
2. Select **Edit > Materials Paintbrush**, or click the Materials Paintbrush button on any tabbed toolbar. 
3. In the catalog panel, select the material you want to apply.

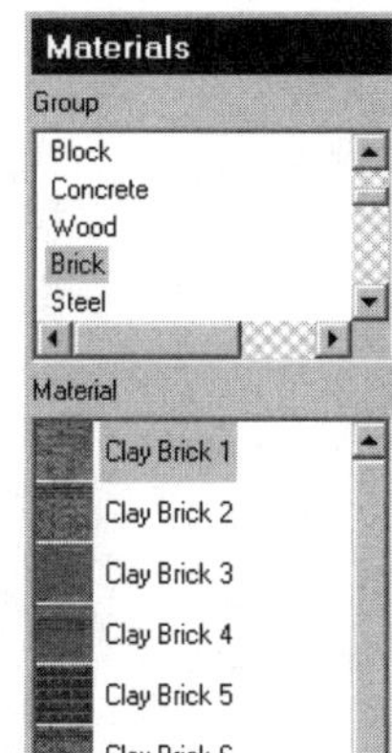

4. Click on the component you want to apply the material to. You can apply different materials to the base, cap and flue.
5. When you are finished applying materials, right-click and select **Finish**.

Moving HVAC Elements

You can move HVAC elements by clicking and dragging them.

To move an HVAC element:

1. Select the HVAC element you want to move.
2. Hover your pointer over the element's center grab handle to display the Move cursor. 
3. Click and drag to move the element.
4. When the element is where you want it, release your mouse button.

Rotating HVAC Elements

You can rotate HVAC elements by clicking and dragging them.

To rotate an HVAC element:

1. Select the element you want to rotate.
2. Hover your pointer over the triangular grab handle to display the Rotate cursor.
3. Click and drag to rotate the element.
4. When the element is at the desired rotation, release your mouse button.

Raising or Lowering an HVAC Element

You can raise or lower an HVAC element using the Elevate tool on the element's right-click menu.

To edit an HVAC element's elevation:

1. Select the element whose elevation you want to edit.
2. Right-click and select **Elevate**, or select **Edit > Modify Elements > Elevate**. The value shown in the **Elevate** dialog is the current elevation of the element.
3. In the **Elevate** dialog, specify the desired elevation of the bottom of the element above the floor.
4. Click **OK**.

Tip: You can also change an HVAC element's elevation by changing the **Distance above current location or terrain** variable on the element's Behavior property page.

Editing the Size of an HVAC Element

You can edit the dimensions of an HVAC element. The more complex an element is, the more variables it will have. A chimney, for example, has separate variables for the base, cap and flue, so you can create the exact look and size you want.

To edit the size of an HVAC element:

1. Select the HVAC element whose properties you want to edit.
2. Right-click and select **Properties**, or select **Edit > Modify Elements > Properties**.
3. Edit the properties as desired.
4. Click **OK**.

Deleting HVAC Elements

You can delete an HVAC element in a couple of easy steps.

To delete an HVAC element:

1. Select the element.
2. Press the **Delete** key on your keyboard, right-click and select **Delete**, or select **Edit > Modify Elements > Delete**.

Part 6

Drawing & Editing Tools

Chapter 22

Drawing Aids

3D Home Architect® Home Design offers a variety of powerful drawing tools that help you insert elements easily and precisely where you want them in your drawing.

If you want you can display a drawing grid in your drawing area, as well as set up a snap grid so that your cursor snaps to the grid when you are inserting elements. The Object Snap feature automatically snaps your pointer to existing objects, and the Angle Snap snaps your pointer to specified angles. The Collision Control feature prevents you from inserting elements where they do not fit.

You can set up drawing aids in your program settings, and toggle them on and off using the buttons on the Status bar.

Setting Up a Drawing Grid

A drawing grid is simply a set of horizontal and vertical lines that can help you orient objects to one another. By default, the spacing between grid lines is 1′, but you can change this if you want. Note that the drawing grid is a visual aid only, and will not be included in printouts.

To set up a drawing grid:

1. Select **Settings > Program Settings** or click the Program Settings button on the Settings toolbar. 
2. In the **Program Settings** dialog, select the Drawing Aids tab.
3. In the *Grid* area, specify the desired distance between vertical grid lines in the **X Spacing** edit box.
4. Specify the desired distance between horizontal grid lines in the **Y Spacing** edit box.
5. By default, the grid is 150′ x 150′, which is the default size of the terrain. To change the overall size of the grid, enter the desired width in the **X Limit** edit box, and the desired height in the **Y Limit** edit box.
6. If you want to turn the grid on, check the **Enable (F7)** check box.
7. Click **OK**.

Turning the Drawing Grid On and Off

You can toggle the drawing grid on and off in one of two ways:

- Press **F7** on your keyboard
- Click the **GRID** button on the Status bar

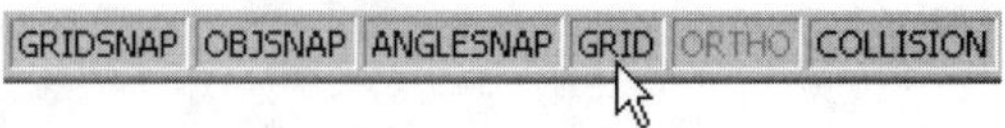

Using the Grid Snap

The Grid Snap feature snaps your pointer to an invisible grid when inserting elements. By default, the spacing between the grid lines in the invisible grid is 1″, but you can change this if you want. If you enable the **Match Grid** option, the invisible snap grid becomes the same size as the drawing grid. This will make it seem like you are snapping to the drawing grid while drawing.

To set up a snap grid:

1. Select **Settings > Program Settings** or click the Program Settings button on the Settings toolbar. 
2. In the **Program Settings** dialog, select the Drawing Aids tab.
3. If you want the snap grid to be the same size as the drawing grid, check the **Match Grid** check box in the *Grid Snap* area.
4. To specify a custom distance between vertical grid lines, enter a value in the **X Spacing** edit box.
5. To specify a custom distance between horizontal grid lines, enter a value in the **Y Spacing** edit box.
6. If you want to turn the grid snap on, check the **Enable (F4)** check box.
7. Click **OK**.

Turning the Grid Snap On and Off

You can toggle the grid snap on and off in one of two ways:

- Press **F4** on your keyboard
- Click the **GRIDSNAP** button on the Status bar

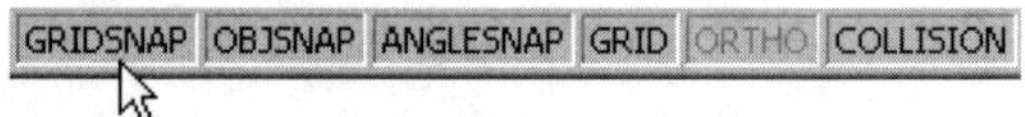

Using the Object Snap

The Object Snap feature makes elements that you are currently inserting automatically snap to existing elements in your drawing. For example, if you are drawing a wall and hover your pointer near an existing wall, your pointer will snap to the existing wall, making it easy to create a wall layout with cleanly intersecting walls.

You can set the pixel search distance for the object snap, which determines how close your pointer needs to be to an element for it to snap to the element.

By default, the Object Snap is enabled, but you can turn it off whenever you want. There are three ways to turn the Object Snap on or off.

To turn the Object Snap on or off:

- Press **F5** on your keyboard
- Click the **OBJSNAP** button on the Status bar

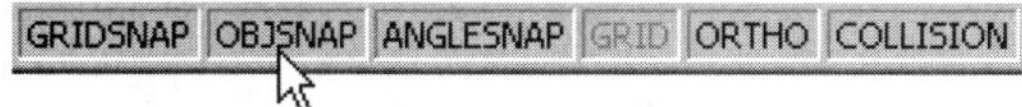

- Select **Settings > Program Settings**, then on the Drawing Aids page, check or uncheck the **Enable (F5)** check box in the *Object Snap* area

To set the pixel search distance:

1. Select **Settings > Program Settings** or click the Program Settings button on the Settings toolbar.
2. In the **Program Settings** dialog, select the Drawing Aids tab.
3. In the Object Snap area, type the desired number of pixels in the **Pixel Search Distance** edit box, or use the arrows to scroll up or down through a list of values.
4. Click **OK**.

Using Ortho

The **Ortho** feature restricts your cursor movement to 90-degree angles when you are inserting elements. This can be especially helpful when drawing elements like walls.

By default, Ortho is enabled. You can toggle it on and off using one of three methods.

To turn Ortho on or off:

- Press **F8** on your keyboard
- Click the **ORTHO** button on the Status bar

- Select **Settings > Program Settings**, then on the Drawing Aids page, check or uncheck the **Ortho (F8)** check box

Using Angle Snap

When the **Angle Snap** feature is turned on, your cursor snaps to specific angles when rotating an element. If you set your snap angle to 10°, for example, your cursor will snap at 10° intervals as you rotate the element.

By default, the Angle Snap is on. You can turn the Angle Snap on and off using one of three methods.

To turn the Angle Snap on or off:

- Press F6 on your keyboard
- Click the ANGLESNAP button on the Status bar

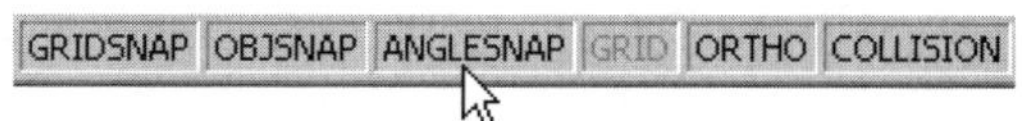

- Select **Settings > Program Settings**, then on the Drawing Aids page, check or uncheck the **Angle Snap (F6)** check box

To change the snap angle:

1. Select **Settings > Program Settings** or click the Program Settings button on the Settings toolbar. 
2. In the **Program Settings** dialog, select the Drawing Aids tab.
3. In the *Ortho / Angle Snap* area, type the desired snap angle in the **Snap Angle** edit box, or use the arrows to scroll up or down through a list of values.
4. Click **OK**.

Disabling/Enabling Collision Control

The program's intelligent **Collision Control** feature prevents objects from being inserted where they do not fit. By default, Collision Control is on, but you can turn it off whenever you like using one of three methods.

To turn Collision Control on or off:

- Press **F9** on your keyboard
- Click the **COLLISION** button on the Status bar

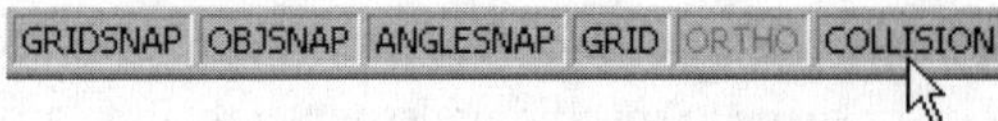

- Select **Settings > Program Settings**, then on the Drawing Aids page, check or uncheck the **Enable Collision Control (F9)** check box

Note: Collision Control affects building elements on the current building location only.

Chapter 23

Measurement

You can change the unit of measure used in a drawing, or select a different level of precision for your measurements.

Once you've drawn something, you can measure it using the Measure tool. You can also use the Area/Perimeter tool to instantly calculate the area of a room or building.

Changing the Unit of Measure

The units of measure used in your project are determined by a template, which by default is either a feet/inches template or millimeters template.

Once you've opened a new project, you can change the units of measure and levels of precision used in that project by making selections on the Units of Measure page of the **Program Settings** dialog.

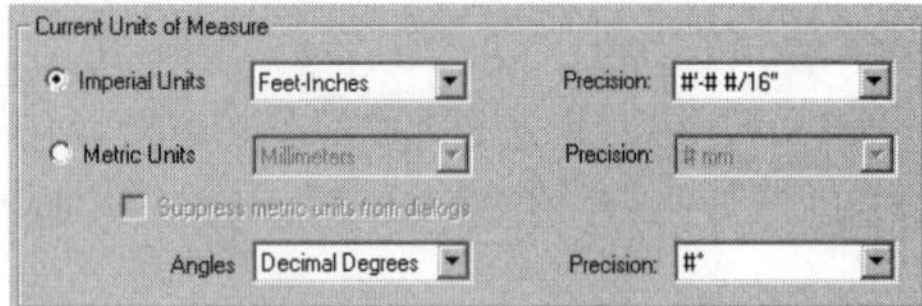

To set your units of measure:

1. Select **Settings > Program Settings** or click the Program Settings button on the Settings toolbar.
2. In the **Program Settings** dialog, select the Units of Measure tab.
3. Select either **Imperial Units** or **Metric Units**, then select the desired units to use.

Measure	Units Available
Imperial	Feet-Inches Inches
Metric	Millimeters Centimeters Meters

4. Select a level of precision for each unit of measure. For example, selecting #'-# #/16" sets the level of precision to 1/16th of an inch when working in feet and inches.
5. Once you've set your units of measure, click **OK**.

Suppressing Metric Units in Dialogs

If you have chosen to work in Metric units, you can choose to suppress units for length/distance, volume, and area measurements shown in dialogs. For example, 1200 mm would appear as simply 1200.

To suppress units:

1. Select **Settings > Program Settings** or click the Program Settings button on the Settings toolbar. 
2. In the **Program Settings** dialog, select the Units of Measure tab.
3. With **Metric Units** selected, enable the **Suppress metric units from dialogs** check box.
4. Click **OK**.

Measuring Distances

Use the Measure tool to measure the distance between any two points in your 2D plan.

To use the Measure tool:

1. Select **Tools > Measure**.
2. Click your first point on the screen.
3. Move your cursor in the direction you want to measure. A ruler is displayed that stretches as you move your cursor.

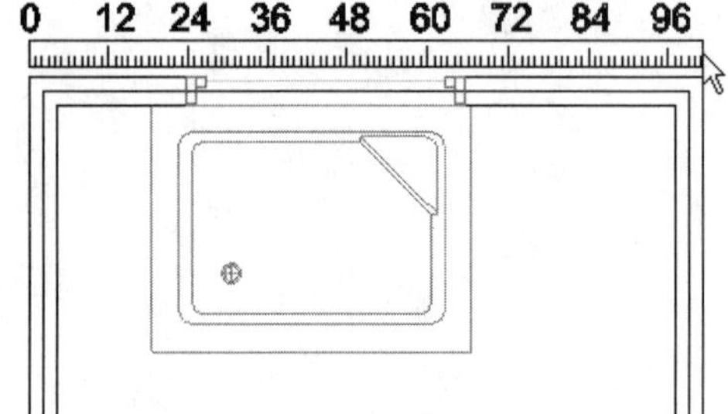

4. Click your second point on the screen. The distance is shown on the ruler as well as on the Status bar at the bottom of the screen.
5. Once you have measured your first distance, you can keep selecting points to measure

additional distances from the last point selected. A running total is displayed on the Status bar.

<Distance6'-10", Total Distance: 12'-8" >

6. When you have finished measuring, right-click and select **Finish**.

Measuring Area and Perimeter

The **Area/Perimeter Calculator** displays the area (e.g. square footage) and perimeter length of each location in your model. It also displays the total area and total perimeter (of all locations). You can use the calculator at any given point in time. The values in the calculator update automatically as your model increases or decreases in size.

Note the calculations are taken from the exterior side of the building's walls.

To measure area:

1. Select **Tools > Calculate/Estimate > Area/ Perimeter**.

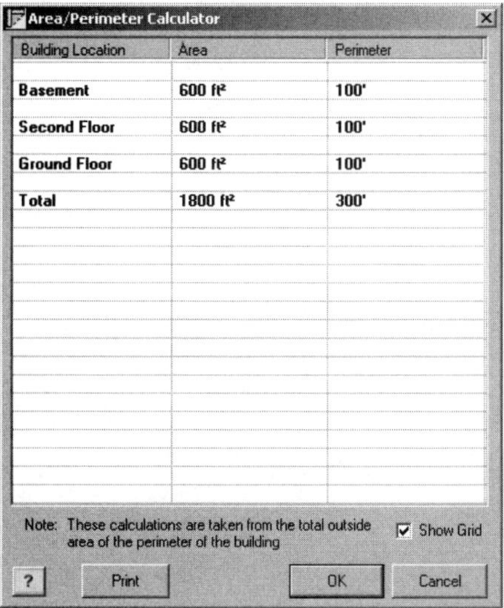

Building Location	Area	Perimeter
Basement	600 ft²	100'
Second Floor	600 ft²	100'
Ground Floor	600 ft²	100'
Total	1800 ft²	300'

2. To turn the grid lines off, uncheck the **Show Grid** check box.
3. To print the calculations, click **Print**.
4. When you are done viewing the area calculations, click **OK**.

Chapter 24

Commander

For very precise control when inserting or editing elements, *3D Home Architect® Home Design* offers a helpful tool called the Commander, which lets you view or enter exact values for distance, direction and angles. It is especially handy for users with some CAD experience.

This chapter tells you how to turn the Commander on, and how to use it.

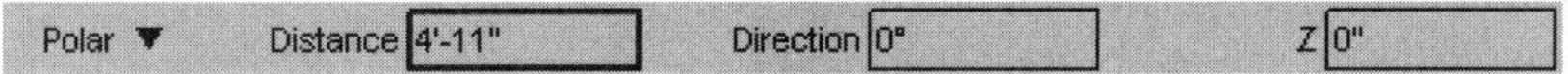

Displaying the Commander

The Commander is a multi-functional tool that lets you enter precise values when inserting or editing elements. Even if you don't need a high level of precision, you may want the Commander displayed so you can see lengths and angles as you draw or edit elements.

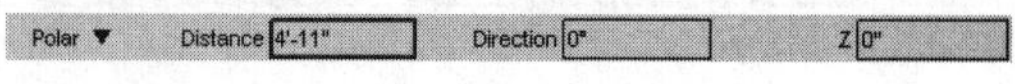

To display the Commander:

1. Select **Settings > Program Settings** or click the Program Settings button on the Settings toolbar.
2. In the **Program Settings** dialog, select the Workspace tab.
3. Check the **Commander** check box.
4. Click **OK**.

The Commander is displayed just below the drawing area, above the toolbar area. Initially the Commander will look grayed out because it is inactive. It will become active when you insert or edit elements.

Using the Commander

The Commander can be a very useful tool when inserting or editing elements. Using the Commander you can:

- Specify the insertion height of an element before it is inserted
- Select a precise insertion point for an element
- Specify a precise length and direction for elements like walls and railings
- Specify a precise distance and direction when stretching or moving an element
- Specify a precise angle when rotating an element
- Specify a precise radius/included angle when curving a wall, deck or opening

Even if you don't want to enter precise values, you can still use the Commander to view measurements as you draw and edit elements. The values in the Commander are linked to your cursor movement and update as you proceed through a command.

The Commander becomes instantly active when inserting elements. It is most useful for things like walls and railings, because it lets you enter a precise length for the element.

The Commander also becomes active when you are moving, stretching or rotating elements. If you have started moving, stretching or rotating an element using your mouse, the Commander displays the move distance or rotation angle as you move your mouse. If you want to be able the enter values in the Commander when moving, stretching or rotating an element, you need to first select an appropriate editing tool from the right-click menu or Edit > Modify Elements menu such as Move, Stretch, Lengthen, or Rotate.

Displaying the Coordinate Icon

The Coordinate Icon marks the current point from which an action will be performed. In other words, it identifies the current reference point when using the Commander. By default, this icon is turned off. If you plan to use the Commander while working, you should turn on the Coordinate Icon.

To display the Coordinate Icon:

1. Select **Settings > Program Settings** or click the Program Settings button on the Settings toolbar.

2. In the **Program Settings** dialog, select the Drawing Aids tab.
3. In the *Visual Aids* area, check the **Show Coordinate Icon** check box.
4. Click **OK**.

Specifying the Insertion Height of an Element Before You Insert It

If you have the Commander turned on, it will display a **Base Height** edit box as soon as an insertion tool becomes active.

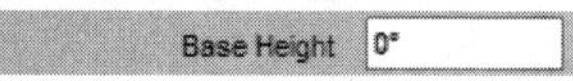

The value shown in the **Base Height** edit box is the height at which the element will insert in your drawing. You can change the insertion height before selecting an insertion point for the element by typing a value in the **Base Height** edit box and pressing ENTER. The height is measured from the floor level of the current building location to the element's insertion point. Most elements have their insertion point at the bottom of the element. Exceptions are windows and wall openings, in which the insertion point is located at the top of the element. In the case of windows and wall openings, the edit box reads "Head Height".

Selecting a Reference Point When Inserting and Editing Elements

To use the Commander, you must first specify a reference point, or base point, from which values can be measured. If you are drawing a wall, for example, the first point you click on the screen is considered the reference point. The Commander then becomes active, and you can enter a Distance and Direction (or X and Y values) for the wall.

If you want to use the Commander to edit an element (e.g. move or rotate it), you must select a point from which to measure the move distance/ direction, or rotation angle. Most often you would select one of the element's grab handles, which are the small blue squares that appear on the major points of an element when you select the element.

There are two ways to select a reference point once you've activated a tool:

- Click the point in your drawing.
- Enter coordinates, or X, Y and Z values, in the Commander. (See *Defining Points in the Cartesian Coordinate System* on page 162.)

Note that even if you choose to click the point in your drawing, you can see the coordinates of your cursor in the Commander as you move your mouse.

By default, coordinates are read from the last point selected in the drawing area. This point is marked by the Coordinate Icon (if enabled).

Entering Values in the Commander

The Commander is intelligent and changes depending on the tool you are using. For example, if you are drawing walls, the Commander's edit boxes become **Distance**, **Direction**, and **Z**. If you are curving walls, however, the edit boxes change to **Radius** and **Included Angle**.

You can move easily from one edit box to the next using your Tab key. Pressing ENTER after typing a value completes the current action.

When entering values in the Commander, especially when inserting or moving elements, it is important to be aware of the current coordinate system in the Commander.

The Commander offers two coordinate systems: Polar and Cartesian. The system you select determines how values are entered in the Commander when you are specifying points or distances.

Note that you can switch between the Polar and Cartesian coordinate system once you have selected a reference point to draw from or move from. You do this by making a selection from the coordinate system drop box on the left side of the Commander.

Note: If moving, stretching or rotating elements, and you want to enter values in the Commander, you need to first select an appropriate editing tool from the right-click menu or Edit > Modify Elements menu such as Move, Stretch, Lengthen or Rotate.

Direction and Angle of Rotation

Direction in a drawing is specified in degrees of an angle. The angle is calculated counterclockwise from the positive X axis.

The Four Primary Drawing Directions

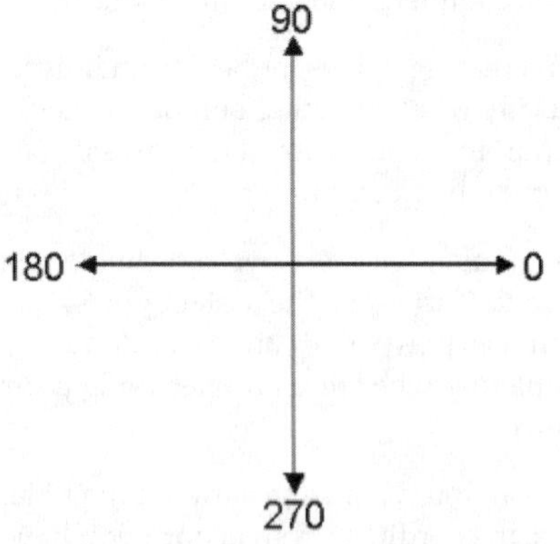

Although the four primary drawing directions are the ones you will probably be working with the most, any angle is possible. If you disable Ortho and Angle Snap, and move an element randomly in your drawing area, there is no restriction on angles at all. Even if Ortho and Angle Snap are enabled, you can enter any angle you want in the Commander.

Defining Points in the Cartesian Coordinate System

Initially when you start an insertion or editing command, the coordinate system is set to Cartesian. This lets you specify a precise reference point to draw or move from by entering X, Y and Z coordinate values in the Commander.

X. Enter an X coordinate to specify a horizontal (left/right) distance in 2D plan view.

Y. Enter a Y coordinate to specify a vertical (up/down) distance in 2D plan view.

Z. Enter a Z coordinate to indicate elevation, or height. If the element is a building element, the Z value is measured from the floor level of the current building location. If the element is a landscape element, the Z value is measured from the terrain.

Remember that the coordinates are measured from the current reference point, which is marked by the Coordinate Icon. (See *Entering Values in the Commander* on page 161.)

In the Cartesian system, you can enter both positive and negative values for any of the coordinates.

Specifying Distance and Direction in the Polar Coordinate System

The Polar coordinate system becomes active once you have selected a reference point to draw from, or start a move from.

In the Polar coordinate system, you specify a distance and direction (angle) when drawing or moving an element.

Distance. Enter a positive value to specify the length of the element, or the move distance.

Direction. Enter the direction you want the element to run, or the direction in which you want to move an element. For information about how direction is specified, see *Direction and Angle of Rotation* on page 162.

Z. Enter the distance you want to move the element vertically. You can enter a positive or negative value to move the element up or down. If the element is a building element, the Z value is measured from the floor level of the current building location. If the element is a landscape element, the Z value is measured from the terrain.

Using the Commander When Rotating Elements

When you select the Rotate tool from the right-click menu or Edit > Modify Elements menu, then select a base point for the rotation, the Commander displays a **Rotation Angle** edit box.

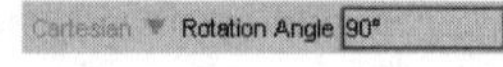

To specify the desired angle of rotation for the element, type the angle in the **Rotation Angle** edit box and press ENTER. For information on how angles are measured, see *Direction and Angle of Rotation* on page 162.

Using the Commander When Curving Elements

When curving an element such as a wall or floor opening, you can use the Commander to specify a precise curve angle.

Radius. The distance from the element (in its uncurved state) to the center point of the curve.

Included Angle. The angle formed between two radius lines extending from the center of the circle implied by the curve out to the endpoints of the arc. The larger the angle, the rounder and larger the curve.

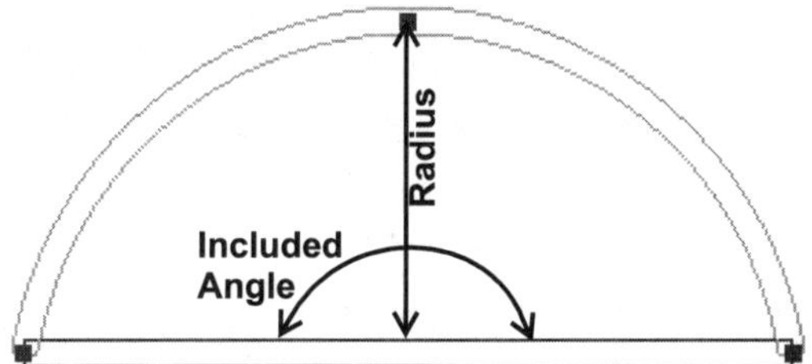

It is not necessary to enter both the Radius and Included Angle values. If you enter one, the program automatically supplies the other. Also, if you enter a value and nothing happens after you press ENTER, then the value is not valid in relation to the dimensions of your element.

Chapter 

Editing Your Design

When you double-click after inserting an element or select **Finish** from the right-click menu, you automatically go into Selection Mode, meaning you can select elements in your drawing area and edit them.

Most elements can be moved, rotated, copied and deleted. Some elements have additional editing commands available. For example, you can lengthen, break and curve walls. All elements have a property sheet where you can change the size or appearance of the element.

To access a menu of editing commands for a selected element, just right-click in the drawing area or select **Edit > Modify Elements**. Certain functions can be performed without selecting any commands at all. For example, you can move and rotate most elements by simply clicking and dragging your mouse.

This chapter describes how to select elements, and use general editing commands like Move, Rotate, Elevate, Duplicate and Delete. It also describes how to access and edit element properties. For information about editing a specific type of element, see the chapter about that element.

Undoing the Previous Action

The Undo tool cancels your most recent action. You can undo as many actions as you have taken since your last save.

To undo an action:

- Select **Edit > Undo**, or
- Click the Undo button on the Standard toolbar, or 
- Press **Ctrl+Z**

Tip: You can use the Redo tool to reapply an action you have canceled using the Undo tool.

Redoing an Undo

The Redo tool reapplies a tool that you have reversed using Undo. Redo will only work directly following an Undo.

To redo a task:

- Select **Edit > Redo**, or
- Click the Redo button on the Standard toolbar, or 
- Press **Ctrl+Y**

Accessing Edit Commands

When you have an element selected, you can access a menu of edit commands by right-clicking in the drawing area, or by selecting **Edit > Modify Elements**.

Menus vary depending on the element selected. Typical commands are Properties, Move, Rotate, Duplicate, and Delete. If two types of elements are selected (such as a floor and a wall), only commands that are common to both element types are available.

Certain functions can be performed without selecting any commands at all. For example, you can move and rotate most elements by simply clicking and dragging your mouse.

Moving Elements

When you select an element, you are automatically in Drag and Drop mode. If the element is a singular, one-click object, like a cabinet or plant, you can move the element by simply clicking and dragging it. If you want to move an area-drawn element, such as a roof, you need to select the Move Whole Element tool before clicking and dragging Otherwise, doing a straight drag-and-drop will only stretch it. If you click and drag a wall, all walls attached to it move with it.

If you have your Commander turned on and would like to be able to enter precise values for the move, you need to select the Move tool instead of doing a straight drag-and-drop.

Note: Elements associated with walls, such as doors and windows, can only be moved within the wall they are in. You cannot move them to another wall.

Doing a Straight Drag-and-Drop

The straight drag-and-drop method is ideal for singular, one-click elements like cabinets and plants.

To move an element using drag-and-drop:

1. Select the element you want to move. You are now in Drag and Drop mode.
2. Hover your pointer over the element's center grab handle to display the Move cursor. 
3. Click and drag to move the element.
4. When the element is where you want it, release the mouse button.

Using the Move Tool

Use the Move tool when you want to be able to specify a precise distance and direction for the move in the Commander.

To move an element using the Move tool:

1. Select the element you want to move.
2. Right-click and select **Move**, or select **Edit > Modify Elements > Move**.
3. Select a base point for the move. The move distance and direction will be measured from this point.

4. Without holding your mouse button down, move your mouse to move the element. Select the point you want to move the element to, or enter a distance and direction in the Commander.

Raising or Lowering an Element

Most elements can be raised or lowered using the Elevate tool on the element's right-click menu. Some elements, such as roofs, do not provide access to the Elevate tool. In the case of a roof, you can raise or lower it by changing the Support Height variable in its properties.

Many block elements (like furniture and appliances) also have a **Distance above current location or terrain** variable in their properties that you can use to raise or lower the element. Walls have an **Extension Below Base** variable, and columns have a **Base Offset** variable in their properties that you can edit.

To raise or lower an element using the Elevate tool:

1. Select the element you want to raise or lower.
2. Right-click and select **Elevate**, or select **Edit > Modify Elements > Elevate**. The value shown in the **Elevate** dialog is the current elevation of the element.
3. In the **Elevate** dialog, specify the desired elevation of the element above the floor. If the element is a landscaping element, the value you specify is relative to the terrain. The distance you enter is the distance from the floor or terrain to the insertion point of the element. For most elements, the insertion point is at the base of the element. For windows and wall openings, however, the insertion point is at the top of the element. Therefore, if you are raising or lowering a window or wall opening, specify the desired distance from the floor to the top of the window or opening.
4. Click **OK**.

To raise or lower a block element by editing its properties:

1. Select the element you want to raise or lower.
2. Right-click and select **Properties**, or select **Edit > Modify Elements > Properties**.
3. In the properties dialog, select the Behavior tab. If there is no Behavior tab, you will need to use the Elevate tool to raise or lower the element.
4. Edit the value in the **Distance above current location or terrain** edit box.
5. Click **OK**.

Rotating Elements in 2D Plan View

Singular, one-click elements like cabinets and furniture can be rotated on the spot by simply clicking and dragging them while in Rotation mode.

Railings can be rotated by clicking and dragging their end points.

For most other elements such as walls, floors, ceilings or roofs, you need to use the Rotate tool. You also need to use the Rotate tool if you want to be able to enter a precise rotation angle in the Commander, or you want to rotate the element about a point other than the center point of the element.

Doing a Simple, On-the-Spot Rotation

If you see a triangular grab handle on an element when it is selected, it can be rotated by simply clicking and dragging it. Using this method, the element is rotated about its center point.

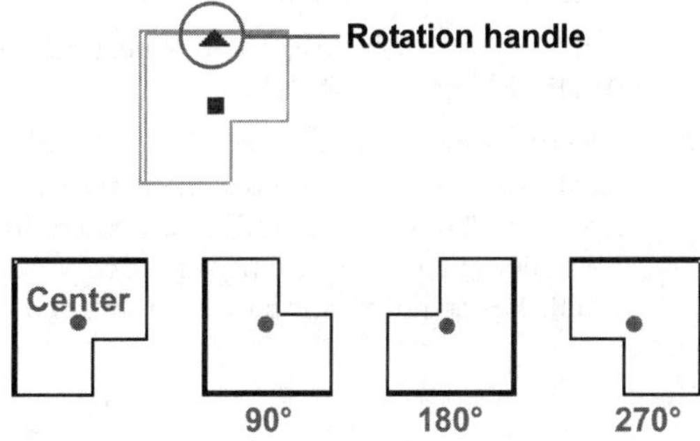

If your Angle Snap is on, the element will rotate in increments of whatever angle is set for the Angle Snap. If the Angle Snap is off, the element will rotate in increments of 1°.

To rotate an element by clicking and dragging:

1. Select the element you want to rotate.
2. Hover your pointer over the triangular grab handle to display the Rotate cursor. If you do not see the triangular grab handle, the element can only be rotated with the Rotate tool.

   Tip: If the square grab handle is in close proximity to the triangular grab handle, you may want to zoom in on the element to distinguish between the two grab handles.
3. Click and drag to rotate the element.
4. When the element is at the desired rotation, release your mouse button.

Using the Rotate Tool

Using the Rotate tool you can rotate an element about any selected base point. You should also use the Rotate tool if you want to be able to enter a precise rotation angle in the Commander.

If your Angle Snap is on, the element will rotate in increments of whatever angle is set for the Angle Snap. If you are using the Commander, you can override the Angle Snap by entering the desired angle in the Commander. If the Angle Snap is off, the element will rotate in increments of 1°.

To rotate an element using the Rotate tool:

1. Select the element to rotate.
2. Right-click and select **Rotate**, or select **Edit > Modify Elements > Rotate**.
3. Select a base point for the rotation. The base point can be any point on the element (e.g. center point or corner point), or any point in the drawing area. The point you pick establishes an automatic baseline that runs through the point at 180°. You can rotate full-circle around this baseline.

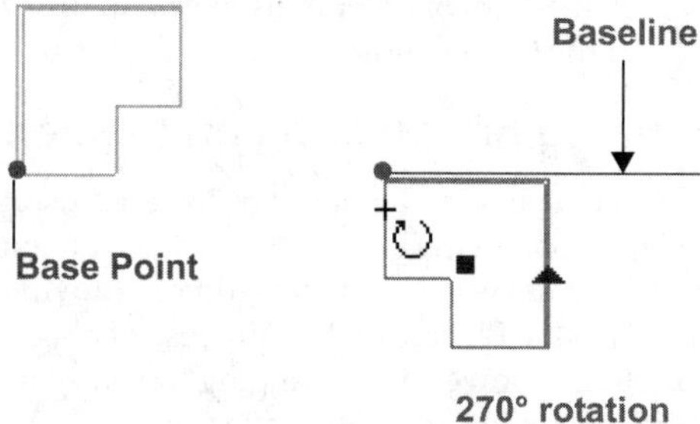

   Tip: If you want to align an element with another element that may be lying at an odd angle, select a base point on the other element, then line up your rotation line with that element.
4. Without holding your mouse button down, move your mouse to rotate the element. The element will rotate from the defined base point in the direction you move the mouse. If the **Commander** is turned on, you can view the angle of rotation as you rotate, or enter a precise angle. Positive angle values are read in a counter-clockwise direction, while negative values are read in a clockwise direction.

Changing an Element's Orientation

Symbol elements, such as furniture and light fixtures, are oriented in a logical fashion when you insert them in your drawing. For example, tables are inserted in a flat, upright position on the floor, and electrical outlets are inserted in a vertical position on the face of walls. You can edit the orientation of most symbol elements. For example, you may want to flip an air register so that you can insert it on the ceiling in your basement.

To change an element's orientation:

1. Select the element.
2. Right-click and select **Properties**, or select **Edit > Modify Elements > Properties**.

3. On the Basic property page, click the appropriate arrow keys in the *Orientation* area to rotate the element.

   (Y, Z) axes: Rotates the element front to back, and vice versa.

   (X, Z) axes: Rotates the element towards its left or right side in 3D.

   (X, Y) axes: Rotates the element left or right in 2D plan view.

Copying Elements on the Same Location

The Duplicate tool creates a copy of a selected element that you can then position where you like on the current location.

To duplicate an element:

1. Select the element to copy.
2. Right-click and select **Duplicate**, or select **Edit > Modify Elements > Duplicate**.
3. Select a base point for the copy movement. Typically you would select one of the element's grab handles, but you can click anywhere in the drawing. The base point is simply a reference point used to define the move distance.
4. Select the point you are copying the element to. You can do this by moving your mouse and then clicking to insert the copy, or by typing a distance and direction in the Commander.

Copying Elements to Other Locations

The Duplicate to Locations tool lets you copy existing elements to other locations. This is useful if the elements you have already drawn will have the same layout on another location. For example, you can copy the exterior walls on the Ground Floor to the Second Floor and instantly create another story.

To copy elements to other locations:

1. Make sure the location you want to copy elements FROM is current.
2. Select the elements you want to copy.
3. Right-click and select **Duplicate to Locations**.
4. Select the target location(s) you want to copy the elements to.
5. Click **OK**.

Note: The location you are copying to must exist in the **Building Locations** dialog. For more information see *Defining Building Locations* on page 18.

Arraying Elements

When you array elements, you create multiple copies of an element at the same time. You can create an array in a single row or column, or a layout of rows and columns. You can also control the spacing between elements in the array, and the array's rotation angle.

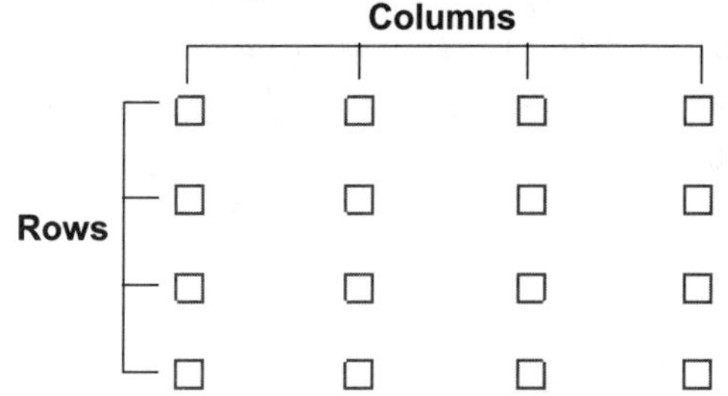

Sample array of posts

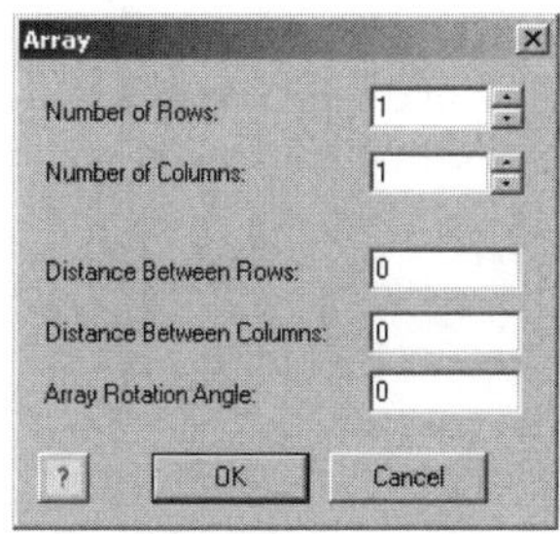

To array an element:

1. Select the element you want to array.
2. Right-click and select **Array**, or select **Edit > Modify Elements > Array**.

3. In the **Number of Rows** box, type the number of horizontal rows you want or use the arrows to select a value.
4. In the **Number of Columns** box, type the number of vertical columns you want.
5. In the **Distance Between Rows** box, type the spacing you want between rows. This determines the distance between elements appearing in columns (vertical spacing).
6. In the **Distance Between Columns** box, type the spacing you want between columns. This determines the distance between elements appearing in rows (horizontal spacing).

   Note: If you are working in Imperial, make sure you include the feet symbol (e.g. 4') if the value is in feet. Otherwise, the value is taken as inches.
7. In the **Array Rotation Angle** box, type the degree of rotation for the array.
8. Click **OK**. The array is created.

Note: The Array tool is only available for certain elements.

Deleting Elements

You can delete an element from your drawing in two quick steps.

To delete an element:

1. Select the element.
2. Press the **Delete** key on your keyboard, or right-click and select **Delete**, or select **Edit > Modify Elements > Delete.**

Editing the Size and Composition of an Element

You can edit the physical make-up of an element as well as its dimensions by accessing the element's Basic property page. Some elements have additional property pages that control its composition. For example, cabinets have Leaf and Details property pages.

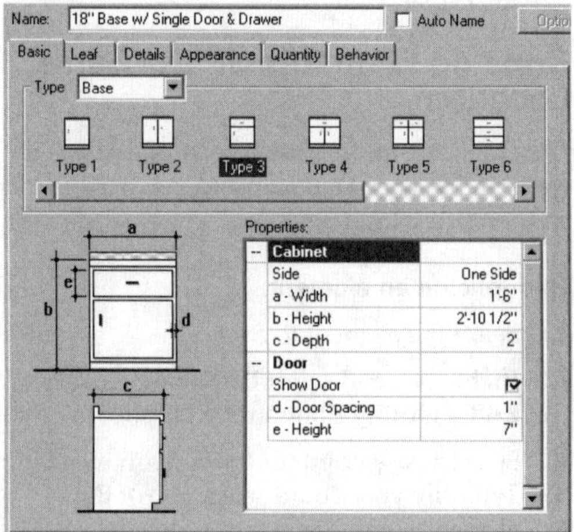

When you edit the properties of elements that exist in your drawing, only selected elements are changed. Other occurrences of the element in your drawing remain unchanged. You can, however, select and edit multiple elements at the same time provided they share the same properties.

To edit the properties of an inserted element:

1. Select the element you want to edit. To select multiple elements, use Shift + click.
2. Right-click and select **Properties**, or select **Edit > Modify Elements > Properties.**
3. Adjust the properties as desired. Clicking a dimension marked with an alphabetical character (a, b, c, etc.) highlights the corresponding dimension in the element graphic, and vice versa, if one exists.
4. Click **OK**. The selected elements are updated in the drawing.

Note: Editing the properties of an element in your drawing has no effect on the element's property definition in the catalog it came from. If you want to edit an element in a catalog, see *Adding and Editing Elements in a Catalog* on page 247. Editing an element in a catalog affects all future insertions of that element in your drawing.

Changing an Element's Material or Color

When you view your design in Rendered or Patterned mode, elements are displayed using materials that are defined in the elements' properties. A material can be a texture, such as brick, or a color. Materials also have a pattern assigned to them, which is what you see when you view in Patterned view. You can select a different material for each of an element's components.

Note: You can't change the way an element looks in 2D plan view.

There are two ways to change an element's material settings: using the Materials Paintbrush, or through the element's Appearance property page.

The Materials Paintbrush is best used in 3D view. It lets you select a material or color in the catalog, then apply it to parts of an element. For example, if you want your table legs to be blue, you can select the Blue Paint material, then click on of the table's legs. All table legs will update automatically. When you use the Materials Paintbrush on an element, the settings on the element's Appearance property page update to match the selections you made with the Materials Paintbrush.

If you choose to edit an element's material through its Appearance property page, you can select different materials for each of the element's parts, rather than just a selected part. It doesn't matter if you're in a 2D view or 3D view.

To use the Materials Paintbrush:

1. Select **Edit > Materials Paintbrush**, or click the Materials Paintbrush button on any tabbed toolbar. 
2. In the catalog panel, select the material you want to apply. There is an incredible selection to choose from, including Wood, Brick, Marble, Concrete, Steel, Carpet, Tile, Roofing and Fabric. If you want to apply a solid color select something from the Paint category.

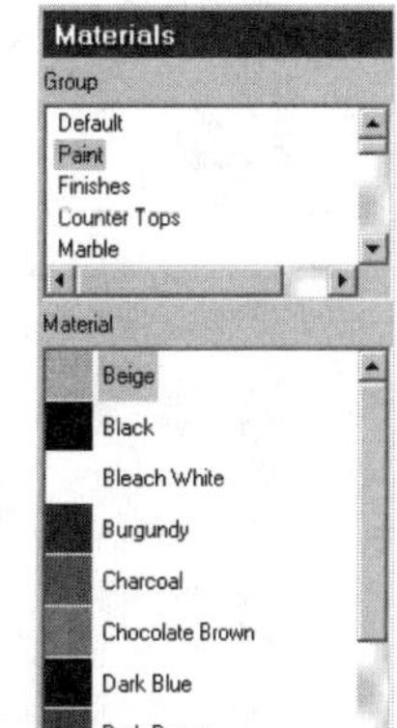

3. In 3D view, click on the element part that you want to apply the material to. The material is immediately applied.
4. Right-click and select **Finish**.

To change an element's material through the Appearance property page:

1. Select the element you want to edit. To select multiple elements, use Shift + click.
2. Right-click and select **Properties**, or select **Edit > Modify Elements > Properties**.
3. Select the **Appearance** tab.

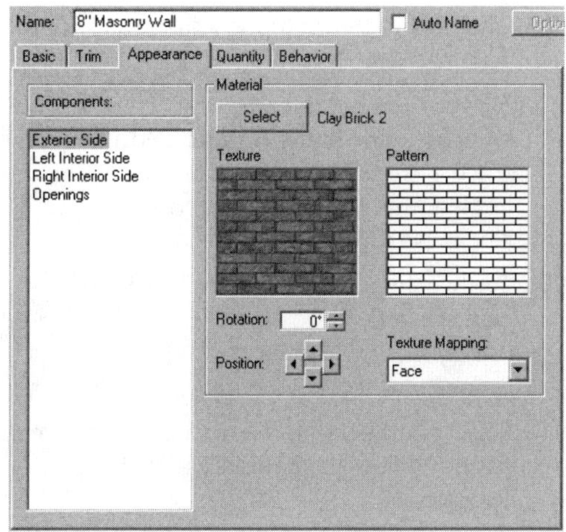

4. In the *Components* pane, select the component whose material you want to change.
5. In the *Material* area, click the **Select** button.

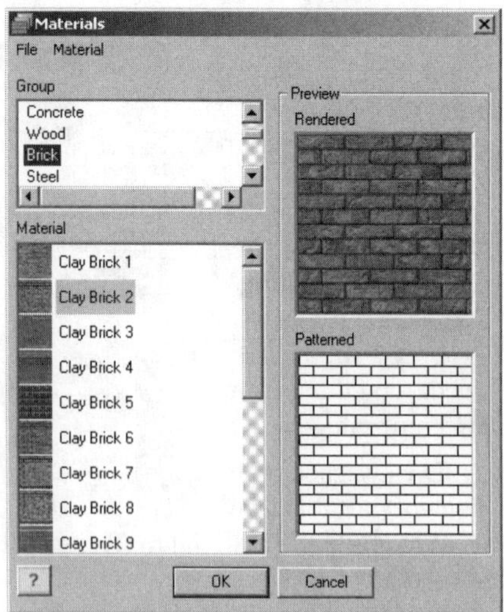

6. In the **Materials** dialog, select the group containing the desired material. If you want to choose a solid color, select the Paint group.
7. Select the material you want to use. The swatches in the preview windows update automatically. If you want to edit the material, click on one of the swatches to access the **Edit Materials** dialog. For information about editing materials, see *Editing Material Properties* on page 261.
8. Click **OK** to return to the Appearance page.
9. If you want to rotate the material on the element, enter an angle in the **Rotation** edit box, or use the arrows to scroll through a list of angles. This rotates the material in a clockwise direction.
10. To shift the material on the element (left, right, up or down), use the **Position** arrows.

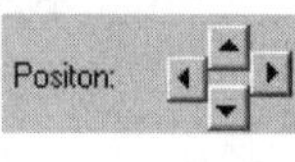

11. Select another component in the *Components* pane and select a material for that component.
12. When all your materials are defined, click **OK**.

Note: When you edit the material of an element in your drawing, the element's material definition in the catalog does not change. The change only applies to the selected element. If you want to change the element's properties in the catalog, see *Adding and Editing Elements in a Catalog* on page 247.

Part 7

Power Tools

Chapter 26

Project Trace Image

Using the Project Trace Image tool you can import a BMP, JPG or TGA file into your drawing space. You can then trace the image using elements from the catalog, creating a true *3D Home Architect® Home Design* model. This is the perfect tool to use if you have sketched out ideas in a drawing program or scanned a floor plan that you have permission to use, and want to recreate the plan in *3D Home Architect® Home Design*.

You can resize the image if you need to before tracing, and delete it once you're done tracing.

Most floor plans are copyrighted, so make sure you have permission to copy them.

Importing an Image to Trace

You can import a BMP, JPG or TGA image, such as a scanned floor plan, and trace it using elements from the catalog, creating a true *3D Home Architect® Home Design* model.

To import an image to trace:

1. In 2D plan view, select **File > Import > Project Trace Image**.
2. In the **Open** dialog, select the file type you are importing from the **File type** drop box. You can import BMP, JPG or TGA files.
3. Locate the file to import, then click **Open**.

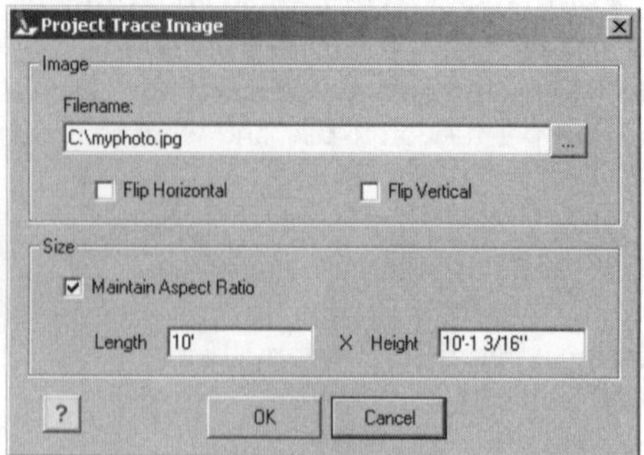

4. If you want to reverse the image (i.e. flip it left to right), enable the **Flip Horizontal** check box. If you want to flip the image vertically (so it is upside down), enable the **Flip Vertical** check box.
5. To change the scale of the image, enter the dimensions in the **Length** and **Height** edit boxes. Typically you would use the overall dimensions shown on the floor plan. For example, if the house is 70′ long, enter 70′ in the **Length** edit box. Keeping the **Maintain Aspect Ratio** check box enabled ensures that the image scales uniformly when one of the dimensions is changed. This prevents the image from becoming distorted.
6. Click **OK**. A bounding box is attached to your cursor.
7. Position the box in your drawing area, then click to insert it. The image is displayed.

Matching the Floor Plan's Drawing Scale

If the floor plan is not the right size, you can scale it up or down to match the plan's drawing scale. Having a correct drawing scale is important for tracing purposes so elements can be created at the correct size.

To resize a project trace image:

1. Select the trace image.
2. Right-click and select **Resize Image**, or select **Edit > Modify Elements > Resize Image**.
3. Find a wall with a known length, then select a point at each end of the wall.

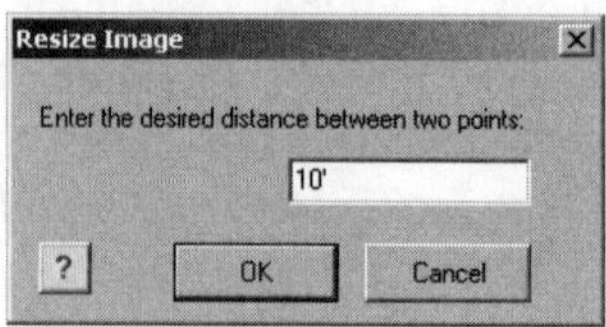

4. In the **Resize Image** dialog, enter the distance between the two points as shown on the floor plan, then click **OK**. The image is scaled instantly.

Tracing the Imported Floor Plan

Tracing an imported image is easy — just use the Insert tools described earlier in this User's Guide.

- To trace foundation walls, see *Creating a Basement or Crawlspace Foundation* on page 46.
- To trace ground floor exterior walls, see *Drawing the Ground Floor Exterior Walls* on page 56.
- To trace interior walls, see *Drawing Interior Walls* on page 59.
- To insert doors, see *Inserting Doors* on page 64.
- To insert windows, see *Inserting Windows* on page 68.
- To insert wall openings, see *Inserting Wall Openings* on page 72.
- To insert stairs, see *Inserting Stairs and Ramps* on page 84.

Deleting a Project Trace Image

Once you're done tracing a floor plan, you can delete the trace image from your drawing, leaving just your *3D Home Architect® Home Design* model on the screen.

To delete a project trace image:

1. Select the trace image.
2. Press the **Delete** key on your keyboard, or right-click and select **Delete**, or select **Edit > Modify Elements > Delete**.

Note: If you prefer you can just hide the project trace image from view instead of deleting it. See *Displaying/Hiding Project Trace Images* on page 37.

Chapter 27

Photo Boards

3D Home Architect® Home Design lets you import digital photographs or scanned images into your work space. The image is oriented vertically in 3D view, much like a billboard. You could, for example, import a picture of your backyard, so when you look out the window, it feels like you're home.

A photo board can be stationary or set to rotate with the camera so it's always facing you. You can also control the height and width of the photo board.

The handy **Photo Board Wizard** steps you through the process quickly and easily.

Importing a Photo Board

A photo board is simply a digital image that is oriented vertically in your 3D workspace. You can import any image you want — your family, pets, neighbor's house — the only limit is your imagination. The handy Photo Board Wizard does it all in a few quick steps.

To import a photo board:

1. Select **File > Import > Photo Board Wizard**.

2. Click **Next**.

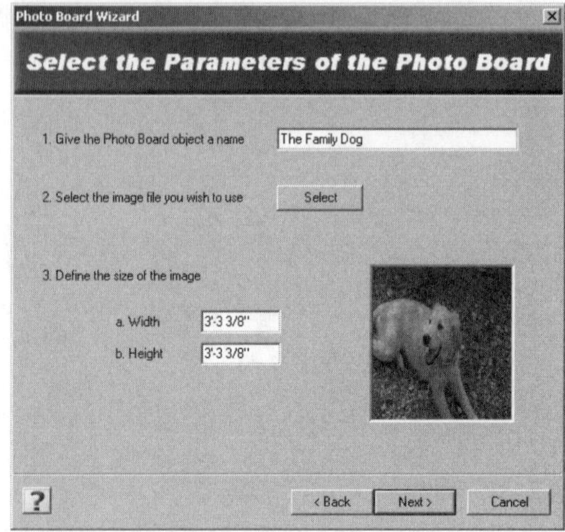

3. Type a name for your photo board.
4. Click the **Select** button, then select the image you want to import. You can import BMP, JPG and TGA files. The image is displayed in the preview window.
5. Define the size of the image by entering values in the **Height** and **Width** edit boxes. Generally you should specify a size that is as close to reality as possible. For example, if the image is of a person who is six feet tall, you should enter a value close to 6′ in the **Height** edit box.
6. Click **Next**.

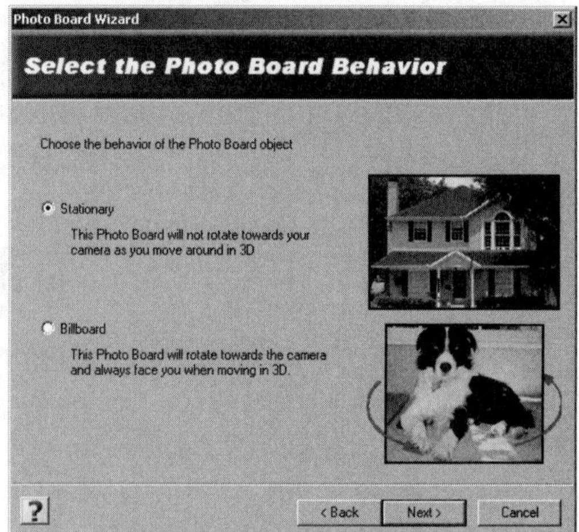

7. Specify whether you want the photo board to be stationary or active. If **Stationary** is selected, the board will always remain oriented the same way, regardless of changes in your camera angle. If **Billboard** is selected, the photo board will rotate toward the camera so it will always face you in 3D.

8. Click **Next**.

9. Click **Finish**. The photo board is attached to your cursor, ready to be inserted.
10. Position the photo board where you want it, then click to insert it.
11. Right-click and select **Finish**.

Adding an Imported Photo Board to Your Catalog

You can save a photo board that you have imported using the Photo Board Wizard to your catalog so you can insert it again in any project.

To save your photo board to the current catalog:

1. Select **File > Catalogs > Save Element to Catalog**. Your pointer changes to a catalog cursor.

2. Click on the photo board in your drawing.

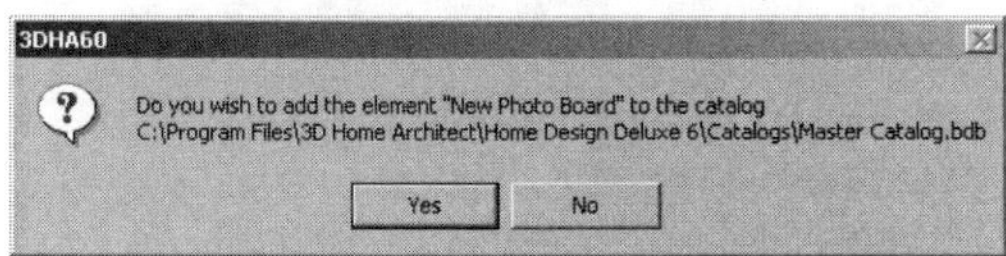

3. Click **Yes** to save the photo board. The photo board is added to the current catalog.

Inserting a Photo Board from the Catalog

The catalog contains a collection of photo boards containing pictures of animals. If you have saved your imported photo board to the catalog, it is also displayed with the existing photo boards in the catalog.

To insert a photo board from the catalog:

1. Select **Insert > Photo Board**.
2. In the catalog panel, select the photo board you want to insert.
3. Position the photo board where you want it, then click to insert it.
4. Right-click and select **Finish**.

Moving a Photo Board

You can move a photo board easily by just clicking and dragging it.

To move a photo board:

1. Select the photo board.
2. Hover your pointer over the board to display the Move cursor.

3. Click and drag to move the board.
4. When the board is where you want it, release your mouse button.

Rotating a Photo Board in 2D Plan View

You can use the Rotate tool to rotate a photo board about a selected point in 2D plan view.

To rotate a photo board:

1. Select the photo board.
2. Right-click and select **Rotate**, or select **Edit > Modify Elements > Rotate**.
3. Hover your pointer over the point you want to rotate the photo board around.
4. Click and drag to rotate the photo board, then release your mouse button.

Changing the Elevation of a Photo Board

You can raise or lower a photo board using the Elevate tool on the right-click menu.

To raise or lower a photo board:

1. Select the photo board.
2. Right-click and select **Elevate**, or select **Edit > Modify Elements > Elevate**. The value shown in the **Elevate** dialog is the current elevation of the photo board.
3. In the **Elevate** dialog, specify the desired elevation of the photo board above the terrain.
4. Click **OK**.

Tip: You can also change a photo board's elevation by changing the **Distance above current location or terrain** variable on the photo board's Behavior property page.

Changing a Photo Board from Stationary to Rotating and Vice Versa

You can choose whether a photo board is stationary or rotating after it has been inserted. A stationary board keeps the same orientation regardless of changes in the camera angle. A rotating board always rotates towards the camera.

To change a photo board's type:

1. Select the photo board.
2. Right-click and select **Properties**, or select **Edit > Modify Elements > Properties**.
3. In the *Type* area, click **Stationary** for a stationary photo board, or **Billboard** for a rotating photo board.
4. Click **OK**.

Editing the Size of a Photo Board

You can edit the height and width of a photo board after it has been inserted.

To edit the size of a photo board:

1. Select the photo board.
2. Right-click and select **Properties**, or select **Edit > Modify Elements > Properties**.
3. Edit the **Height** or **Width** in the Properties area. If **Maintain Aspect Ratio** is checked, the height will automatically change if you edit the width, and vice versa. This ensures the image doesn't get distorted.
4. Click **OK**.

Deleting a Photo Board

You can delete a photo board in a couple of easy steps.

To delete a photo board:

1. Select the photo board.
2. Press the **Delete** key on your keyboard, right-click and select **Delete**, or select **Edit > Modify Elements > Delete.**

Creating Transparency in Photo Board Images

You may find that you want to make portions of your photo board image transparent for a more realistic effect. If the image is of a person, for example, you may want to make the background in the image transparent so that when you insert the photo board in your drawing, you see just the person in your 3D view.

To create transparency in your photo board image, you need to use a graphic editing program such as Microsoft® Paint to apply a magenta color to those portions you want to make transparent.

The RGB color settings for magenta are as follows:

Red: 255 **Green**: 0 **Blue**: 255

Once you have finished editing the image in the graphic editing program, you can re-import the image into *3D Home Architect® Home Design* using the Photo Board Wizard.

Photo board with no transparency

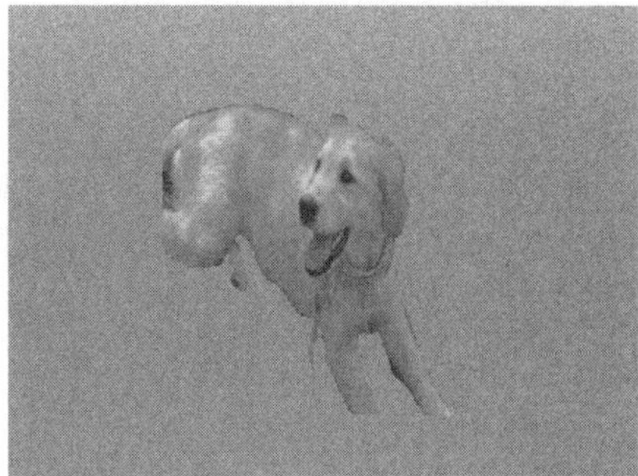

Photo board with transparency

Chapter 28

Text & Dimensions

Using text tools you can add text to any area of your drawing. You may want to add a title to the plan, or label rooms or specific elements. You can use whatever fonts and colors you want.

Dimensions are used to convey precise measurements. You can dimension the exterior of your design instantly, and quickly insert interior dimensions with a few simple mouse clicks.

This chapter describes all text and dimension tools.

Adding Text to Your Drawing

You can add text of varying size, color and font to your drawings. Text can be moved and rotated after it has been inserted, just like most other elements.

To add text to your drawing:

1. Select **Tools > Text > Add Text**, or click the Add Text button on the Notation toolbar.

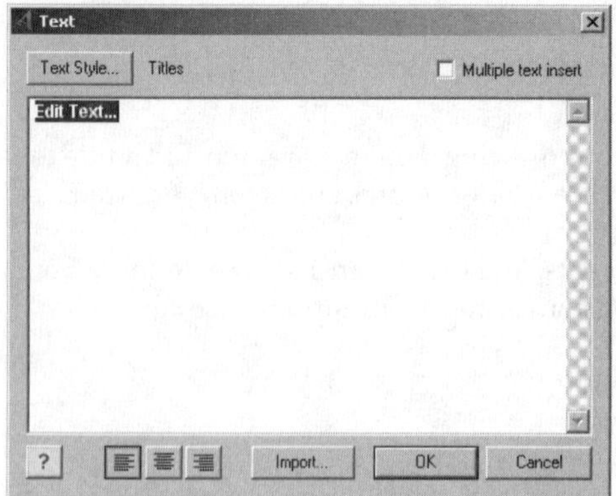

2. In the **Text** dialog, type the text you want to add. If you want to import a text (*.txt) file, click **Import**, then select the file to import.
3. To select a style for the text, click the **Text Style** button and select or create a text style in the **Text Styles** dialog.
4. By default, text is left justified. For multi-line text, this means that text lines will line up on the left, and be ragged on the right. If you want to change the justification of the text, click the appropriate button in the bottom left corner of the dialog.

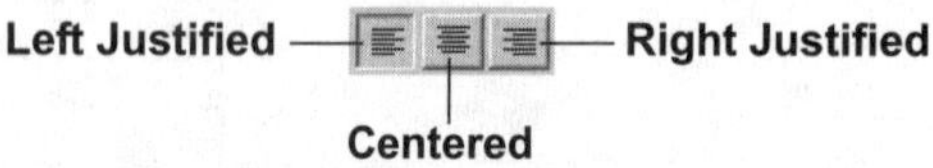

5. If you want to automatically return to the **Text** dialog after you have inserted the current text, enable the **Multiple text insert** check box. This is ideal when you want to insert different pieces of text in your drawing without having to select the **Add Text** tool again.
6. Click **OK**. The text is attached to your cursor.
7. Position the text where you want it, then click to insert it.

Moving Text

You can move text by simply clicking and dragging it.

To move text:

1. Select the text you want to move.
2. Position your pointer over the blue grab handle to display the Move cursor.
3. Click and drag to move the text, then release your mouse button.

Rotating Text

You can change the angle of text using the Rotate tool.

To rotate text:

1. Select the text you want to rotate.
2. Right-click and select **Rotate**, or select **Edit > Modify Elements > Rotate**.
3. Hover your pointer over the point you want to rotate around — typically the blue grab handle.
4. Move your mouse to rotate the text in the desired direction.
5. When the text is at the desired rotation, click to set the position.

Editing Text Content

You can edit the content of a text element by accessing its properties.

To edit text:

1. Select the text you want to edit.
2. Right-click and select **Properties**, or select **Edit > Modify Elements > Properties**.
3. In the **Text** dialog, edit the text in the text window.
4. Click **OK**.

Changing the Style of Text

Text style settings include font, font style, size, and color. You can select a different text style for selected text, or edit individual text style properties.

To change the style of text:

1. Select the text whose style you want to change.
2. Right-click and select **Properties**, or select **Edit > Modify Elements > Properties.**
3. In the **Text** dialog, click **Text Style.**

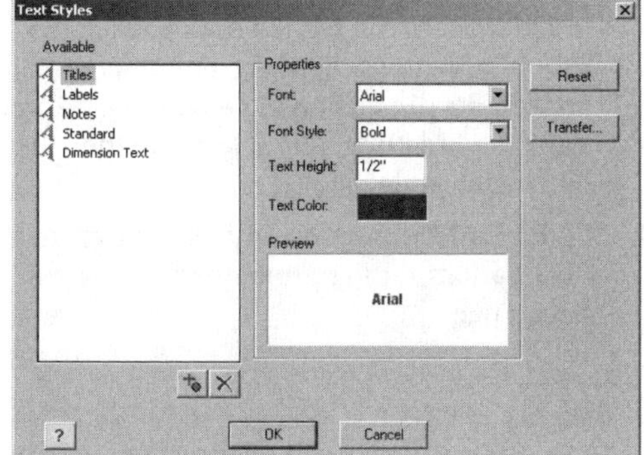

4. In the **Text Styles** dialog, select a new text style, or edit the individual properties of the current text style.

   You can also create a new text style by clicking the Add Item button. 

   Font. A set of text characters in a specific style and size.

   Font Style. The style of text. Choices can include Regular, Italic, Bold, and Bold Italic.

   Text Height. The size of text.

   Text Color. The color of text. Click the swatch to access the **Color** dialog and select a color.
5. Click **OK** in the **Text Styles** dialog.
6. Click **OK** in the **Text** dialog. The text is changed automatically.

Note: Text styles that are edited or added through inserted text are saved with the current project only. If you want to save them in the text styles library file, so that they can be made available in other projects, see *Saving Customized Text Styles to the Text Styles Library File* on page 275.

Changing the Justification of Multi-line Text

You can change the way multiple lines of text are aligned.

To change the justification of text:

1. Select the text you want to edit.
2. Right-click and select **Properties**, or select **Edit > Modify Elements > Properties.**
3. In the **Text** dialog, click the appropriate justification button below the editing window.

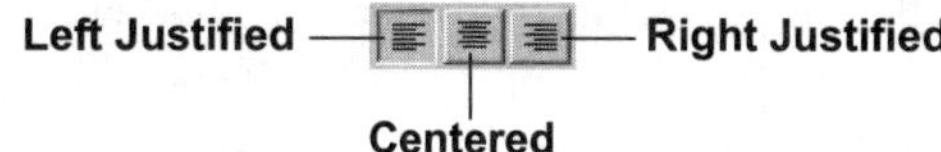

4. Click **OK**.

Deleting Text

You can delete selected text from your drawing in a couple of easy steps.

To delete text:

1. Select the text you want to remove. You can select multiple entries using Shift+click.
2. Press the **Delete** key on your keyboard, or right-click and select **Delete**, or select **Edit > Modify Elements > Delete.**

Adding Text with a Leader

You can insert text with an arrow attached to it that points to a particular element or area in your drawing. The leader has two segments and can be oriented in any fashion.

To add a text with leader:

1. Select **Tools > Text > Add Text with Leader**, or click the Add Text with Leader button on the Notation toolbar.

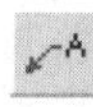

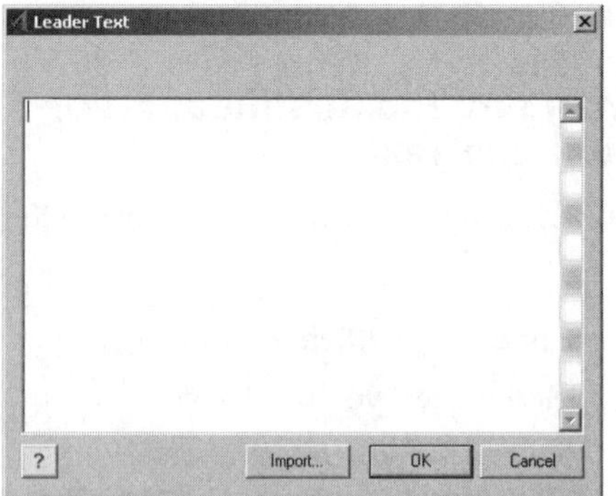

2. In the **Leader Text** dialog, type the text you want to appear with the leader, then click **OK**.
3. In the drawing area, select the point where you want the arrowhead to appear.
4. Move your pointer to stretch the leader, then select the middle point of the leader.
5. Select a third point for the leader. The text is inserted.

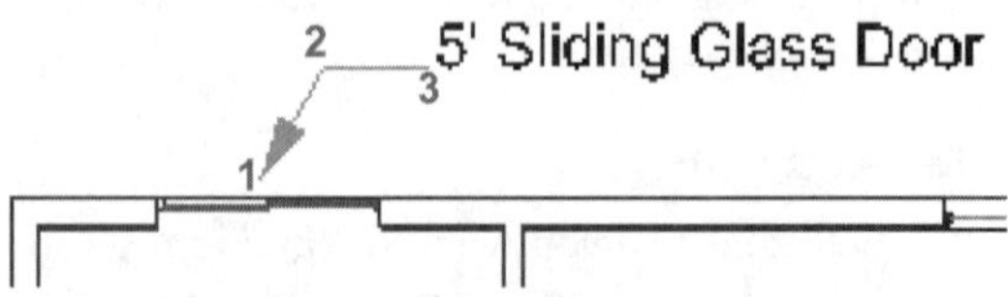

Moving and Stretching a Leader

You can move or stretch a leader by clicking and dragging its grab handles.

To move/stretch a leader:

1. Click on the text with leader to select it. Grab handles appear on the leader.
2. Click and drag a grab handle to move the handle, then release your mouse button.

Changing the Leader Arrow Style

The leader arrow style is determined by the current dimension style, which by default is the Standard dimension style. You can change the style of the leader arrow by editing the properties of the dimension style, or by selecting a dimension style with the desired arrow style setting.

To change the style of a leader arrow:

1. Click on the text with leader to select it.
2. Right-click and select **Properties**, or select **Edit > Modify Elements > Properties.**
3. In the **Dimension Styles** dialog, click the **Edit** button. (Alternatively, if you have imported a dimension style with the desired arrow style setting, just select it in the dimension style list.)
4. In the **Edit Dimension Styles** dialog, enable the **Leaders** radio button on the *Lines and arrows* page.

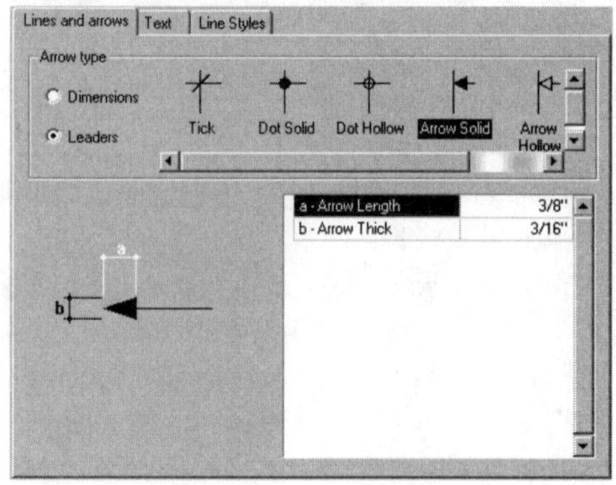

5. Select the desired arrow style in the *Arrow type* area. You can change the dimensions of the arrow in the parameters window.
6. Click **OK** in the **Edit Dimension Styles** dialog.
7. Click **OK** in the **Dimension Styles** dialog.

Moving Leader Text

If you have inserted text with a leader, you can move the text independently of the leader.

To move leader text:

1. Click on the text with leader to select it.
2. Right-click and select **Move Text**, or select **Edit > Modify Elements > Move Text**.
3. Click and drag the text to move it, then release your mouse button.

Editing Leader Text

If you have inserted text with a leader, you can change the text to whatever you want.

To edit leader text:

1. Click on the text with leader to select it.
2. Right-click and select **Edit Text**, or select **Edit > Modify Elements > Edit Text**.
3. In the **Leader Text** dialog, edit the text as desired, then click **OK**.

Deleting Text with a Leader

You can delete text with a leader in a couple of easy steps.

To delete a leader with text:

1. Click on any part of the leader or text. The entire leader with text is selected.
2. Press the **Delete** key on your keyboard, or right-click and select **Delete**, or select **Edit > Modify Elements > Delete**.

Dimensioning

3D Home Architect® Home Design automatically displays on-screen dimensions as you draw, making it easy to draw walls at correct lengths, and insert elements like doors and windows precisely where you want them. These dimensions are drawing aids only that disappear once you have inserted the element.

Using *3D Home Architect® Home Design*'s selection of Dimension tools, you can add fixed dimensions to your drawing to convey the precise measurements of your floor plan. You can control the style of these dimensions, and move and stretch them if you need to.

Setting the Current Dimension Style

When you add dimensions to your drawing, they use the current dimension style, which by default is the Standard dimension style. To view the properties of the current style, or select a different style to use, you need to access the Dimension Styles library for the current drawing.

To set the current dimension style:

1. Select **Settings > Dimension Styles**.

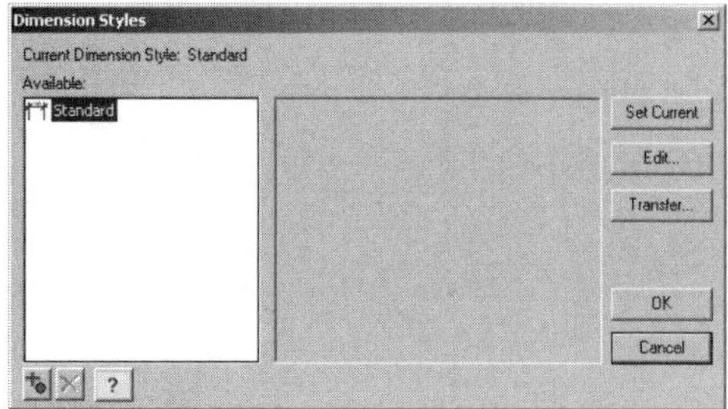

2. Select the style you want to use. To view or edit the properties of the style, click **Edit**. See *Dimension Style Properties* on page 194 for more information.
3. Click **Set Current** to set the selected style as current.
4. Click **OK**.

Creating Automatic Exterior Dimensions

The Apply Auto Exterior Dimensions tool automatically dimensions the exterior walls of your home. By default, three dimension strings are created: one for openings, one for wall segments, and an overall dimension for each side of the model.

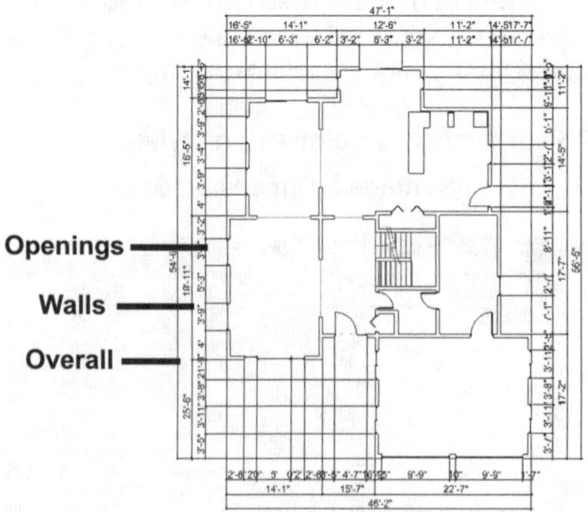

Note: You can control which dimension strings are created, as well as how walls and wall elements are dimensioned. You must specify these settings before the dimensions are created. See *Specifying Exterior Dimension Settings* on page 190.

To create automatic exterior dimensions:

1. Select **Tools > Dimensions > Apply Auto Exterior Dimensions**, or click the Apply Auto Exterior Dimensions button on the Notation toolbar. 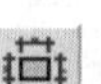

Specifying Exterior Dimension Settings

Before using the Apply Auto Exterior Dimensions tool to create automatic exterior wall dimensions, it is a good idea to specify the settings for the exterior dimensions. These settings control how the walls and wall elements (doors, windows, openings, etc.) are dimensioned.

To specify exterior dimension settings:

1. Select **Settings > Auto Dimension Settings**.

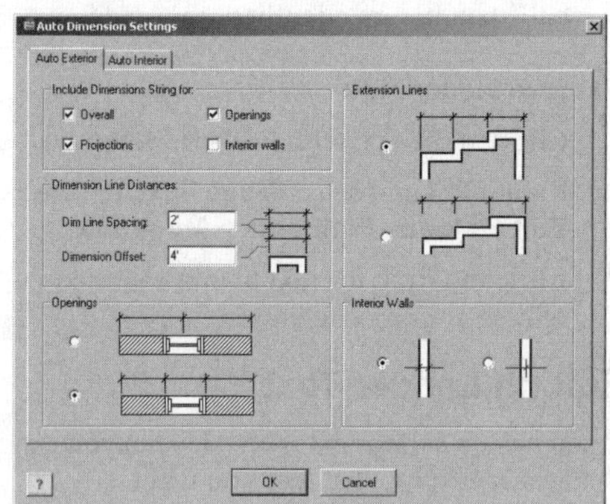

2. In the **Auto Dimension Settings** dialog, specify your settings on the Auto Exterior page. They are described below.

Include Dimension String for:

Overall. The outermost dimension string that dimensions the overall length of each exterior wall.

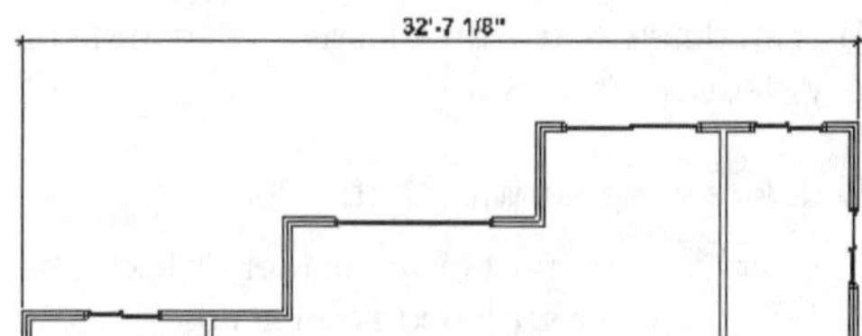

Projections. String that dimensions all projecting points along an exterior wall. If a wall has no projections, this string will be identical to the overall dimension string.

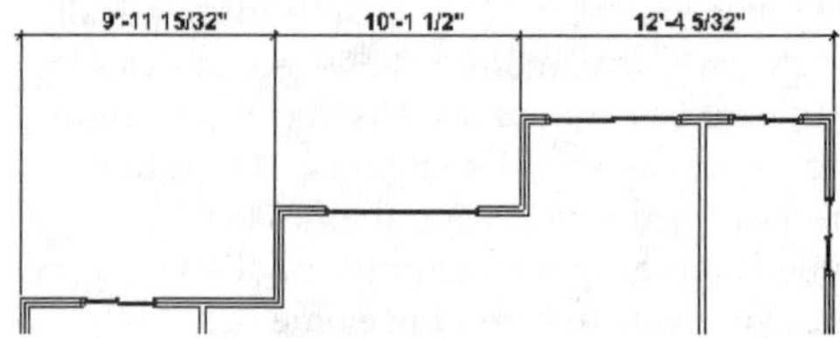

Openings: String that dimensions all major projections and all openings in the exterior walls, including door and window openings. Openings can be dimensioned on center, or to the outside edges (see the **Openings** area of the dialog).

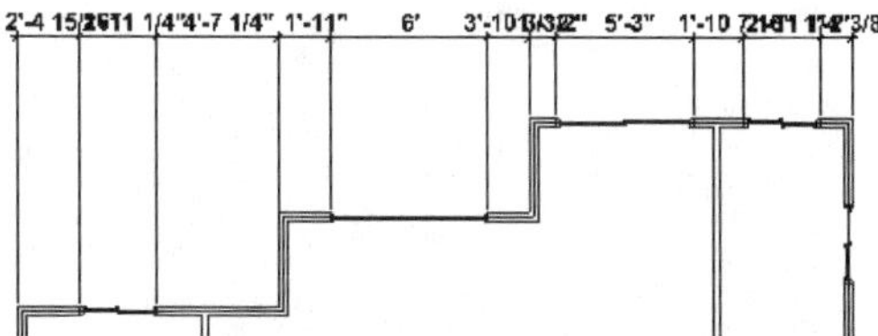

Interior Walls: String that dimensions to all major projections and each interior wall that projects into the exterior wall. Interior walls can be dimensioned on center, or to the walls' outside edges (this is specified in the **Interior Walls** area of the dialog).

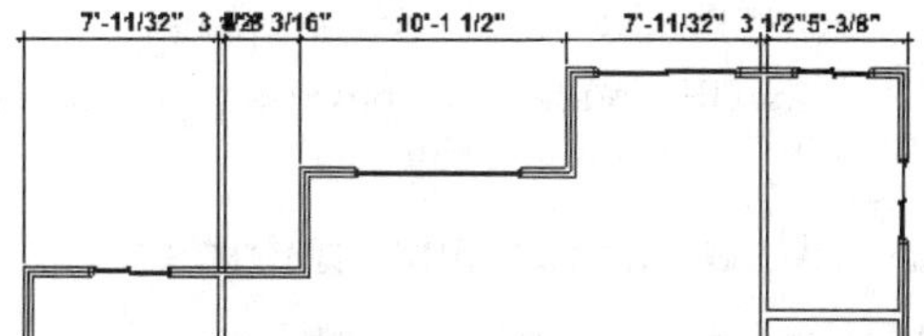

Dimension Line Distances

Dim Line Spacing: The spacing between successive dimension lines (when two or more strings are used).

Dimension Offset: The distance between the first dimension string and the walls.

Openings

If you are including a dimension string for openings, you can specify whether you want the openings to be dimensioned on center, or to the edges of the openings.

Extension Lines

Extension lines extend from the dimension line toward the walls being dimensioned. In situations where dimension points are not parallel with each other, you can specify whether you want the extension lines to extend all the way to the dimension points, or whether you want them to line up with the shortest dimension point.

Interior Walls

If you are including the **Interior Walls** dimension string, you can specify whether you want the walls to be dimensioned on center, or to the walls' outside edges.

Creating Auto Interior Dimensions

The Auto Interior Dimensions tool automatically dimensions interior walls in your model.

To create automatic interior wall dimensions, you draw a base line through your model. Dimensions are created for any walls along that line (running in the same direction as the line).

Before creating automatic interior dimensions, you may want to specify the interior dimension setting, which determines exactly how the walls are dimensioned. See *Specifying Interior Dimension Settings* on page 192.

To create automatic interior dimensions:

1. Select **Tools > Dimensions > Auto Interior Dimensions**, or click the Auto Interior Dimensions button on the Notation toolbar. 
2. Select a start point for the base line that is outside of the model.

3. Select an end point for the base line that is outside of the model. Dimensions are created along that line.

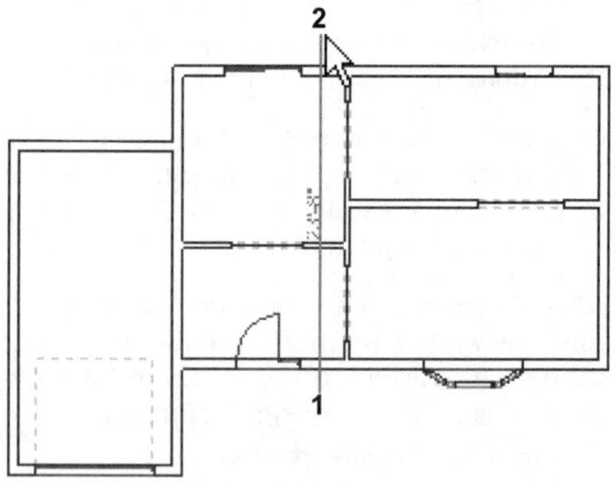

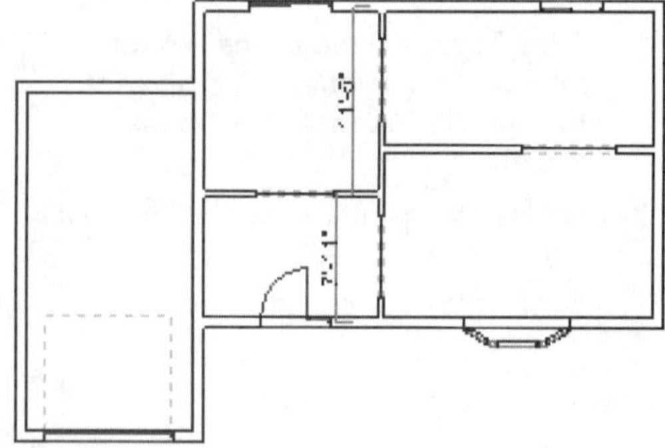

4. Right-click and select **Finish**.

Specifying Interior Dimension Settings

If you are using the Auto Interior Dimensions tool to create automatic interior wall dimensions, you can specify how you want the walls dimensioned before creating the dimensions. By default, walls are dimensioned on center. If you prefer you can dimension walls to one side or both sides.

To specify the auto interior dimension setting:

1. Select **Settings > Auto Dimension Settings**.
2. In the **Auto Dimension Settings** dialog, select the Auto Interior tab.

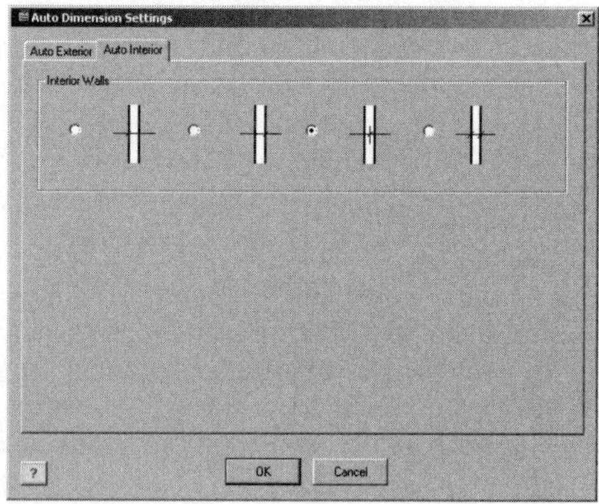

3. Select the desired dimension option.
4. Click **OK**. You can now proceed with creating auto interior dimensions.

Creating Linear Dimensions

A linear dimension is a horizontal or vertical dimension with extension lines going vertically (for a horizontal linear dimension) or horizontally (for a vertical linear dimension) to the origins of the extension lines, which define the endpoint of the dimension.

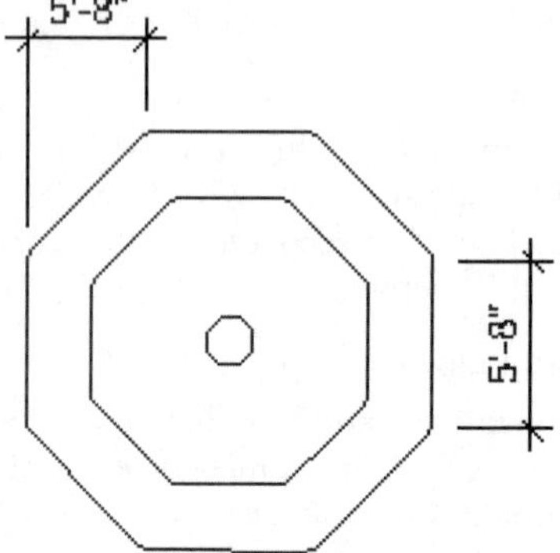

This tool is ideal for creating interior dimensions, or dimensions on a landscape plan.

To create linear dimensions:

1. Select **Tools > Dimensions > Linear Dimensions**, or click the Linear Dimensions button on the Notation toolbar. 
2. Click a point in your drawing to begin the dimension line.
3. Move your mouse (you do not have to hold the mouse button down) to a second point and click. A dimension line including offsets, arrows and a numerical value is added to your drawing.
4. Move your mouse away from the dimension line to stretch your extension lines. When the extension lines are the desired length, click to finish the dimension.

Creating Aligned Dimensions

An aligned dimension is similar to a linear dimension, except it tilts to the same angle as the element you are dimensioning, making it the ideal choice for elements that are not horizontal or vertical.

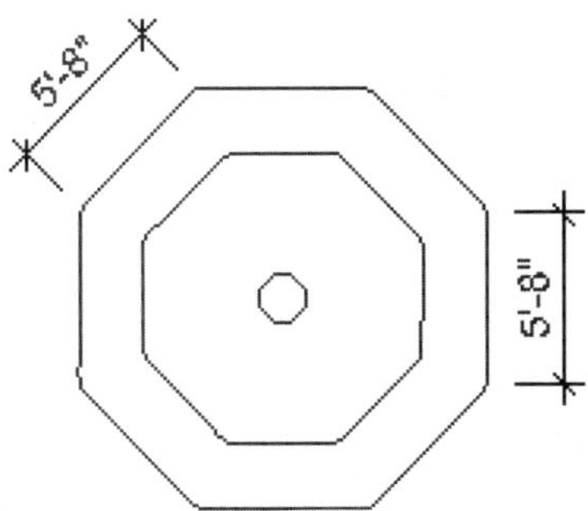

To create aligned dimensions:

1. Select **Tools > Dimensions > Aligned Dimensions**, or click the Aligned Dimensions button on the Notation toolbar. 
2. Click a point in your drawing to begin the dimension line.
3. Move your mouse (you do not have to hold the mouse button down) to a second point and click. A dimension line including offsets, arrows and a numerical value is added to your drawing.
4. Move your mouse away from the dimension line to stretch your extension lines. When the extension lines are the desired length, click to finish the dimension.

Moving a Dimension Line

You can move a dimension line using the Move Dimension Line tool. When you move a dimension line, the extension lines stretch to accommodate the move.

To move a dimension line using the Move Dimension Line tool:

1. Select the dimension.
2. Right-click and select **Move Dimension Line**, or select **Edit > Modify Elements > Move Dimension Line**.
3. Click any point to serve as the base point for the move.
4. Move your mouse in the direction you want to move the dimension line.
5. Click to finish the move.

Stretching Dimensions

You can make a dimension longer or shorter, or stretch either of its extension lines. When you stretch the length of a dimension, the dimension value updates automatically to reflect the new length.

To adjust the length of a dimension:

1. Select the dimension.
2. Click on one of the lower extension grab handles, then drag the dimension to stretch it. Note that it is possible to stretch the extension line at the same time.

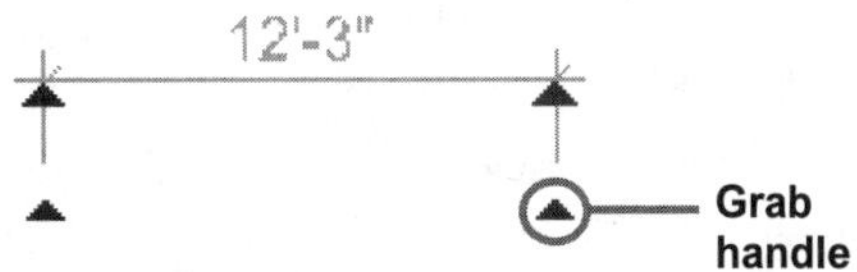

3. Release your mouse button.

To adjust the length of extension lines:

1. Select the dimension.
2. Click the grab handle at the end of the extension line, then drag to stretch the extension line.
3. Release your mouse button.

Changing the Style of a Dimension

You can change a dimension's line, arrow and text style by applying a different dimension style to it, or by editing dimension style properties.

To change the style of a dimension:

1. Select the dimension. You can select multiple dimensions using Shift+click.
2. Right-click and select **Properties**, or select **Edit > Modify Elements > Properties**.

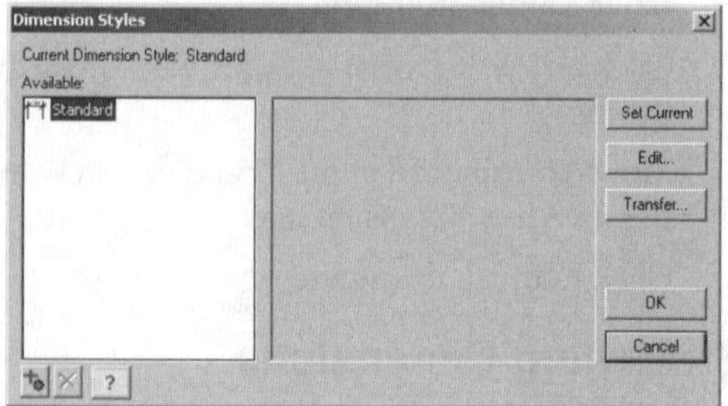

3. In the **Dimension Styles** dialog, select the style you want to apply to the dimension.

   To create a new dimension style, click the Add Item button, then type a name for the style and press ENTER.

   To edit the properties of the currently selected dimension style, click **Edit**, then make your changes in the **Edit Dimension Styles** dialog. See *Dimension Style Properties* on page 194.
4. With the desired style selected, click **Set Current**.
5. Click **OK**.

Note: Dimension styles that are edited or added through inserted dimensions are saved with the current project only. If you want to save them in the dimension styles library, so they can be made available in other projects, see *Saving Customized Dimension Styles to the Dimension Styles Library File* on page 279.

Deleting a Dimension

You can delete a dimension in a couple of easy steps.

To delete a dimension:

1. Select the dimension.
2. Press the **Delete** key on your keyboard, or right-click and select **Delete**, or select **Edit > Modify Elements > Delete**.

Dimension Style Properties

You can control a dimension's line, arrow and text style properties.

Anatomy of a Dimension

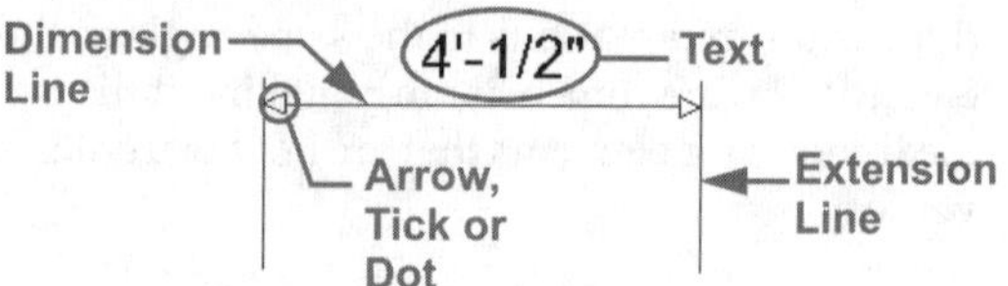

Lines and Arrows

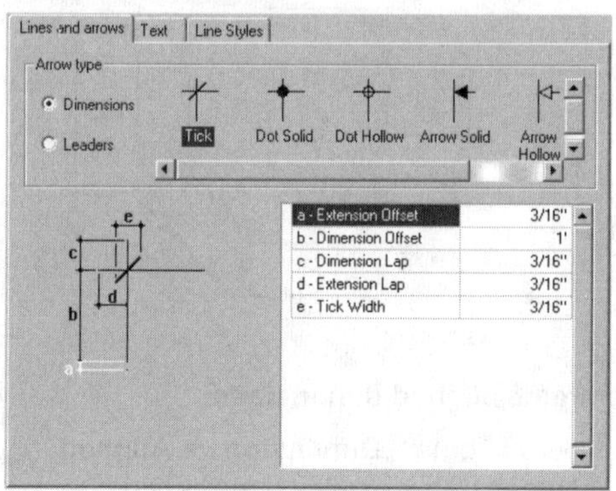

Arrow Type

You can specify an arrow type for dimensions and leaders (leaders are used with the Text with Leader tool). Choose an arrow, dot or tick for your arrow type.

The properties below the *Arrow Type* selection window (Extension Offset, Dimension Offset, etc.) vary depending on the arrow type selected. As you make different selections, the dimension updates in the preview window.

Dimension Text

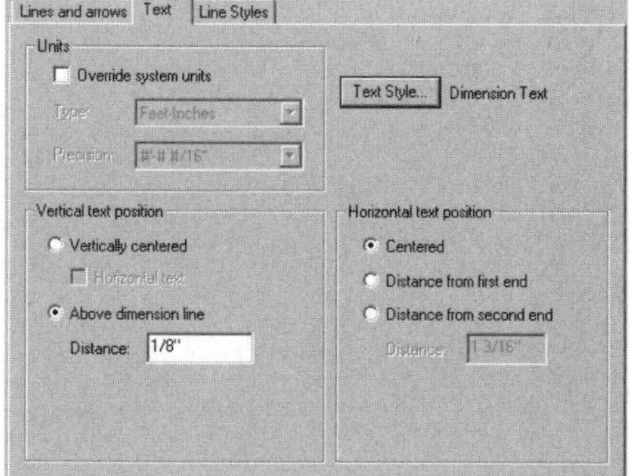

Units

The units (e.g. feet and inches) and precision used to display the dimension value.

Override system units: Uses the unit of measure specified in the **Edit Dimension Styles** dialog instead of the unit of measure specified in the program settings.

Type: Choose from Feet-Inches, Millimeters, Centimeters, Meters or Inches.

Precision: For Feet-Inches, the choices are whole units (0, 1/2, 1/4 and so on). For metric units, the choices are number of decimal places you can use.

Text Style

Refers to the font, font style, text height and color of the dimension text. Click **Text Style** to select a style.

Vertical Text Position

This is the vertical position of the dimension text relative to the dimension line.

Vertically Centered: Text is placed inside the dimension line.

Horizontal Text: Forces the dimension text to always be horizontal, regardless of the dimension line's angle.

Above Dimension Line: Text is placed above the dimension line.

Distance: Distance between the text and the dimension line when placing text above the dimension line.

Horizontal Text Position

This is the position of the dimension text relative to the ends of the dimension line.

Centered: Centers the text inside the dimension line.

Distance from first end: Places the text a specific distance from the first end of the dimension. Specify the distance in the Distance edit box.

Distance from the second end: Places the text a specific distance from the second end of the dimension. Specify the distance in the Distance edit box.

Line Styles

You can select a different line style for the dimension line, extension lines and arrows. A line style determines the line type and color.

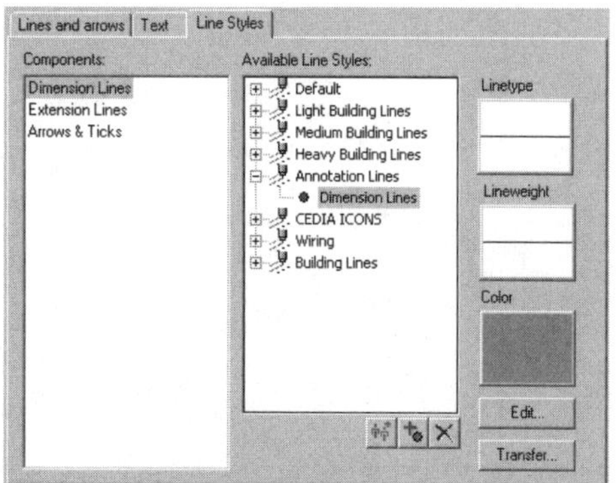

To assign a different line style to a dimension component, select the component in the left pane, then select the desired line style in the right pane.

For information about creating custom line styles, see the Linestyles chapter on page 267.

Chapter 29

Project Estimate

3D Home Architect® Home Design keeps track of all the materials you use to build your home as you design it. You can generate a project estimate with a single mouse click. The resulting estimate is displayed in a detailed spreadsheet that can be saved and printed. You can even choose what locations you want included in the estimate.

Sample unit prices are provided for your convenience, but you can specify custom pricing directly from your suppliers. The grand total is calculated for you automatically, making estimating a breeze!

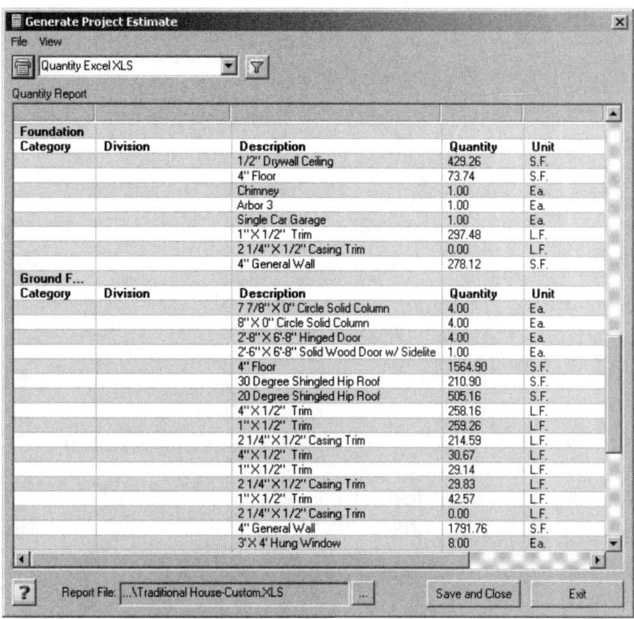

Generate Project Estimate
File View
Quantity Excel XLS
Quantity Report
Foundation
Category Division Description Quantity Unit
1/2" Drywall Ceiling 429.26 S.F.
4" Floor 73.74 S.F.
Chimney 1.00 Ea.
Arbor 3 1.00 Ea.
Single Car Garage 1.00 Ea.
1"X 1/2" Trim 297.48 L.F.
2 1/4"X 1/2" Casing Trim 0.00 L.F.
4" General Wall 278.12 S.F.
Ground F...
Category Division Description Quantity Unit
7 7/8"X 0" Circle Solid Column 4.00 Ea.
8"X 0" Circle Solid Column 4.00 Ea.
2'-8"X 6'-8" Hinged Door 4.00 Ea.
2'-6"X 6'-8" Solid Wood Door w/ Sidelite 1.00 Ea.
4" Floor 1564.90 S.F.
30 Degree Shingled Hip Roof 210.90 S.F.
20 Degree Shingled Hip Roof 505.16 S.F.
4"X 1/2" Trim 258.16 L.F.
1"X 1/2" Trim 259.26 L.F.
2 1/4"X 1/2" Casing Trim 214.59 L.F.
4"X 1/2" Trim 30.67 L.F.
1"X 1/2" Trim 29.14 L.F.
2 1/4"X 1/2" Casing Trim 29.83 L.F.
1"X 1/2" Trim 42.57 L.F.
2 1/4"X 1/2" Casing Trim 0.00 L.F.
4" General Wall 1791.76 S.F.
3'X 4' Hung Window 8.00 Ea.
Report File: ...\Traditional House-Custom.XLS
Save and Close
Exit

Generating a Project Estimate

You can view an accurate project estimate at any time during a design session. The estimate includes a list of materials, the quantities used, and pricing. The estimate is always up-to-date and reflects your project in its current state.

To generate a project estimate:

1. Select **Tools > Calculate/Estimate > Generate Project Estimate.**

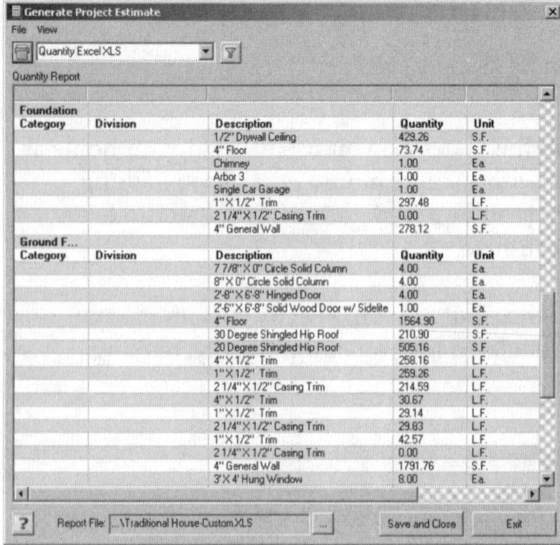

By default, the estimate is shown in *Microsoft® Excel* XLS spreadsheet format. You can switch it to a standard column report format, which can be saved as a TXT file. If you want you can remove the grid lines from the display.

Materials are grouped by location, and there is a terrain category for landscaping materials. You can choose to omit selected locations from the estimate if you want.

The estimate can be printed and saved.

To switch to a standard column report format:

1. In the **Generate Project Estimate** dialog, select **Standard Report Form** from the report form drop box.

To turn grid lines off:

1. In the **Generate Project Estimate** dialog, select **View > Show Grid.**

To filter locations from the estimate:

1. In the **Generate Project Estimate** dialog, click the Filter Report button beside the report form drop box. 

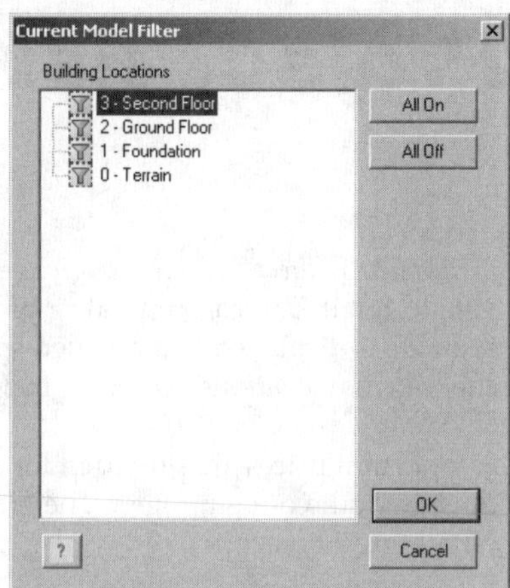

2. To omit a location and its elements from the project estimate, click the location's filter icon.
3. Click **OK**. The estimate is updated.

To print the estimate:

1. In the **Generate Project Estimate** dialog, select **File > Print**, or click the Print button to the left of the report form drop box. 
2. In the **Print** dialog, select the printer you want to use, then click **Print.**

To save the estimate:

1. In the **Generate Project Estimate** dialog, select **File > Save and Close**, or click the **Save and Close** button at the bottom of the dialog.

Note: By default, the estimate is saved in the same directory where the project is saved.

To save using a different file name or save location:

1. Click the Browse button next to the **Report File** edit box at the bottom of the **Generate Project Estimate** dialog.
2. In the **Report Filename** dialog, select the location where you want to save the estimate.
3. In the **File name** edit box, type the name you want to save under.
4. Click **Save**. The estimate is saved under the specified name and location.

To open the estimate in the associated editor:

1. Select **File > Open with Associated Editor**. If you haven't saved the estimate yet, it is saved for you. The estimate is then opened in the associated editor. For estimates in the XLS format, the estimate opens in *Microsoft® Excel*. For estimates in the Standard Report (TXT) format, the estimate opens in a text editor such as *Notepad*.

To close the Generate Project Estimate dialog:

1. Select **File > Exit**, or click the Close button in the top right corner of the dialog.

Opening a Saved Estimate

Once you have saved an estimate, you can open it any time in its associated editor (*Microsoft® Excel* or *Notepad*). You can then edit and print the estimate if you want.

To open a saved estimate:

1. Select **Tools > Calculate/Estimate > View Project Estimate**.

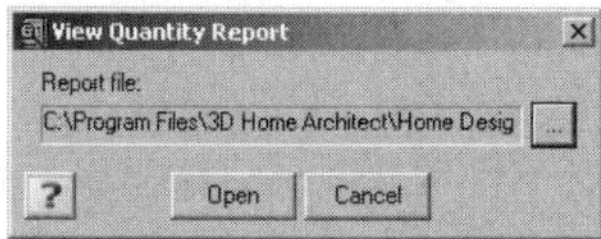

2. Click the Browse button, then locate the file to open.

3. Click **Open**. XLS files open in *Microsoft® Excel*, and TXT files open in a text editor such as *Notepad*.

Editing Material Pricing

Most elements have a default unit price set for them in their properties. These prices are used in the project estimate.

If you have already created your design, you can edit the prices of inserted elements by selecting them in the drawing, then editing their properties. Alternatively you can generate and save a project estimate, then edit the pricing in *Microsoft® Excel* or *Notepad*, depending on the report format you choose.

If you edit the price of any element in the catalog, the price change will affect all new insertions of the element.

To edit the price of an inserted element:

1. Select the element in your drawing. You can select multiple elements of the same type using Shift+click.
2. Right-click and select **Properties**, or select **Edit > Modify Elements > Properties**.
3. In the properties dialog, select the Quantity tab.

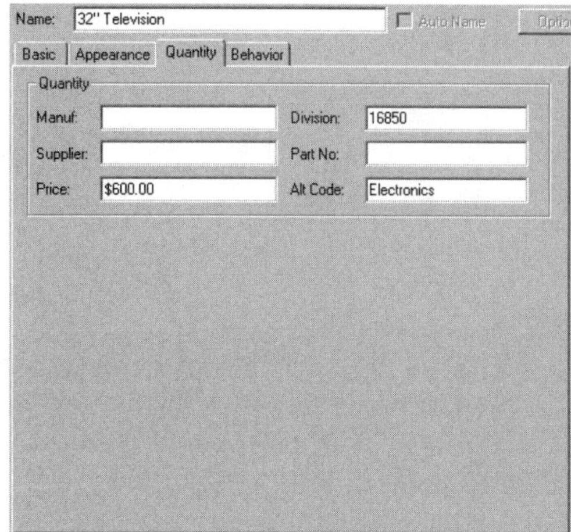

4. Edit the value in the **Price** edit box. Note that prices are unit prices. For a carpet, for example, you would enter the price per square foot, not the price of the entire carpet.
5. Click **OK** in the properties dialog.

To edit material pricing in the catalog:

1. Select **File > Catalogs > Catalog Manager**, or right-click and element in the catalog and select **Catalog Manager**.
2. From the **Element** drop box, select the element type you want to edit.
3. In the *Select a Type* window, select the group containing the element you want to edit.
4. In the *Select an Element* window, select the element to edit.
5. Select **Catalog > Element Properties**, or right-click and select **Properties**.
6. In the properties dialog, select the Quantity tab.
7. Edit the value in the **Price** edit box. Note that prices are unit prices. For a carpet, for example, you would enter the price per square foot, not the price of the entire carpet.
8. Click **OK** in the properties dialog.
9. Click **OK**.

Chapter 30

3DTrueView™

3D Home Architect® Home Design incorporates powerful 3DTrueView™ rendering technology. 3DTrueView™ rendering adds light and shadow to a textured 3D view to achieve stunning, photo-realistic images of both the interior and exterior of your home. These images can be printed directly from the screen. You can also choose to save the rendered image to a bitmap (BMP) or JPG file that you can then open in most graphic editing applications.

Creating a 3DTrueView™ rendering involves nothing more than a single mouse click. Just sit back and watch your design come to life!

How 3DTrueView™ Rendering Works

A rendered view is a photo realistic view that includes light and shadows. When you render a 3D scene, the program performs a series of lighting calculations to determine the lighting in a scene. These are also called *radiosity* calculations. Once a final result is met, the scene is *ray traced*, or rendered. Ray tracing works by tracing the path taken by a ray of light through the scene, and calculating the ray's reflection, refraction, or absorption whenever it intersects an element in the scene.

Material properties define how light reflects off a surface. Direct light and ambient light levels define the light that is reflected. Direct light is light that is emitted from light fixtures. It has a specific color, intensity and direction. Ambient light can be thought of as a general level of light that is everywhere in the scene. Every light in a scene contributes to the overall ambient light in a scene.

The first part of the radiosity process involves finding those element surfaces that are visible to direct light and calculating how much light is transferred to each element. Some elements will receive more light than others depending on their surface properties, and different surfaces will reflect different amounts of light. Still, each element will absorb some of the light, so the total amount reflected back into the scene will be less than that emitted by the light fixtures.

The next part of the process involves finding the element that reflects the most light, and repeating the process. The element is considered a secondary light source, so we need to calculate how much of its light is transferred to other elements in the scene. The process is repeated, one step at a time, until the amount of light remaining in the scene is negligible in comparison to the light originally emitted by the light fixtures. We then say that the radiosity calculations have converged to a solution, and that's when ray tracing begins.

Setting the Viewpoint for the Scene

When you create a 3DTrueView™ rendering, your model is captured at the angle currently shown on the screen. In most cases, the best type of view for 3DTrueView™ rendering is a Perspective view, because it is the most realistic. For information about 3D viewing, see *2D and 3D Viewing* on page 27. Specific topics you might want to look at:

- *Viewing in 3D* on page 29
- *Changing Your Viewpoint* on page 234
- *Selecting a Preset Camera Angle* on page 236
- *Changing the Viewing Field Angle* on page 237

Setting the Scene

Even though creating a 3DTrueView™ rendering involves nothing more than a mouse click, there are a few things you should consider beforehand.

Note: It doesn't matter what display mode (wireframe, patterned, etc.) you're currently in. 3DTrueView™ renderings will always be textured.

Exterior Shots

If you want to do an exterior shot, the most important factor to consider is sunlight. This is determined by your global position and time of day. By adjusting these settings, you control how much sunlight is in the scene, and from what angle it shines. See *Defining Your Location and Time of Day* on page 203.

Night Shots

To create a night shot, you need to first set your background to a night scene. See *Selecting a Background for 3D Views* on page 239. Once your background is set, all you need to do is set the time to a time of day when there is no sun.

Interior Shots

When creating interior shots, light comes from light fixtures that you have inserted in the room, and can also come through the windows if it is daytime. You can turn lights on and off as well as change their light bulbs for different light intensity and effect. For information about interior light fixtures, see *Interior Lighting* on page 129. To speed up the rendering process, you may want to turn off daylight temporarily so that only light from light fixtures is considered in the calculation. This is ideal when a room has small or covered windows, or no windows at all. See *Turning Daylight Off* on page 205.

Defining Your Location and Time of Day

You can define where your model is located in the world, as well as set the time of day. This determines how much daylight there will be in the scene.

To define your location and time of day:

1. Select **View > 3DTrueView > 3DTrueView Options**, or click the 3DTrueView Options button on the 3DTrueView toolbar.

2. In the **Program Settings** dialog, select the **Global Settings** tab.

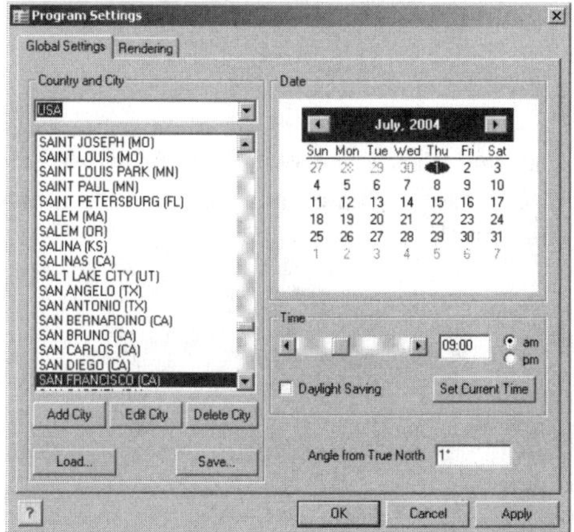

3. Select a country and city from the appropriate drop boxes. You can add or edit a city if needed. Just click the **Add City** or **Edit City** button. You will need to know the longitude, latitude and time zone of the city.

   You can save new or edited cities to the city template for use in other projects if you want.

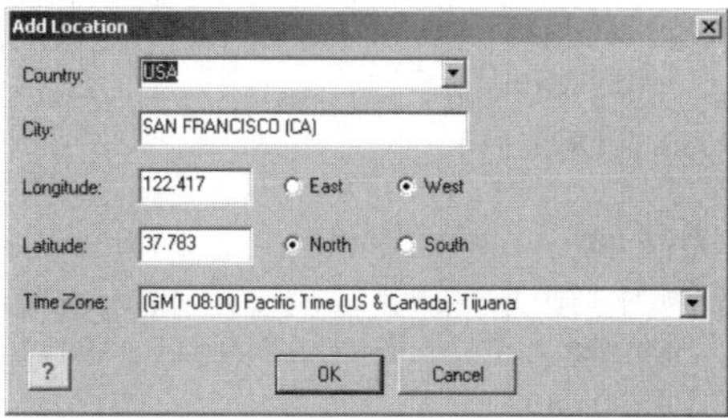

4. To set the month and day, select a month by clicking the arrows on the month bar at the top of the calendar, then click a number on the calendar.
5. To set the time of day, enter a time in the **Time** edit box, or use the slider to select a time. Enable either the **am** or **fm** radio button. Clicking **Set Current Time** reads the current time set in your computer system and defaults to the next smallest 5-minute increment of time. For example, 12:04 becomes 12:00.
6. To keep track of changes in time due to daylight savings, enable the **Daylight Saving** check box.
7. To set the angle from True North, enter a value in the **Angle from True North** edit box. This is the "geographic" North, as opposed to the "magnetic" North which you see on a compass. The value you specify determines where North is on your screen, and affects the angle of the sun for daylight rendering. The number in degrees that you enter is in relation to the 90° perpendicular orientation of your drawing. A value of 1° makes the top of the screen North. A value of 90° makes the top of the screen East, and the left side of the screen North.

   For more information, see "Specifying the Angle of True North" in the Online Help (enter the keywords "true north").

   It is assumed that information regarding building orientation to True North can be taken from, or calculated from, a surveyor's certificate. However, True North can be calculated from a Magnetic North reading taken at your building site. For more information, see "Calculating True North from Magnetic North" in the Online Help (enter the keywords "true north").

8. Click **OK**.

To save new or edited cities:

1. On the Global Settings page of the **Program Settings** dialog, click the **Save** button below the city list.
2. In the **Save As** dialog, select the *timezone.cty* file in the program's templates folder.
3. Click **Save**.
4. Click **Yes** to replace the original city template.

To load a saved city template into other projects:

1. On the Global Settings page of the **Program Settings** dialog, click the **Load** button below the city list.
2. In the **Open** dialog, select the *timezone.cty* file in the program's Templates folder.
3. Click **Open**. The city list is updated automatically.

Creating a 3DTrueView™ Rendering

Creating a photo realistic 3DTrueView™ rendering involves only a simple menu selection or mouse click. Rendered views are displayed instantly on the screen once they've been calculated. If you enable the Render to File option in your render options, the image will also be saved to a BMP or JPG file for later access. For more information see *Saving a 3DTrueView™ Rendering to a File* on page 207.

To create a 3DTrueView rendering:

1. Make sure you have set the 3D scene exactly how you want it.
2. Select **View > 3DTrueView > Render 3DTrueView**, or click the Render 3DTrueView button on the 3DTrueView toolbar. The solution begins.

Before the rendered view is generated, the program goes through a process of calculating light in the scene. These are called *radiosity* calculations. Basically, it determines how much light is given off by the sun or by lighting fixtures, and how much light is reflected off the surface of elements. The view is updated at regular intervals during these calculations. A dialog appears on the screen that shows you the progression of the radiosity calculations.

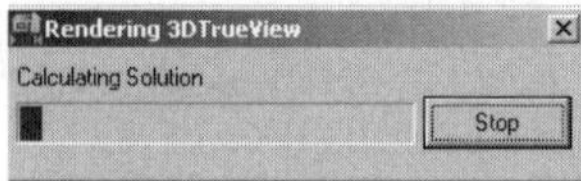

If you click **Stop** during the solution stage, radiosity calculations will stop, and the scene will be instantly rendered. This may be fine if the process seems to be taking a long time, but you may not get the result you want.

3. Once the radiosity calculations are complete, rendering begins. Please wait while the image is generated.

Once the rendering is complete, it fills your current view window. The **Rendering 3DTrueView** dialog tells you that the image is complete.

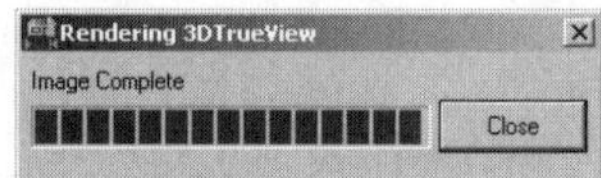

At this point you can print the view if you want.

4. When you are finished viewing the 3DTrueView™ rendering, click **Close** in the **Rendering 3DTrueView** dialog. The view returns to its original, pre-rendered state.

If you selected the **Render to File** option before rendering, the image is saved in the same directory your project is located in. For more information, see *Saving a*

3DTrueView™ Rendering to a File on page 207.

Adjusting the Rendering Quality

By default, the quality level chosen for 3DTrueView™ renderings is Level 1 - Lowest (fastest). You can select an increased quality level before rendering if you want. Note that the higher level of quality you choose, the longer the rendering process takes.

To adjust the rendering quality:

1. Select **View > 3DTrueView > 3DTrueView Options**, or click the 3DTrueView Options button on the 3DTrueView toolbar.
2. In the **Program Settings** dialog, select the Rendering tab.
3. Select the quality level you want from the **Quality Level** drop box.

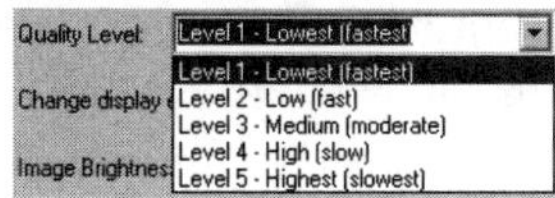

4. Click **OK**.

Changing the Refresh Rate During Lighting Calculations

As the program performs lighting calculations, the view updates at regular intervals to reflect calculations up to that point. You can change the interval at which the view refreshes by increasing or decreasing the number of steps between visual updates.

To change the refresh rate during radiosity calculations:

1. Select **View > 3DTrueView > 3DTrueView Options**, or click the 3DTrueView Options button on the 3DTrueView toolbar.

2. In the **Program Settings** dialog, select the Rendering tab.
3. Edit the value in the **Change Display Every _ Steps** edit box. Fewer steps increase the frequency of visual updates, but can increase rendering time.
4. Click **OK**.

Adjusting the Brightness of the Rendered Image

The program's "virtual camera" works in a manner similar to actual point-and-shoot cameras. It automatically calculates the correct "exposure" for the lighting situation and produces a view with infinite depth of field (i.e. everything is in focus). However if, in exceptional circumstances, you want to brighten or darken a rendering, you can use the Image Brightness option to manually override the automatic exposure. Brightness can be increased or decreased.

To adjust image brightness:

1. Select **View > 3DTrueView > 3DTrueView Options**, or click the 3DTrueView Options button on the 3DTrueView toolbar.

2. In the **Program Settings** dialog, select the Rendering tab.
3. Specify the amount you want to increase or decrease the brightness in the **Image Brightness** edit box, or use the arrow buttons to scroll up or down. A positive value increases the brightness, while a negative values decreases it.
4. Click **OK**.

Turning Daylight Off

By default, daylight is included in radiosity calculations, even for indoor scenes (light can come through a window). You can turn daylight off if you want. This basically omits daylight from the lighting calculations, and can speed up rendering.

Note: The Enable Daylight option should always remain on for exterior shots, even if it is a night shot. If you want to create a night shot, change your time of day instead. See *Defining Your Location and Time of Day* on page 203.

To turn daylight off:

1. Select **View > 3DTrueView > 3DTrueView Options**, or click the 3DTrueView Options button on the 3DTrueView toolbar.
2. In the **Program Settings** dialog, select the Rendering tab.
3. Uncheck the **Enable Daylight** check box.
4. Click **OK**.

Using Antialiasing to Reduce Jagged Edges

Antialiasing blends pixels in areas where two colors or two materials meet to reduce artifacts (or "stair steps") and produce a more natural look to the scene. By default, antialiasing is disabled to increase rendering speed. You can select varying levels of antialiasing.

To use antialiasing:

1. Select **View > 3DTrueView > 3DTrueView Options**, or click the 3DTrueView Options button on the 3DTrueView toolbar.
2. In the **Program Settings** dialog, select the Rendering tab.
3. Use the up arrows key next to the **Antialiasing** check box to increase the level of antialiasing. The higher the level, the cleaner the image, but the longer the rendering process takes. The highest level is 4.
4. Click **OK**.

Creating a Fog Effect

To create a fog effect in your rendering, you need to turn on the Fog option in your rendering settings before rendering the view.

To create a fog effect:

1. Select **View > 3DTrueView > 3DTrueView Options**, or click the 3DTrueView Options button on the 3DTrueView toolbar.
2. In the **Program Settings** dialog, select the Rendering tab.
3. In the *Effects* area, check the **Enable** check box.
4. Enable the **Fog** radio button.
5. In the **Density** edit box, specify the desired thickness of the fog. The higher the percentage, the thicker the fog.
6. Click **OK**.

Creating a Smoke Effect

To create a smoke effect in your rendering, you need to turn on the Smoke option in your rendering settings before rendering the view.

To create a smoke effect:

1. Select **View > 3DTrueView > 3DTrueView Options**, or click the 3DTrueView Options button on the 3DTrueView toolbar.
2. In the **Program Settings** dialog, select the Rendering tab.
3. In the *Effects* area, check the **Enable** check box.
4. Enable the **Smoke** radio button.
5. In the **Density** edit box, specify the desired thickness of the smoke. The higher the percentage, the thicker the smoke.
6. Click **OK**.

Adjusting the Light Coming from Light Fixtures

To adjust the color or intensity of light coming from a light fixture, you can add light bulbs, change a light bulb to a different type, adjust the intensity of the light, select a different color for the light, or turn a light off completely.

See the following topics:

Editing a Light Fixture's Light Source on page 131

Turning a Light On or Off on page 132

Editing the Surface Properties of Materials

Different materials have different finishes. Surface finishes include Dull, Low Gloss, Semi Gloss, High Gloss, Liquid, Fully Reflective, Partially Reflective, Shiny, Fully Transparent, Partially Transparent, and Varnished. The finish determines how much a material reflects, emits and absorbs light. These factors can affect the lighting in a rendered scene.

To edit the surface properties of an element's materials:

1. Select the element in your drawing.
2. Right-click and select **Properties**, or select **Edit > Modify Elements > Properties**.
3. In the properties dialog, select the Appearance tab.
4. On the Appearance page, click the **Select** button, or click the Texture swatch to access the **Materials** dialog.
5. In the **Materials** dialog, click the Rendered swatch to bring up the **Edit Materials** dialog.
6. To change the surface finish of the material (dull, shiny, etc.), make a selection from the drop box in the *Surface Properties* area. If you want to specify a custom surface finish, select *Custom* in the list, then click the **Advanced** button.
7. If creating a custom finish, specify its properties. These are described below.

   Specular. Reflection that creates highlights on materials, making them appear shiny.

   Emissive. The amount of light given off by a material. The more emissive a material is, the more self-luminous it appears.

   Transparency. The degree to which a material is pervious to light.

   Color Bleed. The degree to which different colors blend where they meet.
8. Click **OK** in the **Edit Materials** dialog.
9. Click **OK** in the **Materials** dialog.
10. Click **OK** in the properties dialog.

Saving a 3DTrueView™ Rendering to a File

Rendered views are displayed instantly on the screen once they've been calculated. If you want the image to be saved to a file, you need to turn on the Render to File option in your render settings before creating the rendering. The image will be saved to a BMP or JPG file that you can open in most graphic editing applications.

To save a 3DTrueView rendering to a file:

1. Select **View > 3DTrueView > 3DTrueView Options**, or click the 3DTrueView Options button on the 3DTrueView toolbar. 
2. In the **Program Settings** dialog, select the Rendering tab.
3. In the *Image Output* area, enable the **Render to File** check box.
4. By default, rendered images are saved in the same directory your projects are stored in. By default, this would be a directory similar to the following:

   C:\Documents and Settings\<Current User>\My Documents\Home Design Deluxe 6\Projects

   To select a different location to save your rendered image in, click the Browse button next to the current output folder path. In the **Open** dialog, navigate to the folder where you want to store rendered images.

   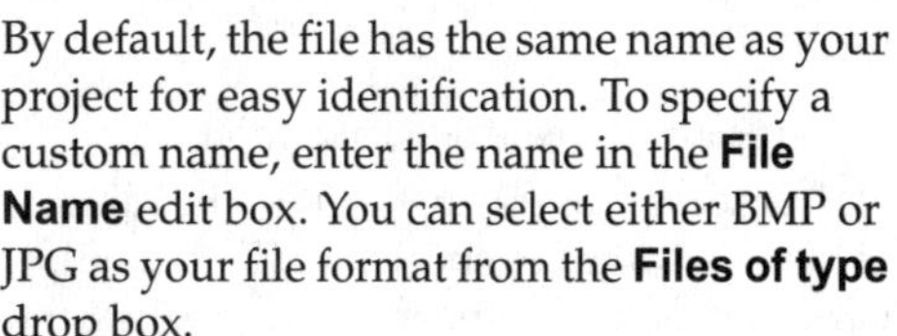

   By default, the file has the same name as your project for easy identification. To specify a custom name, enter the name in the **File Name** edit box. You can select either BMP or JPG as your file format from the **Files of type** drop box.
5. Click **OK**.

Specifying the Output Size of Rendered Images

By default, 3DTrueView™ images fill the view window they are created from. If you enabled the Render to File option in your rendering settings, the image is also saved at that size. You can select another output size if you want.

To specify an output size for rendered images:

1. Select **View > 3DTrueView > 3DTrueView Options**, or click the 3DTrueView Options button on the 3DTrueView toolbar.
2. In the **Program Settings** dialog, select the Rendering tab.
3. In the *Image Output* area, select the desired size from the **Size** drop box. The default selection is *Current View Size*, which saves the image at the size currently shown on the screen. Pre-defined sizes include 640 x 480, 800 x 600, and 1024 x 768. Selecting the *Custom* option lets you define a custom size by entering values in the **Width** and **Height** edit boxes.
4. Click **OK**.

Creating Multiple 3DTrueView™ Renderings in the Same Project

If you enable the Render to File option before creating a rendering, the image is saved to a BMP or JPG file in your projects directory. The file has the same name as your project. If you create another 3DTrueView™ rendering in the same project, the file from the previous rendering is overwritten.

If you want to create and save more 3DTrueView™ renderings within the same project, you need to specify a different output name for each new image before creating the rendering.

To create and save an additional 3DTrueView rendering:

1. Select **View > 3DTrueView > 3DTrueView Options**, or click the 3DTrueView Options button on the 3DTrueView toolbar.
2. In the **Program Settings** dialog, select the Rendering tab.
3. In the *Image Output* area, make sure **Render to File** is checked.
4. Click the Browse button next to the current output folder path.

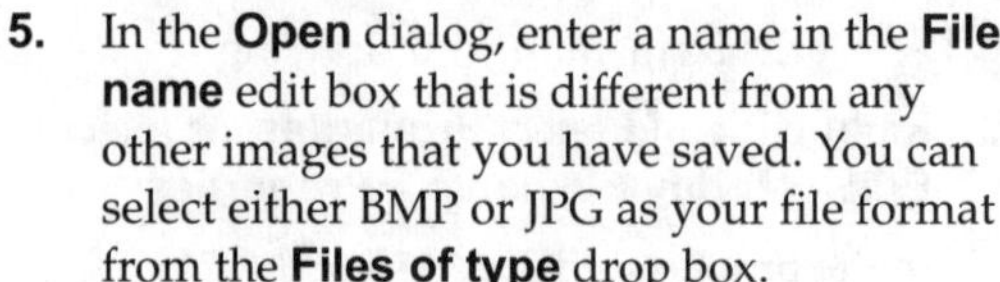

5. In the **Open** dialog, enter a name in the **File name** edit box that is different from any other images that you have saved. You can select either BMP or JPG as your file format from the **Files of type** drop box.
6. Click **Open**.
7. Click **OK** in the **Program Settings** dialog.

   The next 3DTrueView™ rendering you create will be saved to the new file name.

Part 8

Managing Files

Chapter 31

Opening, Saving & Printing

Once you have started and saved a project, you can work on it whenever you like. You can open a saved project by selecting the Open a Saved Project button in the startup dialog, or by selecting Open on the File menu if the program is already running. Once you have opened a project, you can edit, save, print and export it, as well as save it as a template for future projects.

You can have more than one project open at a time. If you have more than one project open, you can switch between projects using the Window menu.

As you edit your drawing, the changes you make are stored temporarily in your computer's memory until you save them. The Save function saves the current project under its current name. You can use Save As to save a project under a different name, and Save All to save all currently open projects. You can also use the Save As tool to save a drawing as a template for use in future projects.

Opening a Saved Project

You can open a saved project (*.bld file) directly from the startup dialog that appears when you start the program. Just click **Open a Saved Project**, then select the project to open.

If the program is already running, you can open a saved project using the Open tool.

To open a saved project if the program is already running:

1. Select **File > Open**, or click the Open button on the **Standard** toolbar.
2. In the **Open** dialog, navigate to the location where you saved the project.
3. Select the project to open, then click **Open**.

Note: You can open drawings from version 5.0 or later of *3D Home Design Suite Professional*, *3D Home Architect®*, or *3D Home Landscape Designer*.

Tip: If the project you want to open is one that your recently worked on, it may be listed in the recently used file list near the bottom of the **File** menu. Just select it to open it.

Viewing Sample Plans

The program ships with a number of sample projects that you can use to see what the program can do, and get design ideas. You can also use a sample project as a template for your own design project.

Sample projects are available for selection in the startup dialog when you launch the program. Just click **View Sample Plans** and select one from the list.

If the program is already running, you can open a sample project using the Open tool.

To open a sample plan if the program is already running:

1. Select **File > Open**, or click the Open button on the **Standard** toolbar.
2. In the **Open** dialog, navigate to the location where you installed the program, then select the **Samples** directory (e.g. *C:\Program Files\3D Home Architect\Home Design Deluxe 6\Samples*).
3. Select the project to open, then click **Open**.

Changing the Number of Files in the Recently Used File List

By default, a maximum of four projects are listed in the recently used file list near the bottom of the **File** menu. You can increase or decrease this number if you want.

To change the number of files in the recently used file list:

1. Select **Settings > Program Settings** or click the Program Settings button on the Settings toolbar. 
2. In the **Program Settings** dialog, select the General tab.
3. Type the maximum number of files to display in the **Recently used file list** edit box, or use the arrows to select a number. You can list a maximum of 9 files.

Repairing Damaged Projects

Occasionally a drawing may become damaged, usually when drawing walls. The Repair Project tool scans the project for elements that have caused damage, and either fixes or removes them.

To repair a damaged project:

1. Select **File > Repair Project**.

If the recovery is successful, the following dialog box appears:

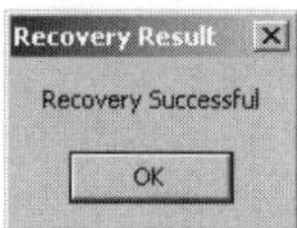

If the recovery is not successful, a dialog appears telling you why it was not successful.

Saving Projects

The program as three save functions: **Save**, **Save As** and **Save All**. They are located on the **File** menu.

- To save the current project under the current name, or to save the current project for the first time, select **File > Save**, or click the Save button on the Standard toolbar. If you are saving for the first time, you are prompted for a file name.
- To save the current project under a different name (i.e. create a copy of it), select **File > Save As**, then specify a name in the **Save As** dialog.
- To save all currently open projects, select **File > Save All**, or click the **Save All** button on the Standard toolbar.

Setting the Automatic Save

The Automatic Save option prompts you to save your project at regular intervals. This is a great way to make sure you save your changes regularly and avoid any loss should a power failure or system error occur. By default, the Automatic Save is enabled.

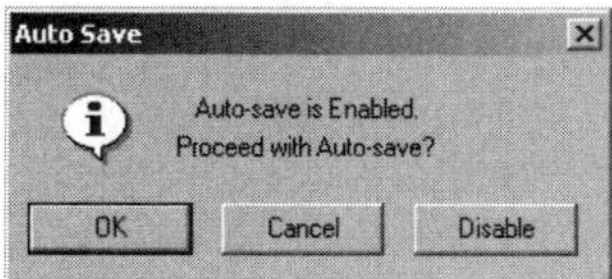

To set the Automatic Save:

1. Select **Settings > Program Settings** or click the Program Settings button on the Settings toolbar.
2. In the **Program Settings** dialog, select the General tab.
3. Enable the **Automatic Save every** check box.
4. In the edit box, specify the save interval in minutes, or use the arrows to select a value.
5. Click **OK**.

Note: When you are prompted to save your project, you can choose not to save at that time by clicking **Cancel** in the prompt dialog. If you want to disable the automatic save prompt, you can click **Disable** in the dialog.

Note: Disabling the Automatic Save applies to the current project only. The Automatic Save is turned on by default for all new projects.

Specifying a Default Save Directory

By default, new (unsaved) projects are saved in the Projects directory created by the program installation. For example,

C:\Documents and Settings\<Current User>\My Documents\Home Design Deluxe 6\Projects

You can specify a different default save directory if you want.

To specify the default save directory:

1. Select **Settings > Program Settings** or click the Program Settings button on the Settings toolbar.
2. In the **Program Settings** dialog, select the **General** tab.
3. In the *File Paths* area, click on the **Projects Directory** to select it.
4. Click **Modify**.
5. In the **Browse For Folder** dialog, select the directory you want to use as your default save directory, then click **OK**.
6. Click **OK** in the **Program Settings** dialog.

Saving a Project as a Template

By default, every new project you start is based on a template. A template determines what settings new projects will have, such as the unit of measure, and building location settings. You can even include building elements in a template if you want.

You can create a template out of any drawing by simply saving it in your Templates directory. To use the template in new drawings you need to select the template in your Startup options.

To create a template:

1. Unless you have already created the drawing you want to use as a template, start a new project (**File > New**).
2. Specify the settings you want to save with the template, such as your building locations and program settings. Note that any elements in your drawing will be saved as well, so unless you want these elements to appear in new projects, you should delete the elements from your drawing.
3. Select **File > Save As**.
4. In the **Save As** dialog, navigate to the program's Templates folder (e.g. *C:\Program Files\3D Home Architect\Home Design Deluxe 6\Templates*).
5. In the **File name** edit box, type a name for the template.
6. Click **Save**.

Selecting a Default Project Template

By default, new projects are based on a default template that ships with the program. If you chose to work in Imperial units during program installation, new projects will be based on the *1-Blank Project (ft & in).bld* template, which is a blank drawing with measurements set to feet and inches. If you chose to work in Metric, new projects will be based on the template, which has its unit of measure set to millimeters. Each template contains three default building locations: Foundation, Ground Floor and Second Floor.

You can select a different template to use as the default template when starting new drawings. You can use one of the templates that ships with the program, or one that you have created yourself.

To select a default project template:

1. Select **Settings > Program Settings** or click the Program Settings button on the Settings toolbar. 
2. In the **Program Settings** dialog, select the General tab.
3. In the *Startup* area, make sure the **Startup using Project Template** radio button is enabled.
4. Click the Browse button next to the current template name. 
5. In the **Open** dialog, select the template you want to use from the Templates directory, then click **Open**.
6. In the **Program Settings** dialog, click **OK**.

Note: You need to start a new drawing to put the new template into effect.

Disabling the Use of Templates

By default, new projects are based on a template that determines the unit of measure used. Templates also have a few pre-defined settings, such as a set of default building locations.

If you prefer you can start new projects without using a template. If you choose to do this, new projects will be blank with no pre-defined settings.

To disable the use of templates:

1. Select **Settings > Program Settings** or click the Program Settings button on the Settings toolbar. 
2. In the **Program Settings** dialog, select the General tab.
3. In the *Startup* area, enable the **Do not use Project Template** radio button.
4. Click **OK**.

Setting the Path to the Templates Directory

By default, the Templates directory is located in the 3D Home Architect Home Design Deluxe 6 program group. If you have moved your Templates directory, or have chosen to store your templates in a different directory, you should reset the path to the template directory in your program settings. The path you set determines the default directory shown when you browse for templates in your *Startup* options on the General page of the Program Settings dialog.

To set the path to your templates directory:

1. Select **Settings > Program Settings** or click the Program Settings button on the Settings toolbar. 
2. In the **Program Settings** dialog, select the **General** tab.
3. In the *File Paths* area, click on the **Templates Directory** to select it.
4. Click **Modify**.
5. In the **Browse For Folder** dialog, select the directory containing your templates, then click **OK**.
6. Click **OK** in the **Program Settings** dialog.

Selecting a Directory for Temporary Files

Certain functions of the program create temporary files which are stored in a directory on your computer system. By default, the path to the temporary directory is as follows:

C:\Documents and Settings\<Current User>\Local Settings\Temp

You can specify a different directory to store your temporary files in if you want.

To set a different temporary files directory:

1. Select **Settings > Program Settings** or click the Program Settings button on the Settings toolbar. 
2. In the **Program Settings** dialog, select the General tab.
3. In the *File Paths* area, click on the **Temporary Directory** to select it.
4. Click **Modify**.
5. In the **Browse For Folder** dialog, select the directory you want to use as your default temporary files directory, then click **OK**.
6. Click **OK** in the **Program Settings** dialog.

Closing Projects

Projects remain open until you close them or exit the program. You can close the active project without exiting the program. If you have more than one drawing open, make sure the drawing you want to close is the active one.

To close a drawing:

1. Select **File > Close**, or click the Close button on the Standard toolbar. 
2. In the dialog, click **Yes** or **No** when you are asked to save changes.
3. If you haven't named the project yet and you clicked **Yes** in the previous step, specify a name for the project in the **Save As** dialog, then click **Save**.

Printing Drawings

The program uses the standard *Windows* **Print** routine with a few added features for your printing convenience.

To print a drawing:

1. Select **File > Print**, or click the Print button on the Standard toolbar. 

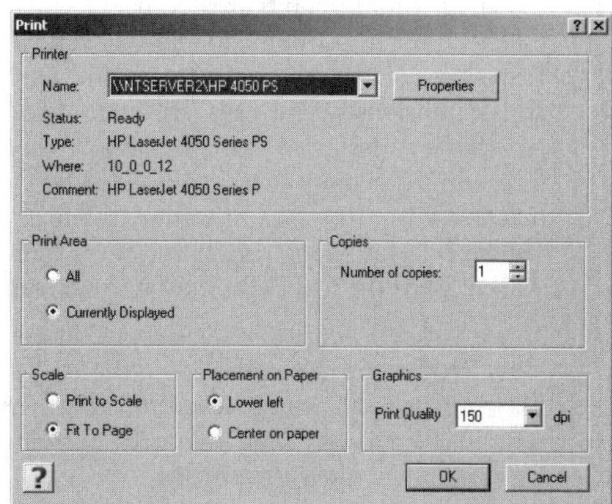

2. In the **Print** dialog, specify your print settings.

Printer. Select a printer from the drop box. Click **Properties** to specify general printer properties.

Print Area. The **All** option prints the extents of your drawing, which is the portion of your drawing that currently contains elements. As you add new elements, the extents update automatically. The **Currently Displayed** option prints exactly what you see on the screen in the current view. If only part of your drawing is currently visible, only that part will appear in the printout.

Copies. Select the number of copies to print from the **Number of copies** drop box.

Scale. The **Print to Scale** option prints the current view according to its defined scale in the view properties, regardless of the paper size. The scale is the ratio of drawing units to real-world units. A scale of 1:1 (12" = 1'- 0") creates a view that is the same scale as the view in the main drawing window. A scale of 1:12 (1" = 1'- 0") creates a smaller-scale view. Note that if you change the scale, the model does not scale on the screen. It will only be scaled on paper when you print the drawing.

However, things like text and dimensions will scale on the screen because they are specified in real-world units, whereas the model on your screen is created using units that are only proportional to real-world units. Regardless of a view's scale, things like text and dimensions will always print out at the size that was assigned to them at the time of insertion. For example, if you inserted text that had a 1/2" text height setting, the text will be 1/2" on paper, regardless of the view scale or what the text looks like on the screen.

To see a view's defined scale, select **Edit > View Properties**, or right-click in the drawing area and select **View Properties**, or right-click on a view's tab below the drawing area and select **View Properties**.

Note that the **Print to Scale** option will not work with most 3D views (unless they are elevation views), since 3D views cannot be scaled.

The **Fit To Page** option scales the drawing to fit the selected paper size. Note that this is the default setting for 3D views, since 3D views are not affected by changes in scale (unless they are elevation views).

Placement on Paper. If you select **Lower left**, the image is printed in the lower left corner of the paper. If you select **Center on paper**, the image is centered on the paper.

Graphics. Choose from three levels of print quality (150, 300 or 600 dpi). A higher resolution (600 dpi) produces graphic images that are sharper and show finer detail, while a lower resolution (150 dpi) permits faster printing and shows less detail.

3. Click **OK**.

Using Print Setup

The program uses the standard *Windows* **Print Setup** for printer and paper selection.

To select a printer and paper for output:

1. Select **File > Print Setup**.
2. Choose the **options** you want.
3. Click **OK**.

Chapter 32

Exporting Files

You can export your drawing to a variety of file formats including DXF, 3DS, WRL, BMP, JPG and TGA.

Exporting Your Model

The Export 3D Model tool lets you export your drawing to three file formats:

- AutoCAD Basic DXF (*.dxf)
- Autodesk 3D Studio (*.3ds)
- VRML (*.wrl)

To export your model:

1. Select **File > Export > 3D Model**.
2. In the **Save As** dialog, click on the **Save as type** drop box and select the file format you want to export to.
3. Locate the directory where you want to save the exported file.
4. In the **File name** edit box, type a file name.
5. Click **Save**. A dialog appears confirming the model has been exported successfully.

6. Click **OK**.

Exporting the Current View

The Export 2D Image tool lets you export the current view to a BMP, JPG or TGA file.

To export a view:

1. Select **File > Export > 2D Image**.
2. In the **Save As** dialog, click on the **Save as type** drop box and select the file format you want to export to.
3. Locate the directory where you want to save the exported file.
4. In the **File name** edit box, type a file name.
5. Click **Save**. The **Export View** dialog appears:

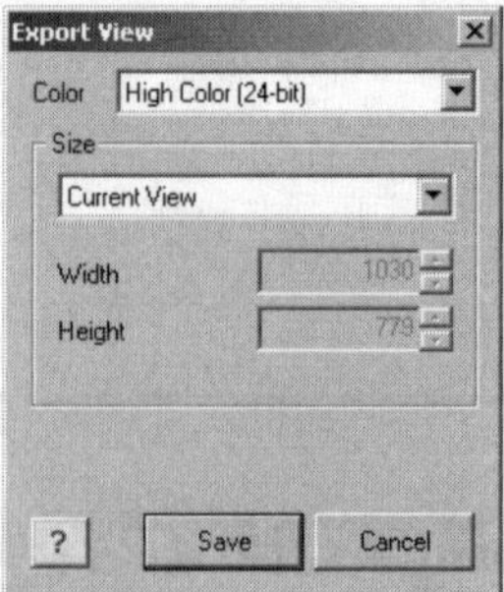

6. From the **Color** drop box, select the desired color setting. Choose from *Grayscale, 256 Color, High Color (16-bit), High Color (24-bit)* or *True Color (32-bit)*.
7. From the **Size** drop box, select the desired output size. By default, Current View is selected, which saves the image at the size currently shown on the screen. You can choose from a list of preset sizes, or select *Custom* and enter the desired values in the **Width** and **Height** edit boxes.
8. Click **Save**. The view is exported.

Part 9

Customization

Chapter 33

Screen Settings

3D Home Architect® Home Design's screen environment is totally customizable, so you can create a work environment that is both functional and comfortable according to your personal needs.

This chapter describes how to display, hide and move screen components, change the color of the drawing area and toolbar areas, and improve graphics display.

Displaying/Hiding Toolbars

There are 10 toolbars available for display. (By default, not all of them are displayed.) You can hide or show individual toolbars by setting your workspace options. When you display a toolbar, it is displayed in one of the toolbar areas which are located directly above and below the drawing area. Note that if you hide a toolbar that is displayed in a tab, the tab is hidden from view as well.

To hide or show toolbars:

1. Select **Settings > Toolbars**.
2. Check the toolbars that you want to display, and uncheck those that you do not want to display.
3. Click **OK**.

Tip: If a toolbar is currently floating freely on the screen, you can hide it by clicking the close button on its title bar, or right-clicking its title bar and selecting **Hide**.

Displaying Toolbars in Tabbed Format

You can display any toolbar in tabbed format, meaning a tab will be added to the row of toolbar tabs below the menu bar.

To display a toolbar in a tab:

1. Select **Settings > Toolbars**.
2. Enable the check box of the toolbar you want to display in a tab.
3. Enable the toolbar's **Tabbed** check box.
4. Click **OK**.

Displaying Toolbars in a Non-tabbed Format

By default, the Building and Interiors toolbars are displayed in tabs below the menu bar. You can change any tabbed toolbar to be displayed as a non-tabbed, free-standing toolbar.

To display toolbars in non-tabbed format:

1. Select **Settings > Toolbars**.
2. Make sure the check box of the toolbar you want to display is enabled.
3. Disable the toolbar's **Tabbed** check box.
4. Click **OK**.

Changing the Background Color of Toolbars

You can change the general background color of individual toolbars by changing your workspace options. This applies to both tabbed and free-standing toolbars.

To change the background color of toolbars:

1. Select **Settings > Toolbars**.
2. Click the Color box next to the toolbar you want to change.
3. In the **Color** dialog, select or create the desired color, then click **OK**.
4. Click **OK** in the **Program Settings** dialog.

Changing the Color of Toolbar Areas

The program has two toolbar areas: one directly above the drawing area, and one directly below the drawing area. By default, the background color of these areas is dark blue. You can change this color in your workspace options.

To change the color of toolbar areas:

1. Select **Settings > Toolbars**.
2. Click the colored box next to the **Toolbar Areas** option.
3. In the **Color** dialog, select or create the desired color for your toolbar areas, then click **OK** to return to the **Program Settings** dialog.
4. Click **OK**.

Moving Toolbars

You can drag any non-tabbed toolbar to any location on the screen. At window edges, the toolbar will automatically dock itself according to the location. For example, if you drag it to the right edge of the screen, it will assume a vertical orientation.

If you drag it into the drawing window, it will float freely. You can then move it by dragging it by its title bar.

To move a toolbar:

1. Click and hold your mouse button over the left grip end of the toolbar (or its title bar if it is currently in the drawing area).

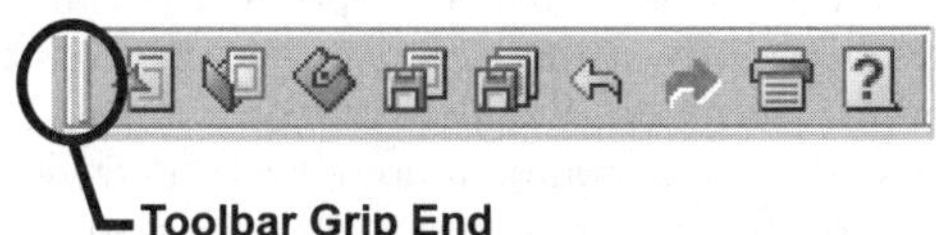

2. Drag the toolbar to the desired location.
3. Release the mouse button.

Displaying/Hiding the Catalog Panel

By default, the catalog panel is displayed on the right side of the screen, as it is an essential component of the program. You can hide the catalog panel from view if you want.

To display or hide the catalog panel:

1. Select **Settings > Toolbars**. Or, select **Settings > Program Settings** (or click the Program Settings button on the Settings toolbar) and select the Workspace tab in the **Program Settings** dialog.
2. In the *Tool Display* area, check or uncheck the **Catalog Panel** check box.
3. Click **OK**.

Resizing the Catalog Panel

When the catalog panel is docked at one side of your screen, you can make it narrower or wider by simply clicking and dragging its edges. If you have moved the catalog panel away from the edge, so it is free-floating, you can resize it by clicking and dragging its corners.

To resize the catalog panel if it is docked:

1. Position your pointer over the panel's left outside edge. (If you have moved the catalog panel to the left side of the screen, position your pointer over the right edge.) Watch for the Resize cursor to appear.

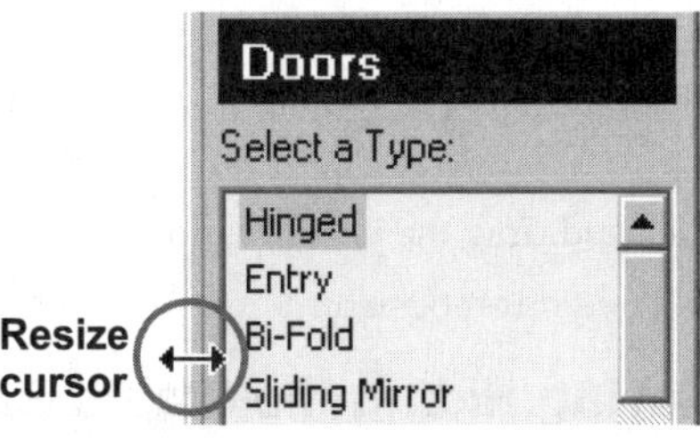

2. Click and drag the edge of the panel to stretch it in the desired direction.
3. Release your mouse button.

To resize the catalog panel if it is free-floating:

1. Position your pointer over one of the panel's corners.
2. Click and drag to stretch the panel.
3. Release your mouse button.

Moving the Catalog Panel

If the catalog panel is docked on one side of the screen, you can move it by clicking and dragging its outside edge. If you move a panel to the side of the screen, it will automatically dock itself to the edge of the screen. Otherwise, the panel is displayed in a free-floating window.

If the panel is free-floating, you can move it by clicking and dragging its title bar.

To move the catalog panel when it is docked:

1. Position your pointer over the panel's outside edge (the edge that is at the side of the screen). Watch for the Move cursor.

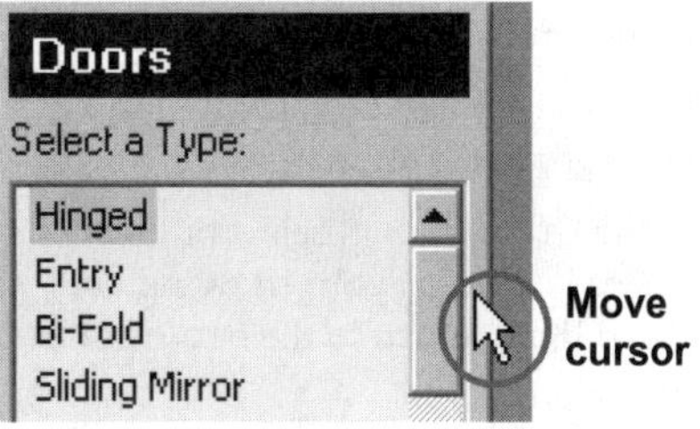

2. Click and drag the panel to move it.

3. Release your mouse button.

To move the catalog panel when it is free-floating:

1. Position your pointer over the panel's title bar.
2. Click and drag the panel to move it.
3. Release your mouse button.

Displaying/Hiding the Status Bar

The Status bar can be toggled on and off as needed.

To display/hide the Status bar:

1. Select **Settings > Toolbars**. Or select **Settings > Program Settings** and select the Workspace tab in the **Program Settings** dialog.
2. In the *Tool Display* area, select or clear the **Status Bar** check box.
3. Click **OK**.

Changing the Background Color of the Drawing Window

By default, the color of the main drawing window is white. You can select a different color if you like. Note, however, that selecting a different background color can make some elements difficult to see depending on their color settings.

To change the background color of the drawing window:

1. Select **Settings > Toolbars**. Or, select **Settings > Program Settings** (or click the Program Settings button on the Settings toolbar) and select the Workspace tab in the **Program Settings** dialog.
2. Click the colored box next to the **Background** option.
3. In the **Color** dialog, select or create the desired color for your drawing area, then click **OK** to return to the **Program Settings** dialog.
4. Click **OK**.

Hardware Acceleration

The **Hardware Acceleration** option controls how your screen responds during a work session. By default, hardware acceleration is enabled.

Hardware acceleration increases the speed of your graphics display. When hardware acceleration is enabled, your computer takes advantage of any installed graphics card that supports hardware acceleration. If no card exists, and the **Hardware Acceleration** option is still enabled, your computer automatically defaults to slower software acceleration, which uses the *Windows* implementation of OpenGL. For detailed information about OpenGL, see the *OpenGL* topic in the online help.

In most cases, it is best to enable the **Hardware Acceleration** option. However, problems sometimes arise with graphics cards on which hardware acceleration is poorly implemented. If you are experiencing display-related problems like scrambled line patterns, see the next topic, *Improving Graphics Display.*

To enable or disable hardware acceleration:

1. Select **Settings > Program Settings** or click the Program Settings button on the Settings toolbar. 
2. In the **Program Settings** dialog, select the General tab.
3. In the *Graphics* area, check or uncheck the **Hardware Acceleration** check box.
4. Click **OK**.

Improving Graphics Display

The type of graphics card you have can affect the way the program's graphics are displayed on the screen. If the display seems unstable or contains some graphic artifacts (e.g. large pixels), here are some tips on how you may be able to improve the display:

1. Disable pre-selection. Pre-selection highlights elements when you hover your pointer over them, and displays tooltips. See *Disabling Pre-Selection* on page 23.

2. Lower your screen resolution (to 1024 x 768, for example). To access this setting, right-click your *Windows* desktop and select **Properties**. In the **Display Properties** dialog, select the **Settings** tab.
3. Lower your color setting in *Windows*. For example, if your colors are set to **True Color (32 bit)**, change the setting to **High Color (16 bit)**. To access this setting, right-click your *Windows* desktop and select **Properties**. In the **Display Properties** dialog, select the **Settings** tab.
4. If the above three methods fail to improve the graphics display, disable Hardware Acceleration in your Program Settings. See *Hardware Acceleration* on page 224.

Chapter 34

Managing View Windows

By default, your project has one view window called Standard. You can create additional view windows using the View Manager. Each view window can have different view settings. For example, you may want to keep the wireframe 2D plan view in the Standard view window, and create a new view window containing a 3D view of the model.

When you create new view windows, you can switch between open view windows using the **Window** menu. You can also turn your view tabs on, which will display a row of tabs below the drawing area. This provides instant point-and-click access to all your view windows.

You can display multiple view windows at the same time using the Tile Open Views and Cascade Open Views tools. View windows can be moved, resized and closed to create the exact arrangement you want.

This chapter describes all the functions of the View Manager, how to navigate between view windows, and arrange view windows.

Using the View Manager

The **View Manager** contains a listing of view windows and lets you open, close, create, and edit views.

By default, your project contains one view window called Standard. The scale of the view in this window is 1:48, or 1/4" = 1'-0".

Using the New View tool you can create new view windows. Each window can have different view settings. For example, you may want to display a wireframe, 2D plan view in the Standard view window, and create a new view window containing a 3D view of your model.

Using the **Window** menu or view tabs you can switch between view windows as needed to see different views of your design. This can eliminate the need to constantly change the current view settings to see a particular view of your design. You can even display two or more view windows at the same time.

You can edit the name and scale of views listed in the **View Manager**.

To access the View Manager:

1. Select **View > View Manager**.

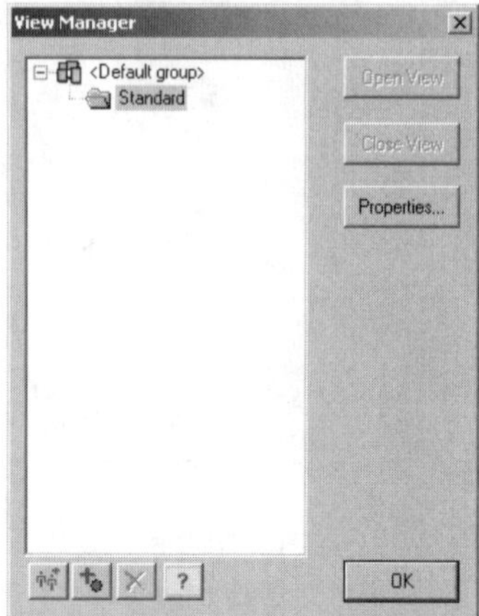

Creating New View Windows

By default, your project contains one view window called Standard. You can use the View Manager to create new view windows and specify different view settings for each window. For example, you may want to create a view window dedicated to 3D viewing only.

Views are stored in groups for easy organization and navigation. You can add view windows to the default group, or create your own groups if you want. For example, you might want to create a group for 3D views only, then add a set of 3D view windows to that group.

To create a new group in the View Manager:

1. Select **View > View Manager**.
2. Click the Add Group button, or right-click in the View Manager's view window and select **Add Group**. A group is added to the list. 
3. Right-click the new group and select **Rename**.
4. Type a name for the group, then press ENTER.

To rename a group in the View Manager:

1. Right-click the group and select **Rename**.
2. Type the new name, then press ENTER.

To delete a group in the View Manager:

1. Make sure the group contains no views.
2. Select the group and click the Delete button, or right-click the group and select **Delete**. 

To create a new view in the View Manager:

1. Select the group you want to add the view to.
2. Click the New View button, or right-click and select **New View**. 
3. In the **View Properties** dialog, type a name for the view window, then select a print scale for the view.

   The scale is the ratio of units on paper to real-world units. If the scale is set to 1:1 (12" = 1'-

0"), twelve inches on paper will represent one foot of your model. This would be a rather large printout. A scale of 1:12 (1" = 1'- 0"), however, would result in a smaller-scale view when the drawing is printed because every foot is represented by only one inch on paper.

4. Click **OK**. The view is added to the View Manager, and becomes the current view window.
5. Click **OK** in the **View Manager** dialog.

   A new view window is created, and becomes the current view window.
6. Select the desired view settings for the new view window.

Turning View Tabs On

When you turn your view tabs on, a row of tabs are displayed below the drawing area. Each tab represents an open view in the View Manager.

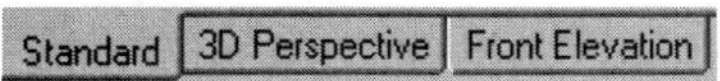

If you have not created any new views in the View Manager, only the Standard view tab is displayed.

To turn view tabs on:

1. Select **Settings > Program Settings** or click the Program Settings button on the Settings toolbar. 
2. In the **Program Settings** dialog, select the Workspace tab.
3. In the *Tool Display* area, check the **View Tabs** check box.
4. Click **OK**.

Switching Between View Windows

When you create a new view in the View Manager, the view appears in the program's **Window** menu.

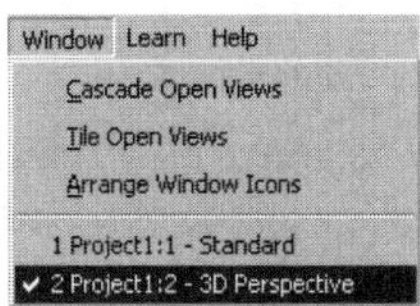

Also, if you have turned your view tabs on, a view tab is created for the new view.

To make a view window the current view window, simply select it from the **Window** menu, or select the view's corresponding view tab below the drawing area.

Tiling View Windows

By default, only one maximized view window is displayed at a time. Using the Tile Open Views tool you can instantly tile all open view windows in the drawing area. This is a great way to see different views of your design while you are working on it. When you make a change in one view window, the design updates automatically in all other view windows.

To tile all open view windows:

1. Select **Window > Tile Open Views**.

Cascading View Windows

By default, only one maximized view window is displayed at a time. Using the Cascade Open Views tool you can instantly display all open view windows in a stacked format, with the current view window on top. Once the view windows are cascaded you can move and resize each one if you want.

To cascade all open view windows:

1. Select **View > Cascade Open Views**.

Returning to a Maximized View

If you have tiled or cascaded your open view windows, you can return to a maximized view (where only one view window is visible) by maximizing one of the open view windows.

To maximize a view window:

1. Click the Maximize button in the view window you want to maximize.

Restoring the Previous Arrangement of View Windows

If you tiled, cascaded or arranged your view windows, then maximized one of them, you can use the Restore Down button to return to the view window arrangement that was displayed before you used the Maximize button.

To restore the previous arrangement of view windows:

1. Click the Restore Down button in the top right corner of the current view window.

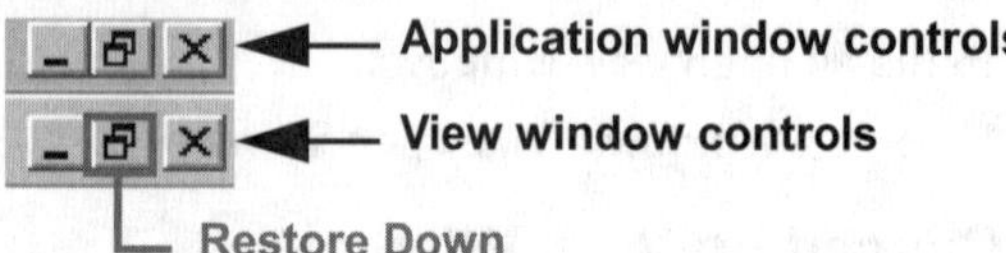

Closing View Windows

By default, the Standard view window is open when you start a project. Also, every time you create a new view window in the View Manager, that window is automatically opened for you. You can close individual view windows using the View Manager's **Close View** button, or by clicking the view window's Close button.

To close a view window from within the window itself:

1. Click the Close button in the top right corner of the view window.

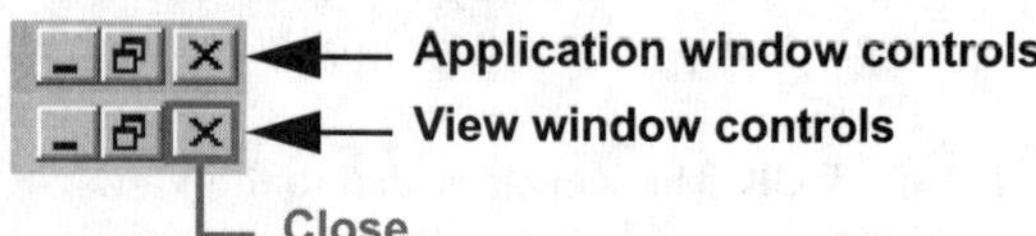

To close a view window using the View Manager:

1. Select **View > View Manager**.
2. Select the view you want to close.
3. Click **Close View**.

Opening View Windows that You Have Closed

If you have closed a view window either through the View Manager or by clicking a view window's Close button, you can open it again using the View Manager's **Open View** button.

To open a view window:

1. Select **View > View Manager**.
2. Select the view you want to open.
3. Click **Open View**. The view window becomes the current view window. It appears on the **Window** menu as well as on a view tab if you have view tabs turned on.

Renaming a View Window

You can edit the name of a view window as it appears in the View Manager, in the program's title bar, and on the view tabs. You can do this in the View Manager, or by accessing the view window's properties.

To rename a view window when it is the current view window:

1. Select **View > View Properties**, or right-click in the view window and select **View Properties**.
2. In the **View Properties** dialog, type the new name in the **Name** edit box.

3. Click **OK**.

To rename a view window in the View Manager:

1. Select **View > View Manager**.
2. Right-click the view you want to rename, then select **Rename**. Or, select the view to rename and click the **Properties** button.
3. Type the new name and press ENTER.
4. Click **OK**.

Editing the Print Scale of a View

You can edit the print scale of a view by accessing the view's properties.

A view's print scale is the ratio of units on paper to real-world units. If the scale is set to 1:1 (12" = 1'- 0"), twelve inches on paper will represent one foot of your model. This would be a rather large printout. A scale of 1:12 (1" = 1'- 0"), however, would result in a smaller-scale view when the drawing is printed because every foot is represented by only one inch on paper.

Note that if you change the print scale, your 2D plan does not scale on the screen. It will only be scaled on paper when you print the drawing. The scale you specify in a view window's properties has a direct link to the **Print to Scale** option in the **Print** dialog.

Changing the print scale has no effect in 3D views, neither on the screen nor in printouts, unless it is an elevation view. This is because a model being viewed in 3D does not have concrete measurements like a flat, 2D view has.

Things like text and dimensions will scale on the screen when you change the scale because they are specified in real-world units, whereas the model on your screen is created using units that are only proportional to real-world units. Regardless of a view's scale, things like text and dimensions will always print out at the size that was assigned to them at the time of insertion. For example, if you inserted text that had a 1/2" text height setting, the text will be 1/2" on paper, regardless of the view scale or what the text looks like on the screen.

To edit a view window's print scale when it is the current view window:

1. Select **View > View Properties**, or right-click in the view window and select **View Properties**.
2. In the **View Properties** dialog, select the desired scale from the **Scale** drop box.
3. Click **OK**.

To edit a view window's print scale in the View Manager:

1. Select **View > View Manager**.
2. Select the view to edit and click the **Properties** button.
3. In the **View Properties** dialog, select the desired scale from the **Scale** drop box.
4. Click **OK**.

Deleting View Windows

You can delete a view window by removing it from the View Manager.

To delete a view window:

1. Select **View > View Manager**.
2. Select the view to delete.
3. Click the Delete button, or right-click and select **Delete**. 
4. Click **Yes** to confirm that you want to delete the view.

Chapter 35

Custom Viewing

You can create your own custom 3D views and edit existing 3D views to suit your needs. For example, you can change the angle of the view, or the camera height. While in 3D view you can use a variety of navigation tools to walk through or fly around your house.

3D Home Architect® Home Design also lets you view instant elevations of your design, and create custom elevations to suit your presentation needs. You can also draw a cut line through your model to create an interesting cross-section view of your model's interior.

Creating New 3D Views

You can create a new 3D view by placing a new camera in your 2D plan view. Once you've inserted the camera, you specify the camera angle and viewing field angle by rotating and clicking your mouse.

To create a new 3D view:

1. While in 2D plan view, select **View > 3D Model View > Place New Camera**, or click the 3D Model View button on the Basic View Control or Advanced View Control toolbar and select **Place New Camera**. A camera is attached to your cursor, ready to be inserted.
2. Click to insert the camera where you want it.
3. Move your cursor in the direction you want to view. Moving the cursor back and forth changes the camera angle.
4. Once you have the desired direction and angle in place, click to select a location for the target.

Once you've defined the position and angle of your camera, the 3D view is instantly displayed.

The view will appear on your **3D Model View** menu and toolbar flyouts for easy access. (By default, the first view you create is called Camera1).

Changing a 3D View

The position of the camera determines the point you are viewing your design from while in 3D view. By moving your camera you can change your viewpoint. See *Changing Your Viewpoint* on page 234.

If you are currently in a 3D view, you can use navigation tools such as Walk Around and Slide to move the camera dynamically. You can find these topics later in this chapter, starting on page 238.

You can also change what you're focused on in a 3D view by moving the target. You can do this by displaying your cameras in 2D plan view and dragging the target icon to a new spot. See *Changing the Target of Your View* on page 235.

You can also change your camera height (page 235), target height (page 235) and viewing field angle (page 237).

Turning Cameras On and Off

Every 3D view is controlled by a virtual "camera". The **Cameras On/Off** function displays a camera icon on the screen. This gives you an idea of where you are viewing from. If you click on a camera, the target and viewing field angle become highlighted. This lets you know what the camera is focused on, and how much of your design is included in the view.

When you have your cameras turned on, you can move cameras and their targets. You can also view the 3D view associated with a camera using the Look Through tool on a camera's right-click menu.

To turn cameras on:

- Select **View > Viewing Aids > Cameras On/Off**, or
- Click the Viewing Aids button on the Basic View Control or Advanced View Control toolbar and select **Cameras On/Off**

In 2D plan view, all cameras for all 3D views are visible. (By default there are two: one for the 3D Perspective, and one for the 3D Overview.) You may need to zoom out to see them.

Changing Your Viewpoint

Moving a camera changes the angle you are viewing from in 3D. You can change the position of a camera by turning your cameras on, then moving the camera in 2D plan view. When you switch back to 3D view, the view will be changed accordingly.

To change your viewpoint for a 3D view:

1. Make sure you are in 2D plan view.
2. Turn your cameras on. (See *Turning Cameras On and Off* on page 234.)

   By default, the camera for the 3D Perspective view is located to the left of the model. The camera for the 3D Overview is located towards the right side of the model.

3. Click on the camera you want to move.
4. Hover your pointer over the camera's blue grab handle to display the Move cursor. Or, right-click in the drawing area and select **Move Camera**.

5. Click and drag the camera to move it where you want it.

Changing the Camera Height

The height of your camera determines the height you are viewing your model from. A positive camera height lets you look down on your model, while a negative camera height lets you look up at your model. A camera height of 0 would be like standing on the ground and looking at your model.

The default camera height in the 3D Perspective view is 5'-6". In the 3D Overview, the camera height is set to approximately 32'.

To change the camera height:

1. With the 3D view displayed, right-click in the drawing window and select **Camera Properties**.
2. In the **Camera Properties** dialog, type the height you want in the **Camera Height** edit box, or use the arrows to scroll up or down through a list of values.
3. Click **Apply** to see the change.
4. If the view is acceptable, click **OK**.

Changing the Target of Your View

The target of a 3D view is the area you are focused on, or looking towards. You can change the position of a target by turning your cameras on, then moving the target in 2D plan view. When you switch back to 3D view, the view be changed accordingly.

To change the target of a 3D view:

1. Make sure you are in 2D plan view.
2. Turn your cameras on. (See *Turning Cameras On and Off* on page 234.)

By default, the camera for the 3D Perspective view is located to the left of the model. The camera for the 3D Overview is located towards the right side of the model.

3. Click on the camera whose target you want to move. The target is usually inside or near your model. It is marked with a blue grab handle.
4. Hover your pointer over the target's grab handle to display the Move cursor. Or, right-click in the drawing area and select **Move Target**.

5. Click and drag the target to move it where you want it.

Changing the Target Height

Raising or lowering your target can increase or decrease the steepness of the angle you are viewing from when looking through the camera.

To change the target height:

1. With the 3D view displayed, right-click in the drawing window and select **Camera Properties**.
2. In the **Camera Properties** dialog, type the height you want in the **Target Height** edit box, or use the arrows to scroll up or down through a list of values.
3. Click **Apply** to see the change.
4. If the view is acceptable, click **OK**.

Viewing in Perspective Mode

When a 3D view is set to a perspective view mode, objects in the scene that are far away appear as if they are smaller; objects closer seem larger. This creates a more realistic view of the model than parallel mode because distance plays a part in the view. By default, the 3D Perspective view has its view mode set to perspective mode.

If the current 3D view is in parallel mode, you can change the view mode to perspective mode if you want.

To change to a perspective view mode:

1. With the 3D view displayed, right-click in the drawing window and select **Camera Properties**.
2. In the **Camera Properties** dialog, enable the **Perspective** radio button.
3. Click **Apply** to see the change.
4. If the view is acceptable, click **OK**.

If you want to change the distance you are viewing from, you need to change the view angle in the camera properties, or move your camera.

Viewing in Parallel Mode

When a 3D view is set to a parallel view mode, the view is set from a common angle, and distance is eliminated from the view. This provides an instant, close-up view of your design. By default, the 3D Overview has its view mode set to parallel mode.

If the current 3D view is in perspective mode, you can change the view mode to parallel mode if you want.

To change to a parallel view mode:

1. With the 3D view displayed, right-click in the drawing window and select **Camera Properties**.
2. In the **Camera Properties** dialog, enable the **Parallel** radio button.
3. Click **Apply** to see the change.
4. If the view is acceptable, click **OK**.

You can change the angle you are viewing from by selecting a preset camera angle in the **Camera Properties** dialog, or by moving the camera.

Selecting a Preset Camera Angle

A convenient and effective way to quickly view your drawing from a number of different angles is to use the Preset Cameras in your camera properties.

The nine preset camera angles show your drawing:

- looking down at an angle from above the four corners
- looking straight on from the four sides
- looking straight down from directly above (90°)

To select a preset Camera angle:

1. With the 3D view displayed, right-click in the drawing window and select **Camera Properties**.
2. In the **Camera Properties** dialog, click on one of the buttons in the *Preset Cameras* area.
3. Click **Apply** to see the change.
4. If the view is acceptable, click **OK**.

Note: You can change your viewing angle to any angle you want by moving the camera or using one of the dynamic navigation tools.

Changing the Viewing Field Angle

The viewing field can only be changed in the 3D Perspective view, or views with their view mode set to Perspective.

The viewing field refers to your field of vision. It works like a camera lens: higher values produce a wide-angle view; lower values produce a close-up view.

Sometimes changing the viewing field angle makes it seem like you are zooming in or out. This is because for wide-angle views, the program needs to shrink the image to provide enough screen space to contain the view. Conversely, the program enlarges the image to fill the screen at smaller view angles, creating a close-up view.

Interior with 45° View Angle

Interior with 120° View Angle

To change the viewing field angle:

1. With the 3D view displayed, right-click in the drawing window and select **Camera Properties**.
2. In the **Camera Properties** dialog, type the desired angle in the **View Angle** edit box, or use the slider to increase or decrease the angle.
3. Click **Apply** to see the change.
4. If the view is acceptable, click **OK**.

Walking Around in 3D View

When you are in a 3D view, you can use the Walk Around tool to walk around your model, or even go right inside it. You can walk forward, backward, left or right.

To walk around in 3D view:

1. Select **View > Zoom and Navigate > Walk Around**, or right-click in the drawing area and select **Walk Around**, or click the Walk Around button on the Zoom and Navigate toolbar.
2. Click and drag in the direction you want to move.
   - To move forward, click and drag upward.
   - To move backward, click and drag downward.
   - To walk left or right, click and drag left or right.

   If you click and drag up to the left, your path of motion will curve upward to the left, and so forth.

Flying Around Your 3D Model

In a 3D view, the Fly Around tool revolves the camera around the target.

To fly around your model:

1. Select **View > Zoom and Navigate > Fly Around**, or right-click in the drawing area and select Fly Around, or click the Fly Around button on the Zoom and Navigate toolbar.
2. Use your mouse button to orbit the camera. Your options are described below.
   - Click and hold the mouse button to slowly rotate the camera around the target on a level plane.
   - Drag toward the top of the screen to make your model tilt downward like a boat coming off a wave.
   - Drag toward the bottom of the screen to make your model tilt up like a boat riding onto a wave.
   - Drag to the right to rotate the model in a clockwise direction.
   - Drag to the left to rotate the model in a counterclockwise direction.

Note: Model direction is the opposite of camera direction. For example, if the model appears to be moving clockwise, the camera is actually moving counterclockwise.

Sliding in a 3D View

In a 3D view, the Slide tool moves both the camera and target at the same time.

To slide in a 3D view:

1. Select **View > Zoom and Navigate > Slide**, or right-click in the drawing area and select **Slide**, or click the Slide button on the Zoom and Navigate toolbar.
2. Once **Slide** is selected, you can do the following:
   - Drag right to move your model view to the left.
   - Drag left to move your model view to the right.
   - Drag up (toward the top of the screen) to move your model view down (toward the bottom of the screen).
   - Drag down to move your model view up.

Note: Model direction is the opposite of camera and target direction. For example, if the model appears to be moving to the right, the camera and target are actually moving to the left.

Spinning the View Using the Look Around Tool

In a 3D view, the Look Around tool revolves the target around the camera.

To spin the view:

1. Select **View > Zoom and Navigate > Look Around**, or right-click in the drawing area and select **Look Around**, or click the Look Around button on the Zoom and Navigate toolbar.

2. Once **Look Around** is selected, you can do the following (presuming that your target is located inside or near the model):
    - Drag right to move the target in a counterclockwise direction. Your model orbits around you in a clockwise direction.
    - Drag left to move the target in a clockwise direction. Your model orbits around you in a counterclockwise direction.
    - Drag up to lower the height and shorten the distance of the target. Your view becomes high-angle, and your model moves toward the top of the screen.
    - Drag down to raise the height and lengthen the distance of the target. Your view becomes low-angle, and your model moves toward the bottom of the screen.

Note: Be careful when using the Look Around tool. It is very easy to lose sight of your model since the camera's "eye" is fixed in one direction only. It does not move to follow the orbiting target. Therefore, your field of vision is limited, and your model can quickly get above, below or behind you.

Resetting the Camera in a 3D View

If you have moved your camera, either by dragging it in 2D plan view or using a navigation tool like Walk Around or Slide, you can use the Reset Camera tool to move the camera back into its original position. Note that this tool is only available when the current view is a 3D view.

To reset the camera to its original position:

1. Select **View > Zoom and Navigate > Reset Camera**, or click the Reset Camera button on the Zoom and Navigate toolbar.

Selecting a Background for 3D Views

By default, a sky image is displayed behind your model when you are in a 3D view. You can select a different image to display, including custom bitmaps that you have imported, or switch to a night scene.

To select a background for the view:

1. Select **Settings > Background Settings**, or click the Background Settings button on the Settings toolbar.

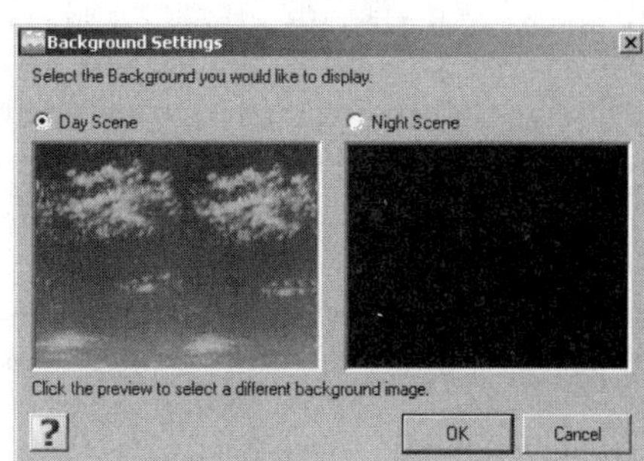

2. In the **Background Settings** dialog, select either the Day Scene or Night Scene radio button. You would want to switch to a night scene if you are doing a nighttime 3DTrueView™ rendering of your model.
3. Click on the current preview to access the **Materials** dialog.

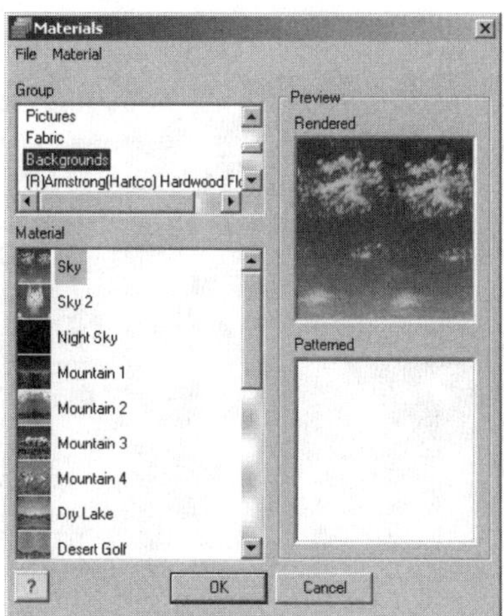

4. In the **Materials** dialog, select a background from the **Materials** list. To add a material to the list (if you have your own bitmap, for example), see *Customizing the Materials Library* on page 260.
5. Click **OK** in the **Materials** dialog.
6. Click **OK** in the **Background Settings** dialog.

Defining the Basic Terrain

By default, a basic 150′ x 150′ grass terrain is displayed in the drawing area. In 2D view, only the boundary of the terrain is shown (you may need to zoom out to see it). Contour lines may also be visible depending on the terrain's defined properties. In 3D view, the terrain is displayed as a solid, 3D object. It can be viewed in wireframe, hidden line or rendered form.

You can control the base level, size (length and width), mesh spacing, and contour interval of the terrain. You can also select a texture to use when displaying the terrain in rendered view (the default is grass).

You can specify whether or not you want the terrain to cut around your building, and select the location that you want the terrain to cut around.

To define the terrain:

1. Select **Settings > Terrain Settings**, or click the Terrain Settings button on the Settings toolbar.

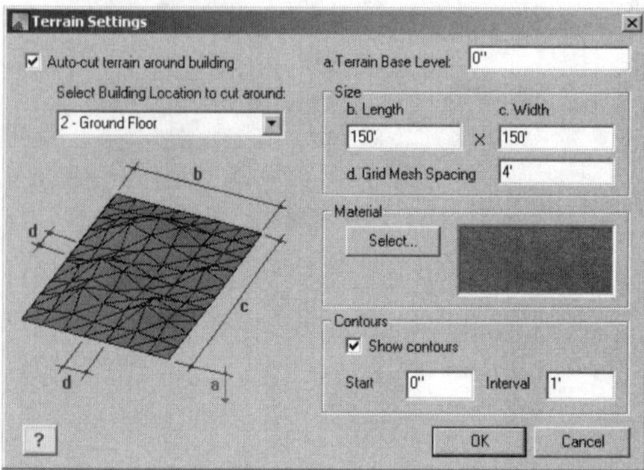

2. In the **Terrain Settings** dialog, set your terrain options:
3. To force the terrain to cut around a building, enable the **Auto-cut terrain around building** check box, then select the building location that you want the terrain to cut around from the **Select Building Location to cut around** drop box.
4. To change the level at which the base of the terrain sits, type the desired value in the **Terrain Base Level** edit box. This value is measured from 0.
5. To change the overall size of the terrain, enter the desired values in the **Length** and **Width** edit boxes.
6. To change the spacing between mesh lines (when viewing the terrain in Wireframe, Hidden Line or Patterned view), enter the desired value in the **Grid Mesh Spacing** edit box.
7. To change the texture used for the terrain, click the Select button in the Material area, then make your selection in the **Materials** dialog.
8. To display contours on your terrain, enable the **Show contours** check box. In the **Start** edit box, enter the elevation of the first contour. In the **Interval** check box, enter the desired spacing between contours.
9. Click **OK**.

Viewing Elevations

Elevations are 2D views that show a particular side of your house (front, rear, left or right) as if you were looking at it face on. While in an elevation view you can zoom in and out as well as change the display type.

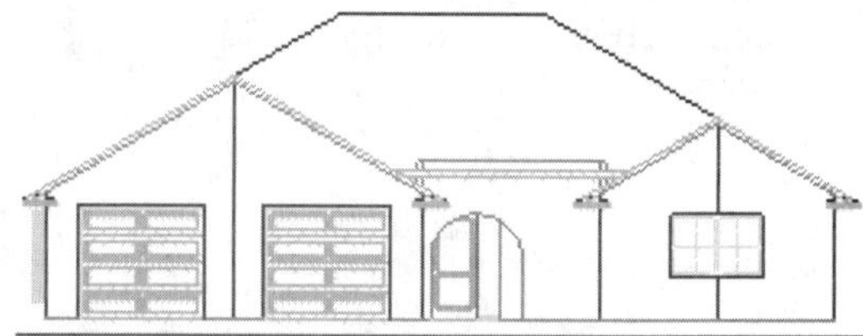

Sample Elevation

To view an elevation:

1. Select **View > Elevation View**, or click the Elevation View button on the Advanced View Control toolbar.
2. From the flyout, select the elevation you want to view (Front, Back, Right or Left).

Tip: If you have your elevation marks turned on in your 2D plan view, you can switch to an elevation view by selecting an elevation mark, right-clicking it, then selecting **View Elevation**.

Turning Elevation Marks On and Off

You can use the Elevation Marks On/Off tool to display elevation marks in your 2D plan view. An elevation mark contains the label given to the elevation in the elevation's properties, as well as a target arrow that identifies the view direction of the elevation.

Back Elevation Mark

By default, four marks are displayed, one for each of the default elevations on the Elevation View menu. If you have created a custom elevation, a mark is displayed for that elevation as well.

To turn elevation marks on or off:

- Select **View > Viewing Aids > Elevation Marks On/Off**, or
- Click the Viewing Aids button on the Basic View Control or Advanced View Control toolbar and select **Elevation Marks On/Off**

The marks are located at the extents of your drawing, so you may need to zoom out to see them.

If you select and right-click an elevation mark, you can access a number of editing tools such as Properties, Move and Move Target. Selecting View Elevation displays the elevation associated with that mark.

Moving Elevation Marks

By default, elevation marks are centered with your model, which means the model is centered on the screen when you view the resulting elevation view. If you move an elevation mark in your 2D plan view, the model may be moved left or right when you display the elevation view. Moving a mark closer to or farther away from the model has no effect on the resulting elevation view.

To move an elevation mark:

1. Select the elevation mark in 2D plan view.
2. Hover your pointer over the mark's blue grab handle to display the Move cursor. Or, right-click in the drawing area and select **Move**.

3. Click and drag the mark to move it where you want it.
4. Right-click and select **View Elevation** to see the resulting elevation.

Changing the Target of an Elevation

By default, elevation marks point straight at your model. The result is a completely face-on view when you display the resulting elevation view. If you rotate an elevation mark, you change the target of the elevation. This focuses the view on a different part of your design when you display the elevation view.

To change the target of an elevation:

1. Make sure your elevation marks are turned on.
2. In 2D plan view, select the mark whose target you want to change.
3. Right-click and select **Move Target**.
4. Click and drag to rotate the mark so it is pointing in a different direction.
5. Right-click and select **View Elevation** to see the result.

Editing Elevation Properties

You can edit the name of an elevation as it appears on the **Elevation View** menu, as well as edit the name and text style of an elevation mark.

To edit elevation properties:

1. If the elevation view is currently displayed, right-click and select **Elevation Properties**. If you are currently in 2D plan view, select the elevation mark, then right-click and select **Properties**.

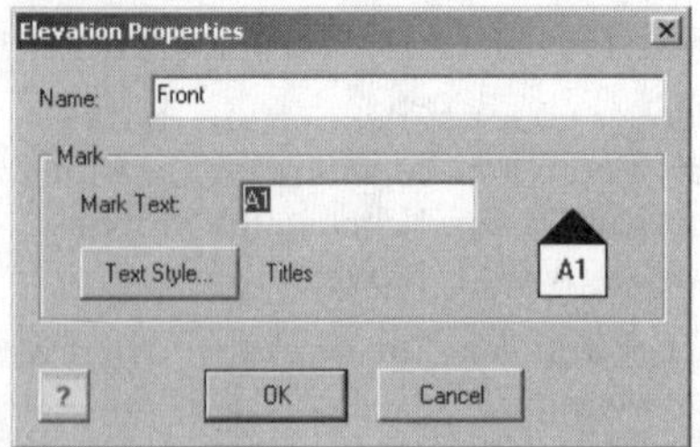

2. To edit the name of the elevation as it appears on the **Elevation View** menu, edit the name in the **Name** edit box.
3. To edit the text that appears on the elevation mark, edit the text in the **Mark Text** edit box.
4. To apply a different text style to the elevation mark, click the **Text Style** button and make a selection from the Text Styles dialog. You can also edit the current text style if you want.
5. Click **OK**.

Deleting an Elevation

You can delete an elevation from the **Elevation View** menu by deleting its corresponding elevation mark in 2D plan view.

To delete an elevation:

1. Make sure your elevation marks are turned on.
2. In 2D plan view, select the mark to delete.
3. Press the **Delete** key on your keyboard, or right-click and select **Delete**.

Creating a Custom Elevation

You can create a custom elevation by inserting an elevation mark in your 2D plan view. Once you've inserted the mark, which represents your viewpoint, you can rotate it using your mouse to define the view direction.

To create a custom elevation:

1. Make sure you are in 2D plan view.
2. Turn your elevation marks on. This is not necessary, but we recommend it so that you can see where other elevation marks are located. The default elevation marks are located at the extents of the terrain, so you may need to zoom out to see them.
3. Select **View > Elevation View > Create New Elevation**, or click the Elevation View button on the Advanced View Control toolbar and select **Create New Elevation**. An elevation mark is attached to your cursor, ready to be inserted.
4. Click to insert the new elevation mark. This represents your viewpoint, so naturally you would select a point in front of the model side you want to look at in your elevation.
5. Move your cursor to rotate the arrow on the elevation mark and define the view direction. Once it is pointing in the desired direction (usually towards your model), click to finish.

Once you've positioned the elevation mark, the resulting elevation is instantly displayed. It is also added to the **Elevation View** menu and toolbar flyout for easy access. (By default, the first view you create is called Elevation1.)

Tip: You can change the name of the elevation as well as edit the elevation mark properties by editing the Elevation Properties.

Creating a Section View

You can cut through any portion of your model to create a section view. Section views are a great way to see the interior features of your model that you are not able to see from the outside.

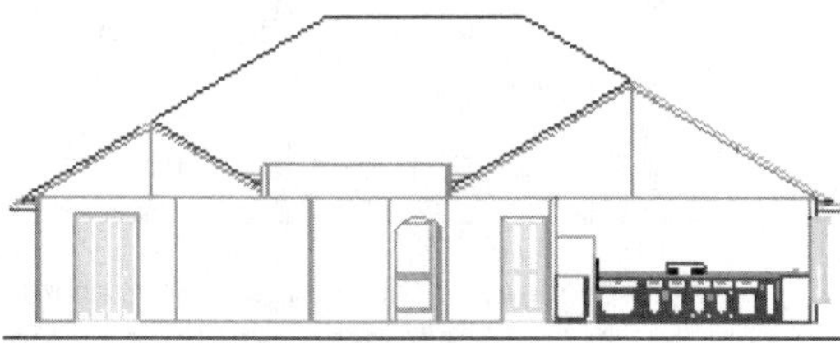

Sample Section

To create a section view, you draw a section line through your model in 2D plan view, then click to define the view direction and depth.

To create a section view:

1. Make sure you are in 2D plan view.
2. Select **View > Section View > Create New Section**, or click the Section View button on the Advanced View Control toolbar and select **Create New Section**.
3. Select two points to draw a line that cuts through your model. This is the line you will be viewing from.
4. Move your cursor in the direction you want to view. The more you move away from the section line, the deeper your view becomes. Once the bounding box is the desired distance and direction from the section line, click to finish.

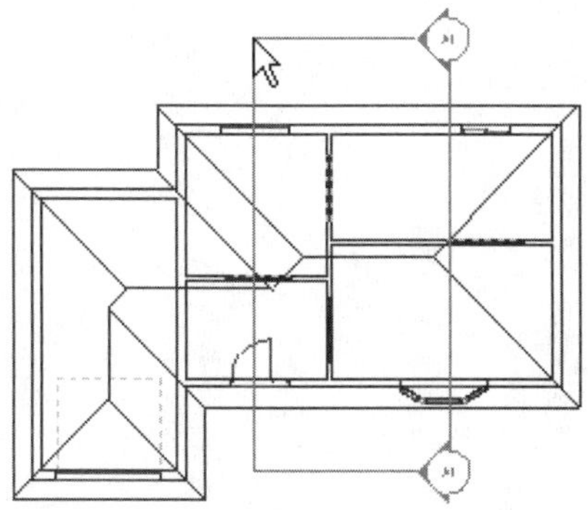

Once you've defined the section mark, the resulting section view is instantly displayed. It is also added to the **Section View** menu and toolbar flyouts for easy access. (By default, the first view you create is called Section1.)

Viewing Section Views

If you have created section views, you can display them at any time using the Section View menu or toolbar.

To view a section view:

1. Select **View > Section View**, or click the Section View button on the Advanced View Control toolbar. 
2. From the flyout, select the section you want to view.

Tip: If you have your section marks turned on in your 2D plan view, you can switch to a section view by selecting a section mark, right-clicking it, then selecting **View Section**.

Turning Section Marks On and Off

When you create a section, a section mark is displayed in the 2D plan view. The section mark contains markers at each end of the section line which indicate the direction of the section view. You can turn section marks on and off using the Section Marks On/Off tool.

To turn section marks on or off:

- Select **View > Viewing Aids > Section Marks On/Off**, or
- Click the Viewing Aids button on the Basic View Control or Advanced View Control toolbar and select **Section Marks On/Off**

Editing a Section View

You can edit a section view by moving the section mark associated with the section view, or by stretching the bounding box attached to the section line. By moving a section mark you are changing your viewpoint. By stretching the bounding box, you are changing the depth of the view.

To change your viewpoint by moving the section mark:

1. In 2D plan view, make sure your section marks are turned on.
2. Click on the section mark.
3. Hover your pointer over the blue grab handle on the section line to display the Move cursor. Or, right-click in the drawing area and select **Move**. 
4. Click and drag the mark to move it where you want it.
5. Right-click and select **View Section** to see the result.

To change the depth of the section view:

1. In 2D plan view, make sure your section marks are turned on.
2. Click on the section mark.
3. Hover your pointer over the blue grab handle on the bounding box line to display the Stretch cursor. Or, right-click in the drawing area and select **Stretch**.
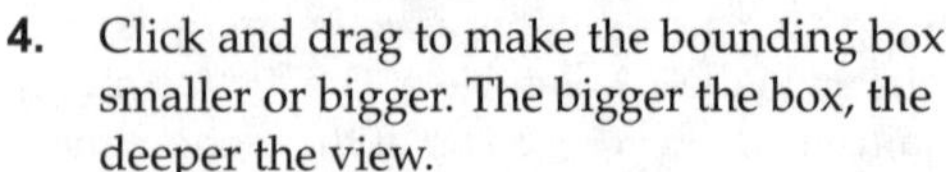
4. Click and drag to make the bounding box smaller or bigger. The bigger the box, the deeper the view.
5. Right-click and select **View Section** to see the result.

Editing Section Properties

You can edit the name of a section as it appears on the **Section View** menu, as well as edit the name and text style of a section mark.

To edit section properties:

1. If the section view is currently displayed, right-click and select **Section Properties**. If you are currently in 2D plan view, select the section mark, then right-click and select **Properties**.

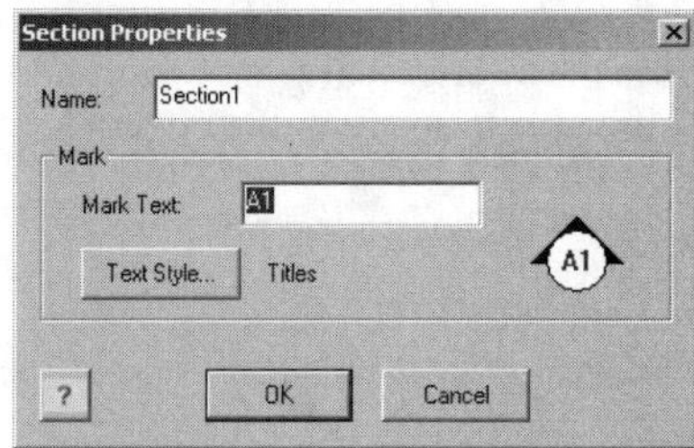

2. To edit the name of the section as it appears on the **Section View** menu, edit the name in the **Name** edit box.
3. To edit the text that appears on the section mark, edit the text in the **Mark Text** edit box.
4. To apply a different text style to the section mark, click the **Text Style** button and make a selection from the **Text Styles** dialog. You can also edit the current text style if you want.
5. Click **OK**.

Deleting a Section View

You can delete a section from the **Section View** menu by deleting its corresponding section mark in 2D plan view.

To delete a section:

1. Make sure your section marks are turned on.
2. In 2D plan view, select the mark to delete.
3. Press the **Delete** key on your keyboard, or right-click and select **Delete**.

Chapter 36

Catalogs & Elements

3D Home Architect® Home Design's Catalog Manager lets you add, edit and delete elements to suit your needs. You can also create new, custom catalogs that contain a specific selection of elements. You can open any catalog you want during a work session to gain access to the elements you want.

Another great feature is Save Element to Catalog, which lets you save an element that you have edited in your drawing to the current catalog.

Using the Catalog Manager

The program's Catalog Manager provides full control of new and existing catalogs.

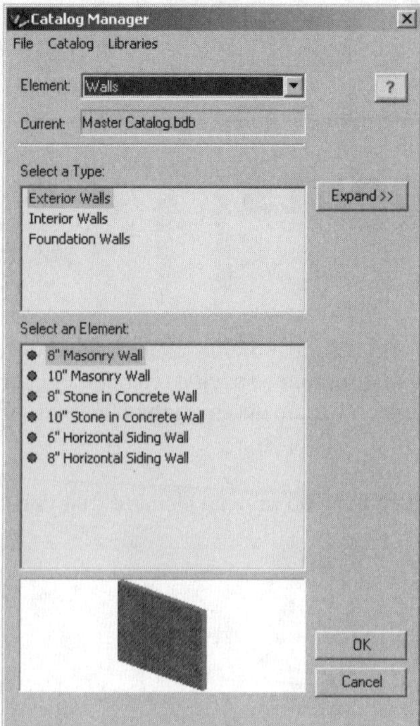

Using the Catalog Manager you can:

- View the contents and properties of any catalog
- Add groups and elements to a catalog
- Delete groups and elements from a catalog
- Edit elements in a catalog
- Import elements into a catalog from another catalog
- Create and save new catalogs

To access the Catalog Manager:

1. Select **File > Catalogs > Catalog Manager**, or right-click an element in the catalog panel and select **Catalog Manager**.

To view a listing of a particular element type:

1. Select the element from the **Element** drop box.

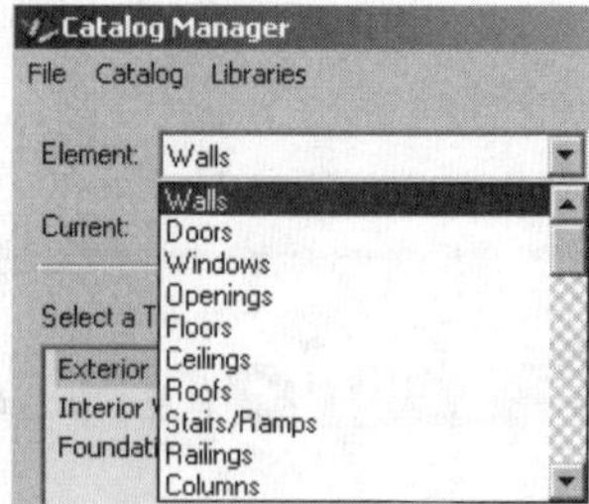

To view the properties of an element:

1. Select the element in the *Select an Element* window.
2. Select **Catalog > Element Properties**, or right-click and select **Properties**.

Adding a Group to a Catalog

All elements are organized by group. For example, walls are grouped under Exterior Walls, Interior Walls, or Foundation Walls. This helps you locate specific element types quickly. You can add groups to any catalog using the Add Group tool.

To add a group to the current catalog:

1. Select **File > Catalogs > Catalog Manager**, or right-click an element in the catalog panel and select **Catalog Manager**.
2. Select the appropriate element type from the **Element** drop box.
3. Select **Catalog > Add Group**, or right-click in the *Select a Type* window and select **Add Group**.
4. Type a name for the group, then press ENTER.
5. Select **File > Save Catalog**.

Renaming a Group in a Catalog

You can change the name of any group in a catalog using the Rename Group tool.

To rename a group:

1. Select **File > Catalogs > Catalog Manager**, or right-click an element in the catalog panel and select **Catalog Manager**.
2. Select the appropriate element type from the **Element** drop box.
3. In the *Select a Type* window, select the group you want to rename.
4. Select **Catalog > Rename Group**, or right-click and select **Rename Group**.
5. Type the new name and press ENTER.
6. Select **File > Save Catalog**.

Deleting a Group in a Catalog

You can delete a group in a catalog provided it contains no elements.

To delete a group in a catalog:

1. Select **File > Catalogs > Catalog Manager**, or right-click an element in the catalog panel and select **Catalog Manager**.
2. Select the appropriate element type from the **Element** drop box.
3. In the *Select a Type* window, select the group you want to delete. Note that the group can only be deleted if it contains no elements.
4. Select **Catalog > Delete Group**, or right-click and select **Delete Group**.
5. Select **File > Save Catalog**.

Adding and Editing Elements in a Catalog

Every element has a number of different properties that determine its size, geometry and appearance. You can edit these properties to suit your needs. If you want you can create a new element instead of editing an existing one.

Note: You can't edit elements in the catalog panel. You need to use the Catalog Manager.

To edit an element in a catalog:

1. Select **File > Catalogs > Catalog Manager**, or right-click an element in the catalog panel and select **Catalog Manager**.
2. Select the appropriate element type from the **Element** drop box.
3. In the *Select a Type* window, select the group containing the element you want to edit.
4. In the *Select an Element* window, select the element to edit.
5. Select **Catalog > Element Properties**, or right-click and select **Properties**.
6. Edit the properties as desired. See *Working with Property Pages* on page 251 for more information.
7. Click **OK** to return to the **Catalog Manager**.
8. Select **File > Save Catalog**.

Note: Editing elements in a catalog has no effect on elements already inserted in your drawing. It only affects future insertions of the element.

To add a new element to a catalog:

1. Select **File > Catalogs > Catalog Manager**, or right-click an element in the catalog panel and select **Catalog Manager**.
2. Select the appropriate element type from the **Element** drop box.
3. In the *Select a Type* window, select the group you want to add the element to.
4. Select **Catalog > Add Element**.

   Elements like furniture, appliances and accessories can be defined based on a set of general parameters, or by importing a 3D

Studio file. If this is the case, you will see a dialog similar to the following:

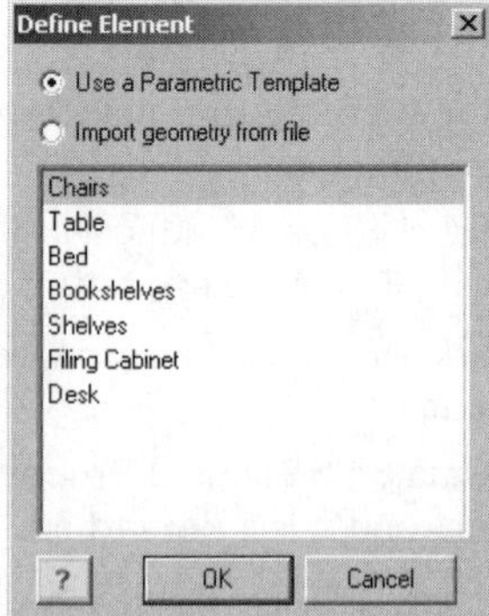

To define the element by specifying size properties, select the **Use a Parametric Template** radio button, select the specific element type you want to create (chair, table, etc.), then click **OK**.

To import a 3D Studio file, select the **Import geometry from file** radio button, click **OK**, then select the desired 3D Studio file. Some elements, like electronics, will prompt you directly for a 3D Studio file because they do not have a parametric template. For more information, see *Importing 3D Studio Files* on page 248.

5. Define the element's properties. (See *Working with Property Pages* on page 251.)

   Note that if the **Auto Name** check box is enabled, the element will be automatically named for you. For example, if you are creating a wall and select Masonry for the wall type, and specify a width of 6", the name automatically becomes **6" Masonry Wall**. For more information about automatic name generation, see *Using Automatic Name Generation* on page 251.)

   If you want to give the element a different name, disable the **Auto Name** check box and type the desired name in the **Name** edit box.

6. Click **OK**. The element is added to the catalog.
7. Select **File > Save Catalog**.

Saving Edited Elements in Your Drawing to a Catalog

If you have edited the properties of an inserted element, you can save that element (and its custom properties) to the current catalog.

To add an edited element from your drawing into the current catalog:

1. Select **File > Catalogs > Save Element to Catalog**. Your pointer changes to a catalog cursor. 
2. Select the element in your drawing.

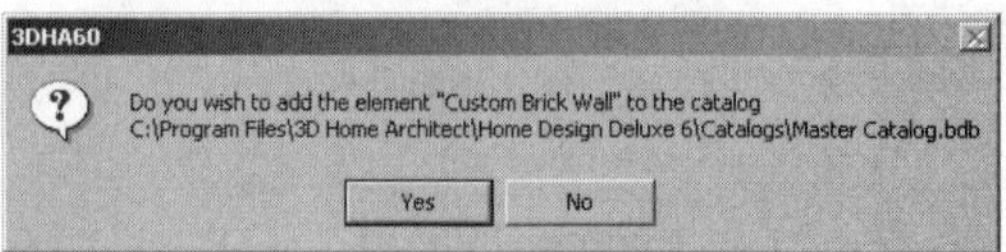

3. Click **Yes** to save the element. The element is added to the current catalog.

Importing 3D Studio Files

Many sites on the Internet offer free downloading of elements in 3D Studio (*.3ds) format. You can easily convert these files for use in *3D Home Architect® Home Design*.

To import a 3D Studio file:

1. Select **File > Catalogs > Catalog Manager**, or right-click an element in the catalog panel and select **Catalog Manager**.
2. Select the appropriate element type from the **Element** drop box (e.g. Furniture).
3. In the *Select a Type* window, select the group you want to add the element to.

4. Select **Catalog > Add Element**. In the **Define Element** dialog, select the **Import geometry from file** radio button.

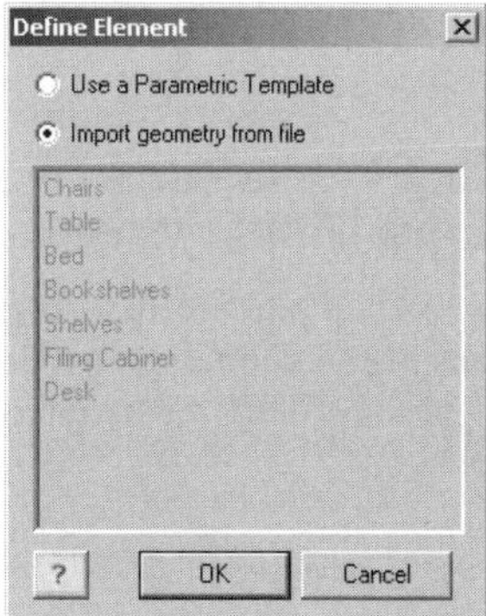

5. Click **OK**.
6. In the **Open** dialog, select the 3D Studio file, then click **Open**.

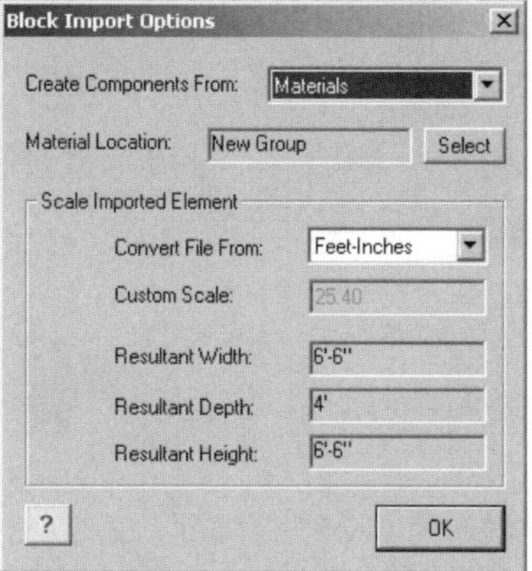

Since *3D Home Architect® Home Design* can only import 3D Studio files, the only selection in the **Create Components From** drop box is *Materials*, since 3DS objects are essentially an assembly of materials.

7. By default, the imported object's materials will be stored in a new group in your materials library. If you want to store them in a specific group, click **Select**, then select the desired group.

8. Click **OK** in the **Material Group(s)** dialog.
9. When you import a 3D Studio block, there is usually no way of knowing what units the designer intended for the block. In the **Block Import Options** dialog, select the unit of measure in the **Convert File From** drop box that will result in a logical Resultant Width, Depth and Height. Selecting *Custom* lets you specify a custom scale in the **Custom Scale** edit box.

   The scale is the multiplication factor of the units used for objects in the block. For example, if you're converting a file that you assume was created in feet and inches, the scale is 25.4.
10. Once logical dimensions are displayed, click **OK** in the **Block Import Options** dialog.
11. In the properties dialog, enter a name for the element in the **Name** edit box.

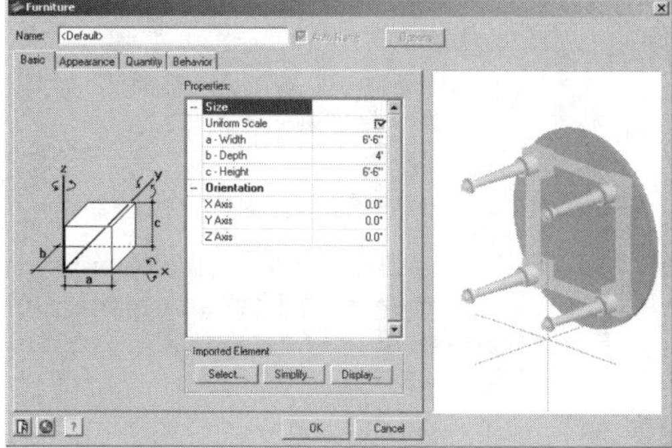

12. Define the element's properties. The element will already have size properties assigned to it that are taken from the 3D Studio file, but you can change these. You may need to edit the orientation of the element so that it inserts correctly in the drawing.
13. If you want to select a different 3D Studio file to apply to your new element, click the **Select** button in the *Imported Element* area of the properties dialog. Repeat steps 7-10.
14. Click **OK**. The new element is added to the catalog.
15. Select **File > Save Catalog**.

Simplifying an Element

If an element looks too complex in the preview window, you can simplify it by reducing the number of polygons used to display it. This applies only to some block elements like furniture and appliances.

To simplify an imported element:

1. Select **File > Catalogs > Catalog Manager**, or right-click an element in the catalog panel and select **Catalog Manager**.
2. Locate the element in the catalog.
3. Select **Catalog > Element Properties**.
4. In the property dialog, click **Simplify**.

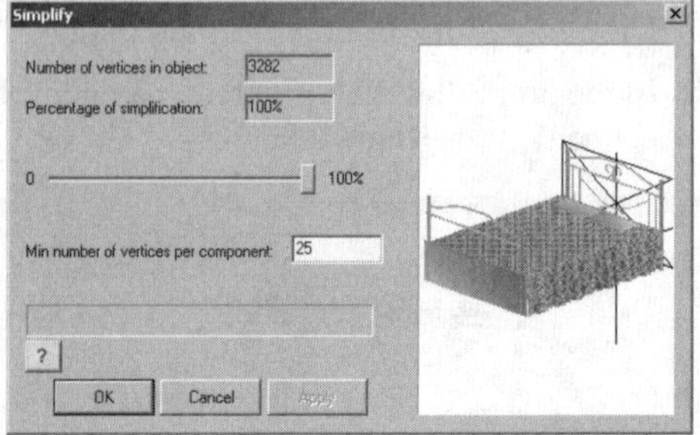

5. To simplify the element, slide the ruler to the left. The **Number of vertices in object** and **Percentage of simplification** values update accordingly.
6. To put a limit on how much simplification can take place, enter a value in the **Min number of vertices per component** edit box. The larger the number, the less simplified the element will become.
7. Click **OK** to return to the properties dialog.
8. Click **OK** in the properties dialog.
9. Select **File > Save Catalog**.

Controlling What Parts of an Element are Displayed

You can hide certain parts of an element from view by changing its display properties. This applies only to some block elements like furniture and appliances.

To control what parts of an element are displayed:

1. Select **File > Catalogs > Catalog Manager**, or right-click an element in the catalog panel and select **Catalog Manager**.
2. Locate the element in the catalog.
3. Select **Catalog > Element Properties**.
4. In the property dialog, click **Display**.

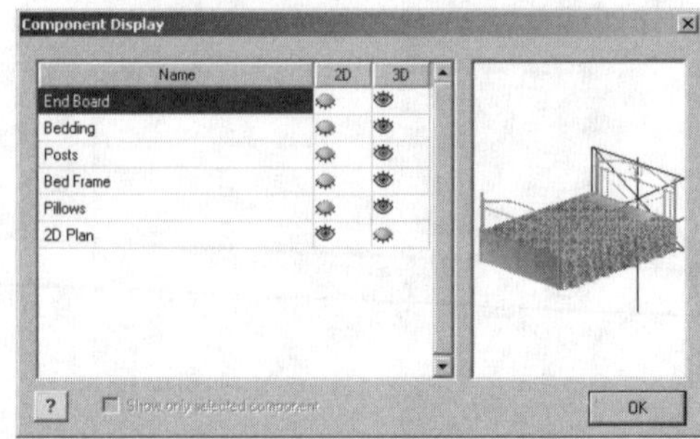

5. To display or hide a component from view in 2D and/or 3D view, select it in the list, then click the appropriate eye icon.

 Component is displayed

 Component is not displayed

6. Click **OK** to return to the properties dialog.
7. Click **OK** in the properties dialog.
8. Select **File > Save Catalog**.

Working with Property Pages

When you access an element's property pages, a multi-tabbed dialog is displayed. The tabs and properties vary depending on the element. The most common property pages are **Basic**, **Appearance**, **Quantity** and **Behavior**. The name, notes and hyperlinks properties are common to all property pages.

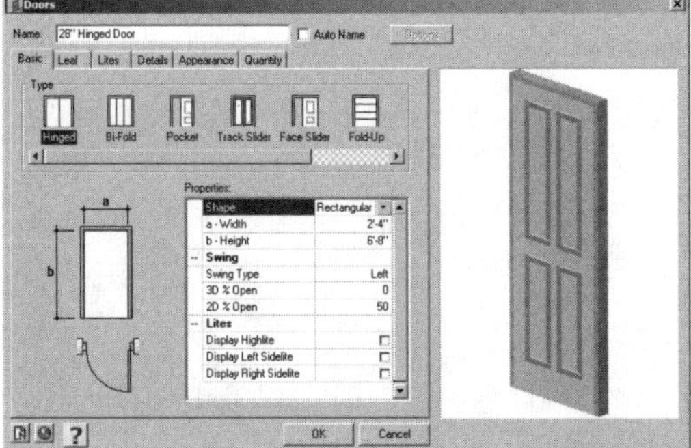

Sample Properties Dialog

A preview of the element is shown in the preview window. By default, the image is displayed in a 3D rendered view. You can switch between 3D and 2D as well as select a different display mode by right-clicking in the preview window and making a selection from the menu.

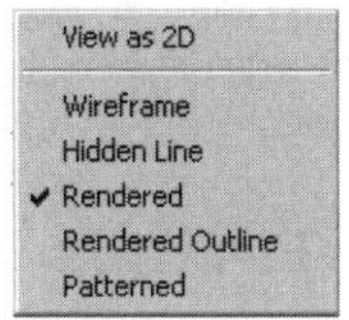

When the image is in a 3D view, you can rotate it around by clicking and dragging with your mouse.

Using Automatic Name Generation

Names of elements are based on pre-defined formulas. The name **8" Concrete Wall** is made up of three variables:

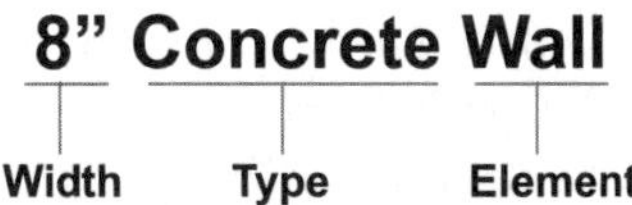

Each variable is separated by a space. These variables and spaces are defined in the name's formula.

If you add or change an element, and select **Auto Name**, the element's name updates automatically in the catalog. For example, if you create a concrete wall, and define a width of 10", the name automatically becomes **10" Concrete Wall**.

Automatic name generation:

- Saves typing a name every time you add or edit an element
- Ensures consistency in catalogs
- Prevents duplicate entries if you forget to change a name

To use automatic name generation when adding or editing an element, enable the **Auto Name** check box next to the **Name** edit box in the element's properties dialog.

Note: If **Auto Name** is not selected, you can type any name you want in the **Name** edit box.

Editing the Name Generation Formula

When you add or edit a catalog element, you can modify the formula used to generate the element's name if you are using automatic name generation. Formulas are made up of variables (like Element Class and Element Type) and separators (spaces, symbols or characters).

Editing an element's name generation formula sets the formula for any new elements you create of that type. For example, if you edit the name generation formula for an 8" Brick Wall, any new walls you add to the catalog will use the new formula if you use automatic name generation.

To modify the formula used for an element's automatic name generation:

1. Select **File > Catalogs > Catalog Manager**, or right-click an element in the catalog panel and select **Catalog Manager**.
2. Select the appropriate element type from the **Element** drop box.
3. Select the element to edit.
4. Select **Catalog > Element Properties**, or right-click and select **Properties**.
5. Click the **Options** button to the right of the **Auto Name** check box. The **Automatic Name Generation** dialog for that element type is displayed. The right pane (titled *Used Variables and Separators*) displays the current formula.

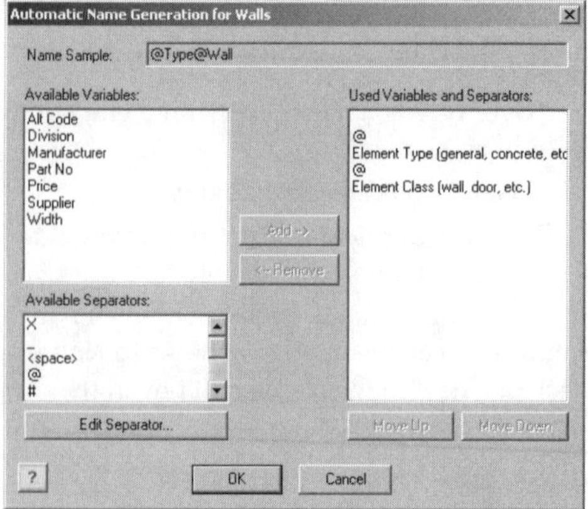

6. To remove a component from the formula, select it and click **Remove**.
7. To add a component to the formula, select the desired variable or separator in the *Available Variables* or *Available Separators* window and click **Add**.
8. To move a component in the formula, select the component and click **Move Up** or **Move Down**.
9. When you have finished modifying the formula, click **OK** to close the **Automatic Name Generation** dialog.
10. Click **OK** to close the element's properties dialog.
11. In the **Catalog Manager**, select **File > Save Catalog**.

Basic Page

Most elements have a **Basic** property page, although the properties on this page will vary according to the element type. Generally there is a **Type** section, where you can select the specific element type, as well as a **Properties** section, where you can specify the dimensions of the element.

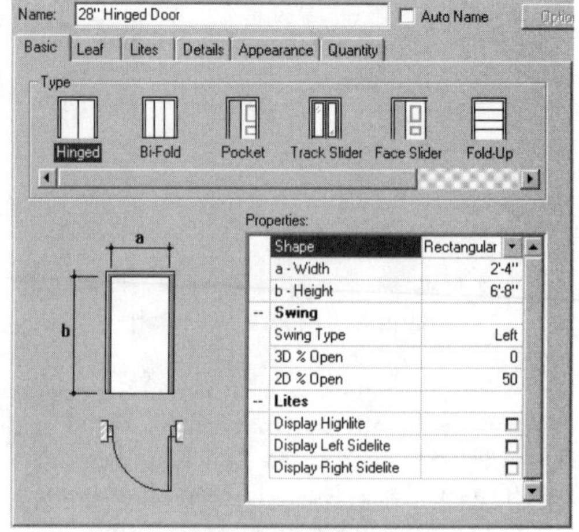

Sample Basic Page

Note: You can find detailed descriptions of size properties for specific element types in their respective chapters.

Changing an Element's Orientation

Symbol elements, such as furniture and light fixtures, are oriented in a logical fashion when you insert them in your drawing. For example, tables are inserted in a flat, upright position on the floor, and electrical outlets are inserted in a vertical position on the face of walls. You can edit the orientation of most symbol elements. For example, you may want to flip an air register so that you can insert it on the ceiling in your basement.

To change an element's orientation:

1. On the Basic property page, click the appropriate arrow keys in the *Orientation* area to rotate the element.

   (Y, Z) axes: Rotates the element front to back, and vice versa.

   (X, Z) axes: Rotates the element towards its left or right side in 3D.

   (X, Y) axes: Rotates the element left or right in 2D plan view.

Appearance Page

The **Appearance** properties page is common to most elements. It provides control over the materials applied to elements, which come into play when you view your model in Rendered or Patterned mode.

A material can be a texture, such as brick, or a color. This is what you see in Rendered mode. Materials also have a pattern assigned to them, which is what you see when you view in Patterned mode.

The contents of the **Components** window varies depending on the element. It contains a listing of the individual components that make up the element, so you can apply a different material to each component.

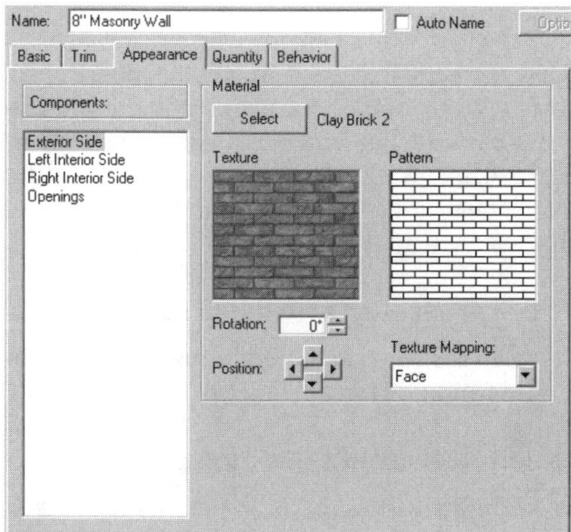

Sample Appearance Page

To change an element's material:

1. In the *Components* pane, select the component whose material you want to change.
2. In the *Material* area, click the **Select** button.

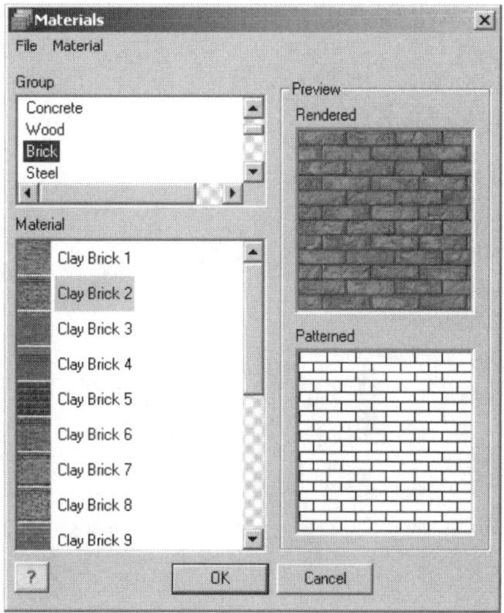

3. In the **Materials** dialog, select the group containing the desired material. If you want to choose a solid color, select the Paint group.
4. Select the material you want to use. The swatches in the preview windows update automatically. If you want to edit the material, click on one of the swatches to access the **Edit Materials** dialog. For information about editing materials, see *Editing Material Properties* on page 261.
5. Click **OK** to return to the Appearance page.
6. If you want to rotate the material on the element, enter an angle in the **Rotation** edit box, or use the arrows to scroll through a list of angles. This rotates the material in a clockwise direction.

   Rotation: 0

7. To shift the material on the element (left, right, up or down), use the **Position** arrows.

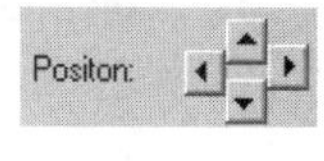

8. Select another component in the *Components* pane and select a material for that component.

9. When all your materials are defined, click **OK**.

Quantity Page

The **Quantity** properties page is common to most elements. It contains information that helps identify the element as a material, such as the manufacturer and price. Some of the information on this page is used in the project estimate.

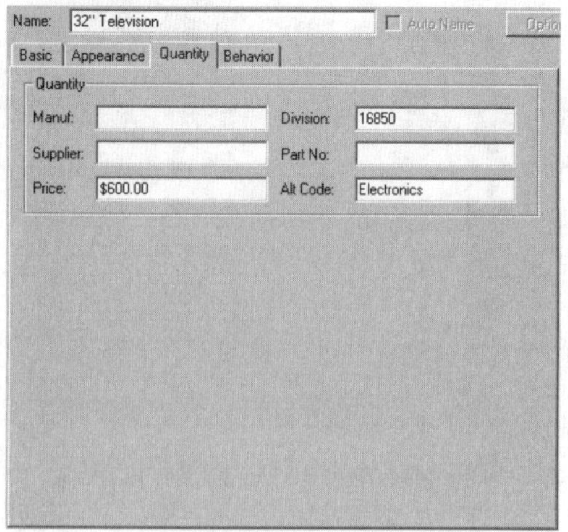

Sample Quantity Page

Manuf: The Manufacturer of the product.

Supplier: The company or store who will be supplying the product.

Price: The unit price of the product.

Division: A construction division identification. In North America, CSI divisions are used.

Part No.: Part Number. A series of numbers that identifies the product.

Alt Code: Alternate Code. An extra identification code that is used to link an element in the program's catalog to the databases of other applications, such as *Timberline.*

Behavior Page

The **Behavior** property page is available for symbol elements like cabinets, furniture and lights.

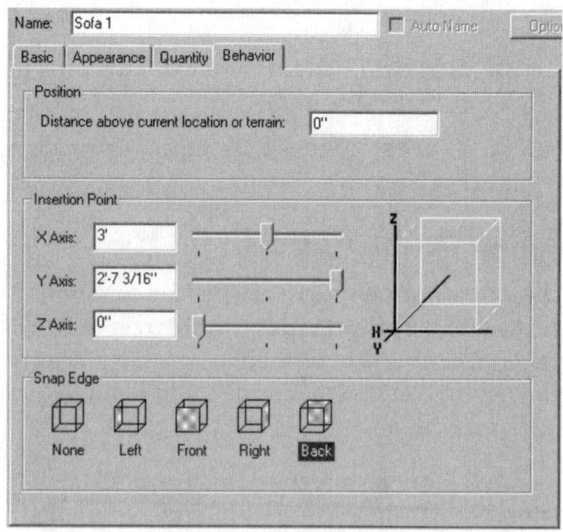

Sample Behavior Page

Usually this page contains a **Distance above current location or terrain** option which lets you control the height at which the element is inserted relative to the floor or terrain. The value entered is the distance from the floor or terrain to the insertion point of the element. (For most elements except windows and wall openings, the insertion point is at the bottom of the element.)

Some elements have a defined **Insertion Point,** which is the point on the element that is attached to the cursor when you are inserting the element. Some elements also have a defined **Snap Edge,** which determines which edge of the element will snap to the wall if you position it near a wall.

To edit an element's insertion height:

1. Edit the value in the **Distance above current location or terrain** edit box.

To edit an element's insertion point:

1. Edit the values in the X Axis, Y Axis and Z Axis edit boxes, or use the sliders beside these edit boxes.

An X value moves the insertion point left or right. A Y value moves the insertion point forwards or backwards. A Z value moves the insertion point up or down on the element.

To edit an element's snap edge:

1. Click on the desired snap edge graphic in the *Snap Edge* area.

Adding Notes to an Element's Properties

The **Notes** function in the properties dialog lets you enter a note about the element. This additional information can be anything you want.

To add a note to an element's properties:

1. Select **File > Catalogs > Catalog Manager**, or right-click an element in the catalog panel and select **Catalog Manager**.
2. Select the appropriate element type from the **Element** drop box.
3. Select the element to edit.
4. Select **Catalog > Element Properties**, or right-click and select **Properties**.
5. In the bottom left corner of the dialog, click the Add Notes button.

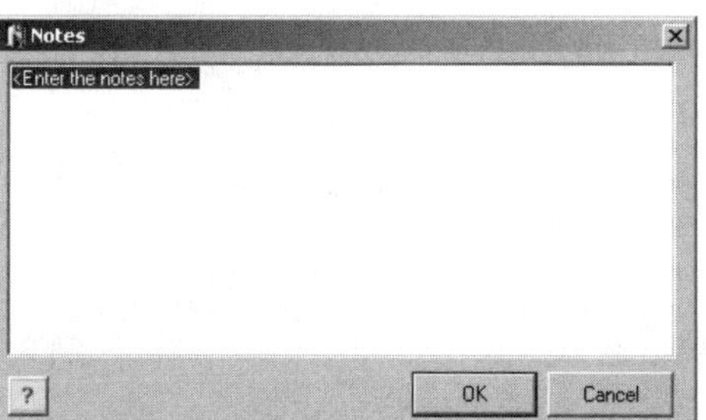

6. Enter your note in the **Notes** dialog.
7. Click **OK**.

Adding Hyperlinks to an Element's Properties

The **Hyperlinks** function in the properties dialog lets you create a link to an external file (e.g. *Word* document) or Web address.

To add a hyperlink to an element's properties:

1. Select **File > Catalogs > Catalog Manager**, or right-click an element in the catalog panel and select **Catalog Manager**.
2. Select the appropriate element type from the **Element** drop box.
3. Select the element to edit.
4. Select **Catalog > Element Properties**, or right-click and select **Properties**.
5. In the bottom left corner of the dialog, click the Add Hyperlinks button.

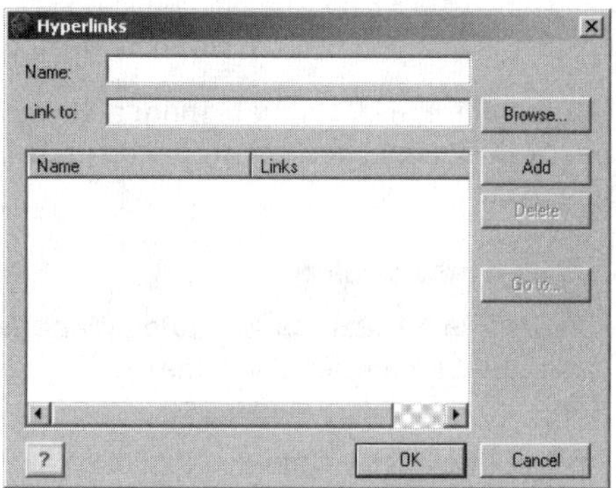

6. In the **Hyperlinks** dialog, specify a name for the hyperlink in the **Name** edit box (e.g. Broderbund Web Site).
7. In the **Link to** edit box, type the web address (e.g. http://www.broderbund.com) or path to the file you are linking to. If you are linking to a file, you can click **Browse** to search through the directories on your computer. Once you've located the file in the **Open** dialog, click **Open**. The path to the file is automatically displayed in the **Link to** edit box.
8. Click **Add** to add the link to the hyperlink window.
9. To view the link, select it in the hyperlink window, then click **Go to**.
10. To delete a hyperlink, select it in the hyperlink window, then click **Delete**.
11. Click **OK**.

Note: You can create a link to another Broderbund® Home Design (*.bld) file. However, if that file uses the same catalog as the current drawing, you cannot access the catalog in the linked file.

Creating a New Catalog

If you plan to edit or add elements in the Master Catalog, you may want to create a new catalog instead of editing the existing one. That way, the custom elements you create are distinguishable from the defaults and are stored in one place. When you create a new catalog, you specify a name and where you want to store the catalog.

When you close the **Catalog Manager**, the new catalog will become the current catalog in the catalog panel.

To create a new catalog:

1. Select **File > Catalogs > Catalog Manager**, or right-click an element in the Catalog panel and select **Catalog Manager**.
2. Select **File > New Catalog**.

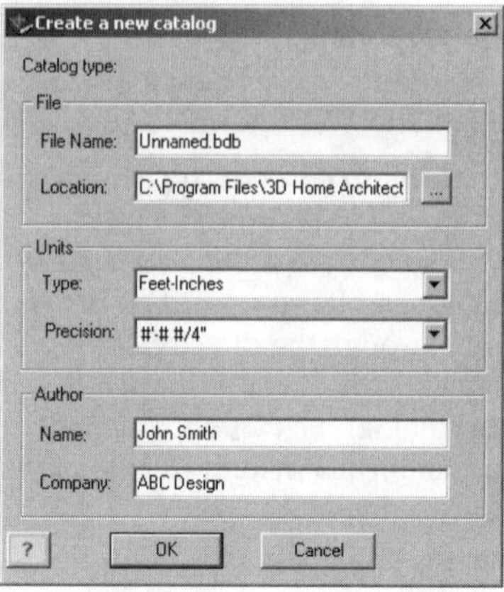

3. In the **Create a new catalog** dialog, type a name (without extension) in the **File Name** box.
4. Click the Browse button next to the **Location** edit box and select the directory where you want to store the new catalog. The default is the program's Catalogs directory, which is where you should store all catalogs.
5. From the **Type** drop box, select the unit of measure you would like to use for elements in the catalog.
6. From the **Precision** drop box, select the level of precision you would like to use for measurements. For example, selecting #'-# #/16" sets the level of precision to 1/16th of an inch when working in feet and inches.
7. In the **Name** edit box, type your name.
8. In the **Company** edit box, type the name of your company, if applicable.
9. Click **OK**. A new, blank catalog is created.

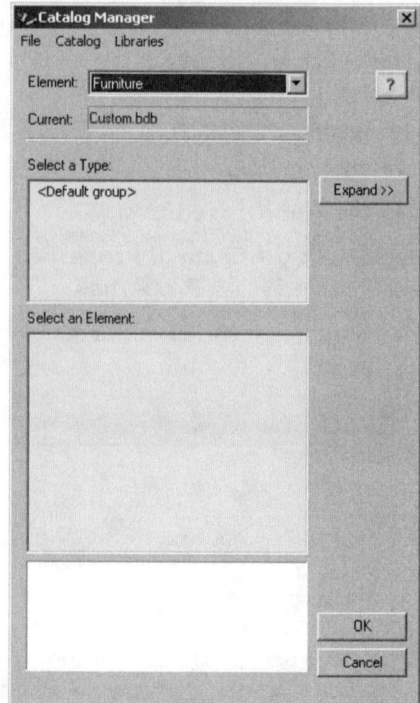

10. Select **File > Save Catalog**.
11. You can now add groups and elements to the catalog, or import elements from another catalog (see *Importing Elements into Catalogs* on page 257). Remember to save the catalog after you make changes to it.

Creating a Copy of a Catalog

You can save a catalog under a different name, which essentially creates a copy of it.

To create a copy of a catalog under a different name:

1. Select **File > Catalogs > Catalog Manager**, or right-click an element in the catalog panel and select **Catalog Manager**.
2. Make sure the catalog you want to save is the current catalog.
3. Select **File > Save Catalog As**.

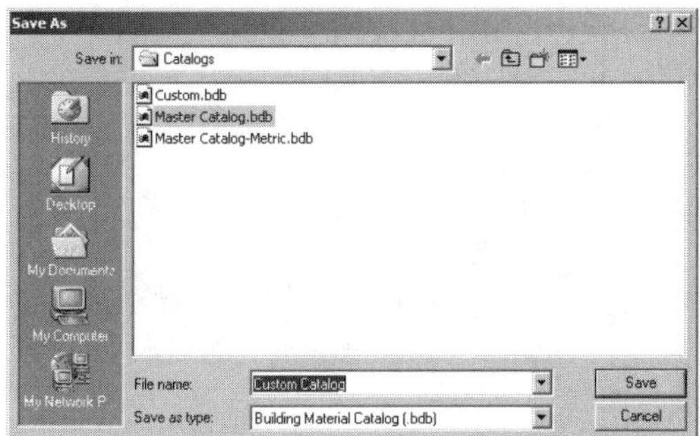

4. In the **File name** edit box, type the name you want to save under (without extension).
5. Click **Save**.

Note: The newly saved catalog becomes the current catalog.

Importing Elements into Catalogs

Using the Catalog Manager you can import elements from another catalog into the current catalog. This feature is often used when you are creating new catalogs.

Note: If you want to import a 3D Studio file, see *Importing 3D Studio Files* on page 248.

To import elements into a catalog:

1. Select **File > Catalogs > Catalog Manager**, or right-click an element in the catalog panel and select **Catalog Manager**.
2. Make sure the catalog you want to import elements into is the currently open catalog.
3. From the **Element** drop box, select the appropriate element type.
4. Click **Expand** to expand the Catalog Manager dialog.
5. On the right side of the dialog, click the Browse button, then select the catalog you want to import elements from. 

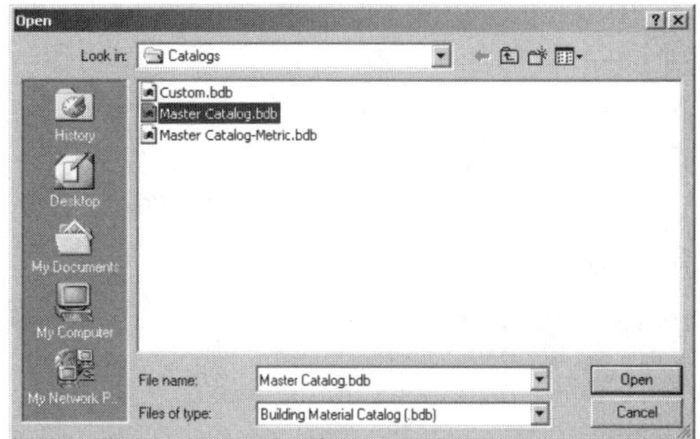

6. In the right-hand window, select an element to import, then click **Import Item**. If you want to import all elements listed, just click **Import All**. The element is imported into the current catalog. Note that the group that the element belongs to is also imported into the current catalog.

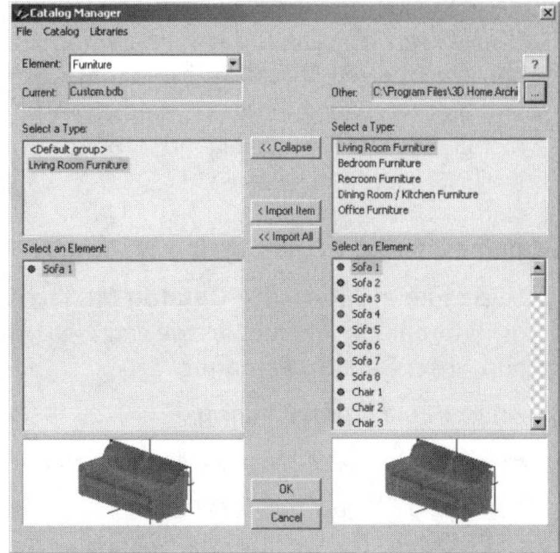

7. When you are done importing elements, click **Collapse** to return to the regular view in the **Catalog Manager**.
8. Select **File > Save Catalog**.

Deleting Elements from a Catalog

You can delete any element from a catalog.

To delete an element from a catalog:

1. Select **File > Catalogs > Catalog Manager**, or right-click an element in the catalog panel and select **Catalog Manager**.
2. Select the appropriate element type from the **Element** drop box.
3. Select the element you want to delete.
4. Select **Catalog > Delete Element**, or right-click and select **Delete Element**.
5. Select **File > Save Catalog**.

Opening a Catalog

You can use the Open Catalog tool to open any catalog and make it the current catalog in the catalog panel. The Open Catalog tool is also available in the Catalog Manager.

To open a catalog for display in the Catalog panel:

1. Select **File > Catalogs > Open Catalog**.
2. In the **Open** dialog, locate the catalog you want to open.
3. Click **Open**. The catalog you opened becomes the active catalog. Note that when you open a catalog, only one element type is displayed. The type displayed depends on the last Insert tool selected.

To open a catalog in the Catalog Manager:

1. Select **File > Catalogs > Catalog Manager**, or right-click an element in the catalog panel and select **Catalog Manager**.
2. Select **File > Open Catalog**.
3. In the **Open** dialog, locate the catalog you want to open.
4. Click **Open**. The catalog you opened becomes the active catalog in the Catalog Manager.
5. Click **OK**. The catalog is now the current catalog in the catalog panel.

Closing a Catalog

You can use the Close Catalog tool to close the current catalog in the catalog panel or the **Catalog Manager** dialog. Note that this leaves the catalog window blank until you open another catalog.

To close the catalog in the catalog panel:

1. Select **File > Catalogs > Close Catalog**.

To close a catalog in the Catalog Manager:

1. Select **File > Close Catalog**.

Viewing Catalog Properties

You can view the properties of the current catalog (file name, location, etc.) using the Catalog Properties tool.

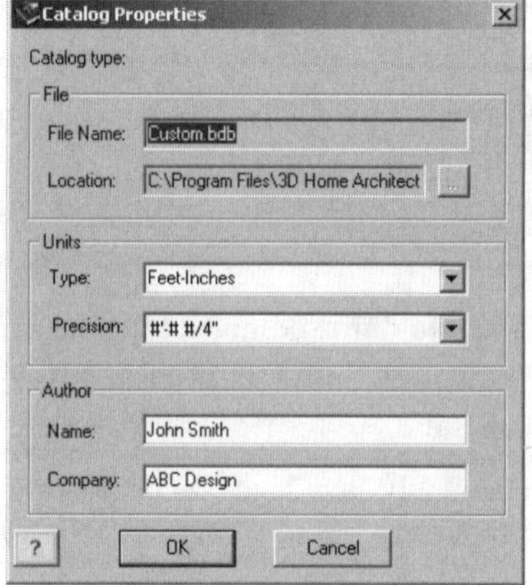

To view the properties of the catalog currently in the catalog panel:

1. Select **File > Catalogs > Catalog Properties**.

To view catalog properties within the catalog Manager:

1. Select **File > Catalog Properties**.

Chapter 37

Materials, Colors & Patterns

Every element has a material assigned to it in the element's property pages. Materials determine what textures, colors and patterns are used to display elements in 3D view. You can edit and create materials on the fly.

All materials are stored in a materials library, called *materials.mlb*. You can create new material libraries containing a specific selection of materials, and load those custom libraries in other projects.

This chapter tells you how to customize materials and work with material libraries.

If you want to edit the material, color or pattern of an inserted element, see *Changing an Element's Material or Color* on page 171.

Things You Should Know About Editing Materials

When you add or edit a material through the Catalog Manager, the custom material is saved with the catalog, and is only available when editing elements in the catalog. If you add or edit a material when editing an element that has been inserted in your drawing, however, the customized material is only available in the current project when editing the properties of inserted elements. The materials library in the catalog remains unchanged. This is because the materials library in the catalog is separate from the materials library in the current drawing.

The reason that there is a project-specific materials library is so that any materials used in your project are always saved with the project, making it possible to share your project with others and always maintain your customized materials.

If you want materials that you have customized in your catalog to be available in your project-specific materials library, or vice versa, you can use the Transfer tool to save the custom materials to the external materials library file (*materials.mlb*), then import the custom materials from the library file into the other materials library.

Customizing the Materials Library

The materials library contains a vast array of materials that you can apply to elements. Even so, you may find that you want to customize it at some point in time.

In the materials library, materials are listed in groups (Concrete, Brick, Wood, etc.) so you can organize and find them easily. You can add, rename and delete groups as needed.

You can add new materials to the library, as well as edit and delete existing materials.

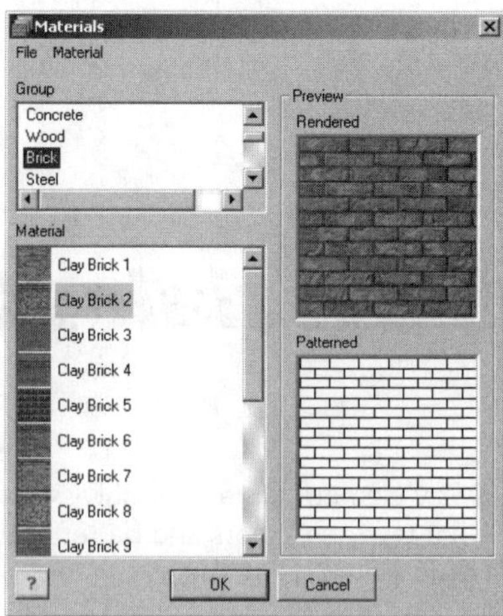

If you customize the catalog materials library (through the Catalog Manager), your change is saved with the catalog.

If you customize the project-specific materials library (by editing an inserted element), your change is saved in the current project only.

To access the catalog materials library:

1. Select **File > Catalogs > Catalog Manager**, or right-click an element in the catalog panel and select **Catalog Manager**.
2. In the **Catalog Manager**, select **Libraries > Materials**. The **Materials** dialog appears.

To access the project-specific materials library:

1. Select an element in your drawing.
2. Right-click and select **Properties**.
3. In the properties dialog, select the Appearance tab.
4. Click the **Select** button. The **Materials** dialog appears.

To add a group to the materials library:

1. Select **Material > Add Group**, or right-click in the *Group* window and select **Add Group**.

2. Type a name for the group, then press ENTER.

To rename a group in the materials library:

1. Select the group in the *Group* window.
2. Select **Material > Rename Group**, or right-click and select **Rename Group**.
3. Type the new name, then press ENTER.

To delete a group from the materials library:

1. Select the group in the *Group* window.
2. Select **Material > Delete Group**, or right-click and select **Delete Group**.

Note: A group cannot be deleted if it contains materials.

To add a new material to the materials library:

1. In the *Group* window, select or create the group you want to add the material to.
2. Select **Material > Add Material**, or right-click in the *Material* window and select **Add Material**.

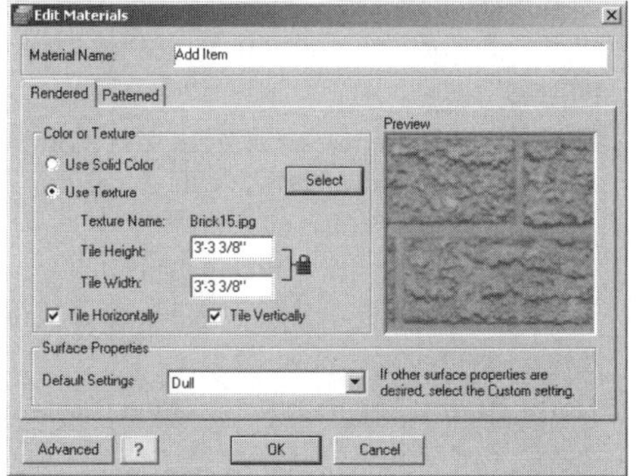

3. In the **Material Name** edit box, type a name for the new material.
4. Specify the material properties. See *Editing Material Properties* on page 261.
5. Click **OK**. The material is added to the library.

To edit a material in the materials library:

1. Select the material in the *Material* window.
2. Select **Material > Edit Material**, or right-click and select **Edit Material**.
3. Edit the material properties in the **Edit Materials** dialog. See *Editing Material Properties* on page 261.
4. Click **OK**.

To delete a material from the materials library:

1. Select the material in the *Material* window.
2. Select **Material > Delete Material**, or right-click and select **Delete Material**.

To save changes to the catalog materials library:

1. Once you've made your changes in the **Materials** dialog, click **OK**.
2. In the **Catalog Manager**, select **File > Save Catalog**.

Editing Material Properties

When you are adding or editing a material in the materials library, you need to specify the material's properties. A material has two main types of properties: *Rendered* and *Patterned*. Rendered properties determine what texture or color is used to display an element in the Rendered or Rendered Outline display mode. Patterned properties determine what pattern is used to display an element in Patterned mode.

To edit the properties of a material:

1. Select the material to edit in the materials list.
2. Select **Material > Edit Material**, or click one of the preview swatches.

To edit Rendered properties:

1. In the **Edit Materials** dialog, select the Rendered tab.

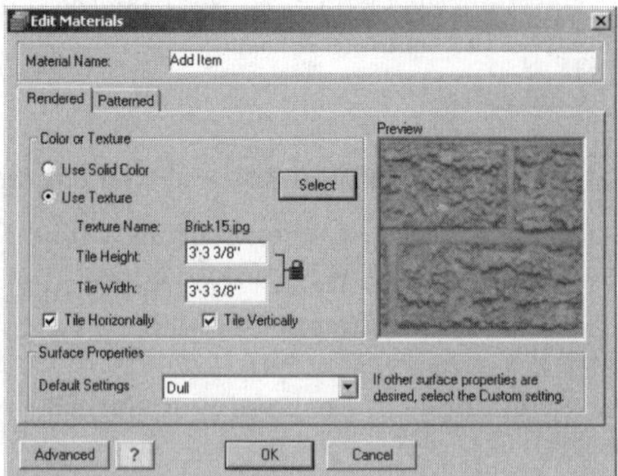

2. If you want to display an element in a solid color in 3D rendered or rendered outline view, enable the **Use Solid Color** radio button. Click the **Select** button, then select the color you want to use in the **Color** dialog.
3. If you want to display an element with a texture applied to it in 3D rendered or rendered outline view, enable the **Use Texture** radio button. Click the **Select** button, then select the texture you want to use. A wide selection of textures can be found in the program's Textures directory. You can use BMP, JPG, TGA and PNG files. If want to use textures from outside sources, see *Using Textures from Outside Sources* on page 263 for guidelines.
4. If you want to change the scale of the texture, enter new values in the **Tile Height** and **Tile Width** edit boxes. Tile height refers to the height of one bitmap tile. The program uses tiled rendering to display images, meaning images are generated in pieces (tiles) vertically and horizontally. Changing the tile height of a brick material, for example, would make the bricks look taller. Changing the tile width would make the bricks look wider.
5. By default, the Tile Height and Tile Width have the Maintain Aspect Ratio lock closed. When the lock is closed, the Tile Width changes to match the Tile Height, and vice versa. This prevents distortion. If you want to specify different values for each, you need to open the Maintain Aspect Ratio lock by clicking on it.

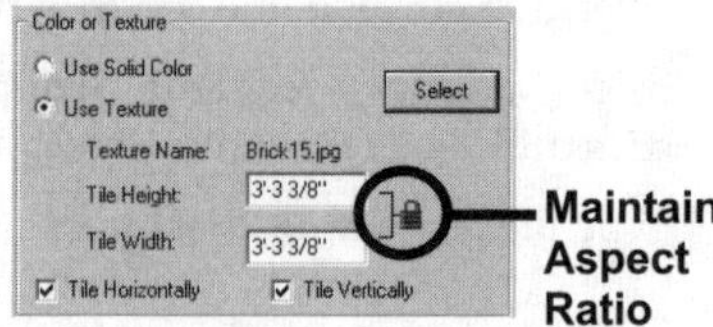

6. To repeat the bitmap tile horizontally, enable the **Tile Horizontally** check box.
7. To repeat the bitmap tile vertically, enable the **Tile Vertically** check box.
8. To change the surface finish of the material (dull, shiny, etc.), make a selection from the drop box in the *Surface Properties* area. This setting will take effect when you create a 3DTrueView. If you want to specify a custom surface finish, select *Custom* in the list, then click the **Advanced** button.
9. If creating a custom finish, specify its properties. These are described below.

   Specular. Reflection that creates highlights on materials, making them appear shiny.

   Emissive. The amount of light given off by a material. The more emissive a material is, the more self-luminous it appears.

   Transparency. The degree to which a material is pervious to light.

   Color Bleed. The degree to which different colors blend where they meet.

   To return to the basic view, click the **Basic** button at the bottom of the dialog.

To edit Patterned properties:

1. In the **Edit Materials** dialog, select the Patterned tab.

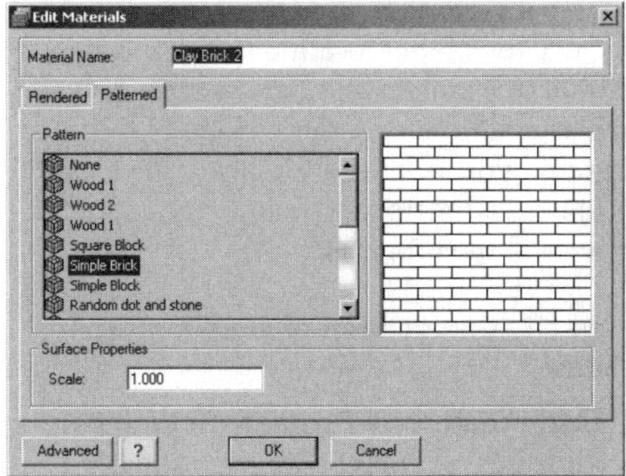

2. To select a different pattern to use in 3D patterned views, select the pattern in the *Pattern* list.
3. To edit the scale of the pattern, edit the value in the **Scale** edit box. A value of 2 doubles the original scale, while a value of .5 halves the original scale.
4. To specify more options, click the **Advanced** button. To edit a pattern, see *Customizing the Patterns Library* on page 265.

Using Textures from Outside Sources

When changing a material's texture assignment, you can use textures from outside sources provided they are appropriately sized and not too large. As a rule, the texture's dimensions should be a multiple of 2:

2, 4, 8, 16, 32, 64, 128, 256, 512, 1024, etc.

If the dimensions are not multiples of 2, the texture will be cropped (from the top and right side) to the next smallest size. For some textures, this will make it look like the texture is cut off.

For example, if your texture is 500 x 500, it will be cropped down to 256 x 256, since 500 is not a multiple of 2. If the texture were 512 x 512, however, it would not be cropped.

Cropping is not that important if the texture is a grid pattern (such as brick), since such a texture is uniform throughout. However, cropping can have an undesirable result if the texture is something like a tree.

Saving Customized Materials to a Materials Library File

If you have added or edited materials in either the catalog materials library or project-specific materials library, you can save the custom materials to the external materials library file (*materials.mlb*). You can then import the customized materials from the library file into any materials library, whether that be the catalog materials library or project-specific materials library. The library file basically acts like a shuttle between libraries.

You can save materials to the default materials library, or create a new library to save them in.

To save customized materials to a materials library file:

1. In the **Materials** dialog, select **File > Transfer**.
2. In the **Open** dialog, select the library you want to export materials to, then click **Open**. The main materials library is called *materials.mlb*.

   Tip: You can create a new library file if you want by entering a name in the **File name** edit box.

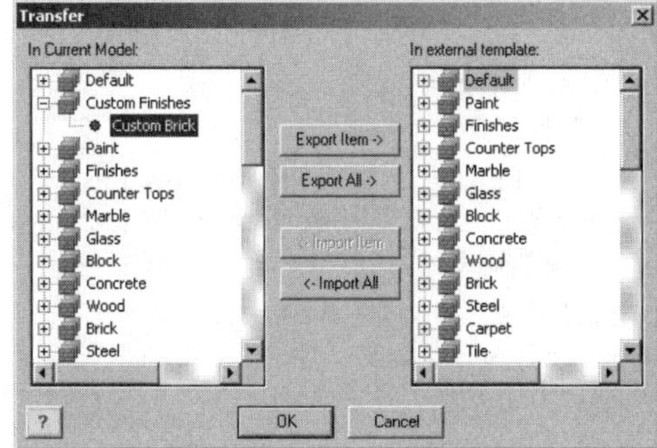

3. In the left pane, select the customized material, then click **Export Item**. The material (and the group it is under) is added to the materials library file. If you wanted

you could also click **Export All** to instantly export the entire materials list to the library file.

4. Click **OK**.

If you want to import the customized materials into your catalog materials library or project-specific materials library, see the next topic, *Importing Materials from a Materials Library File.*

Importing Materials from a Materials Library File

If you have saved customized materials to the materials library file, you can import the materials into your catalog materials library or any project-specific materials library.

To import materials from a library file:

1. In the **Materials** dialog, select **File > Transfer**.
2. In the **Open** dialog, select the materials library (e.g. *materials.mlb*) that you want to import materials from, then click **Open**.

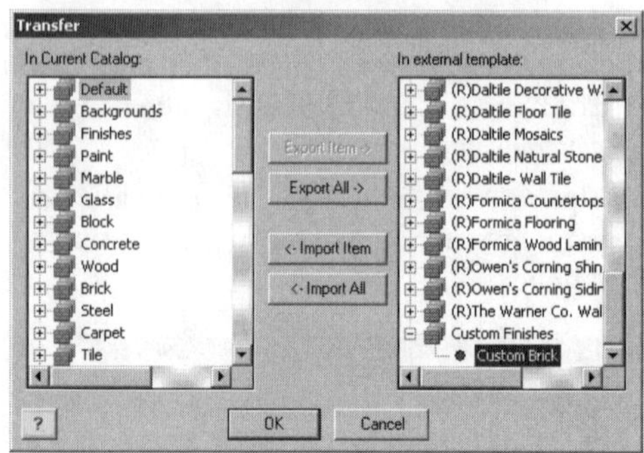

3. In the right pane, select the material to import, then click **Import Item**. Or, just click **Import All** to import the entire list.
4. Click **OK**.

Specifying the Location of the Textures Directory

By default, textures are located in the program's Textures directory. If you move your textures directory to another location on your system, or would like to link to another Textures directory (such as one from an older version of the program), you will need to specify the location of the Textures directory so that textures appear properly in the program.

To specify the location of your Textures directory:

1. Select **Settings > Program Settings** or click the Program Settings button on the Settings toolbar. 
2. In the **Program Settings** dialog, select the **General** tab.
3. In the *File Paths* area, click on the **Textures Directory** to select it.
4. Click **Modify**.
5. In the **Browse For Folder** dialog, locate the folder containing your textures, then click **OK**.
6. Click **OK** in the **Program Settings** dialog.

Note: If you set your path to the Textures directory of an older *3D Home Design* program, the catalog in version 6 will have no textures in it until you switch the path back to the Textures directory of version 6. To alleviate this problem you can copy your old textures into your new Textures directory and leave the path set to the new Textures directory. You will then be able to open drawings from an older version and have all your textures applied, as well as leave the textures in the catalog intact.

Customizing the Patterns Library

The patterns library contains an excellent selection of pre-defined patterns that you can apply to materials.

You can edit patterns to suit your needs.

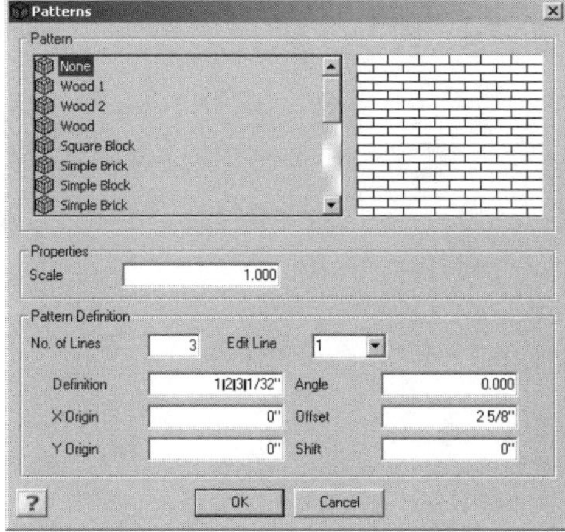

To access the patterns library:

1. Select **File > Catalogs > Catalog Manager**, or right-click an element in the catalog panel and select **Catalog Manager**.
2. In the **Catalog Manager**, select **Libraries > Patterns**. The **Patterns** dialog appears.

Note: You can also access the patterns library when editing the Patterned properties of a material, by clicking the pattern swatch in the **Edit Materials** dialog.

To edit a pattern:

1. Select the pattern in the list.
2. To edit the scale of a pattern, enter a value in the **Scale** edit box. A value of 2 doubles the original scale, while a value of .5 halves the original scale.
3. To edit the pattern's line definition, click the **Advanced** button at the bottom of the dialog. A number of properties pop up that let you define the pattern.

No. of Lines. The number of lines that will repeat in the pattern. Usually, this will be 1 or 2, but it could be more depending on the complexity of the pattern.

Edit Line. The line you are currently editing.

Definition. Generally, the segment lengths and spaces in the line's pattern.

A single value (other than 0) creates a solid line. (See Example 2 on page 265.)

For dashed patterns, segments and spaces can be different lengths, but spaces must be preceded by a negative sign to indicate they are spaces.

For example, a definition of 20,-5,10,-5 (in Metric) creates the following pattern: 20 mm dash, 5 mm space, 10 mm dash, 5 mm space. (See Example 1 on page 265.)

X Origin. The point on the X axis the line passes through.

Y Origin. The point on the Y axis the line passes through.

Angle. The angle of the line in degrees.

Offset. The spacing between lines as the line is repeated (offset) parallel to the original throughout the pattern.

Shift. The distance each offset line is shifted (left or right) from the origin of the previous line. This creates a staggered effect. (See Example 3 on page 266.)

Example 1 (single line pattern)

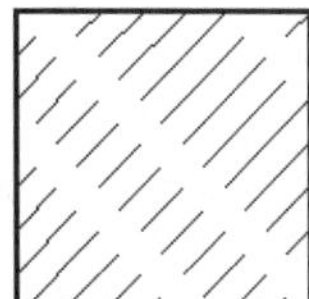

No. of Lines: 1

Line Definition: 20,-5,10,-5

Angle: 45°

Offset: 5

Example 2 (multi-line pattern)

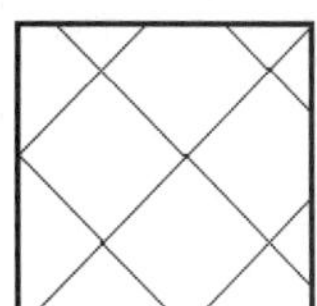

No. of Lines: 2

Line Definition: 1.00 *(both lines)*

Angle: 45° *(line 1)* and 135° *(line 2)*

Offset: 20 *(both lines)*

Example 3 (pattern with a shift)

No. of Lines: 1
Line Definition: 10,-5
Angle: 0°
Offset: 5
Shift: 5

Chapter 38

Line Styles

A line style defines the type and color of a line. Line styles are applied when you insert electrical wiring in your drawing. They are also part of a dimension style's definition.

You can customize the line styles and linetype libraries to suit your needs.

If you want to change the line style of electrical wiring that you have already inserted, see *Changing the Line Style of Wiring* on page 138.

To change the dimension style of an inserted dimension, see *Changing the Style of a Dimension* on page 194.

Things You Should Know About Editing Line Styles

Line styles are used by electrical wiring and dimension styles. When you add or edit a line style through the Catalog Manager, the custom line style is saved with the catalog, and is only available when editing dimension styles in the catalog. If you add or edit a line style when editing electrical wiring or the style of a dimension in your drawing, however, the customized line style is only available in the current project when editing the properties of inserted wiring or dimensions. The line styles library in the catalog remains unchanged. This is because the line styles library in the catalog is separate from the line styles library in the current project.

The reason that there is a project-specific line styles library is so that any line styles used in your project are always saved with the project, making it possible to share your project with others and always maintain your customized line styles.

If you want line styles that you have customized in your catalog to be available in your project-specific line styles library, or vice versa, you can use the Transfer tool to save the custom line styles to the external line styles library file (*linestyles.klb*), then import the custom line styles from the library file into the other line styles library.

Customizing the Line Styles Library

The line styles library contains a wide selection of line styles that you can apply to electrical wiring and dimension styles. You may find that you want to customize the library at some point in time.

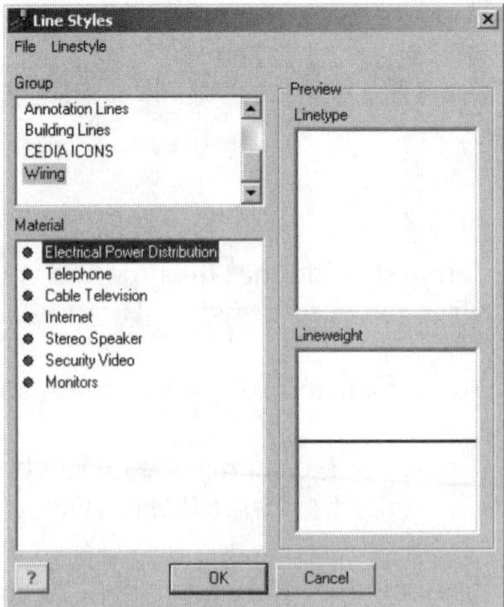

In the line styles library, line styles are listed in groups so you can organize and find them easily. The Wiring group contains an assortment of wiring styles. You can add, rename and delete groups as needed.

You can add new line styles to the library, as well as edit and delete existing line styles.

When you edit the line styles library in your catalog, the line styles are saved with your catalog. If you edit line styles while editing your drawing, the line styles are saved in the current drawing only.

To access the line styles library in the Catalog Manager:

1. Select **File > Catalogs > Catalog Manager**, or right-click an element in the catalog panel and select **Catalog Manager**.
2. In the **Catalog Manager**, select **Libraries > Line Styles**. The **Line Styles** dialog appears.

To access the line styles library through inserted electrical wiring:

1. Select the wiring in your drawing.
2. Right-click and select **Properties**, or select **Edit > Modify Elements > Properties**. The **Line Styles** dialog appears. This is your project-specific line styles library.

To access the line styles library by editing a dimension style:

1. Select **Settings > Dimension Styles**. Or, select a dimension in your drawing, then right-click and select **Properties**.
2. In the **Dimension Styles** dialog, click **Edit**.
3. In the **Edit Dimension Styles** dialog, select the **Line Styles** tab. This is your project-specific line styles library.

To add a group to the line styles library:

1. Select **Linestyle > Add Group**, or right-click in the *Group* window and select **Add Group**.
2. Type a name for the group, then press ENTER.

To rename a group in the line styles library:

1. Select the group in the *Group* window.
2. Select **Linestyle > Rename Group**, or right-click and select **Rename Group**.
3. Type the new name, then press ENTER.

To delete a group from the line styles library:

1. Select the group in the *Group* window.
2. Select **Linestyle > Delete Group**, or right-click and select **Delete Group**.

Note: A group cannot be deleted if it contains line styles.

To add a new line style to the line styles library:

1. In the *Group* window, select or create the group you want to add the line style to.
2. Select **Linestyle > Add Linestyle**, or right-click in the *Material* window and select **Add Linestyle**.

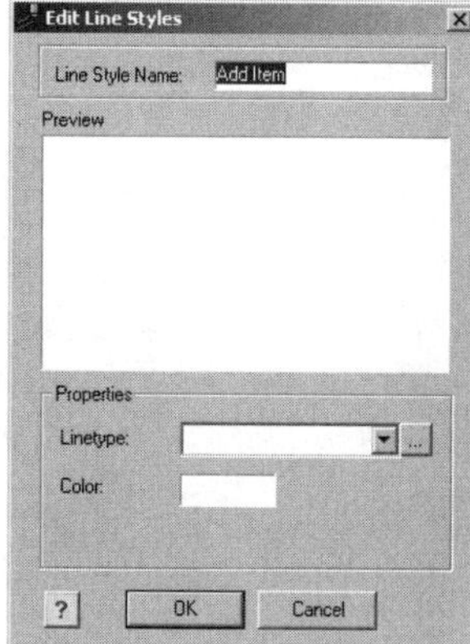

3. In the **Line Style Name** edit box, type a name for the new line style.
4. To select a linetype for the line style, click the Browse button next to the **Linetype** edit box. Select a linetype from the **Linetypes** dialog. If you want to add or edit a linetype, see *Customizing the Linetypes Library* on page 271.
5. To select a color for the line, click the **Color** box in the **Edit Line Styles** dialog, then select the color you want from the **Color** dialog.
6. Click **OK**. The line style is added to the library.

To edit a line style in the line styles library:

1. Select the line style in the *Material* window.

2. Select **Linestyle > Edit Linestyle**, or right-click and select **Edit Linestyle.**

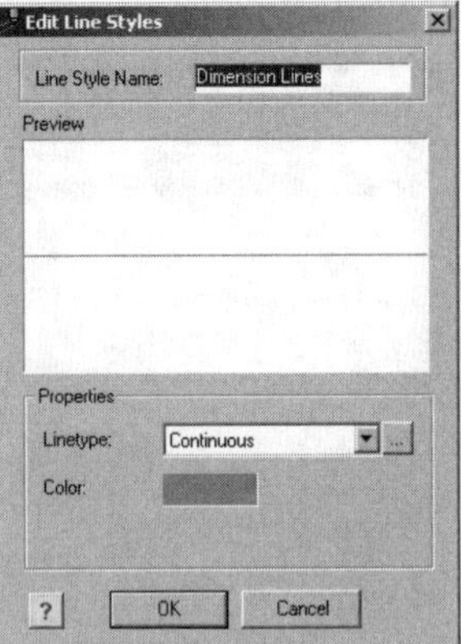

3. In the **Edit Line Styles** dialog, select the desired linetype and color.
4. Click **OK**.

To delete a line style from the line styles library:

1. Select the line style in the *Material* window.
2. Select **Linestyle > Delete Linestyle**, or right-click and select **Delete Linestyle**.

To save changes to the line styles library in the catalog:

1. Once you've made your changes in the **Line Styles** dialog, click **OK**.
2. In the **Catalog Manager**, select **File > Save Catalog**.

Saving Line Styles to a Line Styles Library File

If you have added or edited line styles in either the catalog line styles library or project-specific line styles library, you can save the custom line styles to the external line styles library file (*linestyles.klb*). You can then import the customized line styles from the library file into any line styles library, whether that be the catalog line styles library or project-specific line styles library. The library file basically acts like a shuttle between libraries.

You can save line styles to the default line styles library, or create a new library to save them in.

To save customized line styles to the line styles library file:

1. In the **Line Styles** dialog, select **File > Transfer**.
2. In the **Open** dialog, select the *linestyles.klb* file (or whatever file you want to save to), then click **Open**.

   Tip: You can create a new library file if you want by entering a name in the **File name** edit box.

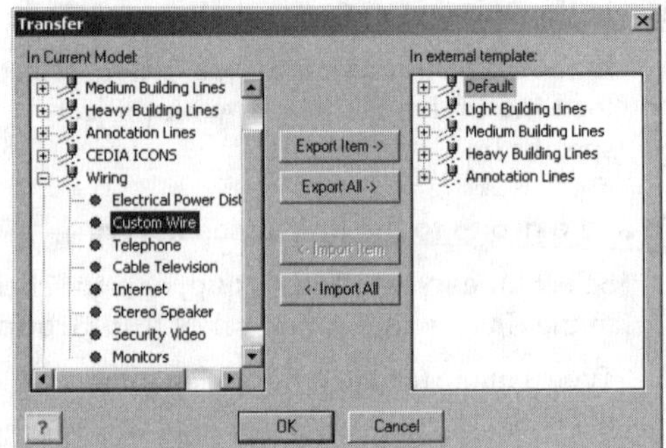

3. In the left pane of the **Transfer** dialog, select the line style you want to save, then click **Export Item**. To export the entire list, just click **Export All**. The library file is updated.
4. Click **OK**.

If you want to import the custom line styles into your catalog line styles library or the project-specific line styles library, see the next topic, *Importing Line Styles from a Line Styles Library File*.

Importing Line Styles from a Line Styles Library File

If you have saved customized line styles to the line styles library file, you can import the line styles into your catalog line styles library or any project-specific line styles library.

To import line styles from a line styles library file:

1. In the **Line Styles** dialog, select **File > Transfer**.

2. In the **Open** dialog, select the *linestyles.klb* file (or whatever file you want to import line styles from), then click **Open**.

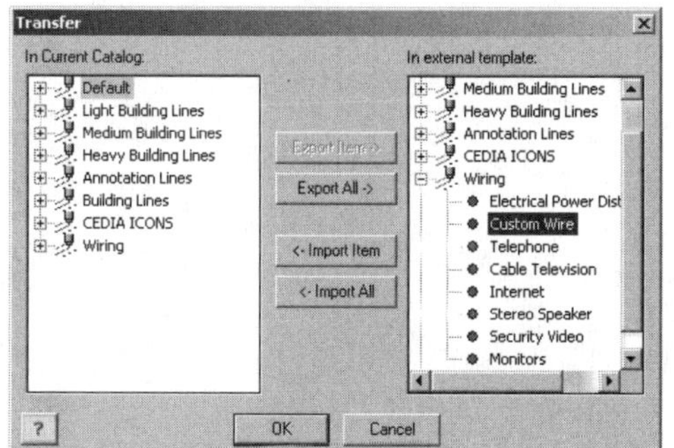

3. In the right pane of the **Transfer** dialog, select the custom line style you want to import, then click **Import Item**. Or, to import the entire list, just click **Import All**. The list in the left pane is updated.
4. Click **OK**.

Customizing the Linetypes Library

The linetypes library contains a list of pre-defined linetypes that you can apply to line styles. You may want to add or edit linetypes to suit your needs.

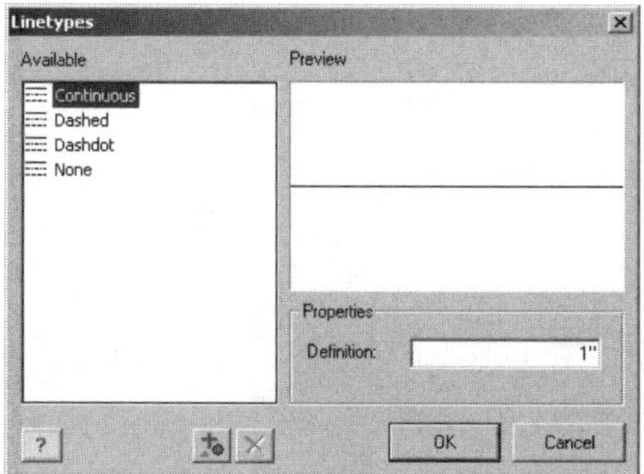

To access the linetypes library:

1. Select **File > Catalogs > Catalog Manager**, or right-click an element in the catalog panel and select **Catalog Manager**.
2. In the **Catalog Manager**, select **Libraries > Linetypes**. The **Linetypes** dialog appears.

Note: You can also access the linetypes library when editing a line style, by clicking one of the swatches, then clicking the Browse button in the **Edit Line Styles** dialog. If you do access the linetypes library this way, new or edited linetypes will be saved with the line style in the current drawing only. The line styles and linetypes libraries in the catalog will remain unchanged.

To edit a linetype:

1. Select the linetype in the list.
2. In the **Definition** edit box, edit the linetype's definition. Lines are defined by a series of distances separated by commas. Each number represents the length of either a line segment or space. Positive numbers create a line segment of the specified length. Negative numbers create a space of the specified length. For example, a dashed line may have a definition like 1/4", -1/4".
3. Once you've edited the linetype, click **OK**.

To add a linetype to the list:

1. Click the Add Item button below the linetypes list, or right-click in the left pane and select **Add Item**. A new entry is added to the list.

2. Type a name for the linetype and press ENTER.
3. In the **Definition** edit box, specify the linetype's definition.
4. Once you've defined the linetype, click **OK**.

To delete a linetype from the list:

1. Select the linetype in the list.
2. Right-click and select **Delete**, or click the Delete button below the linetypes list.

Note: You cannot delete the existing, pre-defined linetypes because they are being used.

To save changes to the linetypes library in the catalog:

1. Once you've made your changes in the **Linetypes** dialog, click **OK**.

2. In the **Catalog Manager**, select **File > Save Catalog**.

Chapter 39

Text & Dimension Styles

When you insert text or dimensions in your drawing, they are always based on a style that determines how they look.

Text and dimension styles are stored in libraries. You can edit and create text and dimension styles to suit your needs.

If you want to change the style of text that you have inserted in your drawing, see *Changing the Style of Text* on page 187. If you want to change the style of a dimension in your drawing, see *Changing the Style of a Dimension* on page 194.

Things You Should Know About Editing Text Styles

When you add or edit a text style through the Catalog Manager, the custom text style is saved with the catalog, and is only available when editing text styles in the catalog. If you add or edit a text style when editing text in your drawing (or an element that uses text), however, the customized text style is only available in the current project when editing text styles in your drawing. The text styles library in the catalog remains unchanged. This is because the text styles library in the catalog is separate from the text styles library in the current project.

The reason that there is a project-specific text styles library is so that any text styles used in your project are always saved with the project, making it possible to share your project with others and always maintain your customized text styles.

If you want text styles that you have customized in your catalog to be available in your project-specific text styles library, or vice versa, you can use the Transfer tool to save the custom text styles to the external text styles library file (*Textstyles.tsl*), then import the custom text styles from the library file into the other text styles library.

Tip: You can save text styles in your template drawing by opening the template drawing, then selecting **Settings > Text Styles** and creating your custom text style in the **Text Styles** dialog. The custom text styles will then be available in the project-specific text styles libraries of future projects that you base on the template drawing.

Customizing the Text Styles Library

The text styles library contains a number of pre-defined text styles that you can apply to text. You can edit the existing text styles, or create your own.

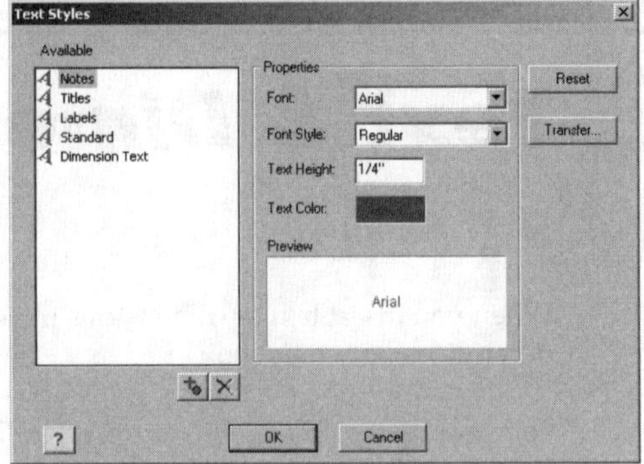

When you edit the text styles library in your catalog, the text styles are saved with your catalog. If you edit text styles while editing inserted text, or an element that uses text, the text styles are saved in the current drawing only.

To access the text styles library in the Catalog Manager:

1. Select **File > Catalogs > Catalog Manager**, or right-click an element in the catalog panel and select **Catalog Manager**.
2. In the **Catalog Manager**, select **Libraries > Text Styles**. The **Text Styles** dialog appears.

To access the text styles library through inserted text:

1. Select the text in your drawing.
2. Right-click and select **Properties**, or select **Edit > Modify Elements > Properties**.
3. In the **Text** dialog, click the **Text Style** button. The **Text Styles** dialog appears. This is your project-specific text styles library.

To access the text styles library through the Settings menu:

1. Select **Settings > Text Styles**. This is your project-specific text styles library.

To add a text style to the library:

1. Right-click in the text style window and select **Add Item**. Or, click the Add Item button below the text style window. A new entry is added to the list.
2. Type a name for the text style and press ENTER.
3. In the *Properties* area, define the text style.

   Font. A set of text characters in a specific style and size.

   Font Style. The style of text. Choices can include Regular, Italic, Bold, and Bold Italic.

   Text Height. The size of text.

   Text Color. The color of text. Click the swatch to access the **Color** dialog and select a color.
4. Click **OK**.

To edit a text style in the library:

1. Select the text style in the list.
2. Edit the properties in the *Properties* area.

   Font. A set of text characters in a specific style and size.

   Font Style. The style of text. Choices can include Regular, Italic, Bold, and Bold Italic.

   Text Height. The size of text.

   Text Color. The color of text. Click the swatch to access the **Color** dialog and select a color.
3. Click **OK**.

Note: Clicking **Reset** will return a text style to the following default values: Arial, Regular, 4", Black.

To delete a text style from the library:

1. Select the text style in the list.
2. Right-click and select **Delete**, or click the Delete button below the text styles window.

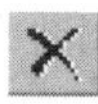

To save changes to the text styles library in the catalog:

1. Once you've made your changes in the **Text Styles** dialog, click **OK**.
2. In the **Catalog Manager**, select **File > Save Catalog**.

Saving Customized Text Styles to the Text Styles Library File

If you have added or edited text styles in either the catalog text styles library or project-specific text styles library, you can save the custom text styles to the external text styles library file (*Textstyles.tsl*). You can then import the customized text styles from the library file into any text styles library, whether that be the catalog text styles library or project-specific text styles library. The library file basically acts like a shuttle between libraries.

You can save text styles to the default text styles library file, or create a new library to save them in.

To save customized text styles to the text styles library file:

1. In the **Text Styles** dialog, click the **Transfer** button.
2. In the **Open** dialog, select the *Textstyles.tsl* file (or whatever file you want to save to), then click **Open**.

   Tip: You can create a new library file if you want by entering a name in the **File name** edit box.

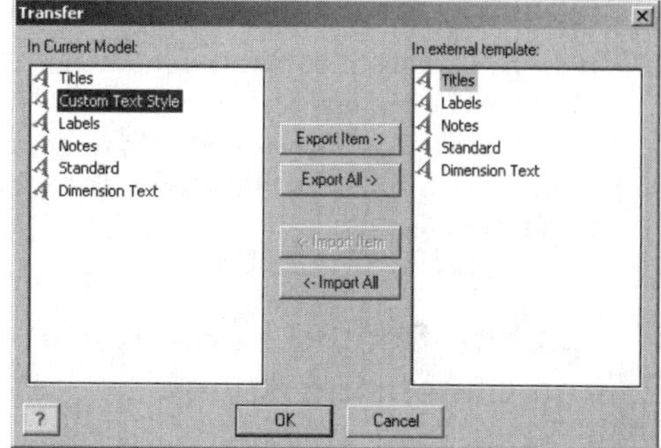

3. In the left pane of the **Transfer** dialog, select the text style you want to save, then click **Export Item**. To export the entire list, just click **Export All**. The library file is updated.
4. Click **OK**.

If you want to import the custom text styles into your catalog text styles library or the current drawing, see the next topic, *Importing Text Styles from a Text Styles Library File.*

Importing Text Styles from a Text Styles Library File

If you have saved customized text styles to the text styles library file, you can import the text styles into your catalog text styles library or any project-specific text styles library.

To import text styles from a text styles library file:

1. In the **Text Styles** dialog, click **Transfer**.
2. In the **Open** dialog, select the *Textstyles.tsl* file (or whatever file you want to import text styles from), then click **Open**.

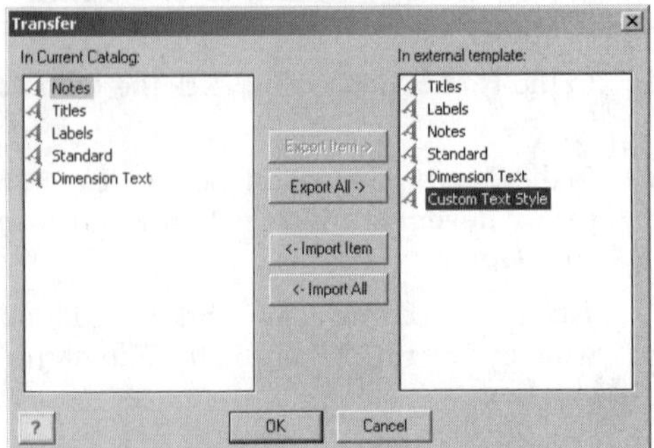

3. In the right pane of the **Transfer** dialog, select the custom text style you want to import, then click **Import Item**. Or, to import the entire list, just click **Import All**. The list in the left pane is updated.
4. Click **OK**.

Things You Should Know About Editing Dimension Styles

When you add or edit a dimension style through the Catalog Manager, the custom dimension style is saved with the catalog, and is only available when editing dimension styles in the catalog. If you add or edit a dimension style when editing dimensions in your drawing, however, the customized dimension style is only available in the current project when editing dimension styles in your drawing. The dimension styles library in the catalog remains unchanged. This is because the dimension styles library in the catalog is separate from the dimension styles library in the current project.

The reason that there is a project-specific dimension styles library is so that any dimension styles used in your project are always saved with the project, making it possible to share your project with others and always maintain your customized dimension styles.

If you want dimension styles that you have customized in your catalog to be available in your project-specific dimension styles library, or vice versa, you can use the Transfer tool to save the custom dimension styles to the external dimension styles library file (*Dimstyles.dlb*), then import the custom dimension styles from the library file into the other dimension styles library.

Tip: You can save dimension styles in your template drawing by opening the template drawing, then selecting **Settings > Dimension Styles** and creating your custom dimension style in the **Dimension Styles** dialog. The custom dimension styles will then be available in the project-specific dimension styles libraries of future projects that you base on the template drawing.

Customizing the Dimension Styles Library

The dimension styles library contains one pre-defined dimension style called *Standard*. This is the default dimension style used when you insert dimensions in your drawing. You can add and edit dimension styles to suit your needs.

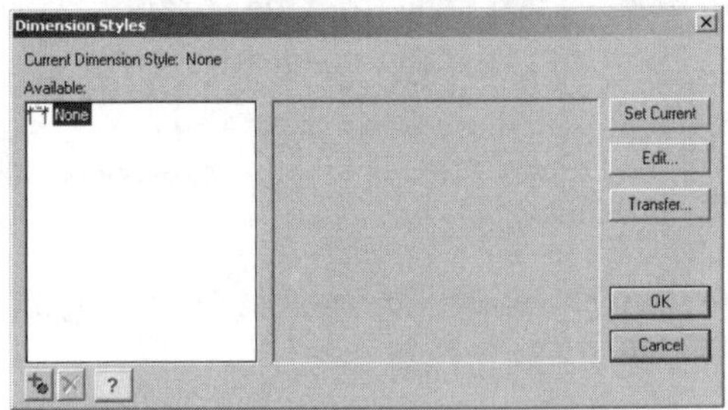

When you edit the dimension styles library in your catalog, the dimension styles are saved with your catalog. If you edit dimension styles while editing inserted dimensions, the dimension styles are saved in the current drawing only.

To access the dimension styles library in the Catalog Manager:

1. Select **File > Catalogs > Catalog Manager**, or right-click an element in the catalog panel and select **Catalog Manager**.
2. In the **Catalog Manager**, select **Libraries > Dimension Styles**. The **Dimension Styles** dialog appears.

To access the dimension styles library through inserted dimensions:

1. Select the dimension in your drawing.
2. Right-click and select **Properties**, or select **Edit > Modify Elements > Properties**. The **Dimension Styles** dialog appears. This is your project-specific dimension styles library.

To access the dimension styles library through the Settings menu:

1. Select **Settings > Dimension Styles**. This is your project-specific dimension styles library.

To add a new dimension style to the list:

1. Right-click in the dimension style window and select **Add Item**. Or, click the Add Item button below the dimension style window. A new entry is added to the list.
2. Type a name for the dimension style and press ENTER.
3. Click the **Edit** button, then define the dimension style. See *Dimension Style Properties* on page 277.
4. Click **OK**.

To edit a dimension style:

1. Select the dimension style in the list.
2. Click **Edit**.
3. Define the dimension in the **Edit Dimension Styles** dialog. See *Dimension Style Properties* on page 277.
4. Click **OK**.

To delete a dimension style from the library:

1. Select the dimension style in the list.
2. Right-click and select **Delete**, or click the Delete button below the dimension styles window. 

To save changes to the dimension styles library in the catalog:

1. Once you've made your changes in the **Dimension Styles** dialog, click **OK**.
2. In the **Catalog Manager**, select **File > Save Catalog**.

Dimension Style Properties

You can control a dimension's line, arrow and text style properties.

Anatomy of a Dimension

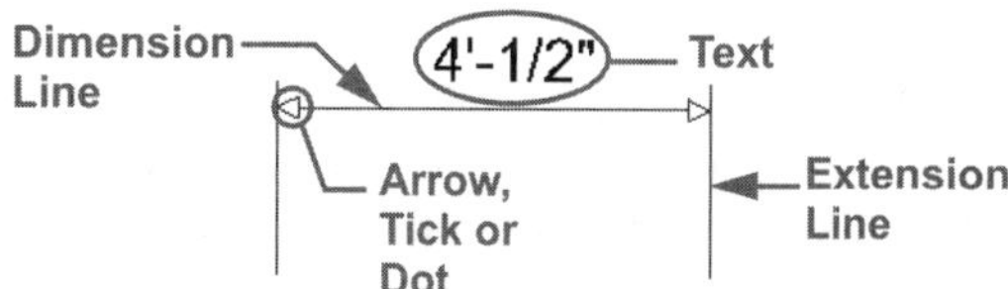

Lines and Arrows

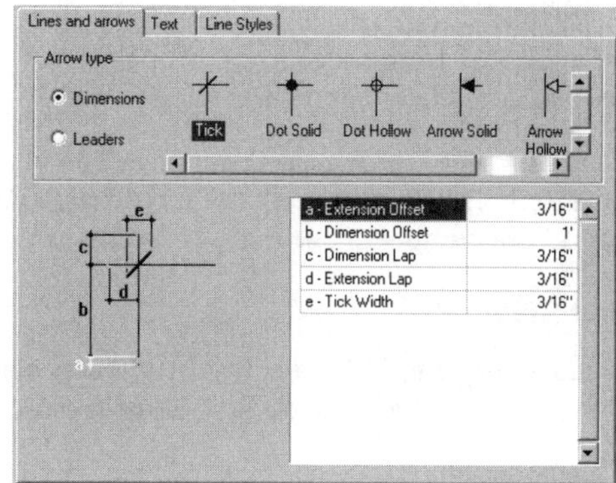

Arrow Type

You can specify an arrow type for dimensions and leaders (leaders are used with the Text with Leader tool). Choose an arrow, dot or tick for your arrow type.

The properties below the *Arrow Type* selection window (Extension Offset, Dimension Offset, etc.) vary depending on the arrow type selected. As you make different selections, the dimension updates in the preview window.

Dimension Text

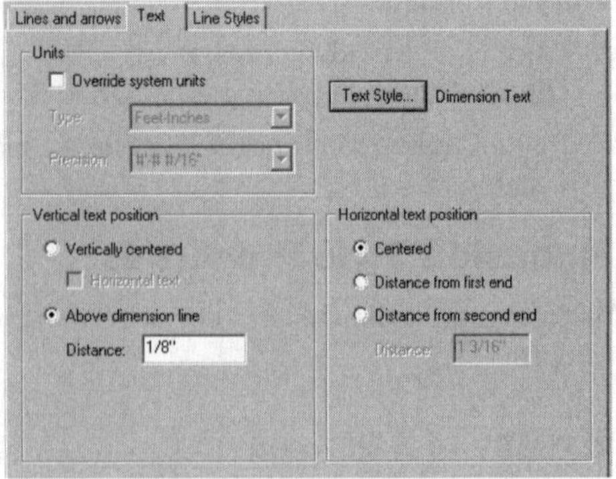

Units

The units (e.g. feet and inches) and precision used to display the dimension value.

Override system units: Uses the unit of measure specified in the **Edit Dimension Styles** dialog instead of the unit of measure specified in the program settings.

Type: Choose from Feet-Inches, Millimeters, Centimeters, Meters or Inches.

Precision: For Feet-Inches, the choices are whole units (0, 1/2, 1/4 and so on). For metric units, the choices are number of decimal places you can use.

Text Style

Refers to the font, font style, text height and color of the dimension text. Click **Text Style** to select a style.

Vertical Text Position

This is the vertical position of the dimension text relative to the dimension line.

Vertically Centered: Text is placed inside the dimension line.

Horizontal Text: Forces the dimension text to always be horizontal, regardless of the dimension line's angle.

Above Dimension Line: Text is placed above the dimension line.

Distance: Distance between the text and the dimension line when placing text above the dimension line.

Horizontal Text Position

This is the position of the dimension text relative to the ends of the dimension line.

Centered: Centers the text inside the dimension line.

Distance from first end: Places the text a specific distance from the first end of the dimension. Specify the distance in the Distance edit box.

Distance from the second end: Places the text a specific distance from the second end of the dimension. Specify the distance in the Distance edit box.

Line Styles

You can select a different line style for the dimension line, extension lines and arrows. A line style determines the linetype and color.

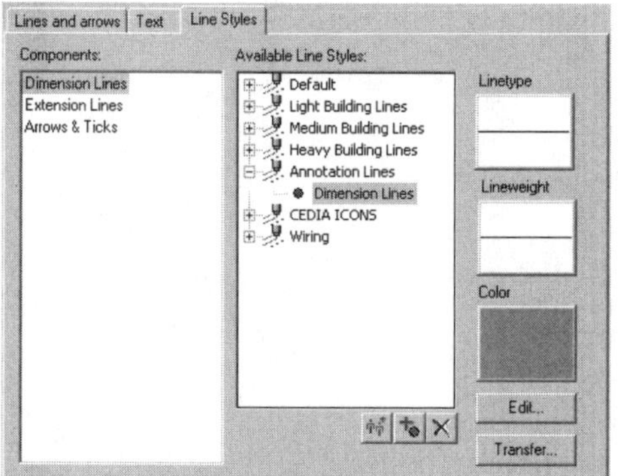

To assign a different line style to a dimension component, select the component in the left pane, then select the desired line style in the right pane.

For information about creating custom line styles, see the Line Styles chapter on page 267.

Saving Customized Dimension Styles to the Dimension Styles Library File

If you have added or edited dimension styles in either the catalog dimension styles library or project-specific dimension styles library, you can save the custom dimension styles to the external dimension styles library file (*Dimstyles.dlb*). You can then import the customized dimension styles from the library file into any dimension styles library, whether that be the catalog dimension styles library or project-specific dimension styles library. The library file basically acts like a shuttle between libraries.

You can save dimension styles to the default dimension styles library file, or create a new library to save them in.

To save dimension styles to the dimension styles library file:

1. In the **Dimension Styles** dialog, click the **Transfer** button.
2. In the **Open** dialog, select the *Dimstyles.dlb* file (or whatever file you want to save to), then click **Open**.

   Tip: You can create a new library file if you want by entering a name in the **File name** edit box.

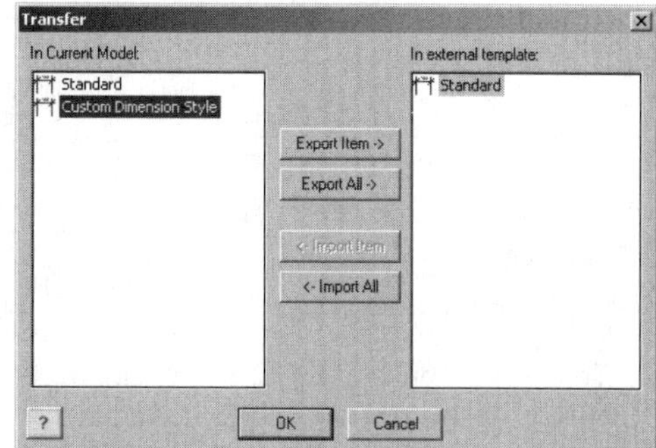

3. In the left pane of the **Transfer** dialog, select the dimension style you want to save, then click **Export Item**. To export the entire list, just click **Export All**. The library file is updated.
4. Click **OK**.

If you want to import the custom dimension styles into your catalog dimension styles library or the project-specific dimension styles library, see the next topic, *Importing Dimension Styles from a Dimension Styles Library File.*

Importing Dimension Styles from Dimension Styles Library File

If you have saved customized dimension styles to the dimension styles library file, you can import the dimension styles into your catalog dimension styles library or any project-specific dimension styles library.

To import dimension styles from a dimension styles library file:

1. In the **Dimension Styles** dialog, click **Transfer**.

2. In the **Open** dialog, select the *Dimstyles.dlb* file (or whatever file you want to import dimension styles from), then click **Open**.

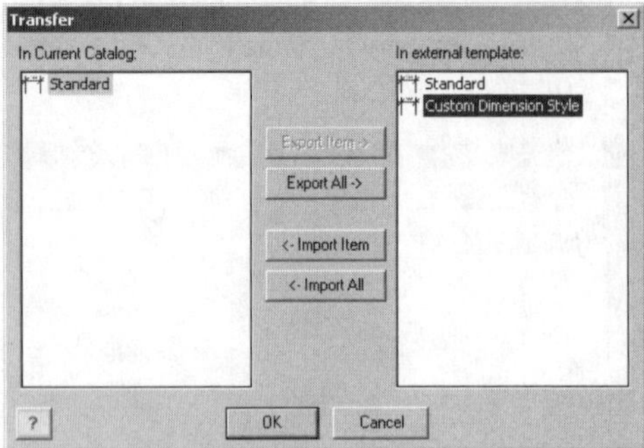

3. In the right pane of the **Transfer** dialog, select the custom dimension style you want to import, then click **Import Item**. Or, to import the entire list, just click **Import All**. The list in the left pane is updated.
4. Click **OK**.

Chapter 40

Light Sources

Light sources are basically light bulbs. Light sources are contained in a light source library which is accessible through the Catalog Manager as well as the Lights property page of light fixtures. You can edit existing light sources as well as import your own light source files into the library.

If you want to change a light fixture's light source, see *Editing a Light Fixture's Light Source* on page 131.

Things You Should Know About Editing Light Sources

Light sources are basically light bulbs. They are applied to light fixtures. When you add or edit a light source through the Catalog Manager, the custom light source is saved with the catalog, and is only available when editing light sources in the catalog. If you add or edit a light source when editing a light fixture that has been inserted in your drawing, however, the customized light source is only available in the current project when editing the properties of inserted light fixtures. The light source library in the catalog remains unchanged. This is because the light source library in the catalog is separate from the light source library in the current drawing.

The reason that there is a project-specific light source library is so that any light sources used in your project are always saved with the project, making it possible to share your project with others and always maintain your customized light sources.

If you want light sources that you have customized in your catalog to be available in your project-specific light source library, or vice versa, you can use the Transfer tool to save the custom light sources to the external light source library file (*Lights.llb*), then import the custom light source from the library file into the other light source library.

Customizing the Light Source Library

The light source library contains an assortment of light sources, mainly fluorescent and incandescent light bulbs, that can be applied to lighting fixtures.

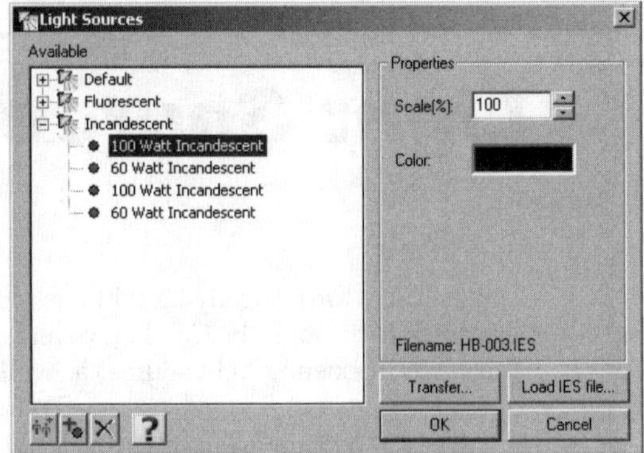

You can customize the light source library by adding and editing light sources. Most manufacturers of lighting equipment provide downloadable .IES photometric data files free of charge on their web sites for use in lighting calculations. Once you've added a light source to your library, you can edit its intensity and color if you want.

Light sources are listed in groups so you can organize and find them easily. You can create, rename and delete groups.

When you edit the light source library in your catalog, the light sources are saved with your catalog. If you edit the light source library while editing an element, the light sources are saved in the current drawing only.

To access the light source library in the Catalog Manager:

1. Select **File > Catalogs > Catalog Manager**, or right-click an element in the catalog panel and select **Catalog Manager**.
2. In the **Catalog Manager**, select **Libraries > Light Sources**. The **Light Sources** dialog appears.

To access the light source library through an inserted light fixture:

1. Select the light fixture.
2. Right-click and select **Properties**, or select **Edit > Modify Elements > Properties**.
3. In the **Lights** dialog, select the Lights tab.
4. Click **Add** or **Edit** to access the light source library.

To add a group to the light source library:

1. Right-click an existing group and select **Add Group**, or click the Add Group button below the light source window. An entry is added to the list.
2. Type a name for the group, then press ENTER.

To delete a group from the line styles library:

1. Select the group to delete.
2. Right-click and select **Delete Group**, or click the Delete button below the light source window.

Note: A group cannot be deleted if it contains light sources.

To add a light source to the list:

1. Select the group you want to add the light source to.
2. Click the Add Item button below the light source window, or right-click in the light source window and select **Add Item**. A new entry is added to the list.

3. Type a name for the light source and press ENTER.
4. Click the **Load IES File** button.
5. Locate and select the *.ies file and click **Open**. The filename is displayed in the right pane of the **Light Sources** dialog.
6. If you want to change the intensity of the light, specify the desired percentage in the **Scale** edit box. For example, if the light source is a 60 Watt bulb, a value of 50% would make the bulb function like a 30 Watt bulb.
7. If you want to change the color of the light, click the **Color** edit box and make a selection from the **Color** dialog.

To apply a different IES file to a light source:

1. Select the light source in the list.
2. Click the **Load IES File** button.
3. Locate and select the *.ies file and click **Open**. The filename is displayed in the right pane of the **Light Sources** dialog.

To edit the intensity of a light source:

1. Select the light source in the list.
2. In the **Scale** edit box, specify how much you want to scale the intensity in terms of a percentage. For example, if the light source is a 60 Watt bulb, a value of 50% would make the bulb function like a 30 Watt bulb.

To edit the color of a light source:

1. Select the light source in the list.
2. Click the **Color** edit box.
3. In the **Color** dialog, select the color you want, then click **OK**.

To delete a light source from the library:

1. Select the light source in the list.
2. Right-click and select **Delete**, or click the Delete button below the light source window.

Saving Customized Light Sources to the Light Source Library File

If you have added or edited light sources in either the catalog light source library or project-specific light source library, you can save the custom light sources to the external light source library file (*Lights.llb*). You can then import the customized light sources from the library file into any light source library, whether that be the catalog light source library or project-specific light source library. The library file basically acts like a shuttle between libraries.

You can save light sources to the default light source library, or create a new library to save them in.

To save light sources to the light source library file:

1. In the **Light Sources** dialog, click **Transfer**.
2. In the **Open** dialog, select the *Lights.llb* file (or whatever file you want to save to), then click **Open**.

   Tip: You can create a new library file if you want by entering a name in the **File name** edit box.

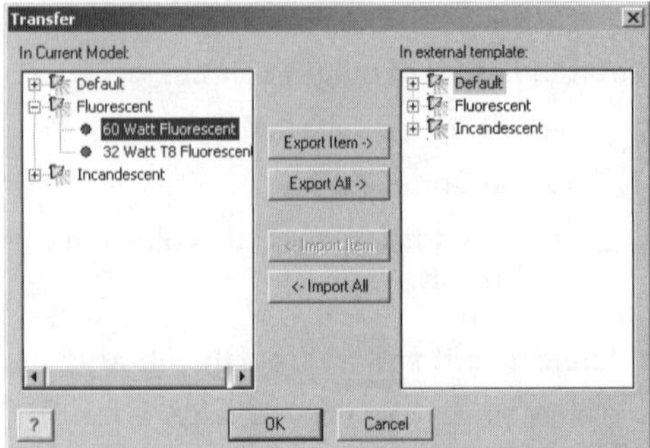

3. In the left pane of the **Transfer** dialog, select the light source you want to save, then click **Export Item**. To export the entire list, just click **Export All**. The library file is updated.
4. Click **OK**.

If you want to import the custom light sources into your catalog light source library or the project-specific light source library, see the next topic, *Importing Light Sources from a Light Source Library File.*

Importing Light Sources from a Light Source Library File

If you have saved customized light sources to the light source library file, you can import the light sources into your catalog light source library or any project-specific light source library.

To import light sources from a light source library file:

1. In the **Light Sources** dialog, click **Transfer**.
2. In the **Open** dialog, select the *Lights.llb* file (or whatever file you want to import light sources from), then click **Open**.

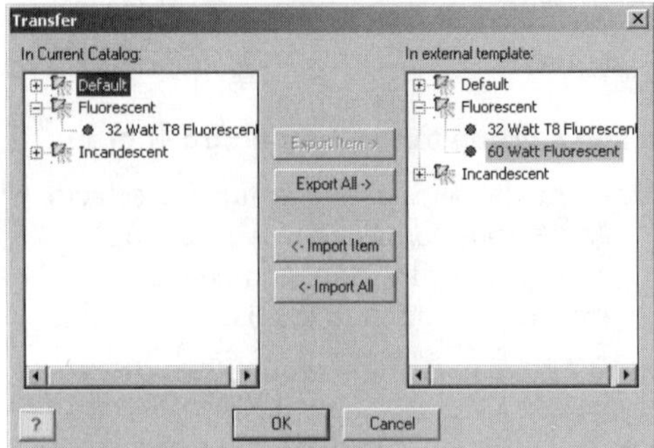

3. In the right pane of the **Transfer** dialog, select the custom light source you want to import, then click **Import Item**. Or, to import the entire list, just click **Import All**. The list in the left pane is updated.
4. Click **OK**.

Specifying the Location of the Light Source Directory

By default, light sources are located in the program's Lights directory. If you move your Lights directory to another location on your system, you will need to specify the location of the Lights directory so that light sources can be accessed by the program.

To specify the location of your Textures directory:

1. Select **Settings > Program Settings** or click the Program Settings button on the Settings toolbar. 
2. In the **Program Settings** dialog, select the **General** tab.
3. In the *File Paths* area, click on the **Lights Directory** to select it.
4. Click **Modify**.

5. In the **Browse For Folder** dialog, locate the folder containing your light sources, then click **OK**.
6. Click **OK** in the **Program Settings** dialog.

Chapter 41

Wizard Configurations

When you run the House Builder Wizard or Kitchen Builder Wizard, you are asked to select a style for your house or kitchen, such as "Country" or "Traditional". The configuration you choose determines the appearance of elements used to build your house or kitchen.

You can specify your own custom configurations that can be used when running the House Builder Wizard or Kitchen Builder Wizard in any project.

Creating a Custom House Builder Wizard Configuration

A House Builder Wizard configuration determines what elements are used for exterior walls, roofs, floors, ceilings, foundation walls and footings. You are asked to select a configuration for your house when you run the House Builder Wizard.

You can edit any of the existing configurations that are available in the House Builder Wizard, or create your own. Customized configurations are saved automatically and will be available when you run the House Builder Wizard in the current project, or any other project.

To access the building configuration library:

1. Select **File > Catalogs > Catalog Manager**, or right-click any element in the catalog panel and select **Catalog Manager**.
2. In the **Catalog Manager** dialog, select **Libraries > Building Configuration**.

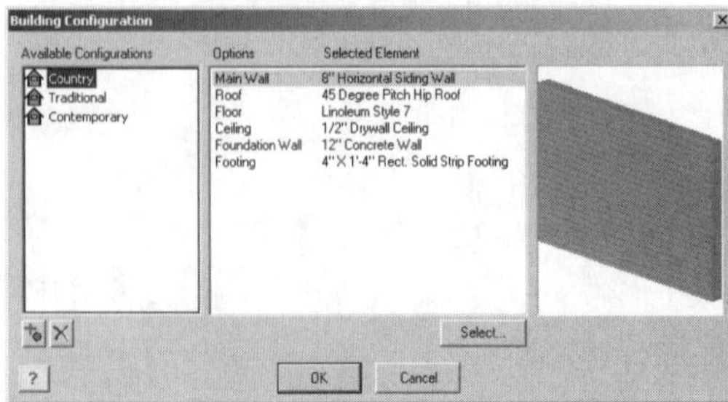

To add a new configuration to the list:

1. Click the Add Item button below the left pane, or right-click in the left pane and select **Add Item**. An entry is added to the list.
2. Type a name for the configuration, then press ENTER.

To edit a building configuration:

1. Select the configuration in the list. The element selections for the configuration are listed in the center pane.
2. In the center pane, select an element type you want to specify a style for.
3. Click the **Select** button.

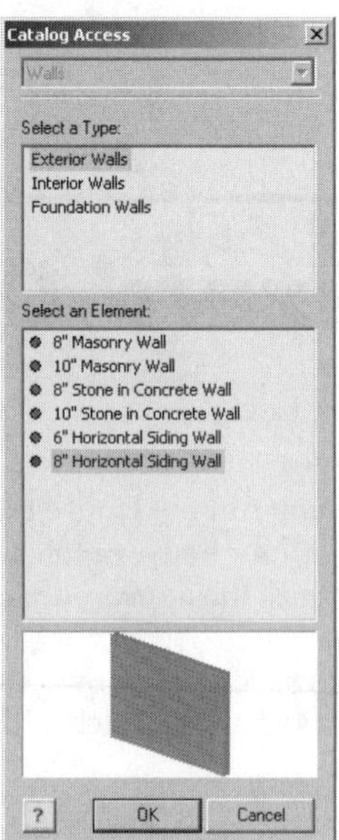

4. In the catalog dialog, select the specific style you want to apply to the selected element type, then click **OK**.
5. Continue selecting styles for the remaining element types.

To delete a configuration from the list:

1. Select the configuration in the list.
2. Click the **Delete** button below the left pane, or right-click in the left pane and select **Delete**.

Creating a Custom Kitchen Builder Wizard Configuration

A Kitchen Builder Wizard configuration determines what types of cabinets and appliances are used in your kitchen. You are asked to select a configuration for your kitchen when you run the Kitchen Builder Wizard.

You can edit any of the existing configurations that are available in the Kitchen Builder Wizard, or create your own. Customized configurations are saved automatically and will be available when you run the Kitchen Builder Wizard in the current project, or any other project.

To access the kitchen configuration library:

1. Select **File > Catalogs > Catalog Manager**, or right-click any element in the catalog panel and select **Catalog Manager**.
2. In the **Catalog Manager** dialog, select **Libraries > Kitchen Configuration**.

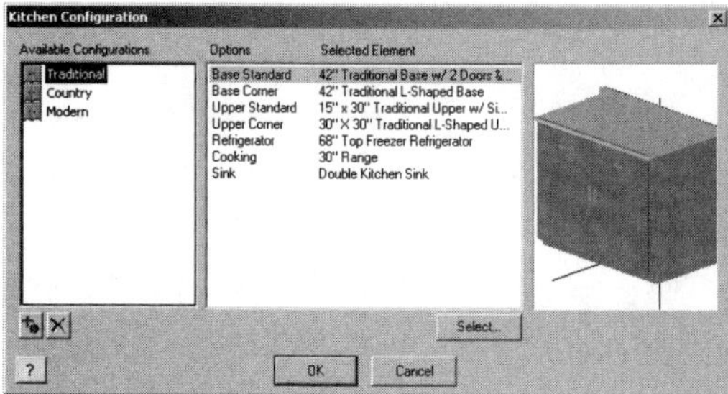

To add a new configuration to the list:

1. Click the Add Item button below the left pane, or right-click in the left pane and select **Add Item**. An entry is added to the list.
2. Type a name for the configuration, then press ENTER.

To edit a kitchen configuration:

1. Select the configuration in the list. The element selections for the configuration are listed in the center pane.
2. In the center pane, select an element type you want to specify a style for.
3. Click the **Select** button.

4. In the catalog dialog, select the specific style you want to apply to the selected element type, then click **OK**.
5. Continue selecting styles for the remaining element types.

To delete a configuration from the list:

1. Select the configuration in the list.
2. Click the **Delete** button below the left pane, or right-click in the left pane and select **Delete**.

Glossary

This handy Glossary contains definitions of construction terms, abbreviations and technical terms used in the program and in this User's Guide. Entries are listed in alphabetical order for your convenience.

Glossary

A

Alt Code – Alternate Code. An extra identification code that is used to link an element in the program's catalog to the databases of other applications.

Ambient – A general level of light that is everywhere in the scene.

Angle Snap – Makes elements move/rotate at specific increments (angles).

Antialiasing – A method of improving image quality by smoothing out jagged edges. This is achieved by adjusting pixel positions or setting pixel intensities so that there is a more gradual transition between the color of a line and the background color.

Array – A method of copying an element into a pattern of rows and/or columns.

Artifacts – Fuzz or distortion in a graphic image or sequence of video images. Large digital pixels ("blocks") and jerkiness in the video stream are examples of artifacts.

Aspect Ratio – The ratio of width to height.

Automatic Save – Saves your drawing for you at specified intervals without prompting.

Awning Window – A window having a sash hinged on pins at the two top or bottom corners of the frame. It opens outward.

B

Backsplash – A vertical surface designed to protect the wall behind a stove or countertop.

Balustrade – A railing consisting of balusters (spindles) attached to a top rail. Used along stairs, landings, porches, decks, etc. Also called a banister.

Baseboard – A board or moulding along the base of a wall. Also called skirting.

Bay Window – A window made up of three sash units that project out from the wall. Usually includes a roof structure.

Beam – In a deck frame, structural member supported by posts that acts to support the deck's floor joists.

Bi-Fold Doors – Narrow doors that are hinged to fold against each other and flat against the jamb.

Bird's Mouth – The notch cut in the lower end of a rafter to fit it to the top plate of a wall.

BLD – BUILD file. The drawing file produced by the program. The extension given to the program's drawing files.

BMP – Bitmap. An image file whose bits are referenced to pixels.

Bow Window – A type of bay window made up of several window units set at slight angles to form a curve.

C

Casement Window – A window having a sash hinged on pins at the top and bottom corners of one side. It opens outward by means of a crank.

Catalog Directory –The directory containing the Master Catalog and other catalogs that you have created.

Catalog Panel – The window on the right side of the screen that displays the contents of the current catalog.

Ceiling Height – The height of the underside of a ceiling surface relative to the floor level.

Chair Rail – A decorative moulding applied horizontally to a wall inside a room at a height of about 3 feet. Used to prevent chairs from marring the wall.

Collision Control – An intelligent drawing aid that prevents elements from being inserted where they won't fit.

Commander – An editing window that appears when certain functions are chosen. It provides precise control over such things as distance and direction.

Complexity – The level of detail shown when elements are displayed.

Cove Molding – A molding with a concave face used as trim.

Crawlspace – The shallow area beneath a house enclosed by the foundation walls.

Crown Molding – A decorative molding along the top of a wall.

Cut Line – The symbol displayed on stairs in Plan view that illustrates the horizontal section cut at eye level.

D

Daylight Saving Time – Time usually one hour ahead of standard time.

Delimiter – A character that marks the beginning or end of a unit of data.

Diffuse – The amount of color that is reflected when an element is illuminated by a light.

Division – A construction division identification. In North America, CSI divisions are used.

DLB File – Dimension Style Library File. Contains Dimension Styles.

Double Roof – A type of hip roof in which the slope to all four sides is broken into two slopes. Both slopes have a pitch.

DPI – Dots per inch. The measurement of resolution for printers.

Drag and Drop Mode – The default mode you are in when you select an element for editing. You can move and rotate elements with your mouse when you are in Drag and Drop Mode.

Drawing Aids – Tools that control the way your cursor works and the way elements are inserted.

Drywall — Gypsum, sometimes with additives, made into paper-covered sheets for use an interior wall or ceiling covering.

Duplicate – Copies a selected element on the same location.

Dutch Gable – A combination of a hip and gable roof. On either end, the lower segment is a hip roof and the upper segment is a gable end. Also known as a Dutch Hip Roof or a Full Return Gable.

DWG – Standard file format for saving vector graphics in applications like AutoCAD.

DXF – Drawing Exchange Format. An ASCII or binary file format of a CAD drawing.

E

Editor – A software application capable of editing text.

Element – A specific type of element, such as a door, having its own distinct properties (size, appearance, etc.).

Elevation – 1. The front, back and side views of a building. 2. The height of an element above the floor or terrain.

Estimate – A report containing a listing of materials, quantities, unit costs, and total cost.

F

Face Slider – Two or more doors that open by sliding to the side in front or behind each other. Also called bypass doors.

Fascia – A flat wood or plywood strip nailed to the overhanging ends of rafters.

Filter – To exclude an element or location from being displayed, quantified or selected.

Fixed Window – A window whose sash is permanently fixed in the frame.

Floor Level – The height of a floor (location) above the ground (0).

Fold-Back Stairs – Stairs that have two flights separated by a landing and that make a complete 180-degree turn. Sometimes called Scissor Stairs.

Fold-Up Door – A door made up of a number of narrow panels that opens overhead by folding up like an accordion.

Foundation – The supporting portion of a structure below the ground floor construction, or below grade, including the footings.

G

Gable Roof – A roof with two sloping sides (as opposed to a Hip Roof, with four sloping sides).

Girt Wall – A wall built up of horizontal structural members that are suspended between vertical columns. Usually found in industrial buildings.

Glass Slider – A door having a wood or aluminum frame fitted with one fixed glass panel and one sliding glass panel. Often called a patio door.

Group – A container for a list of specific element types. For example, doors are organized in groups such as Bi-fold and Single Hinged.

H

Hatching – A pattern of lines used to fill a particular area of your drawing and to represent the material used for that area (e.g. concrete).

Head Height –The height at which the tops of openings, doors and windows are located relative to the floor level.

Header – The structural members placed horizontally over doors, windows and wall openings.

Hidden Line – A view mode where hidden lines are removed from the view, leaving only surfaces displayed.

Highlite – A pane of glass located at the top of a window or door.

Hinged Door – Any type of door that swings open.

Hip Roof – A roof with four sloping sides (as opposed to a Gable Roof, with two sloping sides).

HLB File – Pattern Library File. Contains hatching patterns.

Hopper Window – A window in which the sash is hinged on pins at the two bottom corners, and which opens inward.

Hung Window – A window having two sashes, and whose lower sash slides up and over the fixed, upper sash on the inside.

Hyperlinks – Jumps (links) to external document files or Web addresses.

I

IES File – Name derived from Illuminating Engineering Society. A photometric data file (Lights file) containing Luminaire definition and information.

Interface – Program components that you see on the screen and use to perform tasks.

J

Jamb – The wood or metal pieces that form the sides and top of a door or window enclosure.

Joist – One of a parallel set of structural members used to support floor and ceiling loads. They, in turn, are supported by beams, girders, or bearing walls.

K

KLB File – Line Styles Library File.

L

Landing – A platform between flights of stairs or at the termination of a flight of stairs.

L-Winder Stairs – Stairs that ascend in an L-shape and that use wedge-shaped treads called winders to change direction.

Line Styles – Settings that determine the color and pattern of a line. Used in electrical wiring and dimension styles.

Lite – A pane of glass in a window or door.

LLB File – Lights Library File.

Locations – Drawing layers containing definitions for wall height, floor level, head height and ceiling level.

Louvre Window – A small, slatted window placed high in a gable end. Used mostly for ventilation.

Lumen – A Lumen is equal to one foot-candle (the amount of light one candle generates one foot away) falling on one SQUARE foot of area.

Luminaire – The international term for a piece of lighting equipment. The complete unit including lamp, fixture, and other parts.

M

Magnetic North – Magnetic North is the magnetic north pole. It is the focus of the planet's magnetic field and is the point magnetic compasses point toward.

Mansard Roof – A type of hip roof in which the slope to all four sides is broken into two slopes. The upper slope is nearly or completely flat, while the lower slope has a sharp pitch. Also known as a French gable roof.

MLB File – Materials Library File.

Mono Footing – A pad of masonry, usually concrete, that is wider than the column it supports. Used to transfer the load of the column.

Mullion – Thin horizontal and vertical members that divide the individual panes of glass in a window.

N

Newel – The main post to which the end of a railing is attached.

NLB File – Linetype Library File.

Nosing – The portion of a stair tread that projects over the riser. Also, the projecting edge of a countertop.

O

Open GL – A 3D graphics Application Programming Interface (API) that includes routines for shading, texture mapping, texture filtering, anti-aliasing, lighting, geometry transformations, etc.

Opening – A cutout in a wall.

Ortho – A Drawing Aid that restricts drawing to straight up, down, left, or right.

Orthogonal View – An alternate name for Parallel View in which all drawing lines are parallel and the effect of distance is eliminated. Contrasts with Perspective View.

Overhang – The part of the roof that extends over the side wall. Also, the distance from the side wall to the fascia.

P

Pan – A control that allows you to move the on-screen view by dragging up, down, left, or right.

Parallel View – A 3D view that eliminates the effect of distance from a view. In Parallel View, all drawing lines are parallel. Contrasts with Perspective View. Parallel View is sometimes called Orthogonal View.

Parametric – Having a set of physical properties that determines the characteristics of an element.

Perspective View – A 3D view in which the scale of an element decreases according to its distance from the viewer. Drawing lines converge to a vanishing point. Perspective View represents the way an element would appear to the human eye.

Photometric Data File – A file that allows you to define complex light distributions based on physical lamp properties. When loading a photometric file, a photometric web is constructed that defines the intensity of light for any direction from a light source.

Pixel – A word invented by combining the two words "picture" and "element". The smallest unit of color on a computer display. Size varies by resolution.

Pixel Search Distance – The Pixel Search Distance determines how close your cursor (which is attached to an element you are inserting) needs to be to an existing element before Object Snap occurs.

Plan View – A flat, 2D view from above.

Plate (Top Plate) – The top member of a framed wall upon which the rafters and ceiling joists rest.

Pocket Door – A door that rolls on an overhead track into a frame or pocket hidden in the wall.

Project Directory – The location of the default directory in which projects are stored.

Project Estimate – A report containing a listing of materials, quantities, unit costs, and total cost.

Q

Quantity Report – A list of the type and quantity of materials in your model. Also known as a Materials List or Bill of Materials.

R

Rafter – Structural members that make up the framing for a roof and roof overhang, and that support the sheathing and roofing materials.

Rake – To incline from the perpendicular.

Render – To display a 3D model with surfaces, textures, lighting and shading.

Rendered Mode – A display mode where solid colors and textures are applied to surfaces, creating a realistic 3D effect.

Rendered Outline Mode – A display mode where solid colors and textures are applied to elements, and surfaces are outlined with a black line for high definition.

Riser – The vertical board placed between the treads of a staircase.

Roller Door – A door made of hinged, horizontal steel or wood panels that move on rollers in overhead and side tracks.

Rough Opening – The opening created in a wall to receive a door or window frame.

S

Saddle – A small, double-sloping roof built behind upper-story walls or the back side of a chimney to divert water around the wall or chimney.

Sash – A frame that holds one or more panes of glass and that is set into the window frame.

Seat Cut – The horizontal cut that is made when cutting a bird's mouth in a rafter.

Shininess – The ability of a texture to reflect light.

Slope – Ground that forms an incline.

Snap Angle – The increment angle your cursor will snap at (if Angle Snap is enabled).

Soffit – The area below the eave and overhang. The underside where the roof overhangs the walls.

Specular – A shininess factor that determines the amount of highlighting you see on an element from light sources.

Split L-Shaped Stairs – Stairs that ascend in an L-shaped direction and whose landing is split on a diagonal to make the change in direction.

Spreadsheet – A table of values arranged in rows and columns.

Status Bar – The bar below the drawing area that contains the Help message for the current state or tool. Also contains drawing aid buttons.

Stringer – The inclined side of a stair that supports the treads and risers.

Strip Footings – A flat, masonry section, usually concrete, that is wider than the wall it supports. Used to transfer the vertical load of the wall.

Studs – Members inserted vertically in a wall frame.

Suspended Ceiling – A grid of T-shaped bars hung on wires from overhead support framing, into which removable panels are inserted to form a finished ceiling that allows easy access to the area above it. Typically found in office buildings and basements.

T

Template – A set of pre-defined properties that determines the setup and outcome of something (like a report).

Temporary Directory – The default directory in which temporary files generated by the program are saved.

Terrain – A piece of land.

Tile Height – The height of one tile in a texture pattern. The program generates large images by "tiling" texture bitmaps horizontally and vertically.

Tilt Door – A door consisting of a single leaf that opens overhead by tilting up (e.g. Tilt Garage Door).

Toe Space – A recessed area between the bottom of a cabinet and the floor that allows you to stand close to the cabinet. Also called a toe kick.

Transom – A member between a door or window and a sidelite or highlite frame.

Transparency – The degree to which a texture can be penetrated by light.

Tread – The horizontal part of a stair that is stepped on.

True North – True North is the geographic North Pole. It is located at 90 degrees North latitude and all lines of longitude converge at the pole.

Truss – A variety of members made up into a series of triangles. Used for constructing roofs.

TSL File – Text Style Library File

U

U-Winder Stairs – Stairs that ascend in a U-shaped direction.

V

View Filter – A dialog used for displaying and hiding elements and/or locations, and controlling the selectability of elements.

Vent Window – A window made up of two or more segments with one segment acting as a vent.

VRML – Virtual Reality Modeling Language. The open standard for virtual reality on the Internet.

W

Winder – One of the wedge-shaped treads that make up a winding or spiral staircase.

Windowing – A selection method where you click and drag a rectangle, from left to right, around elements you want to select.

Wireframe View – The default 3D view where all lines making up elements are displayed. It allows you to see through elements.

WRL File – WORLD file. Capable of being viewed in VRML viewers.

X

X Axis – One of the three drawing axes. An X coordinate specifies a horizontal distance.

Y

Y Axis – One of the three drawing axes. A Y coordinate specifies a vertical distance.

Z

Z Axis – One of the three drawing axes. The Z coordinate indicates either elevation or depth.

Z Buffer – A block of memory used to store the Z-axis value of a pixel on the screen. Higher depth values improve detail of 3D display but may slow the system.

Zenith - Culminating point.

Zoom Realtime – Magnifies or shrinks the view as you click and drag with your mouse.

Zoom to Fit – Zooms the drawing to the extents of the drawing area, creating a maximized view of your entire design.

Zoom Window – Magnifies an area of your drawing that you select by windowing.

Catalog Index

When you want to know where to find something in the catalog, this is the place to look. The Catalog Index contains a list of interior elements — everything from air hockey tables to water heaters — and tells you what tool to select to access each one, and what group to select in the catalog. Items are listed in alphabetical order for your convenience.

Catalog Index

Items	Tool to Select	Catalog Groups
Air Hockey Table	Insert > Interiors > Furniture	Recroom Furniture
Air Returns	Insert > Interiors > HVAC	Ventilation
Aquariums	Insert > Interiors > Accessories	Aquariums
Area Rugs	Insert > Interiors > Accessories	Area Rugs
Armchairs	Insert > Interiors > Furniture	Living Room Furniture
Armoire	Insert > Interiors > Furniture	Bedroom Furniture
Barstools	Insert > Interiors > Furniture	Recroom Furniture
Basinet	Insert > Interiors > Furniture	Bedroom Furniture
Bathroom Vanities	Insert > Interiors > Cabinets	Bathroom Vanities
Bathtubs	Insert > Interiors > Plumbing Fixtures	Tubs and Showers
Beds	Insert > Interiors > Furniture	Bedroom Furniture
Beer Bottle	Insert > Interiors > Furniture	Recroom Furniture
Benches, interior	Insert > Interiors > Furniture	Living Room Furniture
Bidets	Insert > Interiors > Plumbing Fixtures	Toilets and Bidets
Billiards Tables	Insert > Interiors > Furniture	Recroom Furniture
Blender	Insert > Interiors > Appliances	Kitchen Appliances
Blinds	Insert > Interiors > Accessories	Window Treatments
Books	Insert > Interiors > Accessories	Decorative
Bookshelves	Insert > Interiors > Furniture	Bedroom Furniture Office Furniture

Catalog Index

Items	Tool to Select	Catalog Groups
Built-in Ovens	Insert > Interiors > Appliances	Kitchen Appliances
Cabinets, base	Insert > Interiors > Cabinets	Single Door Base Cabinets Double Door Base Cabinets Base Drawer Units Base Corner Cabinets Base Island Cabinets Bathroom Vanities
Cabinets, upper	Insert > Interiors > Cabinets	Upper Corner Cabinets Upper Cabinets Upper Island Cabinets
Cable Outlets	Insert > Interiors > Electrical	Outlets
Candle Sticks	Insert > Interiors > Accessories	Decorative
Card Table	Insert > Interiors > Furniture	Recroom Furniture
CD Stands	Insert > Interiors > Furniture	Living Room Furniture
Ceiling Fans	Insert > Interiors > Lighting	Ceiling Lights
Chairs, living room	Insert > Interiors > Furniture	Living Room Furniture
Chairs, recroom	Insert > Interiors > Furniture	Recroom Furniture
Change Screen	Insert > Interiors > Furniture	Bedroom Furniture
Change Table	Insert > Interiors > Furniture	Bedroom Furniture
Chests	Insert > Interiors > Furniture	Bedroom Furniture
Chimney	Insert > Interiors > HVAC	Ventilation
Clocks	Insert > Interiors > Electronics	Clocks
Closet Rods/ Shelves	Insert > Interiors > Furniture	Bedroom Furniture
Coffee Tables	Insert > Interiors > Furniture	Living Room Furniture

Catalog Index

Items	Tool to Select	Catalog Groups
Computer	Insert > Interiors > Electronics	Computer Components
Cooktops	Insert > Interiors > Appliances	Kitchen Appliances
Cribs	Insert > Interiors > Furniture	Bedroom Furniture
Cubicals	Insert > Interiors > Furniture	Office Furniture
Cups	Insert > Interiors > Accessories	Dining Room/Kitchen Accessories
Curtains	Insert > Interiors > Accessories	Window Treatments
Dart Board	Insert > Interiors > Furniture	Recroom Furniture
Desks	Insert > Interiors > Furniture	Office Furniture
Dining Sets	Insert > Interiors > Furniture	Dining Room/Kitchen Furniture
Dishes	Insert > Interiors > Accessories	Dining Room/Kitchen Accessories
Dishwasher	Insert > Interiors > Appliances	Kitchen Appliances
Door mats	Insert > Interiors > Accessories	Decorative
Down Spout	Insert > Interiors > Plumbing Fixtures	Exterior Plumbing Fixtures
Drapes	Insert > Interiors > Accessories	Window Treatments
Dressers	Insert > Interiors > Furniture	Bedroom Furniture
Dry Bars	Insert > Interiors > Furniture	Recroom Furniture
Dryers	Insert > Interiors > Appliances	Laundry Appliances
DVD Player	Insert > Interiors > Electronics	Televisions
End tables	Insert > Interiors > Furniture	Living Room Furniture

Catalog Index

Items	Tool to Select	Catalog Groups
Entertainment Units	Insert > Interiors > Furniture	Living Room Furniture
Faucets	Insert > Interiors > Plumbing Fixtures	Faucets/Fixtures
Fax Machine	Insert > Interiors > Electronics	Communications
Filing Cabinets	Insert > Interiors > Furniture	Office Furniture
Fireplaces	Insert > Interiors > HVAC	Heating
Floor Registers	Insert > Interiors > HVAC	Ventilation
Flower Pots, indoor	Insert > Interiors > Accessories	Decorative
Foosball Table	Insert > Interiors > Furniture	Recroom Furniture
Furnace	Insert > Interiors > HVAC	Heating
Futon	Insert > Interiors > Furniture	Living Room Furniture
Garbage Bin	Insert > Interiors > Accessories	Dining Room/Kitchen Accessories Bathroom Accessories
Islands, kitchen	Insert > Interiors > Cabinets	Base Island Cabinets Upper Island Cabinets
Kitchen Tables	Insert > Interiors > Furniture	Dining Room/Kitchen Furniture
Knife Sets	Insert > Interiors > Accessories	Dining Room/Kitchen Accessories
Lamps	Insert > Interiors > Lighting	Lamps
Light Switches	Insert > Interiors > Electrical	Switches
Lights	Insert > Interiors > Lighting	Ceiling Lights Lamps Wall Lights
Loveseats	Insert > Interiors > Furniture	Living Room Furniture
Medicine Cabinet	Insert > Interiors > Accessories	Bathroom Accessories

Catalog Index

Items	Tool to Select	Catalog Groups
Microwaves	Insert > Interiors > Appliances	Kitchen Appliances
Mirror, standing	Insert > Interiors > Furniture	Bedroom Furniture
Mirrors, wall	Insert > Interiors > Accessories	Decorative
Nightstands	Insert > Interiors > Furniture	Bedroom Furniture
Office Tables	Insert > Interiors > Furniture	Office Furniture
Ottoman	Insert > Interiors > Furniture	Living Room Furniture
Outlets	Insert > Interiors > Electrical	Outlets
Ovens	Insert > Interiors > Appliances	Kitchen Appliances
Pantry Cabinets	Insert > Interiors > Cabinets	Pantry Cabinets
Phone	Insert > Interiors > Electronics	Communications
Phone Jacks	Insert > Interiors > Electrical	Outlets
Photo Copier	Insert > Interiors > Electronics	Communications
Pianos	Insert > Interiors > Furniture	Living Room Furniture
Pictures	Insert > Interiors > Accessories	Decorative
Pillows	Insert > Interiors > Accessories	Decorative
Ping Pong Table	Insert > Interiors > Furniture	Recroom Furniture
Pool Tables	Insert > Interiors > Furniture	Recroom Furniture
Pot Racks	Insert > Interiors > Furniture	Dining Room/Kitchen Furniture
Pots & Pans	Insert > Interiors > Accessories	Dining Room/Kitchen Accessories

Catalog Index

Items	Tool to Select	Catalog Groups
Printer	Insert > Interiors > Electronics	Computer Components
Range Hoods	Insert > Interiors > Appliances	Kitchen Appliances
Ranges	Insert > Interiors > Appliances	Kitchen Appliances
Refrigerators	Insert > Interiors > Appliances	Kitchen Appliances
Registers, floor	Insert > Interiors > HVAC	Ventilation
Rugs, area	Insert > Interiors > Accessories	Area Rugs
Sconces	Insert > Interiors > Lighting	Wall Lights
Screen, change	Insert > Interiors > Furniture	Bedroom Furniture
Shelves, closet	Insert > Interiors > Furniture	Bedroom Furniture
Shelving Units	Insert > Interiors > Furniture	Living Room Furniture Office Furniture
Shower Curtain	Insert > Interiors > Accessories	Bathroom Accessories
Showers	Insert > Interiors > Plumbing Fixtures	Tubs and Showers
Shutters	Insert > Interiors > Accessories	Dining Room/Kitchen Accessories
Sinks	Insert > Interiors > Plumbing Fixtures	Sinks
Smoke Detector	Insert > Interiors > Electrical	Sensors and Controls
Snooker Table	Insert > Interiors > Furniture	Recroom Furniture
Sofas	Insert > Interiors > Furniture	Living Room Furniture
Switches	Insert > Interiors > Electrical	Switches
Tables, coffee	Insert > Interiors > Furniture	Living Room Furniture
Tables, end	Insert > Interiors > Furniture	Living Room Furniture

Catalog Index

Items	Tool to Select	Catalog Groups
Tables, kitchen	Insert > Interiors > Furniture	Dining Room/Kitchen Furniture
Tables, office	Insert > Interiors > Furniture	Office Furniture
Telephone	Insert > Interiors > Electronics	Communications
Television Stands	Insert > Interiors > Furniture	Living Room Furniture
Televisions	Insert > Interiors > Electronics	Televisions
Thermostats	Insert > Interiors > Electrical	Sensors and Controls
Toaster	Insert > Interiors > Appliances	Kitchen Appliances
Toilet Paper Dispenser	Insert > Interiors > Accessories	Bathroom Accessories
Toilets	Insert > Interiors > Plumbing Fixtures	Toilets and Bidets
Towel Racks/Rings	Insert > Interiors > Accessories	Bathroom Accessories
Track Lighting	Insert > Interiors > Lighting	Ceiling Lights
Trash Compactor	Insert > Interiors > Appliances	Kitchen Appliances
Valance	Insert > Interiors > Accessories	Window Treatments
Vanities, bathroom	Insert > Interiors > Cabinets	Bathroom Vanities
Vases	Insert > Interiors > Accessories	Decorative
VCR	Insert > Interiors > Electronics	Televisions
Washers	Insert > Interiors > Appliances	Laundry Appliances
Water Heater	Insert > Interiors > HVAC	Heating
Wood Stove	Insert > Interiors > HVAC	Heating

Index

1-2-3

A

B

C

D

E

F

G

H

I

N

O

P

Q

R

S

T

U

V

W

X

Z